# SOCIAL WORK PRACTICE WITH CLIENTS WHO HAVE ALCOHOL PROBLEMS

# SOCIAL WORK PRACTICE WITH CLIENTS WHO HAVE ALCOHOL PROBLEMS

*Edited By*

**Edith M. Freeman, Ph.D.**

*School of Social Welfare*
*University of Kansas*
*Lawrence, Kansas*

CHARLES C THOMAS • PUBLISHER
*Springfield • Illinois • U.S.A.*

*Published and Distributed Throughout the World by*

CHARLES C THOMAS • PUBLISHER
2600 South First Street
Springfield, Illinois 62717

© *1985 by* CHARLES C THOMAS • PUBLISHER

ISBN 0-398-05107-0

Library of Congress Catalog Card Number: 84–26790

*Printed in the United States of America*
*SC-R-3*

**Library of Congress Cataloging in Publication Data**
Main entry under title:

Social work practice with clients who have
    alcohol problems.

    Includes bibliographies and index.
    1. Social work with alcoholics—United States—
Addresses, essays, lectures.    2. Alcoholism—Treatment
United States—Addresses, essays, lectures.    I. Freeman,
Edith M.    [DNLM: 1. Alcoholism—prevention & control.
2. Alcoholism—rehabilitation.    3. Community Mental
Health Services.    4. Social work.    WM 274 S6775]
HV5279.S63   1985        362.2'9286        84–26790
ISBN 0-398-05107-0

# CONTRIBUTORS

**MIRIAM AARON, R.N., B.A.,**

*Treatment Unit Director*
*New York State Division of Alcoholism and Alcohol Abuse*
*New York City, New York*

**SANDRA C. ANDERSON, Ph.D.,**

*Associate Professor*
*School of Social Work*
*Portland State University*
*Portland, Oregon*

**BETTY BLACKMON, M.S.W., J.D.,**

*Director of Johnson County Mental Health Substance Abuse Division*
*Shawnee, Kansas*

**E. THOMAS COPELAND, Jr., Ph.D.**

*Chief Psychologist*
*State Reception and Diagnostic Center*
*Topeka, Kansas*

**EILEEN M. CORRIGAN, D.S.W.,**

*Professor*
*School of Social Work*
*Rutgers University*
*New Brunswick, New Jersey*

**LINDA DENNISTON, M.S.W.**

*Coordinator of Substance Abuse Services*
*Northeast Kansas Mental Health and Guidance Center*
*Leavenworth, Kansas*

**CHRISTINE HUFF FEWELL, M.S.W.**

*Private Practice*
*New York City, New York*


**JOHN W. FINNEY, Ph.D.**

*Department of Psychiatry and Behavioral Sciences*
*Veterans Administration and Stanford University Medical Center*
*Palo Alto, California*


**EDITH M. FREEMAN, Ph.D.**

*Associate Professor*
*University of Kansas School of Social Welfare*
*Lawrence, Kansas*


**WENDY GAMBLE, Ph.D.**

*Department of Psychiatry and Behavioral Sciences*
*Veterans Administration and Stanford University Medical Center*
*Palo Alto, California*


**EUNICE GARCIA, M.S.S.W.**

*Field Practicum Specialist*
*School of Social Work*
*University of Texas*
*Austin, Texas*


**JOHN F. GUNTHER, D.S.W.**

*Assistant Professor*
*School of Social Work*
*University of Oklahoma*
*Norman, Oklahoma*


**DAVID R. GLASS, JR., Ph.D.**

*Center for Family Research*
*Department of Psychiatry and Behavioral Sciences*
*George Washington University*
*School of Medicine and Health Sciences*
*Washington, D.C.*

**THOMAS C. HARFORD, Ph.D.**

*Division of Biometry and Epidemiology*
*National Institute on Alcohol Abuse and Alcoholism*
*Rockville, Maryland*


**JEFFREY JAY, Ph.D.**

*Center for Family Research*
*Department of Psychiatry and Behavioral Sciences*
*George Washington University*
*School of Medicine and Health Sciences*
*Washington, D.C.*


**ERIC J. JOLLY (OOLOOTEEKA), Ph.D.**

*Assistant Professor*
*Department of Psychology*
*Eastern New Mexico University*
*Portales, New Mexico*


**JOHN W. JONES, Ph.D., C.A.C.**

*Chief Psychologist*
*The Saint Paul Companies*
*St. Paul, Minnesota*


**WALLACE MANDELL, Ph.D., M.P.H.**

*School of Hygiene and Public Health*
*Johns Hopkins University*
*Baltimore, Maryland*


**RUTH G. MC ROY, Ph.D.**

*Assistant Professor*
*School of Social Work*
*University of Texas*
*Austin, Texas*


**RUDOLF H. MOOS, Ph.D.**

*Department of Psychiatry and Behavioral Sciences*
*Veterans Administration and Stanford University Medical Center*
*Palo Alto, California*

**JO ANNE M. PILAT, M.S.W., C.A.C.**

*Regional Manager of Counseling Services*
*A. T. & T. Employee Assistance Program*
*Chicago, Illinois*


**MARY ROHMAN, M.A.**

*Research Coordinator*
*The Medical Foundation, Inc.*
*Boston, Massachusetts*


**CLAYTON T. SHORKEY, Ph.D.**

*School of Social Work*
*University of Texas*
*Austin, Texas*


**DANIELLE L. SPIEGLER, B.A.**

*Research Psychologist*
*Division of Biometry and Epidemiology*
*National Institute of Alcohol Abuse and Alcoholism*
*Rockville, Maryland*


**MARION L. USHER, M.S.S.W.**

*Center for Family Research*
*Department of Psychiatry and Behavioral Sciences*
*George Washington University*
*School of Medicine and Health Sciences*
*Washington, D.C.*


**HENRY WECHSLER, Ph.D.**

*Director of Research*
*The Medical Foundation, Inc.*
*Boston, Massachusetts*


**KENNETH WEDEL, Ph.D.**

*Professor & Dean*
*School of Social Work*
*University of Oklahoma*
*Norman, Oklahoma*

**ANN WEICK, Ph.D.**

*Associate Professor*
*University of Kansas School of Social Welfare*
*Lawrence, Kansas*

**JANET M. WRIGHT, M.S.S.W.**

*Rural Outreach Worker*
*Dane County Advocates for Battered Women*
*Madison, Wisconsin*

# PREFACE

The alcoholism treatment field is one of several specialized practice areas that are in transition currently. There are many reasons for the current turmoil in this field. As the field developed, it was assumed that practitioners would develop effective approaches for helping clients with alcohol problems to resolve those problems, and for decreasing the number of people who potentially might develop such problems in the future. The hoped for collaboration between prevention and treatment practitioners to achieve these goals has not occurred to the extent desired. Additionally, recidivism and drop-out rates for treated alcoholics and increases in the number of people who have become alcoholic have raised serious questions about the effectiveness of prevention and treatment efforts to date.

Other factors have also contributed to the increased focus on this practice area. They include the following: increased financial and human costs from alcohol-related problems in critical areas such as industry and traffic accidents; increased awareness in the general public and the development of special interest groups, such as MADD and SADD;[1] growing numbers of alcohol problems in population groups not previously identified as being at-risk, such as women and the elderly; the federal and state governments' efforts to target alcohol problems as an area for priority funding; state-of-the-art changes in many of the professional disciplines that serve as "feeder systems" for this practice area; and conflicts within the alcoholism treatment field itself about what constitutes adequate credentials, training, and intervention techniques in this field.

The idea for this book developed out of that turmoil-filled

---

[1]These organizations are Mothers Against Drunk Driving (MADD), and Students Against Drunk Driving (SADD).

context. It has been planned and written with the idea of capturing the current status of practice in this field, the factors described above that have impacted on the current transitional phase, and all of the many other social changes that have also affected practice in this specialized area. The focus of the book is on four areas relevant to practice in this area: prevention, treatment, research, and training for the area. These divisions are to facilitate clarity only, since the four areas are closely interrelated in actual practice.

The book is intended to be used primarily by mental health students and practitioners in alcoholism treatment and prevention programs; in many other social agencies such as hospitals, mental health centers, family service agencies, probation offices, and schools; in state alcohol problem control agencies; and in private agencies that provide consultation, program development and evaluation services to alcohol programs. These practitioners include social workers, psychologists, doctors, nurses, alcoholism counselors, and aides. It is assumed that most of the practitioners in this target audience have backgrounds in practice theory and a beginning competence in doing practice. At the same time, the book includes some basic background information about practice in this field that should be helpful to the students who will also be using it and to educators who wish to use it for assigned readings.

The contributing authors represent a similar broad range of professional backgrounds although social workers are predominant in numbers. A range of roles are also represented by these authors since they include practitioners, educators, and researchers. This broad range of backgrounds and roles in these authors has contributed to what I hope is the richness and practical nature of this book.

Edith M. Freeman

# INTRODUCTION

The purpose of this book is to present a clear description of effective practice with clients who have alcohol problems given the numerous factors that are impacting this practice area during the current transitional phase. The clients involved range from problem drinkers to alcohol abusers to those who are alcohol-dependent. These clients are often difficult to work with because of the intractibility of alcohol problems. Another contributing factor is the impossibility of isolating those problems from related problem areas and from many complex environmental factors which help to maintain the problems.

For these reasons, the book's examples of effective practice with this client group can contribute significantly toward efforts to improve practice in this specialized area. The issue of what constitutes good practice is dealt with on three levels. Specific content areas about alcohol problems are presented for knowledge building in this practice area. A number of practice principles are also presented, such as the need to explore with elderly clients all prescription and nonprescription drugs being used including alcohol. Third, practice approaches and specific techniques are discussed in some chapters along with case examples which illustrate how they can improve practice with particular clients.

This book should be extremely useful for additional reasons. It makes use of the social work frame of reference for assessing and resolving alcohol problems. Alcohol use and recovery are viewed within a context so that the latter is not equated with abstinence only. Instead, it is also equated with concommitant changes in alcohol-related problems such as coping with stress without alcohol, communication patterns, and appropriate use of leisure time. In this sense, it emphasizes the importance of viewing clients wholistically, including a focus on their social context or environment. Familial and peer relationships as well as factors in work, school, and other environments which impinge on clients' problems with alcohol are all deemed important in assessment and treatment. Thus, the person-in-environment perspective and a de-emphasis on the individual deficit perspective are the unifying principles of practice as described throughout the book.

The book's emphasis on systematic practice is another advantage. It presents a systematic view of assessment, treatment, and evaluation procedures, and points out the importance of selecting the treatment approach based on the needs in each case rather than selecting one approach or technique for all clients who have alcohol problems.

Finally, this book is useful because it describes and in some cases offers suggestions about how to deal with some of the major practice issues involved in work with these clients. These issues include: the efficacy of preventive efforts, abstinence vs. controlled drinking, the consequences of using the medical disease model and others in conceptualizing alcoholism, self-help organizations such as AA vs. formal treatment programs, differential selection of treatment modalities, dealing with the range of diversity among alcoholics including gender and racial differences, how to work with mandatory referrals, the differential use of staff in programs, the use of drugs to aid recovery, and the relative importance of evaluation and how it should be done. These are issues that will continue to dominate and impact on this field of practice.

Edith M. Freeman

# ACKNOWLEDGMENTS

In the process of editing this book, I have become more aware of how much this kind of endeavor is dependent on the cooperation and assistance of many people. I wish to thank the contributing authors for their support, goodwill, and written contributions. In particular, I am grateful to Ruth McRoy, Betty Blackmon, JoAnne Pilat, and Ann Weick for their suggestions after reading the plan for this book or portions of the book.

Finally, I am most grateful to my family for their patient and enthusiastic support throughout the planning and completion of this book.

E. M. F.

# CONTENTS

# SOCIAL WORK PRACTICE WITH CLIENTS WHO HAVE ALCOHOL PROBLEMS

# PART ONE: PREVENTION SERVICES

# OVERVIEW

EDITH M. FREEMAN

The four chapters in this section are focused on prevention services in circumstances involving population groups that are high-risk for alcohol abuse or dependency. These circumstances offer opportunities for prevention at several levels depending on the needs of the population groups involved. In her book on generic clinical practice, Helen Northen noted that primary prevention is based on the assumption that particular conditions or events affect large numbers of people in somewhat similar ways. She indicated that people are likely to cope with those conditions more adequately and to prevent potential problems if they have been prepared to anticipate and face them.[1]

Thus in terms of alcoholism, primary prevention seeks to reduce the incidence of this disease through intervention before problem drinking and related dysfunctions occur. The chapter by Spiegler, Harford, and Freeman describes important components for primary prevention programs with adolescents. It also includes an analysis of research focused on the impact of selected environmental factors on alcohol use and the complexity of prevention efforts with this age group. Aaron's chapter on EAP's highlights particular groups of employees such as women, licensed professionals, and executives who are high risk for stress and alcohol misuse. She proposes that primary prevention can be done via educational sessions and the provision of support groups in the work place.

Secondary prevention is possible when early warning symp-

---

[1]Northen, Helen: *Clinical Social Work*. New York, Columbia University Press, 1982.

toms occur prior to the onset of the disabling effects of alcoholism, while the purpose of tertiary prevention is to overcome or reduce those effects after they occur. The chapters on DUI clients and domestic violence by Denniston and Wright respectively, illustrate how prevention on those two levels can be done. The recommended strategies for work with the clients involved are all the more useful because these clients are often nonvoluntary. Denniston uses case examples to illustrate how to integrate prevention and intervention with DUI clients, and recommends that a next step is the development of procedures for evaluating prevention efforts. Wright notes how collaborative efforts between agencies can enhance prevention services.

*Chapter One*

# AN ECOLOGICAL PERSPECTIVE ON ALCOHOL USE AMONG ADOLESCENTS: IMPLICATIONS FOR PREVENTION

DANIELLE L. SPIEGLER, THOMAS C. HARFORD,
AND EDITH M. FREEMAN

It has been well established in numerous surveys of alcohol use among teenagers that a substantial proportion of young people consume alcoholic beverages at least occasionally. About 8 out of 10 high school students in a 1978 national survey of adolescent drinking practices reported experimenting with alcohol.[1] Approximately 60 percent reported monthly alcohol use and about 25 percent reported weekly use. One in three 10th to 12th graders were classified as moderate/heavier or heavier drinkers.

Many factors influence the use of alcohol by adolescents. A number of these may be categorized as psychological. Others relate to the availability of alcohol in society and the broader sociocultural fabric of population subgroups with different traditions concerning alcohol use. This chapter reviews the literature on the relationship between adolescent drinking and four categories of environmental influences: sociodemographic, parental, peer, and contextual factors. Relevant data obtained from a 1978 national survey of high school students in the United States[2] are highlighted, and new analyses are presented comparing the relative influences on adolescent drinking patterns of the environmental factors under consideration. These factors are relevant to alcohol prevention programs for adolescents. Therefore, based on this review of the literature and analysis of the 1978 survey, some implications for the design of prevention programs will also be presented.

## REVIEW OF ENVIRONMENTAL FACTORS

It should be noted at the outset that assessment of the environmental factors which influence adolescent drinking practices is a complicated task. First, a conceptually adequate definition of the environment is not easily specified. Second, the multiplicity of environments is complicated by their differential proximity to behavior. For example, demographic variables are conceptually more remote from drinking behavior than the number of drinking companions present. Third, environmental factors act in concert with personality variables and are often mediated by persons acting in a particular context. Despite these difficulties, and to help elucidate underlying related structures, it can be extremely valuable to identify factors in the environment which relate to and influence the frequency and level of alcohol consumption in adolescents. Further, such an approach is consistent with an ecological perspective on prevention and treatment of alcohol problems in this age group.

### Sociodemographic Variables

Studies of adolescent drinking have consistently shown associations between various demographic factors and adolescent drinking.[3] The 1978 national survey found that older adolescents are more likely to drink than younger ones; boys drink more often and in larger amounts than girls; black youths drink less than white youths; alcohol use is least prevalent among teenagers affiliated with Protestant denominations and most prevalent among Catholic youth; it is more prevalent in urban than in rural communities and in larger rather than smaller communities; Northeast and North Central regions have the lowest proportion of abstainers; and there is no correlation between socioeconomic status and teenage drinking.[4]

As will be seen later in this chapter, demographic variables, while significant, account for only a small proportion of the variance in adolescent drinking practices. These variables are conceptually more remote from drinking behavior than many other environmental factors, and whatever influence they exert is probably associated with other environmental factors.

### Parental Influences

Studies concerning the influence of parental factors on adolescent drinking have considered the influence of the general parent-child relationship, parental attitudes toward drinking, and actual parental drinking practices. Data concerning the influence of the general parent-child relationship are not consistent. One study found that heavier teenage drinkers were less likely than moderate drinkers to report being "very close" to their families.[5] Another study reported that perceived parental attitudes and behaviors toward the child, particularly maternal control, correlated strongly with adolescent drinking behavior.[6] However, Smart et al. found that parental rejection and control had very little association with adolescent drinking behavior.[7] Marguiles et al. found that neither family closeness nor perceived parental control significantly influenced the onset of drinking.[8] However, the relative closeness to parents and to peers did predict onset of drinking, with adolescents closer to peers more likely to start drinking.

Jessor and his colleagues have shown that drinking behavior is less problematic when adolescents report similar interests and common expectations between parents and friends and when the views and opinions of parents are more influential than those of friends.[9] When adolescents report that their parents have a more tolerant attitude toward teenage drinking, alcohol is more likely to be used by adolescents. The relationship between parental attitudes and adolescent drinking practices is not a simple one, however, and not one of a linear relationship. There is some evidence that more restrictive and disapproving attitudes by parents may result in a decrease in overall drinking but an increase in the amounts of problem drinking.[10] Davies and Stacey found that abstainers, occasional drinkers, and heavy drinkers perceived their parents' attitudes toward drinking as being negative, whereas light and moderate drinkers perceived their parents' attitudes as being positive.[11] However, Rachal et al. report consistency between teenagers' drinking and their parents' approval or disapproval of drinking.[12] Fewer abstainers reported parental approval than reported disapproval. Almost exactly the reverse was true for heavier drinkers.

Most of the literature on parental influences on adolescent drinking focuses on the relationship between actual parental drinking practices and adolescent drinking behavior. A number of major surveys of adolescent drinking in the 1950's and 1960's reported a relationship between parental and adolescent drinking practices. (See Blane and Hewitt for a comprehensive review of the literature.[13]) More recent studies continue to indicate such a correspondence between parental and adolescent behaviors.[14] Adolescent girls were found to be more susceptible to the examples of significant others (parents or peers) than were boys.

The national survey conducted in 1974 reports that students whose parents drank were almost twice as likely to be heavier drinkers than students with abstinent parents (27% vs. 14%).[15] Thirty-five percent of the abstainers and 11 percent of the heavy drinkers reported that their parents were abstainers. Eighteen percent of abstainers and 42 percent of heavy drinkers reported regular drinking by their parents. Kandel et al. report even more dramatic differences.[16] Seventy-two percent of the families in which parents were abstainers had children who also abstained and 81 percent of the families in which both parents drank had children who also drank.

The national survey conducted in 1978 also found that teenage drinking was related to perceptions of parental alcohol use, with abstainers being more likely to report abstention by their parents.[17] However, heavier drinkers were less likely to report consistency between their own and their parents' drinking. These results parallel the findings of Davies and Stacey regarding the nature of the relationship between adolescent drinking and parental attitudes towards drinking.[18]

### Peer Influences

The attitudes and drinking behaviors of one's peers have long been recognized as important environmental structures relating to both onset of drinking and the maintenance of drinking. Studies generally indicate that peer influences have even more of an impact on adolescent drinking than parental influences. Several different aspects of peer influences on adolescent drinking have been investigated, including peer pressure, peer behavior, and peer relationships in general.

With the exception of one study,[19] there is little evidence for the effect of direct peer pressure on adolescent drinking practices.[20] Instead, peer influence seems to take the more subtle form of peer modeling and networking. Studies consistently find that adolescent drinking becomes more prevalent, frequent, heavier, or more problem-related as the extent of drinking among friends increases.[21] In a longitudinal study of junior and senior high school students, it was found that perceived peer support for drinking was the most important variable accounting for a subject's change in drinking status from abstainer to drinker during a one-year period.[22]

Results from the 1978 national survey support these findings. An adolescent's drinking behavior is strongly related to the drinking behavior and attitudes of his or her peers. Seventy percent of the abstainers "hang around" with other abstainers, whereas only 1 percent of the heavier drinkers associate with nondrinkers. Most heavier drinkers associate with other drinkers. The higher the drinking level, the more likely that peers are perceived as approving of teenage drinking.

There is also evidence that mere involvement with peers is a significant variable in the drinking behavior of adolescents. It has been found that drinking correlates with the amount of time spent with friends[23] and with participation in peer activities in general.[24] In fact, in a study comparing the relative influence of peers and parents with respect to initiation into the use of hard liquor, the single most important predictive variable was the degree of adolescent involvement in peer activities, e.g., attending parties, getting together with friends, and dating.[25]

While it has been found repeatedly that adolescents demonstrate drinking behaviors similar to those of their friends, the dynamics of this relationship are not yet clear. An individual adolescent, who for his or her own personal reasons has decided to drink, may seek social support for that drinking behavior by befriending other adolescents who drink. It is also quite possible that the mere existence of peer groups serves as an incentive to drinking, as an expression either of cohesiveness or of rebellion towards parents. This is clearly an area warranting further investigation.

## Contextual Factors

Among the environmental factors considered in this chapter, drinking contexts are the most immediate or proximal to behavior. Surveys of adolescent drinking patterns indicate that most teenagers are introduced to alcohol at home in the presence of their parents.[26] The most commonly reported occasions on which teenagers are likely to drink, however, are at parties attended by peers with no adult supervision.[27] Studies also indicate that heavier or more frequent drinkers are more likely to report using alcohol in peer settings than in the context of the family. The 1974 national survey indicated that the great majority of heavy drinkers (80%) drank mostly with peers while only a small proportion of the infrequent drinkers (6%) reported drinking mostly with peers.[28] As drinking level increased, the proportions of students drinking most of the time with peers also increased.

Further analysis of these data found that 51 percent of the students drank both at home and in peer settings, 36 percent drank only at home, and 13 percent drank only with peers.[29] While the proportion of students who drank exclusively at home decreased with age, the proportion who drank both at home and with peers or exclusively with peers increased with age. Students who drank exclusively in peer settings drank less frequently than students who drank both at home and in peer settings but the amounts consumed per occasion were similar. Boys and girls at the junior high level had similar patterns. However, at the senior high level, more boys than girls drank at teenage parties when adults were not present.

While evidence exists that relates contexts of drinking to overall patterns of consumption, there are very few data on the frequency and amount of drinking that occurs in specific contexts. In a Scottish survey of 14- to 17-year olds, Davies and Stacey found that more teenagers drank in the parental home (92%) than in the home of a friend (71%) or outside the home (66%), but the amounts of alcohol consumed at home were significantly less than in the other two contexts.[30] The largest amounts were consumed outside the home (i.e., at a dance, in a hotel or pub, outdoors, or somewhere else). The quantities consumed in each of the three settings increased as a function of age. However, there was a noticeable shift, particularly among boys, from drinking in the home context to drinking away from home.

More recent data from the 1978 national survey suggest a strong relationship between adolescent drinking contexts and overall patterns of consumption.[31] Approximately three-fourths of the frequent-heavy drinking boys drank mostly at teen parties whereas only a quarter of them drank mostly in adult contexts. A similar pattern was present among heavy drinkers who drank less frequently. It may be inferred that teenage parties where adults are not present represent the drinking context which draws upon heavy drinking boys. The exact relationship must be inferred since the quantity data are not context-specific assessments.

There is also evidence to suggest that problems associated with drinking may be linked to situational factors. A study of students in a southern abstinence community found that students who drank with friends or alone were more likely to be problem users while those who drank with parents or relatives were more likely not to be problem users.[32] In a survey of high school students in Ontario, it was found that scores on a problem-drinking scale were more strongly correlated with situational factors than other types of peer or parental influences.[33] Problem drinkers had their first drinks away from home and usually drank in cars. Other studies indicate that teenagers whose early use of alcohol occurs with peers rather than parents may also experience more problems with alcohol or with society in general. Two studies found that the majority of nondelinquent youth took their first drinks with parents or relatives and continued to drink predominantly with family members, while delinquent youth generally took their first drink with friends and continued to drink predominantly with friends.[34]

One consequence of alcohol misuse often reported in teenage surveys is the reported frequency of drunkenness.[35] Times drunk may be viewed as an extension of the drinking quantity variable (i.e., heavier drinkers get drunk more frequently than light drinkers), but it also serves to define a greater state of risk regarding negative behavioral consequences of drinking. It can therefore be a useful marker variable for targeting those teenagers who are likely to experience alcohol-related problems. In the 1978 survey it was found that frequency of times drunk was highly correlated with reports of problems related to drinking.

Approximately 30 percent of the 1978 student sample reported being drunk six or more times during the past year. There was a strong relationship between times drunk and the percentage of students who drink mostly at teenage parties with no adults present. The majority of students who frequently get drunk drink mostly at teen parties with no adults present, rather than mostly in other settings. For example, among boys who reported getting drunk 52 or more times, 76 percent drank mostly at home. Among students who report never having gotten drunk, 39 percent never drink at teen parties. For students who reported getting drunk only once in the past year, only 16 percent report never drinking in this context. (As was the case for drinking patterns, the report of drunkenness by students who drink mostly in a given context does not indicate that drunkenness occurred in that context.)

To further elucidate the relationship between drinking context and drunkenness, Harford and Spiegler derived three mutually exclusive categories from the four context items under investigation.[36] Among teenagers who drink exclusively at home, the majority report never having been drunk (72% of the boys and 76% of the girls). Boys and girls who drink both at teenage parties and at home had the highest proportion of times drunk. Students who did not drink at home but did drink at parties with or without adults present had distributions that were more similar to the second group than the first.

These data suggest that a strong relationship exists between adolescent drinking contexts and overall patterns of consumption. Teenage parties when adults are not present are related to patterns of frequent and heavy consumption among boys and girls. Social controls for teenage drinking are most likely to be exercised in the home of parents where access to alcohol is generally under the supervision of parents or other adult relatives. Outside the parental home, drinking appears to be under the control of teenagers themselves. The present data, however, do not isolate direction or causality of the relationship. While it can be argued that the absence of adult supervision at teenage parties contributes to excessive consumption, it is equally tenable that these occasions tend to draw upon a heavier drinking group of adolescents.

### Relative Contributions of Environmental Factors

A variety of factors have been shown to differentially impact on the level of teenage alcohol use. Jessor and Jessor have found that variables such as sociodemographic status are less directly related to teenage drinking than are factors in the more immediate environment such as peer drinking models and teenage marijuana use.[37] In order to determine the contributions of various environmental influences on the drinking behavior of the adolescents in the 1978 national survey, four sets of drinking measures (typical frequency, typical quantity, times drunk, and problem drinking) were regressed separately on four sets of environmental variables (sociodemographic characteristics, parental influences, peer influences, and drinking contexts). The standardized regression coefficients (Beta) for each of the four regression analyses and the per cent of variability explained ($R^2$) are presented in Table I. Each coefficient reflects the effects of a particular variable after the effects of the other variables in the regression equation are controlled.

Overall, the variables most significantly related to drinking pattern are number of friends drinking, social functions of drinking, and drinking at teen parties with no adults present. For each of the drinking measures, sociodemographic characteristics and parental influence only accounted for a small proportion of the variation although the latter did account for 14 per cent of problem drinking. Drinking contexts accounted for the highest proportion of the variance for all four measures: 49 percent of typical frequency, 46 percent of typical quantity, 42 percent of times drunk, and 18 percent of problem drinking. As might be expected, problem drinking is a more difficult outcome to predict than either the quantity or frequency of drinking.

TABLE 1-1.
STANDARDIZED REGRESSION COEFFICIENTS FOR VARIABLES
RELATED TO TYPICAL DRINKING FREQUENCY,
TYPICAL DRINKING QUANTITY, FREQUENCY OF TIMES DRUNK,
AND PROBLEM DRINKING INDEX

| | Typical Frequency | Typical Quantity | Times Drunk | Problem Drinking |
|---|---|---|---|---|
| | | Beta | | |
| Sociodemographic Factors | | | | |
| Grade in school | −.12** | −.07** | .06** | .15** |
| Gender | .12** | .18** | −.12** | −.15** |
| Black | −.05* | .00 | .02 | .00 |
| Size of town | .05** | −.03* | −.01 | .06** |
| White | .08** | .20** | −.11** | −.11** |
| Religious Affiliation | −.03 | −.02 | .01 | −.01 |
| Socioeconomic status | −.01 | .02 | .01 | .00 |
| Region | −.01 | .04 | −.07** | −.01 |
| Total Variance (R²) | .04 | .08 | .04 | .06 |
| Parental Influences | | | | |
| Attitudes re boys drinking | .26** | .21** | −.19** | −.16** |
| Paternal drinking | .12** | .11** | −.09** | −.06** |
| Maternal drinking | .10** | .05** | −.05** | −.01 |
| Attitudes re girls drinking | .00 | −.07** | .04 | .04 |
| Total Variance (R²) | .14 | .06 | .06 | .03 |
| Peer Influences | | | | |
| Number friends drinking | −.42** | −.41** | .38** | .23** |
| Social functions | −.30** | −.32** | .35** | .19** |
| Conforming functions | .08** | .06** | −.08** | −.01 |
| Number at school drinking | .06** | .05** | −.07** | −.03 |
| Peer approval for drinking | .03 | .02 | −.03** | .05** |
| Status functions | .03 | .02 | −.05* | .01 |
| Total Variance (R²) | .34 | .36 | .34 | .14 |
| Drinking Contexts | | | | |
| At home with parents | −.18** | −.06 | .00 | −.02 |
| Teen parties with adults | −.16** | −.09 | .14** | .13** |
| Teen parties—no adults | −.51** | −.61 | .56** | .34** |
| Total Variance (R²) | .49 | .46 | .42 | .18 |

*p < .05
**p < .01

These findings have highlighted environmental factors that
significantly influence drinking patterns among adolescents. Some
of these factors may also affect whether prevention programs for

this population can change their knowledge, attitudes, and behaviors related to alcohol use in the desired direction.

## IMPLICATIONS FOR PREVENTION PROGRAMS

Peer influences and drinking contexts have been found to have the most impact on the drinking patterns of adolescents. It is clear that efforts to prevent problem drinking in adolescents require changes in the social norms surrounding drinking and in the process through which adolescents become drinkers. Logically, goals for prevention programs should reflect an awareness of these factors by: (1) encouraging peer groups of adolescents to decide if and how they will drink, (2) providing adequate information for them to make those decisions, and (3) helping them to identify beliefs and attitudes toward alcohol that can affect those decisions.

These goals are part of a range of program components that should be considered in developing a prevention program for adolescents. It is important to clarify how programs can be structured to achieve effectiveness in light of the environmental factors noted previously. Consequently, the following components will be discussed here: participants and settings, content areas, instructional methods, program trainers, evaluation, and collateral training.

### Participants and Settings

Findings from the 1974 and 1978 national surveys indicate that older adolescents are more likely to drink and to be problem-drinkers than younger ones. These findings indicate a greater potential for primary prevention with younger adolescents and preadolescents. Therefore, separate prevention services should be provided for these two age groups, as well as for older adolescents. An additional reason for separating adolescents in these age groups is to prevent alcohol misuse in older adolescents from becoming a model for younger adolescents.

Programs for adolescents in the same age range should include natural peer groupings in the same sessions. More prevalent, frequent, and heavier drinking occurs in adolescents as the extent of drinking among friends increases. Those peer influences that typically support increased drinking could be utilized in sessions to support responsible use of alcohol or abstinence. In order to impact effectively on this peer culture, programs should involve at least 15 to 20 sessions.

Schools are optimal settings for these sessions, since students spend approximately 50 percent of their waking hours and form the majority of their peer relationships there. Prevention programs should be integrated into the regular curriculum within the natural context of education for living. To reach those adolescents who are turned off by school or who have dropped out of the educational system, other settings should also be used. These include community centers, neighborhood houses and churches — settings where indigenous peer groups congregate and attend teen parties. Since teen parties are the context in which adolescents most frequently drink larger quantities of alcohol, the settings mentioned may provide opportunities for more direct impact on adolescent drinking behavior.

## Content Areas

Regardless of the kinds of settings used for prevention programs, there are some basic content areas that should be included across all settings. Areas to be covered are based on findings about factors that influence frequency, quantity, times drunk and problem drinking in adolescents. They are also based on the three goals discussed previously. Content areas include:

1. Basic knowledge about alcohol usage, the alcoholic content of various beverages, short- and long-term effects of alcohol (physical, social, emotional), and the multiple determinants of alcoholism.
2. Information on the progression from responsible usage to problem usage, how to assess a drinking problem in general and among the participants, and treatment methods for alcohol problems.
3. Evaluation of the meaning of alcohol use and its role in adolescent subcultures, drinking models in peer and paren-

tal relationships, and other factors such as drinking contexts that influence drinking patterns in adolescents and other age groups.

4. Decision-making processes related to responsible and irresponsible alcohol use, alternatives to drinking, values clarification about drinking including relevant beliefs and values, how to cope with pressures to drink and factors that influence drinking patterns in adolescents.

The organization and sequence of these content areas into specific sessions can be varied based on the ages of participants and current drinking patterns. The perspective from which the content is presented should also vary based on those same factors. Other areas of content may be used as supplementary material for these major areas.

### Instructional Methods

As with the four major content areas, the instructional methods chosen should engage the participants' interests and involvement. Short lecturettes combined with large group discussions encourage knowledge building and the sharing of attitudes and beliefs about drinking between peers. Additionally, exercises, role playing, small group discussions, and tasks performed between sessions can impact on those peer influences and drinking contexts that typically support drinking.

For example, structured exercises and small group discussions can be used to simulate important drinking contexts such as teen parties without adult supervision. These methods can heighten awareness about consequences, increase decision-making skills, and develop peer supports for responsible use of alcohol. Role playing can provide related opportunities to apply new knowledge and practice in handling real situations that influence drinking. It may also reveal attitudes, values, and beliefs that affect how adolescents handle pressures related to drinking and teach them alternative ways to respond. All of these methods can be integrated into regular sessions, and used in a more formal way after units of content have been presented to test learning. Wodarski and Hoffman have noted that a game format is very effective for this latter purpose.[38]

## Program Trainers

The skills necessary for using these varied instructional methods should be considered in the selection of trainers. Trainers should be taught about the specific prevention program involved. In addition, because of the importance of factors that influence drinking, they should understand the ecological perspective, alcohol treatment and prevention issues, the dynamics of "normal" adolescent development, and the impact of this subculture on drinking. They should also have knowledge and skills related to group process. Lastly, trainers should be clear about their own attitudes towards drinking. The findings from the 1978 survey indicate that restrictive attitudes in adults have been correlated with problem drinking in adolescents, so trainer attitudes could affect whether or not program outcomes are positive.[39]

Trained peer co-leaders who have previously participated in the prevention program involved can be used also to effect positive outcomes. Since perceived support for drinking has been correlated with heavier and more frequent drinking in adolescents, peer co-leaders may be more influential than adults in supporting decreased drinking.[40] As co-leaders, they can be utilized to teach specific content such as the effects of beliefs and attitudes about alcohol on drinking patterns, and to lead small group discussions or exercises.

## Evaluation

The effects of using peer co-leaders as well as other specific program components should be evaluated in a systematic manner. Both the long- and short-term effects of these components should be evaluated. Additionally, evaluation should be used to identify high risk adolescents and those who are already problem-drinkers or alcoholics for supplemental follow-up services.

Evaluation can be accomplished through the development of clear behavioral objectives that can be used to monitor and measure responses by the participants. These objectives should focus on changes in the participants' knowledge, attitudes, and behaviors related to alcohol use. Because changes in the manner in which adolescents respond to factors that influence drinking may be very subtle and complex, it may be necessary to measure very specific variables. Therefore, experimental methods should be used: matched control groups, pre- and post-scales or question- naires that measure subtle changes in participants' knowledge, attitudes, and behaviors associated with alcohol use (including frequency, quantity, times drunk, and problem-drinking), and periodic structured follow-up contacts at 3 months, 6 months, 1 year, 2 years and so on to evaluate the maintenance of changes.[41]

If the circumstances are structured and rated objectively at specific periods in the program, participants' responses to simula- tions and exercises can be used for ongoing evaluation of changes. Results from these methods can be compared with self-report data (on the questionnaires and scales) about changes in alcohol use that occur outside of the sessions.

### Collateral Training

Changes in alcohol use by adolescents in their natural environ- ments are the focal point of evaluation. However, parental and peer influences and drinking contexts may affect the extent to which changes occur or can be maintained. Prevention programs for key individuals in an adolescent's environment may therefore be very useful in reinforcing positive changes that occur in his or her use of alcohol.

Adolescents are most often introduced to alcohol at home in the presence of parents. Parents need to be aware of the impact which this process and their attitudes and use of alcohol have on the subsequent drinking patterns of their children. Parents should also be aware that more problem-drinkers are introduced to alco- hol away from home in the company of peers and that more problem drinking occurs among adolescents who drink only in that context. Information about these issues along with the con- tent areas discussed for adolescents could help parents, teachers, and other adults in the environment to support responsible use of alcohol in adolescents.

## SUMMARY AND CONCLUSIONS

This chapter has examined the associations between selected environmental factors (demographic, parental, peer, and contextual) and various measures of alcohol consumption. Of the environmental influences considered, the circumstances in which adolescents consume alcohol were found to be the most important in predicting heavier levels of alcohol consumption. Contextual factors also help direct attention to antecedent conditions which structure the environment of the adolescent, and to ways in which problem-drinking can be prevented. Prevention programs have a greater potential for primary prevention with younger adolescents who as a group drink less than older ones. Providing separate programs for these two age groups may increase the likelihood of success with both groups. This issue, along with other program components, have been discussed in terms of the factors that most significantly influence drinking in adolescents.

Additional research is needed regarding the manner in which environmental factors specifically influence drinking among adolescents in supervised situations. Further, in view of the frequency of drinking in nonadult contexts, and its connection to heavy and problem drinking, more detailed studies are needed to identify the critical variables in peer contexts which influence heavier consumption. Teenage parties vary considerably with respect to several dimensions: formal and informal occasions, the number of persons present, the specific location, the sex ratio and age ratio of those present, access to alcohol, and friendship patterns. Research is necessary to determine the roles these factors play in the level of consumption, and how they may affect adolescents' responses to prevention efforts.

## REFERENCES

1. Rachal, J. V., Maisto, S. A., Guess, L. L., and Hubbard, R. L.: *Alcohol Use Among Youth.* In Alcohol and Health Monograph No. 1. Washington, D.C., DHHS Publ. No. (ADM)82-1190, 55–95, 1982.

2. Ibid.
3. See for example, Blane, H. T., and Hewitt, L. E.: *Alcohol and Youth: An analysis of the Literature 1960–1975.* Final report submitted to the National Institute of Alcohol Abuse and Alcoholism under Contract No. (ADM)281-75-0026, 1977; Mandell, W. and Ginsberg, H. M.: Youthful alcohol use, abuse and alcoholism. In Kissin, B., and Begleiter, H., (Eds.): *Social Aspects of Alcoholism.* New York, Plenum, 1977; Marden, P. G., and Kolodner, K.: *Alcohol Use and Abuse Among Adolescents.* NCAI Report to NIAAA, NCA 1026533, 1977; and Schuckit, M. A.: *Alcohol Patterns and Problems in Youth.* Unpublished conference manuscript. Alcoholism and Drug Abuse Institute, University of Washington, 1978.
4. Rachal, Maisto, Guess, & Hubbard, op. cit.
5. Wechsler, H. and Thum, D.: Teenage drinking, drug use, and social correlates. *Quarterly Journal of Studies on Alcohol, 34:*1220–1227, 1973.
6. Prendergast, T. J., Jr., and Schaefer, E. S.: Correlates of drinking and drunkenness among high school students. *Quarterly Journal of Studies on Alcohol, 35:*232–242, 1974.
7. Smart, R. G., Gray, G., and Bennett, C.: Predictors of drinking and signs of heavy drinking among high school students. *International Journal of Addictions, 13:*1079–1094, 1978.
8. Margulies, R. Z., Kessler, R. C., and Kandel, D. B.: A longitudinal study of onset of drinking among high-school students. *Journal of Studies on Alcohol, 38:*897–912, 1977.
9. Jessor, R., and Jessor, S. L.: *Problem Behavior and Psychosocial Development: A Longitudinal Study of Youth.* New York, Academic Press, 1977. See also Donovan, J. E., and Jessor, R.: Adolescent problem drinking: Psychosocial correlates in a national sample study. *Journal of Studies on Alcohol, 39:*1506–1524, 1978.
10. Globetti, G.: Social adjustment of high school students and problem drinking. *Journal of Alcohol Education, 13:*21–29, 1967.
11. Davies, J., and Stacey, B.: *Teenagers and Alcohol. Vol II.* London, Her Majesty's Stationery Office, 1972.
12. Rachal, Maisto, Guess, & Hubbard, op. cit.
13. Blane & Hewitt, op. cit.
14. Margulies, Kessler, & Kandel, op. cit. See also Forslund, M. A., and Gustafson, T. J.: Influence of peers and parents and sex differences in drinking by high school students. *Quarterly Journal of Studies on Alcohol, 31:*868–875, 1970.
15. Rachal, J. V., Williams, J. R., Brehn, M. L., Cavanaugh, B., Moore, R. P., and Eckerman, W. C.: *A National Study of Adolescent Drinking Behavior, Attitudes, and Correlates.* Research Triangle Park, N.C., Research Triangle Park Center for the Study of Social Behavior, 1975.
16. Kandel, D. B., Kessler, R. C., and Margulies, R. Z.: Antecedents of adolescent initiation into stages of drug use: A developmental analysis. In Kandel, D. B. (Ed.), *Longitudinal Research on Drug Use: Empirical Findings and Methodological Issues.* New York, John Wiley and Sons, 1978.

17. Rachal, Maisto, Guess, & Hubbard, op. cit.
18. Davies & Stacey, op. cit.
19. Forslund & Gustafson, op. cit.
20. Rachal, Williams, Brehn, Cavanaugh, Moore, & Eckerman, op. cit. See also Maddon, G. L. and McCall, B. C.: *Drinking among teenagers: A sociological interpretation of alcohol use by high-school students.* Monograph No. 4. New Brunswick, N.J., Rutgers Center of Alcohol Studies, 1964; and Mandell, W., Cooper, A., Silberstein, R. M., Novick, J., and Koloski, E.: *Youthful Drinking, New York State, 1962.* Staten Island, N.Y., Staten Island Mental Health Society, Wakoff Research Center, 1963.
21. Wechsler & Thum, op. cit.; Jessor & Jessor, op. cit.; Rachal, Williams, Brehn, Cavanaugh, Moore, & Eckerman, op. cit.; and Kane, R. L., and Patterson, E.: Drinking attitudes and behavior of high school students in Kentucky. *Quarterly Journal of Studies on Alcohol, 33:* 635–646, 1972.
22. Jessor, R., Collins, M. J., and Jessor, S. L.: On becoming a drinker: Social-psychological aspects of an adolescent transition. *Annals of the New York Academy of Science, 197:*199–213, 1972.
23. Ibid.
24. Margulies, Kessler, & Kandel, op. cit.
25. Kandel, Kessler, & Margulies, op. cit.
26. Davies & Stacey, op. cit.; and Maddon & McCall, op. cit.
27. Ibid.
28. Rachal, Williams, Brehn, Cavanaugh, Moore, Eckerman, op. cit.
29. Harford, T. C., and Spiegler, D. L.: Developmental trends of adolescent drinking. *Journal of Alcohol Studies, 44:*181–188, 1983.
30. Davies & Stacey, op. cit.
31. Rachal, Maisto, Guess, & Hubbard, op. cit.; and Harford, T. C., and Spiegler, D. L.: Environmental influences in adolescent drinking. In *Alcohol and Health Monograph No. 4.* Washington, D.C., DHHS Publ. No. (ADM)82-1193, 167–193, 1982.
32. Globetti, G.: Problem and non-problem drinking among high school students in abstinence communities. *International Journal of Addictions, 7:*511–523, 1972.
33. Smart, R. G., and Gray, G.: Parental and peer influences as correlates of problem drinking among high school students. *International Journal of Addictions, 14:*905–917, 1979.
34. MacKay, J. R., Phillips, D. L., and Bryce, F. O.: Drinking behavior among teenagers: A comparison of institutionalized and noninstitutionalized youth. *Journal of Health and Social Behavior, 8:*46–54, 1967; and Pearce, J., and Garrett, H. D.: Comparison of the drinking behavior of delinquent youth versus non-delinquent youth in the states of Idaho and Utah. *Journal of School Health, 401:*131–135, 1970.
35. Jessor & Jessor, op. cit.
36. Harford & Spiegler, op. cit.

37.  Jessor & Jessor, op. cit.
38.  Wodarski, J. S., and Hoffman, S. D.: Alcohol education for adolescents. *Social Work in Education,* 6:69–92, 1984.
39.  Rachal, Maisto, Guess, & Hubbard, op. cit.
40.  Ibid.
41.  McCarty, D., Morrison, S., and Mills, K. C.: Attitudes, beliefs, and alcohol use: An analysis of relationships. *Journal of Studies on Alcohol,* 44:328–341, 1983.

*Chapter Two*

# DOMESTIC VIOLENCE AND SUBSTANCE ABUSE: A COOPERATIVE APPROACH TOWARD WORKING WITH DUALLY AFFECTED FAMILIES

JANET WRIGHT

Although domestic violence has been a problem for as long as we have had history and probably before, only more recently have we become aware of its massive proportions. It is now estimated that one out of two women have or will experience some violence in their adult relationships.[1] Considering the fact that substance abuse is adversely affecting over one-quarter of all Americans,[2] one can imagine the huge overlap that must occur between these two issues. Research shows that somewhere between 50 and 95 percent of all women who suffer from domestic violence also live in homes where substance abuse is a problem.[3] In other words, there could potentially be 10 to 20 million American families which are dually affected by these problems. The numbers are staggering. Consider these research statistics: (1) 1 in 10 Americans are problem drinkers.[4] (2) According to the FBI, every 18 seconds a woman is beaten in her own home in the U.S.A.[5] (3) For every alcohol abuser, there are an estimated five other persons who suffer directly.[6] (4) A Louis Harris poll published in 1979 found that one out of ten women had been abused by their husbands *within that year.*[7]

## THEORETICAL BASIS

There are several theories that attempt to clarify the connection between domestic violence and substance abuse.[8]

The theoretical concept of disavowel involves the assumption that men beat women because they know that being drunk releases them from responsibility by their partners and by the rest of society. Our society has not been consistent or clear in determining just how responsible an alcoholic is for his or her behavior.

A battered woman once described how she changed her own perception of this responsibility. She had never really held her husband responsible for her beatings because he was always drunk. Then one hot summer day, her husband was drunk as usual and in his undershorts when he beat her. After the beating, he went into the bedroom, pulled on his pants, got his wallet and keys and left. She thought if he was so out of control, how did he know it wasn't okay to go outside in his underwear? Other examples include drunk husbands who manage to beat their wives where it won't show or who aim for the abdomen of their pregnant wives.

The disinhibition theory has an underlying assumption that alcohol acts to lessen inhibitions so that people who drink lose their inhibitions toward aggressive behavior including domestic violence. However, many alcoholics are not violent. Fewer women are violent when drinking, and individuals from various cultures show differing amounts of violence when drinking.

Learned behavior theory postulates that people who are violent when drinking have learned through cultural or familial norms that violence and drinking go together. This theory provides the most useful explanation because it helps account for the intergenerational factor in domestic violence, the fact that abusers are more likely to come from families that used violence as a control.[9]

This theory also places emphasis on cultural values that teach violence against women. This explanation is the one most widely accepted by grass roots agencies organized by and for battered women since 1965. It will be discussed in greater detail shortly.

### SIMILARITIES AND DIFFERENCES

All of these theories may be enlightening in different situations and should be looked at in terms of treatment procedures. However, none of them address the fact that substance abuse and woman abuse are two separate but related problems. Substance abuse does not cause violence, and violence does not cause substance abuse. Violence is not just a symptom on the progression chart of alcoholism. If a woman is helped to deal with the violence in her life, but she is also addicted to Valium®, she won't necessarily suddenly stop taking that Valium. Or, as was so aptly stated in an AA meeting once, "If we sober up a wife-beater, we have in most cases a sober wifebeater."

There are some similarities between substance abusing families and those involving domestic violence.[10] Both abuses: (1) resolve conflict temporarily, (2) force reactions in others, (3) block feelings and intimacy, (4) mask depression and fear, (5) create rigid family patterns, (6) have an addictive quality for the abuser, and (7) generally keep the woman in the relationship. These similarities may make it seem that we could use the same prevention and intervention tactics for both problem areas.

However, there are some very important differences between the two kinds of abuses. Substance abuse is more likely to occur in different locations so that other people are likely to become aware of the problem, at home, on the job, while driving, at parties, or at the neighborhood bar. For this reason, the technique of having friends and family confront the abuser with his or her abuse may be a successful early secondary prevention tactic. Domestic violence is much more likely to occur only within the confines of the home, with the victim and perhaps the children as the only witnesses. It is not likely to come to the attention of the employer, law enforcement, friends, or even neighbors unless the victim approaches them for assistance.

Secondly, substance abuse affects others, but it affects them secondarily. Domestic violence is an act perpetrated on someone else and affects her primarily. If there are children, the violence may also be directed against them or they may be affected secondarily as witnesses. Substance abuse becomes more like domestic violence when the abuser is driving under the influence. Then he or she can affect another's life primarily. Penalties for this behavior have recently become stricter.

A third difference is that substance abuse affects both men and women. Statistics on alcoholism are now approaching a one-to-one ratio between men and women, although men may still be slightly more affected. However, with domestic violence, by far the most serious violence resulting in injuries is directed against women. This factor has a serious influence on how prevention is approached.

There are also similarities and differences among families affected by both problems. It is essential when working with these families that we take all of their unique characteristics into consideration. A black battered woman's experience is similar in many ways to a white woman's, but there are important differences. Black women have to cope with the additional problem of racism. They have different pressures from the community, especially if they go to a predominately white shelter. They may have fewer options for getting out of their marriage if they are also poor. If this is not taken into account, treatment may be more damaging than helpful. A woman going into substance abuse treatment has different needs and a different reality than a man going into treatment. A woman whose husband is violent toward her *and* abuses alcohol has different needs from a woman whose husband is not violent but abuses alcohol. All of the similarities and differences discussed in this section help create a structure for looking at prevention and intervention with dually affected families.

### PREVENTION

One of the first questions to address when one looks at prevention is why is the problem occurring? Why do people abuse drugs? And why do men beat women? The reasons for abusing drugs range from the belief that it is a biochemical and perhaps genetic disease to the belief that it is simply a bad habit that can be broken. A complicating issue is society's acceptance of drug use and encouragement to abuse drugs. Most prevention and treatment personnel, however, ascribe to the belief that alcoholism is a disease. Prevention, then, lies in early intervention and abstention.

A more accurate term for this second kind of abuse is woman abuse, instead of spouse abuse or family violence. Although husband abuse has increased, an estimated 95 percent of serious violence between adult partners is directed against women.[11] This happens because women have a different status from men in our society. Women have been seen in the past as possessions of their fathers and then husbands. It was legal for men to beat, discipline, and chastize their wives. The expression "rule of thumb" originated from an old English law which stated that a man could not beat his wife with a stick that was thicker around than his own thumb.[12]

While the laws have changed, attitudinal changes lag behind. In a 1970 study of attitudes of mental health workers, they were asked to write traits of healthy females, healthy males, and healthy adults.[13] The healthy male and adult traits were identical. Healthy females were associated with stereotypic negative traits. So women must choose between the adult and female status. No wonder so many women call themselves girls.

In an examination of rape-free and rape-prone societies, Beryl Benderly found that the incidence of rape was directly related to the following factors: the status of women, the values that govern the relations between the sexes, and the attitudes taught to boys.[14] Societies with a high incidence of rape tolerate violence and encourage men and boys to be tough, aggressive, and competitive. Men have special politically important gathering spots which are off limits to women. Women take little or no part in public decision-making or religious rituals. Men mock or scorn women's practical judgement. They also demean what they see as women's work and remain aloof from childbearing and rearing. These groups usually trace their beginnings to a male supreme being. The opposite is true of rape-free societies.

Power and violence go hand in hand in our society. Violence is our method of choice for emphasizing and insuring control. In our society that means men over women, men *and* women over children, white over black, etc. The way that we define and act out power in this society is unhealthy for all of us. Any efforts directed toward prevention must address these issues.

### The Medical Model

Looking at the differences in causes of substance abuse and woman abuse, one can understand the necessity for some different approaches to prevention and intervention. Substance abuse has generally been approached using the medical model. This model focuses on the treatment of sick individuals and their families. The goal is to help individuals and their families fit into society better and to be happier within that society.

In the woman abuse field, the focus has more often been on the fact that society is sick and needs changing. The attempt has been to change society to help make individuals within it function better and be happier.

There is and should be some overlap between models used for both kinds of abuse. Substance abuse workers recognize the insidious messages conveyed by the media which encourage the use of drugs. Prevention efforts have been increased to counteract this influence, including the development of curricula for schools and materials for the media to refute the idea that substances lead to instant maturity, beauty, and sexual attractiveness. However, a vast amount of resources continue to be used for individual and family treatment based on the disease model. The disease model in substance abuse presents a no fault model. Substance abuse is a disease. It has predictable symptoms, is progressive, chronic, and fatal. The dependent person is ill and in need of treatment. Medical treatment is often a necessary part of recovery, along with therapy and self-help groups.

### Social Change Model

On the other hand, the woman abuse field generally recognizes that a person initiates violence towards others in order to achieve, demonstrate, or assert control or dominance over them. If violence is a disease, it is a social disease, and society, not the battered woman, is the enabler through the transmission of cultural sanctions for aggressive behavior toward women. The best cure for violence is the consistent societal and personal message that it is not okay and that the abuser will face unpleasant consequences.

Unfortunately, there is very little funding available for social change which is really the focus of primary prevention. However, many battered women's programs are funded to provide services to individuals for secondary and tertiary prevention through shelters, crisis lines, and counseling. These services are crucial for preventing the escalation of these problems in each situation. It is equally important to continually focus on the reasons why women end up needing these services to begin with because of oppression within our society.

Primary prevention of woman abuse lies in changing oppressive attitudes toward women and the services or *lack* of services based on these attitudes. Women stay in battering relationships and other unhealthy relationships primarily because their options elsewhere are limited. For example, women earn on the average 59 cents for every dollar that men earn. Women need hard resources such as job training, jobs, adequate child care services, affordable housing, child support, equity in settlements from divorces, flexible and creative employment situations such as job sharing, and affordable and competent legal advice. Counseling is also important, but these other needs must be met on a priority basis. As in Maslow's self-actualizing theory, survival needs must be satisfied first.[15] It is pointless to work on parenting issues unless a woman's desperate need to find housing has been met first or simultaneously.

In a similar vein, treatment programs for men who batter have been touted as the new prevention programs. While treatment programs for men who batter are very important for those men at a secondary or tertiary prevention level, they can presently make very little difference in terms of primary prevention.

To summarize, a first step in the prevention area is the provision of educational services to the general public to address oppressive attitudes toward women and to teach functional and nondestructive ways to resolve individual and familial stresses. A second step is to provide the hard resources for single and/or working women that were described earlier in this section. Providing crisis services, including counseling and shelter, is a third step. These three steps involve prevention at primary and secondary levels. A fourth step is for society to validate the seriousness of this crime and to let it be known that woman abuse will not be tolerated through the enactment of tougher and more consistently enforced laws. This last preventive step at the tertiary level may aid in early identification and treatment of families in which woman abuse is occurring.

## EARLY IDENTIFICATION AND INTERVENTION PLANNING

The first step to intervention with dually affected families is early identification of potential or existing abuse situations. The obvious key to identification is in *asking*. Understanding the huge overlap between the two problems, every substance abuse worker should be asking about violence and every woman abuse worker should be asking about substance abuse. Workers in both fields often use a funneling technique when assessing a potential problem, starting broad and narrowing in. For example, a series of questions for substance abusers around violence might be: Do you and your partner ever argue? Do you yell at each other when you fight? Have either of you ever hurt the other one when you are fighting? Have you ever slapped your wife? ... and so on. Or, questions for a potentially abused woman include: Do you and your partner ever argue? Do you yell at each other when you fight? Have either of you ever hurt the other one when you were fighting? Have you ever been slapped, shoved, or kicked? ... etc.

The most important issue with identification however is simply the asking itself. By asking, one recognizes that it is a common issue, that it is an issue of concern, and that the practitioner is not afraid of hearing the answer. With the victim, reactions must be nonjudgmental and informative. It is not her fault. This happens to a surprisingly large number of women. There is help available. She should be aware of these resources.

With the abuser, reactions should be empathic of the feelings but confrontive of the actions. He must have really been angry when his wife nagged at him, you can understand that, but he should know that it is not okay to hit her. He can change. There is help available. He should be aware of these resources.

Woman abuse is not something that either the abused or the perpetrator usually brings up. In fact, they will often go to great lengths to avoid it. Even if the questions asked are denied, asking will open the door so this person knows that he or she can talk with you about this issue in the future.

Once a dually affected family is identified, the question often asked is, "Which is the primary problem? Which should be treated first?" First it is important to keep in mind that both substance abuse and woman abuse are serious problems. Both need to be addressed. If a child is in a car accident and has a badly broken leg and internal injuries, the physician doesn't decide to treat one and hope the other will go away. She or he decides what is the most immediate, life-threatening problem and deals with that. Then she or he takes care of the other problems. That is how one must look at these families.

There are two common configurations of dually-affected families. Possible plans for the abuser and the victim will be outlined. First, the situation where the man abuses his partner as well as substances (Type A). And secondly, the situation where the woman abuses substances and her partner abuses her (Type B).

### Man Abuses Substances and is Violent: Type A Plan

Violent behaviors can terminate before sobriety, but without a program for achieving and maintaining sobriety, chances of violent behavior recurring are high.

Plan for the abuser in Family Type A:

1. He must be told immediately that the violence is not okay; that it will not be tolerated; and that he must stop.
2. He must receive treatment for his substance abuse.
3. Before this treatment is terminated, he should begin treatment for his violence.
4. He should get ongoing support around both issues.
5. Family treatment is appropriate only if both partners want to reconcile and if the violence has stopped. This issue will be addressed in more detail later.

Plan for the victim in Family Type A:

1. She and her children must find a safe place away from the abuser to stay.
2. She will have to work on the issues which the violence has created: legal, financial, employment, housing, child care, etc.
3. She will need information and probably counseling regarding the impact of substance abuse on herself and her family.

4. She will need ongoing support regarding the violence and possibly the substance abuse (such as Al-Anon).
5. Family treatment should be provided if it is desired.

### Woman Abuses Substances and is Victim of Violence: Type B Plan

Plan for the violent person in Family Type B:

1. He must be told that the violence is his responsibility and he needs treatment for it.
2. He should be given information and possibly counseling regarding the substance abuse of his wife.
3. He should receive ongoing support for both issues.
4. Couple/family counseling should be offered if it is desired.

Plan for the substance abuser/victim of violence in Family Type B:

1. She and her children must find a safe place away from the abuser to stay.
2. She will need a combination of treatment for her substance abuse and support for the issues she must deal with as a result of the violence.
3. She should receive ongoing support for both issues.
4. Couple/family treatment should be offered if it is desired.

### THE PROCESS OF TREATMENT

The process of treatment can involve possible conflicts for practitioners. Substance abuse treatment focuses on the chemically-dependent individual, but most programs now emphasize that the family's involvement in treatment is crucial in the abuser's recovery. One example of what is called professional enabling is the practice of seeing substance abusers by themselves. Their delusions help them to avoid seeing the truth. Now here is the bind. When there is violence in the family, it is pointless to do couple/family therapy until the violence has stopped. Not only is it simply pointless, but it is dangerous as well. The woman has too much fear and pain to be honest and to trust.

In one city, when a group working with violent men began,

they did couple counseling. But they discovered the women were being beaten on the way to the parking lot after sessions. Or women colluded in lying about the violence in order to protect themselves. Violent families need to be disrupted until the violence stops. Substance abuse workers and women abuse workers need to sit down together and discuss how to overcome this apparent conflict. It can no longer be ignored. Most workers in the battered women's movement agree that couple or family counseling is generally ineffective at best and dangerous at worst until the violence has stopped and the individuals have some degree of confidence that the abuser can control it. Individual or group counseling with the victims of domestic violence can be useful in the meantime, if it is done in consideration of the unique needs of this client group.

### Confrontation

Confrontation is a technique often used in substance abuse treatment. It can work to break down barriers, delusions, and denial that keep abusers from participating in their own recovery. Alcoholics who are confronted with their destructive behavior may be hearing this directly for the first time. One of the ways people change is by creating dissonance. For example, they may say as a result of a confrontation, I really like and respect Janet, but I don't like what she is saying ... but maybe I should at least think about it. However, we need to understand that battered women live with confrontation daily. In the beginning, being confrontive toward a battered woman about her enabling behavior will only serve to increase her self-blame and self-doubt. A battered woman needs liberal doses of support, belief and encouragement before she can begin to confront her own dysfunctional behaviors with the help of the practitioner.

### Enabling

Enabling is an important construct in the substance abuse model. Enablers react to the symptoms of the illness of substance abuse in such a way as to shield substance abusers from experiencing the full impact of the harmful consequences of the disease. The abuser thus loses the opportunity to gain some important insights into the severity of his or her problem. The treatment of enablers is based on helping them to let go of the responsibility they feel for the abuser, helping enablers to understand that they cannot control the behavior of someone else.

This kind of consciousness-raising for the enabler is not really that different from the goal of many shelter programs for battered women, i.e., to help them understand that they cannot change the abuser's behavior, and that only *he* is responsible for his violence and only *he* can change it.

There is a crucial difference, however. The battered woman is not an enabler of her abuser's violence any more than Jews, gays, and retarded individuals were enablers of Nazi violence, just as blacks have not been enablers of Ku Klux Klan violence. Looking at the definition of enabling, a battered woman cannot shield her abuser from the harmful consequences of his violence, because there are no harmful consequences for him. The harmful consequences are for her and her children. In most cases, he is not in danger of losing his job, his money, or even his friends or children as a consequence of his violence. He can only lose her. But she can lose her financial support, her children, her friends, her home, her business, her life.

Many parents use the theory of natural and logical consequences.[16] They allow children to suffer the natural consequences of their behavior. The theory, as stated by Theodore Dreikers, goes like this: Alfred is in the habit of forgetting his school lunch. Mom yells at him whenever she has to deliver it to school, but the yelling does no good. So one day she adopts the natural consequence, she lets Alfred go without lunch. Alfred learns his lesson. This generally works when there are natural consequences. However, we don't use natural consequences when there are none or when they are life-threatening. We don't let Susie run into a street, saying, "When she gets hit by a car, she'll learn!" So we have logical consequences. There are no natural consequences for violence. The *logical* consequence and treatment strategy is to isolate that person or put that person in a situation where he cannot be violent through the use of restraining orders, arrest, jail, and deferred prosecution. Those options or consequences are an integral part of prevention and treatment.

### CONCLUSIONS

Working with dually affected families creates new issues and new problems. These problems can only be overcome through the close cooperation of workers in the substance abuse field and the woman abuse field. Mistrust and misunderstanding between the two fields has been high. Approaches can, on the surface, seem irreconcilable. However, if effective prevention and treatment services are to be provided to dually affected families, differences must be confronted and resolved.

Primary prevention is a natural place for cooperation. School curricula which emphasize respect for individual differences, critical assessment of media messages, sound development of values, problem solving skills, verbal negotiation skills, building of self-esteem, relaxation skills, and equality between the sexes will benefit programs for battered women and those for substance abusers. Criminal justice codes which leave no doubt as to the responsibility of the abuser are necessary to prevent the epidemic of both abuses. Child protection laws and systems focused on incest and sexual abuse are important to both problem areas.

In intervention and treatment, cooperation is also crucial. Local treatment programs should begin with collaborative training programs aimed at increasing practitioners' knowledge of both areas, enhancing assessment skills, increasing cross-referrals, increasing awareness of existing programs, changing attitudes, increasing understanding, and hopefully leading towards more collaboration.[17] Such training should include an experiential component so that practitioners can actually participate in practice activities such as assessment, shelter intakes, intakes for halfway houses, and telephone crisis shifts in both types of programs. Participation greatly increases understanding. Cooperation between practitioners in both practice areas can increase also the quality of services to families currently experiencing violence and to potential victims as well.

# REFERENCES

1. Langley, Roger and Levy, Richard C.: *Wife Beating: The Silent Crisis.* New York, E. P. Dutton, 1977, p. 4.
2. Royce, James E.: *Alcohol Problems and Alcoholism.* New York, The Free Press, 1981, p. 29.
3. Langley & Levy, op. cit., 1977. Also Royce, op. cit., p. 29.
4. Johnson, Vernon E.: *I'll Quit Tomorrow.* San Francisco, Harper & Row Publishers, 1980, p. 1.
5. Federal Bureau of Investigation, Uniform Crime Reports, 1979.
6. Beckman, Linda: Women alcoholics. *Journal of Studies on Alcohol, 36*:797–824, 1975.
7. Shulman, Mark: A survey of spousal violence against women in Kentucky. Washington, D.C., Government Printing Office, 1979.
8. Coleman, Diane Hoshall and Strauss, Murray A.: Alcohol abuse and family violence. Paper presented at the American Sociological Association Annual Meeting, University of New Hampshire, 1979, Revised, 1980.
9. Star, Barbara: *Helping the Abuser.* New York, Family Service Association of America, 1983, p. 35.
10. Flanger, Jerry: The vicious circle of alcoholism and family violence. In Royce, James (Ed.): *Alcohol Problems and Alcoholism.* New York, The Free Press, 1981.
11. Schecter, Susan: *Women and Male Violence.* Boston, South End Press, 1982, p. 214.
12. Langley & Levy, op. cit., pp. 33–34.
13. Broverman, Inge, Broverman, Donald M., Clarkson, Frank E., Rosenkrantz, Paul, and Vogel, Susan R.: Sex role stereotypes and clinical judgments of mental health. *Journal of Consulting and Clinical Psychology, 34*:1–7, 1970.
14. Benderly, Beryl Lieff: Rape free or rape prone. *Science,* 40–43, 1982.
15. Maslow, Abraham Harold: *Toward a Psychology of Being.* Boston, Van Nostrand, 1968.
16. Dreikurs, Rudolf with Soltz, Vicki: *Children: The Challenge.* New York, Hawthorne Books, Inc., 1964.
17. Wright, Janet: *Chemical Dependency and Violence: Working with Dually Affected Families.* Madison, Wisconsin Clearinghouse, 1982.

## Chapter Three

## EMPLOYEE ASSISTANCE PROGRAMS*

Miriam Aaron

Employee Assistance Programs (EAP's) provide services designed for identification, assessment, referral and follow up with employees who need assistance. These programs may operate at the work location or at a site separate from the work place. Services are available for employees with problems that include, but are not limited to, familial/marital, emotional, legal, financial, compulsive gambling, alcoholism, and alcohol abuse or abuse of other mood altering substances. These problems are generally termed behavioral/medical problems and interfere with an employee's ability to function appropriately on the job.

### OVERVIEW

Intervention provided through an EAP generally results in early case-finding or prevention before an employee loses a job and before an employer loses a valued worker. Benefits of such early intervention include: a high degree of compliance with recommended care, decreases in employee absenteeism, increases in morale and productivity and cost savings to unions, employers and employees.

The development of EAP's is spreading rapidly in the United States. Programs have been developed by individual companies, unions and occupational groups. According to the National Institute of Alcohol Abuse and Alcoholism, there were approximately

*Some of the materials in this chapter were developed as a part of work for the New York State Division of Alcoholism and Alcohol Abuse.

30 effective programs in the nation in 1972.[1] In 1980, there were more than 5000 such programs. Evaluation of some of these programs has shown that many of them are effective.[2] Work settings in which programs have been established report a high rate of recovery from conditions underlying work performance problems.

The activities that are undertaken in company or union based programs generally do not include direct treatment services but rather consist of a system that leads to identification of employees who need help, assessment to determine the type of help needed and contact with community-based services where treatment or other helping services can be obtained by employees referred for care. It is important for staff in these programs to have a broad understanding of a variety of human services so that appropriate assessments are made and referrals are compatible with needs. Moreover, within EAP's it is essential to emphasize skillful exploration with employees who are affected by alcoholism or abuse of other mood altering substances, since their presenting problems may have developed in association with addictions to alcohol and/or other substances.[3]

While treatment is not included generally in most EAP's, these programs provide an invaluable means for continuity of care. The follow-up provided increases opportunities for identifying additional services which an employee may need following an initial referral, as well as assessing compliance with recommended helping resources.

Program services can be utilized by employees who voluntarily seek assistance or who are referred by a supervisor or union representative. Important features in any EAP include insuring that any information pertaining to program participants is kept confidential and an employee's standing in the work organization or promotional opportunities are not jeopardized as a result of program participation. These programs do not replace existing disciplinary procedures within the work setting; they are established as a means for providing labor and management with a system for dealing with employees who have behavioral/medical problems at the workplace with a minimum of disruption. An additional benefit involves the training of supervisory personnel and union representatives to delineate their roles and responsibilities in making referrals for program services. This training not only clarifies what the program is designed to accomplish but also reinforces some fundamental and sound work practices. Most programs also seek to educate the general workforce about various problems and community resources as a form of prevention. This provides a positive normative perspective on common but often undiscussed problems.

### RATIONALE FOR PROGRAM DEVELOPMENT

Employees with behavioral/medical problems are a legitimate concern within the work setting. Such employees are absent more frequently than others, are involved in a greater number of accidents both on and off the job, and generally evidence an erratic pattern in their job performance and interpersonal relationships. These patterns can cause disruption and low morale, both for themselves and those around them.[4]

While the traditional focus of managers and supervisors has been on job skill performance, it is becoming increasingly apparent that in order for employees to function appropriately at work, other factors must be considered. The employee who is distracted because of a difficult home situation, financial worries, legal problems, or child care concerns is likely to be absent often, report to work late and, once there, be unable to concentrate on the demands of the job. Similarly, the employee who is affected by alcoholism, alcohol abuse, or dependence on other mood altering substances will be unable to function well. These factors provide a basis for on-the-job services, but until recently little has been done formally and systematically to assist employees with these problems.

### OCCUPATIONAL ALCOHOLISM PROGRAMS

Early attempts by some employers to assist alcoholic employees were largely unsuccessful. They lacked knowledge about the disease as well as knowledge about treatment or rehabilitation resources. Then in the early 1940's, when Alcoholics Anonymous gained recognition as an effective aid for helping alcoholics to achieve and sustain sobriety, some employers developed company sponsored programs to deal with alcoholic employees. A major difficulty in those early programs was the tendency of supervisors to diagnose alcoholism on the basis of overt symptoms such as blood-shot eyes, staggering gait, and the smell of liquor on the breath. This approach identified only those employees who were already in late stages of the disease when their capacity to function had already deteriorated drastically. Often, these employees were terminated rather than treated. Consequently, these programs did not provide an effective means for prevention and early intervention with alcoholic employees but instead came to be regarded as "witch hunts."[5]

The concept that serves as a basis for today's occupational alcoholism programs evolved in the early 1970's. The impetus for the growth and development of these programs was provided by the federal government. In 1971, funding was provided for two consultants from each of the fifty states whose job was to encourage the development of work-based intervention programs and to assist in their development. With the recognition that alcoholics usually evidence signs of deteriorating work performance, behavioral signs associated with such deterioration were observed and categorized.[6]

Some of these signs include the following:

- Excessive absenteeism, especially on Monday, Friday or on the day after payday;
- Erratic work performance patterns, an employee sometimes performs very well and at other times does not;
- Declining performance—An employee who has been a good performer shows signs of deterioration in the ability to perform;
- On the job absenteeism, reporting to work but frequently being absent from the work station;
- Increased use of health benefits;
- Frequent accidents, these may occur on or off the job.

Experience in various work settings has shown that intervention based on a recognition of deteriorating work performance is more effective than earlier attempts to identify the early stage alcoholic employee and to provide motivation for treatment and rehabilitation. For many alcoholics, the threat of job loss is an incentive for accepting a referral for treatment.

### Supervisory or Administrative Roles

The supervisor or manager plays a critical preventive role in these programs by helping to identify the early stage alcoholic. This is accomplished by maintaining one of the key roles of the supervisor, that of monitoring job performance. When the supervisor notes that a formerly effective employee is beginning to show signs of deteriorating work performance, this pattern of deterioration is documented. Such documentation may be noted on standardized organizational evaluation forms, or informal notes may be kept in the supervisor's desk. When sufficient data are available, the supervisor meets with the employee and presents evidence of the deterioration in job performance, punctuality, attendance, or behavior. The supervisor is careful not to try to diagnose the cause of the problem(s), or to become involved in an attempt to solve personal problems. This applies even for supervisors who have a clinical specialty and who are professionally competent to provide clinical services. Attempting to solve personal problems compromises his or her effectiveness both as a clinician and supervisor.

Instead, the availability of the program as a resource for assessing the nature of problems and recommending appropriate care should be made known. The supervisor can explain the manner in which the program operates and its' guarantee of confidentiality. If at that time, the employee states that the problem can be handled without assistance, the supervisor sets a time limit by which work performance must return to an acceptable level. If deterioration persists, or if there is some improvement for a short while followed by further decline, the employee should be confronted again. At that time, the employee should be offered the alternative of disciplinary consequences for unacceptable or substandard performance, or a referral. It should be clearly stated by the supervisor that any disciplinary action is based on performance criteria only. It has been the experience in most programs that when an employee is offered this choice, acceptance of the referral is often likely.

Many programs report that 65 to 85 percent of employees who are confronted will opt for treatment referrals.[7]

## The Follow-Up Process After Referral

Alcoholic employees may initially report to the EAP with the expectation of manipulating the staff and maintaining their denial. It is the responsibility of the professional EAP staff to diagnose the problem, make an appropriate referral to a community resource, and monitor progress through treatment and follow-up on the employee's progress after he or she returns to work. Most important, the staff is often able to motivate the employee to recognize and accept the underlying problem(s) that caused the performance difficulties and to acknowledge the need for accepting treatment.

The nature of the diagnosis, the treatment plan as well as all information about program participation are kept strictly confidential. The referring supervisor is informed only that the employee is participating in the program, and when appropriate, the length of time he or she will be away from work. No notations are entered into the employee's personnel file, and information may only be released by EAP personnel with a release signed by the employee.

Employees can use program services before any disciplinary action takes place by voluntarily seeking out program staff. Voluntary referrals or self-referrals can be initiated by employees themselves or as a result of encouragement by family members, peers, union representatives, or medical department staff. In the case of voluntary program participation, the supervisor is not informed that program services have been sought, except if indicated by the need for time away from work. If that is necessary, a signed release must be obtained from the employee before any information is disclosed to the supervisor or others designated. Moreover, even with a signed release, only information that the supervisor must have in order to reschedule workloads is disclosed; diagnosis, treatment or other personal data remain confidential.

For employees who are covered under collective bargaining agreements, union representation may be indicated at the time of supervisory confrontations. It is helpful when the union is supportive of the program and there is coordination and cooperation between labor and management throughout the referral and follow-up process.

## FROM OCCUPATIONAL ALCOHOLISM
## TO EMPLOYEE ASSISTANCE PROGRAMS

As work-based programs began to develop, it became apparent that some employees with problems other than alcoholism were also being identified by supervisors and referred for assessment through the established process. This occurred because supervisors were being taught not to diagnose the underlying cause of problems, but to make referrals on the basis of difficulties in work performance. Persons with marital, financial, legal, and compulsive gambling problems often display difficulties on the job that are manifested in the same manner as alcoholism. In response to these needs, many programs expanded their range and scope of services for alcoholics to include many of these other employee problems. These programs came to be known as EAP's, this title more accurately reflects the broad range of services and activities provided. These programs will be described in terms of program types, elements, and organization.

### Types of Programs

There are at least three different program types that operate under the general heading of EAP.

1. Occupational Alcoholism Programs—where the major emphasis is on services to alcoholic employees or alcohol-related problems involving supervisory or administrative case finding and referral.
2. Employee Assistance Programs—where the emphasis is on services to employees with a broad range of problems involving supervisory or administrative case finding and referral.
3. Employee counseling programs—where therapeutic counseling as well as referral services are furnished, often without the work-based activities that involve supervisory or administrative case finding and referrals.[8]

Each of these programs provides valuable services. However, to achieve the goal of prevention and early intervention and to optimize program services for the work setting, the activities involving supervisory case finding and referral to the EAP must be included. An employee counseling service that does not include those components can provide help, but only after the employee requests services. Even with these components, intervention with alcoholic employees often occurs only in late stages of the disease when signs of alcoholism can no longer be hidden or ignored.

### Program Elements

Since no two work settings are exactly alike, no two programs are identical. However, there are basic elements that are needed in any program if it is likely to be effective. In order to operate with any degree of success, a program should be fully integrated into the structure and function of the organization which it serves and should include the following elements:

- An identified program coordinator—In a program serving 3,000 or more employees, this should be a full time position; for smaller work settings, a part-time coordinator may be used. This position involves planning, coordinating and evaluating program activities, and coordinating the work of the EAP with other company departments. It also involves delegation of assignments to other EAP staff for assessment, referral, follow-up, training for old and new staff in other departments, and consultation for program development, and establishment of program evaluation procedures. The position requires skills in administration; an understanding of labor/management relations; and an understanding about substance abuse, addictions, and other behavior/medical problems which occur in work settings.
- A policy statement—The policy statement should clearly define the support of labor and management, provide assurance of confidentiality, and provide the overall parameters of the program. The policy statement should also include a clearcut definition of the program and its scope.

- Procedures—There should be written guidelines to facilitate implementation of program policies. Procedures should contain a description of steps that can be utilized in seeking program services on a voluntary basis or through a referral by a supervisor.
- Confidentiality—Rules should be established and included in the policy statement, specifying how records are to be maintained, who will have access to them, and guidelines for confidential release of information. Federal regulations governing confidentiality of alcohol and drug abuse information should be considered by all programs. These regulations must be followed by any direct or indirect recipient of federal funding.
- A committee of concern composed of representatives from management and labor where appropriate may be designated to provide advocacy and support for the program.
- Training—Training is needed for program staff. There is also a need for ongoing training and educational activities for managers, supervisors, union representatives and the general workforce related to the program and other topics.
- Insurance—As a program is established, there should be a review of the benefits. Adjustments should be made to insure that available plans adequately cover the costs incurred in the diagnosis and treatment of problems referred to the EAP. Periodic reviews are needed to update coverage.
- Resources—A list of available community resources that provide services for the problems referred to the EAP should be developed during the program planning phase. Personal contact is desirable to identify how, and under what circumstances a resource can best be used. Personal contact should be maintained by program staff with representatives from each resource used by the program. The list should be reviewed and revised at regular intervals.
- Evaluation and data collection—There should be a periodic review of the program to provide an objective evaluation of its operation and performance. All information gathered in this process must be handled in a confidential manner. Program modifications should be made on the basis of evaluation of data. Information collected should include the following, in addition to data specifically suited to the needs of the organization

served by the program: Number of clients seen, diagnosis/ presenting problem(s), activities conducted by program staff, e.g., orientation, training, promotional activities, source(s) of referral to the EAP, number of employees referred for services, type of services to which referrals were made, and demographic data of employees utilizing program services, e.g., age, sex, length of employment, ethnic background.[9]

### Program Organization

As stated earlier, as EAP's are developed, they assume the definition, characteristics, and services deemed necessary by the organization which they serve. The professional selected as program coordinator, the background and experience of program staff, and organizational mandates all play a role in determining what a developing program will be like. The decision on how to organize a program to fit a specific setting is based on several factors. Some of the factors to be considered include the following: Number of employees served by the program, employee services that are already available, budgetary considerations, and geographic location(s) of employees covered by the program.

There are basically four different ways to organize these programs. They are: an internal model based within the work setting, an internal union-based model, a consortium, and a single agency serving multiple work locations. There are some important similarities and differences between these models that can affect service delivery. For example, all require a designated program coordinator and related staff, and all involve the basic functions of assessment, referral and follow-up, and training.

Differences involve the location of the program and administrative responsibility for the program. The internal models both provide services to the company or union, but one is located in and is responsible to a company unit, while the other is responsible to the union. Therefore, service priorities may be different in the two internal models. The external consortium model usually involves two or more companies, each with 1500 or fewer employees, with the EAP located in one of those companies or in a different site, and with a liaison from each company participating in the consortium. The single agency serving multiple work locations provides services on a contractual basis, and is housed in the host setting or in a location specifically rented for the EAP. Administrative responsibility within this model is with the EAP agency itself.

## PREVENTION SERVICES FOR HIGH-RISK EMPLOYEES

The programming activities described in the previous sections provide a sound foundation for effective intervention with employees who need assistance, while at the same time minimizing the disruption that can be created by such employees in the work place. However, it is becoming apparent that not all employees respond in the same ways. For example, program directors report that the factory worker who has no opportunity for advancement and who believes that a similar job is available elsewhere, is apt to be more willing to give up the job than alcohol.

This type of employee and others are less likely to be referred early enough for prevention services, or to refer themselves. Employees such as women, executives, and licensed professionals may be high-risk for this reason, and may require special efforts to help them to prevent problems.

For example, women in unskilled low salaried jobs may be viewed as easily replaceable and may be fired rather than confronted with evidence of poor job performance. Women in responsible middle or upper management positions may be assumed to have obtained the positions through affirmative action programs. Consequently, there may be some reluctance to confront them around performance problems for fear of being accused of discrimination. On the other hand, supervisors may be protective of female heads of households and hold off confronting them to keep from "adding to their problems."

All of these circumstances prevent women from getting the help which they need. EAP's can prevent some of these difficulties from developing by providing training to supervisors on the needs and problems of women in these circumstances and on assumptions and stereotypes about working women. Additionally, women's support groups can be developed in work settings to help the women involved become aware of how to deal with stresses at work, alcoholism, depression, loneliness, sexual identity problems, marital difficulties, and other problems that affect job performance.[10]

Frequently, it is assumed that executives are exempt from referral for program services. It is often not possible to document their work performance, and it is difficult to refer them to an EAP whose administrator is usually of a lower rank in the hierarchy. Therefore, it is often helpful to use outside consultants to provide services to troubled executives. Techniques aimed at prevention can involve monitoring the range of plans and level of goals set by the executive, and then intervening as needed. In many cases, rather than experiencing a decrease in performance, troubled executives exhibit a decrease in their aspirations over time. They meet their goals, but the goals are set much lower than in the past.

While most states have rules and regulations which govern the behavior of licensed professionals, the reluctance of colleagues and supervisors to be the cause of a loss of license and the ease with which these professionals can change jobs, represent a major barrier to prevention services. One organized preventive approach used increasingly by professional organizations is the peer intervention program. These programs are an adjunct to EAP's and provide an opportunity for licensed professionals who practice while they are impaired to "voluntarily" seek treatment services.

On a voluntary basis, colleagues meet with the professional who needs help, assess the person's needs and make recommendations for prevention, treatment, and/or other services. Generally, there is a hot line telephone service available for callers who wish to refer colleagues or themselves.

## SUMMARY

EAP's offer a valuable service for labor and management by providing interventions with employees who have personal problems that interfere with their on-the-job functioning. Effective programs include trained staff, a policy statement, operating procedures and a system for education and training of all personnel in the work organization served by the program.

Program staff must be competent in the techniques needed to conduct training activities, assess human problems, provide pretreatment counseling which may be needed to motivate an employee to accept a referral, and determine the appropriate referral resource once a problem has been identified. An ability to collaborate with other units within the work setting as well as staff in outside treatment agencies is also needed. The potential impact of EAP's is not only in the work place. The community where the company or union program is located and the communities where the employees who benefit from the program reside, benefit indirectly from program services at preventive and interventive levels.

## REFERENCES

1. U. S. National Institute on Alcohol Abuse and Alcoholism. Occupational alcoholism: Some problems and some solutions. DHEW Pub. No. HSM-73-9060, Rockville, Md, 1973.
2. U. S. National Institute on Alcohol Abuse and Alcoholism. Occupational alcoholism programs bibliography. DHEW Pub. No. ADM.-80-943. Washington, D.C., U.S. Govt. Print. Off., 1980; Wrich, J.: The *Employee Assistance Program.* Center City, Minn., Hazelden, Foundation; Revised 1981; and Fourth special report to the U. S. Congress on Alcohol and Health, from the Secretary of Health and Human Services, January 1984.
3. Ibid.
4. Reichman, Walter and Aaron, Miriam: Early intervention for alcohol abusers at the workplace. Paper presented at the International Congress on Drugs and Alcohol, Jerusalem, Israel, September, 1981.
5. Trice, H. M. and Roman, P. M.: *Spirits and Demons at Work: Alcohol and Other Drugs on the Job.* Ithaca, Cornell University, New York State School of Industrial and Labor Relations, 1972.
6. U. S. National Institute on Alcohol Abuse and Alcoholism. Alcohol and health: New knowledge. Second special report to the Congress. DHEW Pub. No. ADM-75-212. Washington, D.C., U.S. Govt. Print. Off., 1975.
7. Beyer, J. M. and Trice, H. M.: *Implementing Change: Alcoholism Policies in Work Organizations.* New York, Free Press, 1978.
8. Wrich, op. cit.
9. Ibid.
10. Guida, Miriam (Aaron): Alcoholism & women at the workplace: An occupational health concern? Report of the Nursing Sub-Committee 1978–1981; Guida, Miriam (Aaron): The nurse's contribution to the health of the worker. Report No. 3, The Health & Safety of Women Workers, August, 1981.

## Chapter Four

# DUI OFFENDERS:
# A FOCUS FOR PREVENTION SERVICES

LINDA B. DENNISTON

U sing identified at-risk groups as a source for prevention is not a new idea.[1] This chapter will focus on the feasibility of prevention programs developed for the identified population of substance users who drive under the influence. These programs can prevent continued driving under the influence, and are also directed toward preventing continued substance abuse when a comprehensive treatment approach is used. In order to have such a program focused on substance abuse, it is necessary to address the issues of court ordered clients who come for evaluation and/or treatment as a result of drunk driving laws. This chapter will examine the process of working with this population of clients from an historical view, some related legislation, techniques for evaluating DUI clients, and finally, actual treatment of these clients with a goal of prevention. Case studies taken from the author's practice are used to illustrate the prevention and treatment methods used.

While terms vary in regard to laws dealing with drunk driving, two common variations appear descriptive—that is, Driving Under the Influence (DUI) and Driving While Intoxicated (DWI). For consistency, the term DUI will be used throughout this chapter to represent the identified population. Further, while drugs other than alcohol offer additional implications for treatment (both legally and therapeutically), much of this chapter will apply to evaluation and treatment of clients who use alcohol only or alcohol in combination with other drugs.

## THE PROBLEM OF DRINKING AND DRIVING

It is estimated currently that 25,000 people are killed annually in the United States as a direct result of accidents due to driving under the influence, and another 75,000 people are injured in traffic accidents related to substance use. Alcohol is involved in 55 percent of all fatal accidents with 50 to 65 percent of fatally injured drivers being intoxicated at the time of the accident. A dollar loss resulting from substance-related accidents is conservatively placed at 15 to 16 billion dollars annually, with this figure estimated to be as high as 24 billion dollars in the Final Report from the Presidential Commission on Drunk Driving.[2] When it is further considered that only 1 in 2000 DUI offenders are actually identified, and that each time a ticket is given it is estimated that the offender has driven 30 to 100 times under the influence without being caught, the extent of this problem and the need for prevention efforts can be clearly seen. Stiffer legislation could result in the early identification of more of those who drive under the influence.

A look at psychosocial factors regarding the DUI offender adds credibility to the above figures and further clarifies the viability of prevention with this identified population. In a comparative study, Bell et al.[3] described a continuum of problems related to substance use between a control group, DUI drivers and alcoholics in treatment, with DUI offenders moving close to identified alcoholics in other life problems. This was demonstrated in their perceptions of a drinking problem (MAST scores) as well as higher incidences of health, family, financial, and job-related problems, with the control group having fewer of these problems. In particular, data related to divorce/separation and employment rates of DUI offenders showed them to have these problems much more frequently than the control group.

## HISTORICAL PERSPECTIVES AND LEGISLATION
### RELATED TO THE PROBLEM

Driving under the influence has long been a problem with the effects noted above. The problem has increased dramatically in the past two decades with an increase in the number of privately owned vehicles and increased availability and use of substances among all segments of society. Efforts to deal with this problem have included the local policeman taking intoxicated individuals to their homes, jailing them for indefinite periods of time and imposing fines, and taking away driving privileges. It was not until the early 1970's that a concerted and somewhat consistent effort was developed for dealing with the problem of drunk driving within the legal system and within the population as a whole. The Alcohol Safety Action Program (ASAP) was formed by the National Highway Traffic Safety Administration with a focus on drugs other than alcohol. It was then changed to the Alcohol-Drug Safety Action Program (ADSAP). The latter program involved minimal prevention with a focus on education.

Then efforts were made to enact consistent legislation by addressing the issue of a legal age for drinking (ranging from 17 to 21 years in the various states), identifying a blood alcohol concentration (BAC) at which drivers' abilities are affected and capacities impaired, and initiating legal consequences for driving under the influence. Individual states began to look at the drunk driving problem with the impact from various interest groups adding impetus to states' efforts. The formation of Mothers Against Drunk Driving (MADD) and Students Against Drunk Driving (SADD) added pressure to legislatures and increased public awareness about the problem. In 1982, more than 700 bills related to drinking and driving were introduced in various state legislatures. Of these 700 bills, 127 were enacted as laws in 39 states, clearly demonstrating increasing efforts to deal with this problem.[4]

## IMPACT OF PREVENTION AND TREATMENT EFFORTS

Up to this point, consideration of driving under the influence as a problem, its impact on society at large, and legal and societal efforts to decrease the problem have been reviewed. In the 1970's it became apparent that more than legal consequences and education were needed in order to prevent escalation of this problem in the population at-risk. Those who use substances and drive were often seen to be in need of treatment to address their abuse of or addiction to the substance(s) they were using. Thus, legal consequences began to include required evaluation and treatment of the individuals' problems related to their use of substances.

While the focus remained on preventing increases in traffic accidents resulting from the use of substances and driving, it became apparent that the legal consequences and educational programs being used could be enhanced by evaluation and treatment. Those who drink and drive began to be identified as more than just social drinkers; they were viewed as abusers or addicts with multiple life problems related to their substance use.[5] This had implications for not only preventing further drinking and driving but also for preventing continued or further substance abuse. It was now apparent that there was an identified high-risk population that could become the focus for effective prevention efforts through evaluation and court-ordered treatment. Thus, DUI programs can be seen as a process for identifying those who abuse or are addicted to substances among the broader category of substance users. Through effective treatment, prevention of continued abuse can occur in addition to prevention of the harmful effects of drunk driving to the offenders and others.

## EVALUATING DUI OFFENDERS

The purpose of court ordered evaluations of DUI offenders is to assess the extent of substance-related problems with individuals and to make recommendations concerning their amenability to treatment and the methods to be used. Outlined below are suggested methods and tools that can be effectively used in the evaluation process.

DUI offenders come to treatment facilities for assessment under court orders and not by personal choice or by recognizing that they have a substance problem. Therefore, resistance and denial are common reactions in individuals who come for court ordered evaluations. A minimum of two appointments are recommended, and additional sessions may be needed to obtain an accurate description of the offender's substance use/abuse. One of these appointments can be used for objective testing; a second can be used for a clinical interview to facilitate a differential diagnosis of the extent of substance abuse or addiction.

## Testing

While three or more testing instruments are often used in the assessment process, two tests most often used and recommended are the Minnesota Multi-Phasic Inventory (MMPI)[6] and the Michigan Alcoholism Screening Test (MAST).[7] The MMPI is seen as an accurate indicator of addiction, in particular when a score of 24 or higher is attained on one of its scales, the MacAndrews Scale. This scale has been shown to be effective in distinguishing alcoholics from nonalcoholics. In addition, it has been effective in identifying alcohol abusers and poly-drug users. Other MMPI scales can identify additional problem areas often associated with substance abuse, such as poor impulse control.

The MAST is an accurate indicator of substance-related problems, particularly with cooperative clients who are open about their prior use. The MAST can be a more accurate indicator if it is administered after a complete client history is obtained, involving the client and significant others as sources of information (spouse, parent, child, etc.). A cut-off score above 4 is indicative of a substance problem. The higher the score on the MAST the greater the extent and severity of life problems related to substance use.[8]

## The Clinical Interview

A clinical interview with the DUI offender should last a minimum of two hours, allowing time for taking a complete history relevant to onset of substance use, and the impact of this use on all aspects of client's life including social, psychological, legal, vocational, physical, and financial areas. This history can often be more accurately obtained in the presence of a significant other and through supporting documents such as a presentence investigation report, arrest report (including client's BAC at the time of arrest), and any other reports which add information to client's history.

## Analysis and Recommendations

After testing and the clinical interview, the evaluator should combine data/information/impressions gathered and assess the client's substance-related problems, making recommendations for treatment or advising against treatment. The following two case studies illustrate how information from the evaluation can be used to analyze whether treatment is needed and the kind of treatment indicated.

> Twenty-one year old K came for evaluation after a DUI arrest. He had no prior arrests, his BAC was .07, the MacAndrews score was 17, and the MAST score was 2. He had a sound work history since age 17, having taken three college courses each semester for two years while maintaining a 3.5 GPA. K had been engaged for two years with plans to marry after graduation. His fiancee came with him for the clinical interview and supported his history of drinking three or four times a year on special occasions such as their engagement anniversary. K related a family history involving an alcoholic father. Based on test scores, family and personal history and the clinician's impressions that this client was very amenable to treatment, K was diagnosed as exhibiting episodic alcohol abuse. It was recommended that he be involved in treatment focused on education about substance use. In addition, six sessions of individual counseling were recommended for focusing on his father's history and how this could impact on the client's problems with alcohol.

In evaluating K, consideration was given to his present life circumstances which indicated an ability to work within limits (college, work), set goals, and form a satisfying personal relationship. He did not have a history of substance-related problems, and test scores further validated K's ability to control his use of alcohol. Based on these factors, it was determined that he would benefit from learning more about substance use and its' effects. Finally, consideration was given to family history, with individual sessions recommended to emphasize his high-risk status and the need for caution in his substance use.

Evaluation in a second case study indicated a more severe level of alcohol problems affecting many more areas of functioning.

> Thirty-six year old D came for an evaluation after a second DUI within a one-year period. His BAC at the time of arrest was .22, he had a MacAndrews score of 33, and a MAST of 12. He had a prior record

consisting of two disorderly conduct arrests and one speeding ticket. D was in his second marriage reporting that "alcohol caused problems in the first one," and he related that his father also had an alcohol problem. D had drunk for more than 10 years. He had tried abstaining on several occasions and had gone to AA for a period of time in the past, which he had found to be helpful. Based on this information, recommendations were made for him to be evaluated for Antabuse®, and that he be involved for eight hours in an information school, on-going group treatment at the mental health center and family treatment to focus on marital issues that had been identified as being related to his drinking. A differential diagnosis of alcohol dependence was given based on this client's increased tolerance over time, and symptoms of withdrawal during periods of abstinence.

Consideration was first given to D's high BAC, which exemplified ingestion of a high amount of alcohol. His test scores and history of other legal and personal problems further substantiated the seriousness of his addiction. A diagnosis of dependence was descriptive of his problem. Because of his long history and severity of substance related problems, Antabuse® was recommended as an adjunct to treatment to facilitate a goal of abstinence. Group therapy was utilized to add additional support and/or confrontation, as needed. Finally, involving D's wife in treatment offered further support and directly addressed their interactions in this drinking relationship that had been noted during the evaluation.

## PREVENTION AND TREATMENT PROGRAMS FOR DUI OFFENDERS

As noted above, identified DUI offenders can be representative of an entire spectrum of substance use, abuse, and addiction. Therefore, no one treatment model or goal can be applied in an effective prevention and treatment program. Just as treatment of substance abuse as a whole calls for a differential approach to treatment, so too does an effective treatment program for DUI offenders.[9] The evaluation of DUI offenders identifies the extent of each individual's problems with substances and facilitates a differential diagnosis and recommendations for treatment. An effective treatment program needs to incorporate a total treatment philosophy capable of addressing the multi-faceted needs of its clients. While one focus will always be to prevent further drinking and driving, there needs to be a focus on preventing continued and further substance abuse on the part of clients and, hopefully, on preventing those around them from having similar problems. The latter could include family members, friends and co-workers who might refrain from driving under the influence due to the DUI offender's participation in treatment or who themselves may be involved actively in the treatment.

Approaches to prevention and treatment include education; individual, group or family treatment; or any combination of these services based on the severity of problems noted during evaluation. Additional considerations include use of Antabuse®, sporadic drug screenings and/or referrals to Alcoholics Anonymous, Narcotics Anonymous, Al-Anon, or Alateen as needed in order to support the achievement of goals involved in prevention and treatment. The following descriptions of services provided in two case situations illustrate the relationship between prevention and treatment with DUI offenders.

> R was a forty-nine year old male who was diagnosed alcoholic after evaluation for a DUI. His BAC was .27, the MacAndrews was 35, and the MAST was 25. This diagnosis was based on extensive personal and legal history of abuse, as well as severe physical problems resulting from prolonged and heavy alcohol use. Antabuse was contraindicated because of his physical deterioration. It was important to prevent escalation of his addiction due to these severe problems and to achieve the necessary goal of abstinence with this client. To facilitate this goal, it was recommended that R attend group treatment once weekly for two hours, focused on his past abuse of substances and alternatives to drinking. He was referred to group after four individual sessions that were designed to provide the support, confrontation and identification which are often a part of the group process with DUI offenders. In addition, he participated in marital counseling twice monthly in order to involve his wife in his treatment as well as prevent the onset of stress resulting from their changing interactions and relationship. AA and Al-Anon were used as adjuncts to treatment, with R attending AA twice weekly and Mrs. R attending Al-Anon. At the end of six months of treatment, the goal of abstinence has been maintained with the clients continuing in treatment focused on other related problems.

R's wife was involved in sessions by the second month of his treatment to add further support for him and to change a drinking relationship to an abstaining one. These sessions and the other identified methods of treatment have seemed to be effective with this client as exemplified by his achieving and maintaining a goal of abstinence after six months of treatment. The on-going multiple support systems being used were identified as crucial elements in R's treatment, based on the extent and severity of life problems related to his substance abuse including his physical problems.

This second case situation illustrates a different set of dynamics related to prevention and treatment with a DUI offender.

> L., age thirty-three, was involved in first individual, and then group treatment after being identified as a substance abuser following his DUI evaluation. While the clinical interview and testing (his MAST was 3 and MacAndrews was 19) did not indicate addiction, L was seen as high risk for alcoholism because he was progressively abusing both alcohol and marijuana. After seven individual sessions, this client continued his use of alcohol and marijuana at the same rate of use prior to his DUI. He had refrained from driving while using but would periodically be under the influence of one or both substances, with this use being problematic in other areas of his life, e.g., in his marriage. He was referred for group treatment and, after seeing others with similar or worse problems became willing to set goals for drinking two times weekly, having only two drinks at those times, and refraining from smoking marijuana. After eight group sessions, he has been able to maintain these goals and is continuing in treatment currently. A specific technique used with L was a daily record count to help him see how often he was under the influence of alcohol and/or marijuana, to identify his patterns of use, and to help him set realistic goals for change.

While L was meeting the goal of not driving under the influence, individual therapy did not seem to impact on changing his continued abuse of substances. He was transferred to group treatment with the aim of addressing this issue of abuse. At this writing, treatment appears effective, exemplified by his achieving the goal of controlled drinking. L has also requested marital counseling in conjunction with this group treatment. This seems appropriate at this time and will be incorporated into his treatment plan. One area of continued focus related to prevention is L's tendency to slowly increase the amount and frequency of his drinking. Sporadic daily record counting will be used to prevent this from occurring, as well as the use of self reports and validations by his spouse.

## SUMMARY

Driving under the influence has been recognized as a very real problem in terms of the human and financial costs to society at large. As a result, state and federal governments have begun a concerted effort to address this problem in the past 10 years by enacting new legislation with a goal of preventing substance abuse and DUI offences. Methods for evaluating and treating this identified high risk group of clients have been described since they facilitate the achievement of goals. Case studies were presented to exemplify a differential approach to diagnosis and treatment of DUI offenders based on the severity of problems and the needs involved in each case. It was shown that this differential approach can result in effective prevention and treatment services with these clients. An area for future focus is the need for more consistent descriptions and evaluations of models being used in these programs for DUI offenders in order to make these services more systematic.

## REFERENCES

1. Nathan, Peter E.: Failures in prevention, *American Psychologist,* 459–467, 1983.
2. See for instance State Legislation on Alcohol and Drunk Driving Enacted During the 1983 Legislative Session, Washington, D.C., National Highway Traffic Safety Administration, September, 1983; Presidential Commission on Drunk Driving, Final Report, November, 1983; and Kansas Governor's Committee on Drinking and Driving, Final Report, December, 1982.
3. Bell, R., et al.: An analytic comparison of persons arrested for driving while intoxicated and alcohol detoxification. *Alcoholism: Clinical and Experimental Research,* 2:141–148, 1978.
4. *A Digest of State Alcohol-Highway Safety Related Legislation, Second Edition.* Washington, D.C., National Highway Traffic Safety Administration, 1983.
5. Panepinto, William C.: A short-term group treatment model for problem-drinking drivers. *Social Groupwork and Alcoholism,* 33–40, 1982.
6. See for instance Swartz, Mark: Construct validity of the MacAndrews Scale. *Journal of Consulting and Clinical Psychology,* 47:1090–1095, 1979; Rich, Charles C. and Davis, Harry G.: Concurrent validity of MMPI alcoholism scales.

*Journal of Clinical Psychology, 25*:425–426, 1969; Lachar, David, et al.: The MacAndrew Alcoholism Scale as a general measure of substance misuse. *Journal of Studies on Alcohol, 37*:1609–1615, 1976; and Clopton, James R.: Alcoholism and the MMPI: A review. *Journal of Studies on Alcohol, 39*:1540–1558, 1978.

7. Selzer, M. L.: The Michigan Alcoholism Screening Test: The quest for a new diagnostic instrument. *American Journal of Psychiatry, 127*:1653–1658, 1971.

8. Ibid.

9. Miller, William R.: *Addictive Behaviors*. Oxford, England, Pergamon Press, 1982, pp. 135–141; Miller, William R.: Treating problem drinkers: What works?. *The Behavior Therapist, 5*:15–18, 1982; and Miller, William R.: Controlled drinking: A history and a critical review. *Journal of Studies on Alcohol, 44*:68–83, 1983.

# PART TWO: TREATMENT SERVICES
*General Issues in Treatment*

# OVERVIEW

## EDITH M. FREEMAN

This section includes chapters focused on treatment. The chapters in the general issues part of the section attempt to demonstrate the importance of systematic practice in work with clients who have alcohol problems. Blackmon's chapter on assessment outlines a clear process of assessment that encourages integration of practitioner's existing skills in assessment with the specific areas of attention involved in the drinking history. It also focuses on the critical area of treatment planning which is dealt with more specifically from a number of different perspectives by the other chapters on groups, practice approaches, and families. Those chapters by Freeman and Usher et al. present specific techniques for working with client systems in group and family modalities.

The other part of this section has chapters that focus on particular population groups that are high-risk for alcohol problems because of environmental factors. Traditionally, many of these groups such as blacks, the poor, women, and the elderly have been viewed from an individual deficit perspective. A common theme in these eight chapters is the emphasis on building on the strengths of these clients and on the impact of biases toward these clients that are sanctioned by societal values.

There are some differences in the approaches which these authors propose for work with the clients included in these chapters. For example, Fewell describes the use of psychodynamic approaches for work with women but also encourages a focus on environmental and interpersonal factors that affect their alcohol problems. Copeland, Blackmon, and Pilat et al. recommend the use of systems approaches with poor clients, the elderly, and the children of alcoholics. On the other hand, McRoy et al. and Gunther et al. recommend several approaches and techniques that can be useful with minority clients in combination. Weick raises issues about an aspect of the environment often ignored, the physical environment, and discusses its impact on alcohol use in teenagers.

## Chapter Five

# ASSESSMENT IN INPATIENT AND OUTPATIENT ALCOHOL TREATMENT PROGRAMS

BETTY BLACKMON

Alcohol abuse and alcoholism have reached epidemic proportions. It is estimated that ten million persons in this country are alcoholic. This may be an underestimation because 75 percent of adults in the United States drink.[1] Researchers in the alcoholism treatment field have not determined to date why some included in this percentage become alcoholic and others do not.

Alcohol is significant in a broad range of social problems based on these statistics. For example, we know that 50 percent of all highway fatalities are attributable to alcohol use or abuse.[2] We also know that alcohol use is involved in 65 percent of all homicides. Further, 33 percent of all inmates imprisoned for a variety of crimes were using alcohol when those crimes were committed. Secondly, the loss of production in industry which is attributed to alcohol use is estimated at 60 million dollars. A large percentage of absentism, on the job injuries, and hospitalizations involve alcohol abuse.[3] However, many of these instances are unnoticed or mislabelled as other problems rather than as alcohol-related.

Third, it is known that many persons who receive care at general hospitals and doctor's offices for anxiety, insomnia, and high blood pressure may be experiencing problems in their use of alcohol. These persons and others with heart disease or diabetes may complicate their physical problems by using alcohol. However, physicians do not always explore whether their patients drink alcohol, or if they do, whether they have stopped drinking.

Education is a fourth area in which problems such as truancy, underachievement, and disruptive behavior often involve alcohol use. Few educators are aware of the magnitude of this problem; it has been found that 80 percent of students on a national level have used alcohol.[4] The role of alcohol in family problems and parent child conflicts is a final area in which alcohol use is often overlooked. Social workers, psychologists, and psychiatrists in mental health centers, child guidance clinics, and other social agencies rarely inquire about each client's alcohol use as a matter of course. Further, some mental patients with severe emotional problems also abuse alcohol. Assessments of these clients rarely include questions about their use of alcohol or treatment for any identified alcohol abuse. Many of these clients also take high dosages of prescribed drugs that should not be mixed with alcohol.

This chapter will include a description of how to do effective assessments with these and other clients whose abuse of alcohol may not be apparent in their presenting problems, as well as with clients whose abuse of alcohol or alcoholism is part of the presenting problems. Specific content areas for assessments including the drinking history will be discussed. Additionally, the importance of linking these assessments to effective treatment planning for outpatient and inpatient services will be included. Finally, the role of social workers and other helping professionals in this process and in making effective referrals will be discussed.

## ASSESSMENT FROM A SOCIAL WORK PERSPECTIVE

A definition that facilitates the assessment of alcoholism and related problems states, assessment is "A collection of facts that are organized in a systematic method that encompasses an individual's social functioning and enables the practitioner to fully understand and identify the situation through a process of analysis."[5]

Thus, assessment as defined here is compatible with the social work frame of reference which places emphasis on persons in their environments.[6] The interactive nature of persons and their environments is of particular importance to the early detection of alcohol abuse and alcoholism because of system inbalances involved in the abuser or alcoholic's life which may help to maintain the problem. Practitioners who focus only on the intrapsychic functioning of individuals will not see other dysfunctional aspects of their environments, and may inadvertently help to exaccerbate problems by not also assessing and intervening in clients' environments.

## THE ASSESSMENT PROCESS

There are numerous content areas one must explore when conducting an adequate assessment in any situation. The assessment of alcoholism is no different. A careful examination of these areas enables practitioners to gain a wholistic view for their analysis and impressions. Every aspect of the person's functioning must be examined. In terms of content, an assessment should include the areas which follow.

### Content Areas

#### *Physical or Medical History*

The person's physical history should include information on the last time a person has seen a physician and the reason for the contact. If for some reason the person is beginning to have physical consequences, the practitioner can be alerted to this. For example, if a person were hospitalized for a broken ankle, the circumstances surrounding the incident may reveal abusive drinking which led to high-risk behavior and the injury. Or the person's equilibrium could have been diminished, thus causing the injury.

Symptoms such as insomnia, decreases in appetite, or gastrointestinal disturbances should be explored as they may be related to alcohol problems. For instance, if a person is experiencing frequent insomnia, a question into what a person uses to get to sleep may reveal that alcohol has been used as a sedative. Although this is not necessarily indicative of alcoholism, a person who is using alcohol to relax and who does so constantly may be in the prestages of alcoholism. Persons who report a loss of appetite, but also report drinking warrant further exploration of their alcohol use.

If the individual has a condition where drinking is contraindicated by a physician and the person continues to use alcohol, a warning flag is automatically raised. For instance, a person who is diabetic and continues to drink may be indicating the importance of alcohol in his or her life. Clients often tell practitioners about the medicinal value of alcohol. It is possible that the "night cap" prescribed by a physician or self prescribed is being misused or abused by those clients.

### Employment History

The employment history is vital information because of the large amount of time spent in work settings. When looking at data collected, frequent job changes, although progressive, may indicate that an individual leaves jobs prior to being terminated because of alcohol abuse. Another symptom seen in the early phase of alcoholism is job dissatisfaction without any basis or a continuous distortion of problems. Poor peer relationships on the job may be a result of coworkers' irritation with the abuser who takes extended lunches for the purpose of drinking, creating more work for them. Underachievement also may be symptomatic of someone who is abusing or is dependent on alcohol, because the preoccupation with alcohol may result in an individual not working up to his or her potential. Terminations, high absenteeism, chronic tardiness, and frequent job changes can all be reliable symptoms of problems with alcohol.

### Marital and Family History

An examination of past and present family relationships is essential in the early detection of alcohol abuse or alcoholism. An examination of the number of divorces and separations is important, but an indepth study of the quality of these relationships and whether they involve alcohol use or abuse is more important. The individual's past relationships should be explored for areas of conflict and strengths. "How much was alcohol involved in the formation and maintenance of the relationship?" is a key question. This information can indicate how alcohol may have created estrangements or provided the total basis for relationships. In addition, whether the client is married or single, information should be gathered about any effects which alcohol has had on specific areas of relationships such as the sexual area.

Information about the individual's original family may reveal an alcoholic parent, grandparent, sibling, or other relative, putting the client in the high-risk category for alcoholism. Persons growing up in alcoholic homes exhibit behavior attributable to the dysfunctional relationships that exist in alcoholic families, especially if the alcoholism is left untreated. Adult children of alcoholics often repeat the drinking patterns of their parents and continue to maintain the same dysfunctional relationship patterns with their own children and with others.[7]

### Social Functioning

Exploration of peer and other social relationships is also important for determining the extent of alcohol problems and other related or nonrelated social dysfunctions. It is important to clarify how the client uses his or her leisure time, who that time is spent with, whether there are nondrinking peers who can support the client's sobriety, and whether alcohol is used with current peers during leisure time. This exploration can also reveal whether the client drinks alone and whether he or she is socially and/or physically isolated in his or her environment. At the same time, it can help to identify who, if anyone, the client depends on for emotional support in his or her social environment, and whether the client is satisfied with those relationships or the lack of relationships.

### THE DRINKING HISTORY

In addition to exploring those content areas of the assessment that were discussed in the previous section, a drinking history should be obtained. This drinking history includes the reasons for using alcohol and its effects, drinking patterns, legal difficulties, and methods of coping with stress.

## Rewards From Alcohol Use

In some instances, the alcohol abuser may constantly seek rewards from alcohol that were not an issue when earlier social usage was involved. These rewards may include relief of discomfort, release of inhibitions, and reduction in anxiety states. The problem has progressed when drinking becomes a means to sociability and drinking occasions are sought out. Activities that were fun formerly may subsequently require the use of alcohol. Intimacy in relationships may diminish because as alcohol usage increases, a lack of trust and defensiveness may increase.

Finding out about the rewards of drinking is critical, especially when it provides the individual with relief from emotional or physical pain. Some persons may reveal that alcohol bolsters self-esteem and provides the motivation to overcome insecurities. Alcohol abuse in persons who are high risk tends to alter their behavior. These individuals are able to do or say things when using alcohol that they feel uncomfortable about when sober.

## Drinking Patterns

Collection of information regarding the quantity, quality, frequency of use, length of alcohol use, and periods of abstinence indicate the clients' drinking patterns. This should also include information about the circumstances in which the client drinks.

It is important to know when the drinking began from first usage. If a client started drinking at age 16 years and is now 32 years old, it is apparent that he or she may have utilized alcohol for 16 years, and that progressive use is probable.

Quality is used as a gauge to see if there is a marked increase or decrease in tolerance, whether it takes more alcohol to have the same desired effects. Marked increases in usage usually indicate frequent use in order to develop this tolerance. Decreased tolerance is often indicative that a person's tolerance has reversed after prolonged use. Quality questions are often relative, because minimizing the amount and frequency usually occurs when clients are in denial about drinking or are having feelings of guilt about their drinking. For these reasons, questions about quantity alone are not sufficient for assessment purposes. Some practitioners find that a clear statement or question about consumption may avoid this kind of denial. For example, when clients are asked how much they drink a day, they usually respond with the amount. When practitioners demonstrate a nonjudgmental and fact finding approach, the client tends to be at ease and reveals more.

### Periods of Abstinence

Finding out if a person has had periods of abstinence may indicate that they have made efforts to control their drinking. Periods of not drinking should be distinguished from abstinence which involves a conscious effort to stop. Clients may have concerns about their alcohol use, and questions about periods of abstinence provide a forum for discussion of these concerns. In addition, if they have made repeated unsuccessful attempts at stopping their alcohol use, this may be a strong indication that they have lost control and are now dependent. The practitioner also needs to follow up to find out what made them return to drinking. This will provide information about precipitating events which usually involve environmental issues that affect alcohol use and maintenance of abstinence. It is also important to find out if they sought or received help during these periods, and what happened when they did.

### Legal Problems

Clients present themselves in various settings with requests for assistance with a variety of presenting problems. A brief exploration of pending legal issues should occur during the first contact. Knowledge about these problems can be helpful in assessment and treatment. For example, violations of the law such as driving under the influence can aid in the assessment of alcoholism and provide the leverage for keeping clients in treatment, especially recent offenders. These violations help practitioners to gauge the extent of alcohol problems and loss of control, and provide the documentation to clients that theirs is a serious problem. Other symptomatic legal problems include child custody issues and assault charges.

## Coping Patterns

An examination of the client's coping skills may reveal maladaptive problem solving. Clients may drink rather than take steps to solve their life problems. Poor impulse control, low self-esteem, grandiosity, and passive aggressive behaviors have been seen in clients who have alcohol problems. Some authors have identified common patterns in the problematic use of alcohol, and have concluded that there is an alcoholic personality. However, it is important not to generalize these characteristics, but to use them as a guide for further exploration of the content areas involved in regular assessments and the drinking history.

## OTHER AIDS TO ASSESSMENT

There are numerous classification systems that can be utilized for the purpose of assessing alcohol abuse and dependency. These systems can be used singularly or in combination, but it is preferable to use more than one. None of them are foolproof, but their criteria can provide guidelines for determining the stage of alcoholism or abuse being experienced by the client, and provide feedback to the client when self administered. A few of these systems and the methods used in many alcoholism programs are included in this section.

## Classification Systems

### Jellinek's System

Jellinek identified a series of progressive stages of alcoholism. According to Jellinek, the stages of alcoholism are divided into the following: pre-alcohol, prodromal, crucial, and chronic.[8] Each stage has certain characteristics which indicate where the individual is in his or her drinking. It is not necessary that a person go through every stage, and many clients don't fit all of the characteristics for any of the stages. When used as an interview guide, this system provides practitioners with a set of characteristics to integrate into their routine assessments.

### Michigan Alcohol Screening Test

The Michigan Alcohol Screening Test is a brief 25 item test in which each item is given different weights.[9] The test was originally used to test persons convicted of driving under the influence, but was later determined to be effective with the general population. In a validation study, the test failed to identify only 15 out of 264 alcoholic clients.[10] The test is quick and may be given to the individual during intake prior to the initial interview. Most clients respond accurately to the items. A discussion of responses often yields additional revealing information. For instance, one question asks, "Do you feel you are a normal drinker?" Whether the question is answered yes or no, the practitioner can explore what is normal to the particular client. Normal to some clients means that they don't get drunk more than a couple of times per month. They may feel that this is normal compared to other heavy drinkers whom they know. This instrument permits the practitioner to explore the thinking of clients regarding their problem. This instrument is weighted toward the long-range consequences of drinking, therefore, it may not detect persons in the earlier stages of alcoholism.

### Diagnostic Statistical Manual III, 3rd Edition

The DSM–III is a handy reference guide to the diagnosis of abuse and alcoholism. The examination of pathological use of alcohol is keyed to impairment in social, employment or vocational, and legal functioning.[11] The duration of the impairment is also assessed along with the severity. However, persons who are in earlier stages of alcoholism may not be identifiable with the DSM–III, especially binge drinkers with very few consequences related to drinking.

### N.C.A. Criteria

The criteria for diagnosis of alcoholism developed by the National Council on Alcoholism's Criteria Committee are descriptive.[12] The criteria focus on signs and symptoms of alcoholism and divide them into two tracks. Track I gives the physical symptoms and Track II provides symptoms that are psychological and attitudinal. Both provide the practitioner with a process for organizing material gathered in the assessment.

### Collateral Information

Collateral information is helpful if one remembers that significant others may not have accurate knowledge of alcoholism. However, practitioners can utilize collaterals to provide facts about the client's behavior that may help in assessment. Employers, health care professionals, and probation officers are also reliable when collecting data relating to alcohol problems. Family members may need to be interviewed jointly as well as individually. The practitioner should explore conflicts in information with the understanding that they may only represent different perceptions about the same issues or real inaccuracies. Even when collateral information from family members does not conflict, it may need to be explored for collusiveness when it involves information related to areas such as periods of abstinence or a potential for violence by the client under the influence.

### FORMULATION OF IMPRESSIONS

After completion of the assessment, the drinking history, and other aids to assessment, impressions must be formulated. Impressions should not be based upon a single isolated fact. All of the factors discussed in previous sections of this chapter must be considered in formulating impressions. Impressions consist of the following areas: the client's strengths and any strengths in the client's environment; the extent of the problems with alcohol, and other related and nonrelated problems; the impact which alcohol has had on the client(s); the prognosis for recovery; and what is recommended to resolve the problems involving the client and his or her environment. This analysis provides the foundation for treatment planning.

## TREATMENT PLANNING

Planning for intervention is the purpose of the assessment process. The treatment or intervention phase with the alcoholic may prove to be frustrating to the practitioner whose assessment is not comprehensive. Exploration of the areas mentioned earlier will usually ensure appropriate treatment planning.

### The Effects of Denial on Treatment Planning

Practitioners must remember that their belief systems about alcohol use may block effective intervention. Examples of value biases that can block intervention include denial of alcoholism as an illness by the practitioner, and treating it as though it is a secondary rather than primary problem. Denial in the practitioner is not the only type of denial encountered. The client often denies the problem on one or more levels and this must be directly addressed in the treatment plan. Clients who are seeking treatment often minimize alcohol problems and deny the efforts required to change. Denial is multifaceted, and it would be simplistic to believe that denial is simply a lack of acceptance by the client. It is complicated by societal views of the alcoholic, which are often accepted by the client indicating he or she is weak, immoral, and hopeless. Also, alcohol interfers with cognitive processes, so clients are not able to clearly think about factors or behaviors that point to their loss of control.

Additionally, denial is seen in the family, because their relationships with the alcoholic are affected. Family members may be resistive to efforts to change them because the alcoholic's behavior masks other problems in the family system including dysfunctional relationships, and usually it is seen as the only problem by the family. The treatment plan must consider this kind of denial also, so that members are able to provide the supports which alcoholic members need to maintain abstinence once those systemic changes occur in relationships due to treatment.

### Treatment Methods

Individuals may need one or more kinds of services in order to achieve and maintain abstinence. Several treatment methods can be used to provide those services, and they may involve individual, family, or group modalities.

### Inpatient Treatment

When evaluating to determine whether an individual needs inpatient treatment, the following factors should be seen as indicators:

1. The client is alcohol dependent or an abuser, and is unable to maintain sobriety—usually the person has tried and failed.
2. Instability in the individual's environment—a pending loss of family, job, or other supports. The fewer supports, the greater the indication that residential treatment is needed.
3. Severe physical withdrawal symptoms—the person is experiencing convulsions, anxiety, delirium tremens, hallucinations or has a prior history of severe withdrawal.

### Outpatient Treatment

Clients should receive outpatient treatment based on the following indicators:

1. Client is alcohol dependent or an abuser and has had periods of sobriety.
2. Social networks, such as family and peers, are stable.
3. Client is employed full time.

### Education Services (Outpatient)

Clients who need education services may have the following characteristics:

1. Clients who are not alcohol dependent but who abuse alcohol.
2. Clients who lack knowledge about alcohol use, abuse, and dependency.
3. Clients who have stable social networks.

## Referrals

The treatment plan should incorporate counseling, education, provision of support groups such as AA, and referrals for important needs to public welfare agencies, emergency shelters, vocational training centers, hospitals, or family service agencies. Just telling the client to call a particular agency is inadequate. The number of clients who do not make the required call, or who do and then are placed on a waiting list is higher than necessary.

A systematic approach to making referrals is essential: obtaining specific knowledge about what resources are provided by each agency, maintaining direct and on-going contacts with staff in those agencies, calling ahead to pave the way for clients, and introducing them to contact persons such as members of an AA group facilitates effective referrals. It may be necessary for social workers, psychologists, alcoholism counselors, and others to advocate aggressively for clients in order to link them with resources for the needs identified during the assessment process.

### SUMMARY AND CONCLUSIONS

This chapter presented an overview of the assessment and treatment planning process with alcoholic clients. The primary focus was on early and accurate identification of alcoholic clients and on the variety of procedures and aids available for facilitating these assessments. Proper identification of alcoholics in the beginning stages of alcoholism is crucial to prevent escalation of this progressive disease. It has been estimated that as many as 20 percent of persons seen in agencies whose primary service is not alcoholism treatment have problems that are alcohol-related but that they are not being identified. Social workers and other staff in those agencies and in alcoholism treatment centers can improve assessment and treatment planning with alcoholic clients by incorporating the type of comprehensive process described in this chapter.

## REFERENCES

1. Dusek, Dorothy and Girdano, Daniel A.: *Drugs, A Factual Account.* Addison-Wesley Publishing Company, 1980.
2. Ibid.
3. Ibid.
4. Free, James L.: *Just One More.* Bull Publishing Co., 1977.
5. Bartlett, Harriet M.: *The Common Base of Social Work Practice.* New York, National Association of Social Workers, 1970.
6. Compton, Beulah Roberts and Galaway, Burt: *Social Work Processes.* New York, The Dorsey Press, 1979.
7. Berenson, David: Alcohol in the family. In Guerin, Philip J. (Ed.), *Family Therapy, Theory and Practice,* Gardner Press, 1976.
8. Jellinek, E. M.: Phases in the drinking history of alcoholics. *Quarterly Journal Studies on Alcohol, 7,* 1946.
9. Selzer, Melville L.: The quest for a new diagnostic instrument. *American Journal of Psychiatry, 127,* 1971.
10. Ibid.
11. *Diagnostic and Statistical Manual of Mental Disorders, 3rd Edition.* New York, American Psychiatric Association, 1980.
12. Criteria for the diagnosis of alcoholism: National Council on Alcoholism. *American Journal of Psychiatry, 129,* 1972.

## Chapter Six

# TOWARD IMPROVING TREATMENT EFFECTIVENESS WITH ALCOHOL PROBLEMS

EDITH M. FREEMAN

Questions have been raised about the effectiveness of treatment approaches used with alcoholic clients for a number of reasons. For example, high dropout rates among alcoholic clients during intake indicate serious problems in engaging some of these clients in treatment. Some authors have estimated that between 52 and 75 percent of these clients drop out by the fourth session,[1] and that less than 25 percent remain in treatment for three consecutive months.[2]

There are questions also about practice effectiveness with those alcoholic clients who remain in treatment beyond these initial sessions. The kinds of treatment approaches that are effective with specific types of alcoholic clients and the extent of their effectiveness need to be identified. Much of the outcome research described in the literature has not provided sufficient data in this area. Often, these studies have had methodological problems such as a failure to clearly describe salient characteristics of the clients and treatment approaches involved, or they have used different standards for acceptable treatment outcomes.[3] High relapse rates among the small percentage of alcoholic clients who complete treatment programs indicate a continuing need for researchers to institute sound experimental conditions and standardized outcome criteria in order to identify examples of good practice. Katherine Wood has noted the need for research itself to be effective in order to document whether the examples of practice being observed are effective.[4]

This chapter will explore how methodological problems in

most of this outcome research and the lack of standardized outcome criteria have limited conclusions that can be drawn about the effectiveness of treatment approaches with alcoholic clients. It will analyze elements of three different approaches that may potentially be effective with particular types of clients, and make recommendations about how those approaches can be evaluated more successfully. This analysis will then be used to recommend guidelines for social workers and other helping professionals in selecting appropriate treatment approaches to use in any given practice situation.

## METHODOLOGICAL PROBLEMS IN OUTCOME RESEARCH

Some authors have noted that the match between treatment approach and client should be increasingly based on research findings if the notion of treatment as an applied science is to have real meaning.[5] However, this use of research findings to inform practice has been hampered by the inadequate quality of most outcome research on alcoholism treatment. For example, Hill and Blane reviewed 49 studies that were published between 1952 and 1963.[6] They noted that they did not summarize their findings about treatment outcomes because the results could have been misleading, given the methodological problems in this research.[7]

Similarly, May and Kuller evaluated some of the outcome research on alcoholism treatment published between 1965 and 1975. They concluded that research designs being used during that period showed almost no improvements. They also highlighted the fact that there was a lack of consensus among researchers about "what constitutes an effective outcome and an effective measurement of that outcome for the alcoholic client."[8]

These reviews and many others have identified some of the consistent methodological problems involved in this research. They include: (1) the lack of prior planning and the use of retrospective treatment outcomes, (2) a failure to collect pretreatment baseline data, (3) inadequate sampling techniques including a failure to randomize subjects, (4) a lack of control groups, (5) the use of unreliable measuring instruments, (6) the use of poorly defined criterion variables, (7) the failure to use objective measures of behavioral change, (8) inaccurate or insufficient collection of data such as reliance on self-report data only, (9) the absence of specific descriptions of populations and treatment approaches being used, (10) a failure to relate sample variations to outcome variations, (11) a rudimentary level of statistical analysis, and (12) a failure to do longterm follow-up for at least 12 months after treatment ends.[9]

It is important to identify these problems since they severely limit conclusions that can be drawn about the benefits of certain approaches. These problems also prevent the identification of certain elements of approaches that may be relatively harmful by retarding improvement.[10] These limitations have resulted in fewer opportunities to systematically analyze and improve the quality of treatment programs available for alcoholic clients.

## LACK OF STANDARDIZED OUTCOME CRITERIA

Although research methodological problems have been major barriers to determining what constitutes practice effectiveness in alcoholism treatment, a related barrier is the lack of consensus about criteria for treatment success. The latter controversial issue has been summarized as follows: "is total and lifelong abstinence the only acceptable goal in treating problem drinkers, or can some clients successfully learn and maintain a pattern of moderate and nonproblem drinking?"[11]

Researchers and practitioners have taken different sides in this controversy based on how they define alcoholism. Some accept Jellinek's definition of five different types of alcoholism, only two of which are regarded as diseases: gamma and delta alcoholism. He characterized gamma alcoholism as a loss of control or the inability to stop drinking once started. Delta alcoholism was characterized as an inability to abstain, involving steady rather than binge drinking.[12]

Jellinek indicated that alpha, beta, and epsilon alcoholism or abnormal drinking do not involve addiction or loss of control, even though they do involve other kinds of dysfunctions.[13] He used the term alcoholism in a general sense to describe all alcohol-related problems with disease and nondisease subtypes included within this broader category. He did not, however, deal explicitly with the question of permanence or irreversibility in relation to the five subtypes or the broader category of alcoholism which he described.[14] Some authors have assumed that nonaddicted problem-drinkers within this broad category can be taught to drink in moderation without problems and that only addicted problem-drinkers must become abstinent.

Others have accepted the more specialized use of the term alcoholism promoted by Alcoholics Anonymous. This definition refers to alcohol dependence or addiction, is distinct from the larger category of problem drinking, and corresponds with Jellinek's definition of gamma alcoholism. It recognizes all alcoholism as an irreversible disease process for which abstinence, rather than moderation, is the only possible goal.[15] To complicate this situation even more, several other well-known definitions have gained acceptance in the alcoholism treatment field.[16]

This lack of consensus about the definition, and whether abstinence, controlled drinking, or both are acceptable outcome criteria have made it difficult to identify studies that are comparable in this regard. Some researchers have responded to this controversy by not stating treatment goals prior to treatment and then developing them retrospectively, or by not stating them at all. The usefulness of this research will continue to be limited until differences in the definition of alcoholism and outcome criteria are somehow reconciled or accepted.

The development of more sophisticated diagnostic procedures may also be helpful by determining whether significant distinctions can be made between subtypes of addicted and nonaddicted problem drinkers. This could provide a basis for exploring differential treatment planning: determining whether different goals and treatment approaches for addicted and nonaddicted problem drinkers are viable and safe. Determining whether abstinence is an important goal for all problem-drinkers at least during treatment could also be explored. Requiring nonaddicted problem-drinkers to become abstinent during treatment may be important for determining how they function when they are alcohol-free, and the longest period of time in which they can remain abstinent successfully.

The lack of standard outcome criteria is a barrier in another way. Until recently, most researchers only explored alcohol consumption rates as outcome criteria. There has been a growing emphasis on exploring other criteria that can affect recovery, and that can be used also to measure whether treatment has been effective. The lack of consensus about including other criteria may have been perpetuated because these criteria often have not been defined in observable and measureable terms.

The multivariate outcomes emphasize an ecological focus on alcoholic clients in their environments rather than in isolation, both before and after treatment ends. They include the following: the rate of legal problems, job stability, social functioning in marital and family roles, the use of abstinent peers as support networks in handling problems, level of self-esteem, and problem-solving skills. Maisto and McCollam indicated that this kind of multivariate conceptualization assumes alcoholism is a part of complex behavioral patterns that have multiple causes. It assumes also that a variety of techniques may be required to affect these multiple areas of functioning with different clients.[17]

### SOME APPROACHES TO TREATMENT

State-of-the-art limitations in treatment advances and outcome research, which have been discussed previously, make systematic comparisons between different treatment approaches difficult at present. In fact, Voris has noted the need for a prerequisite step: the development of research that focuses on client-treatment-outcome interactions, rather than on the main effects of one or more treatments on outcomes.[18] This kind of research, involving a factor analysis of the elements of an approach, could identify the relative effects of these elements on particular kinds of alcoholic clients.

This section will focus on three commonly used treatment approaches and elements of those approaches which might be effective with certain groups of clients. It will also note how experimental evaluation of these approaches could be improved. The approaches are: Alcoholics Anonymous, behavioral approaches, and systems approaches.

## Alcoholics Anonymous

Alcoholics Anonymous is thought to be the most widely used treatment and self-help community resource for alcoholics in the United States today. In addition, the organization has grown to approximately one-half million members in 90 countries since it began in this country in 1935.[19] As mentioned previously, this organization views alcoholism as a disease which the alcoholic cannot handle alone and which cannot be cured. It is assumed that the alcoholic can never return to social or controlled drinking. A life-time affiliation in AA is encouraged, although some recovering alcoholics only attend periodically during stressful periods once a stable period of abstinence has been established.

The specific interventions that are a part of AA may vary from group to group, but there are some common elements involved in this approach. These elements include: the provision of role models, provision of a support group, a focus on small manageable goals, and a supportive philosophy for successful recovery.

Role modeling occurs in each meeting when alcoholics with longer periods of abstinence repeat their admissions of past failures and describe how they overcame their loss of control to alcoholism. This process is usually reinforcing for both old and new members. Role modeling also occurs when each new member is assigned an old member as a sponsor to help with problems that block recovery, in an on-going manner and during crisis periods. Meetings are available from group to group every night; thus they provide support by reducing the amount of unstructured time available to alcoholics during which they are more vulnerable to relapse. Parallel involvement of family members in Al-Anon and Alateen meetings can provide additional support for the alcoholic and his or her family by effecting important individual and family system changes. AA meetings are also the media in which members provide active support and encouragement to other members who maintain their abstinence from day to day or to members who relapse.

Members are told consistently to set small goals: to avoid drinking one day at a time rather than to swear off drinking forever. This process can increase confidence, self-esteem, and optimism about recovery. The organization's philosophy is consistent with this focus on small goals. This philosophy is embodied in twelve steps which clarify what an alcoholic must do to recover successfully. The steps include members admitting their powerlessness to control drinking and the need for turning over their lives to a higher power, confessing their wrongdoing, establishing faith in a higher power, making amends, and sharing their spiritual awakening with others.[20]

The emphasis in this philosophy is on the here and now; members are told to take responsibility for maintaining their abstinence currently (with some help from others). The past is emphasized only to the extent of noting how the disease of alcoholism robbed the individual of this ability to take control of his or her life previously.

These interventions, especially the provision of role models and a support network, are likely to be more beneficial to clients who are isolated socially and without external supports. Long-term alcoholics might also benefit more from this approach because its positive philosophy about outcomes can counteract their ten or more years of alienation and skepticism about recovery.

On the other hand, the goal of abstinence may discourage young alcoholics who find it difficult to contemplate not using alcohol during the large number of years remaining in their lives. The AA philosophy may also discourage some alcoholics who cannot maintain abstinence at first, or those who relapse and then return to abstinence. AA views these kinds of relapses as failures (while continuing to offer support), but they can also be viewed as small steps toward the long-term goal of unbroken abstinence. Similarly, nonaddicted problem-drinkers who are able to drink moderately without problems after treatment may view themselves as failures in terms of this philosophy.[21] Some gay clients, elderly, women, and racial minorities may find it difficult to identify and use role models effectively based on the traditional membership in some AA groups.

Systematic research on the AA approach is very sparse, and more studies are needed to clarify how this approach works with different groups of clients.[22] Further, studies that have been done have relied heavily on self-report data without supplemental data from other sources. They have also used very brief follow-up periods in which to collect data, focused on affiliation with AA as a dependent variable instead of actual attendance rates or level of involvement, and have not examined drop-outs who may comprise a distinctly different group of alcoholic clients. Exploration of this latter group could not only provide feedback about elements of this approach which interact negatively with specific characteristics of drop-outs, but could also affect undocumented success rates for AA which range from 40 to 70 percent.[23]

Studies on the AA approach could be improved by correcting these methodological problems. In addition, a more clear description of this approach needs to be operationalized. AA groups may differ in some of the interventions used and the manner in which they are used, and this can affect the outcomes reported. For example, various AA sponsors may provide support in different ways and with different effects.[24] Similarly, the characteristics of clients who are involved in AA successfully should be described and explored more thoroughly. The effects of this approach on clients could be documented more adequately by collecting data on treated and untreated alcoholics, and by collecting pre and post data on drinking patterns rather than just on abstinence rates. Other outcome criteria that can be defined behaviorally should also be explored in terms of this approach. These behavioral definitions are more commonly used in the next approach to be discussed.

### Behavioral Approaches

A number of behavioral approaches have been used in the treatment of alcoholism including rational emotive therapy (RET), social skills training, assertiveness training, covert sensitization and other forms of aversive conditioning, systematic desensitization, relaxation or self-control techniques, and didactic training in the application of behavioral principles. All of these approaches are based on social learning theory; an underlying assumption is that all behavior is learned and therefore can be unlearned by the same process.[25]

Consequently, drinking behavior is seen as being learned and maintained through rewards and reinforcers. Rewards include pleasureable physiological changes that result from using alcohol, psychological changes such as removal of anxiety, the control of someone else's behavior, peer approval, and the opportunity to participate in adult behaviors. In essence, an implication of this theory is that people begin drinking, become alcohol abusers or alcohol dependent, and remain alcoholics because it serves some useful purpose for them. The theory also involves the assumption that nonaddicted clients can be taught to control their drinking so that abstinence does not have to be the goal in all situations.

Recovery is accomplished in a number of related ways with these approaches. For example, alternative prosocial behaviors may be developed in assertiveness or social skills training, systematic desensitization, or self-control techniques.[26] In addition, other techniques are used to inhibit anxiety which has triggered substance abuse episodes in the past. In aversion therapy, classical conditioning is used to associate actual drinking behavior with unpleasant chemical or electrical stimuli.[27] The negative physical reaction that occurs when clients on Antabuse try to drink alcohol is a form of classical conditioning. Similarly, this process is also used to pair imagined aversive stimuli with the imagined use of alcohol in covert sensitization, a verbal aversion technique.

Cognitive approaches such as RET are used to help alcoholic clients develop a new belief system about stressful situations and alcohol use. Clients are taught that it is what they tell themselves about these situations, their emotional reactions to this irrational self-talk, and their use of alcohol to hide these emotional reactions that are problematic rather than the situations themselves. Clients are taught how to attack and change their former belief systems and emotional reactions through the use of exercises and practice. They also learn to develop rational self-talk statements based on the new belief system and other concrete ways to handle stress.[28]

All of these behavioral approaches are different and any one of them may be used differently by various practitioners. There are some areas of agreement across these approaches, however. Alcoholic clients are counseled individually, and as couples, families, and groups. Further, some common elements have been identified across these approaches that could be potentially effective. They include: a behavioral assessment, a written contract, a broad-spectrum behavioral treatment plan, homework assignments, graphs and other concrete aids for providing feedback on the client's progress, and the use of environmental reinforcers.[29]

Situations in which drinking behavior and the stimulus events which follow this behavior occur most frequently vary from individual to individual. Therefore, behavioral assessments involve a careful functional analysis with the client of the behavior-controlling stimuli in each individual situation. This practice encourages the practitioner to focus on the client as an individual and on the way in which drinking behavior functions within each unique client system. Such a focus can potentially increase the accuracy of assessments. The written contract, which is based on these assessments, makes the focus for change and the specific details related to that process explicit. It encourages the alcoholic client, who needs to assume full responsibility for his or her recovery in the here and now, to be an active participant in this process.

Broad-spectrum behavioral treatment is a more sophisticated response to the problem of alcoholism than dependence on one particular delimited approach in all situations. Complex problems in all life domains, including drinking patterns, are broken into separate behavioral components—each of which is then modified by using these approaches either singularly or in combination.[30] Homework assignments are used to help clients achieve small incremental changes in themselves and their environments to facilitate the recovery process. Using "I" statements to discuss a conflict situation with a family member, or developing a list of progressively difficult but unavoidable social situations in which drinking is expected and which clients will attempt in the future can help them to develop important recovery skills.

The process of treatment and its effects on drinking patterns and other outcomes are monitored through graphs and other aids which clients are taught to use during didactic training for applying behavioral principles. This visual feedback can help to increase motivation and reinforce efforts to abstain in situations that typically evoke drinking and related problem behaviors. Environmental reinforcers such as social interactions with friends, relatives, and community groups with whom alcohol use is not tolerated are also used to maintain the effects of treatment.

Behavioral approaches involving elements such as written contracts may be most useful with alcoholic clients who are concrete thinkers and with nonvoluntary clients. The latter are more likely to respond positively and less suspiciously to an explicit contract than they are to a situation that involves unclear expectations. Graphs and other concrete tools may be useful to these clients also if they are responsive to visual feedback.

Homework assignments may be particularly helpful to clients whose family situations involve role and interpersonal dysfunctions, whether or not the other family members are involved directly in treatment. When possible, they should be involved in treatment with these approaches to influence system changes more effectively.

When used alone, behavioral approaches may be less effective with some clients who have complex intangible problems such as projection of their feelings onto others in addition to alcohol-related problems. Behavioral approaches, other than cognitive approaches such as RET, may also be less effective with clients who are insight-oriented. In addition, clients who are too focused on the impact which the past may have on their current problems with alcohol may not benefit as much from these approaches because of the here and now emphasis. Clients who do not have the external supports that are needed for ongoing recovery may not be appropriate for these approaches either, unless supplemental interventions are used.

Research on the use of behavioral approaches with alcoholic clients has been very extensive with success rates of up to 50 percent reported in studies involving both abstinence and controlled drinking as outcomes.[31] These studies have indicated that teaching alcoholics how to monitor their own progress within their natural environments in concrete ways, such as counting instances in which they experience an urge to drink or keeping a record of what happens when they drink, have increased abstinence rates. The development of alternative behaviors to drinking such as relaxation and assertiveness, and the use of environmental reinforcers for abstinence have been found to be effective also.[32]

Generally, the specific behavioral approaches used in these

studies have been clearly described, as the treatment outcomes have been. Pre and post data have usually been collected systematically; some studies have also included follow-up data for up to six months to a year after treatment ended.[33] Since behavioral research usually involves single subject designs, the sample sizes for these studies usually have been small, ranging from one to 25. This factor could have provided opportunities for the client-treatment-outcome analyses recommended by Voris,[34] except important client characteristics have not been described thoroughly enough in many of these studies.

In other studies, treatment goals have not been specified, so rates for controlled drinking or abstinence have been reported without analyzing them against a goal or standard outcome criteria. Related to this problem, in some situations in which abstinence was a specified goal, clients who achieved a controlled drinking status were not evaluated sufficiently to determine the reasons the goal was not achieved or whether the goal of abstinence was appropriate. In addition to the need to correct these methodological problems, this research could be improved by comparing treatment and no treatment conditions with controls, and by exploring the use of these approaches with larger samples and different kinds of alcoholic clients.

### Systems Approaches

Systems approaches are based on general systems theory which consists of a series of related definitions, assumptions, and postulates about all levels of systems from atomic particles to galaxies. These approaches are more directly related to a subcategory of this theory, general behavior systems theory, which deals with living systems ranging from the individual to society. Some of these living systems are open systems, and are responsive to inputs and changes in contrast to closed systems which are much more resistive to change. Despite the greater possibilities of change in open systems, change is a difficult and complex process based on this theory. Both open and closed systems maintain dynamic steady states or homeostasis, which gives them the appearance of being stationary. After any disturbance, all systems tend to reestablish their steady state through a process of self-regulation.[35]

In certain interactional systems such as individuals or families, for example, alcohol can begin to play a critical role in day-to-day behavior. "It can become a central organizing principle around which consistent patterns of interaction within systems are shaped."[36] Other interactional systems in which alcohol can similarly become a dysfunctional organizing principle include the social domain and work relationships with peers.[37] This quality of adaptability in systems, maintaining homeostasis while also accommodating alcoholism behaviors, indicates that the sobriety of one member cannot be attained without related changes in other parts of the systems involved. Even with the individual client (system); sobriety cannot be achieved just by giving up alcohol unless other dysfunctional alcohol-related behaviors are given up also.

Even after sobriety is attained, alcohol can become a functional rather than dysfunctional organizing principle within some systems. Steinglass noted that in these situations, family life may continue to be organized around alcohol to maximize prevention of relapse to a wet state. All social life and family rituals are restructured with the alcoholism component in mind; family members are active in AA, Al-Anon, or Alateen, and family members make career changes that incorporate this focus on alcoholism such as becoming activists for treatment resources or alcoholism counselors. Steinglass labelled this kind of family system a stable-dry family.[38] This description also fits other types of systems such as AA and some informal peer relationships.

A number of different approaches comprise the broad category of systems approaches. They include family systems approaches (such as structural, strategic, developmental, communications, intergenerational) and the life model.[39] There are a number of differences between these approaches, in particular between family systems approaches and the life model. The life model is a more recently developed approach, and fewer of its abstract concepts have been operationalized into observable behaviors or interventions. But there are some similarities in these approaches. The individual's problems are reframed into systems' problems, to which all subsystems have probably reacted in ways that may have contributed to the development of alcoholism and in which they must be involved to resolve the problems.[40]

This ecological perspective means that assessment and treatment are focused on the individual alcoholic client, the systems involved, and the interface between these interacting systems. In terms of treatment, several common elements may be productive in problem resolution: the individual, peer, family, work, or other systems involved are used as the vehicles for change; specific tools are used to illustrate roles and relationships graphically; the concepts of family rituals, rules, myths, and secrets are analyzed to identify how they accommodate alcohol-related behaviors; and homework assignments are provided to effect changes within systems in their natural environments.

The system as the vehicle for change can be a particularly powerful element. Both within and outside of treatment sessions, the alcoholic system is assumed to present all of the symptom behaviors that contribute to its dysfunctional steady state. The practitioner can use these symptoms or examples of dysfunctional interactional patterns as opportunities to change the system on the spot. An effort is made to help members of the system learn to accommodate abstinence rather than drinking behavior, and to become more open to other necessary changes in interactional patterns that will support sobriety. The practitioner demonstrates within sessions how the system can change its way of functioning and yet survive.

Tools that are used to illustrate roles and relationships help to achieve these productive changes. They are used for assessment and goal setting, for planning and implementing treatment, and for evaluating the effects of treatment; but not all of them are used in each of these approaches. They include: the ecomap and genogram, sculpting, role-playing, communication games and other structured exercises, and the portrayal of structural issues such as boundary infringements and triangulation involving subsystems.[41] All of these tools operate on the same principle; they illustrate graphically to the system and practitioner patterns of interactions that maintain alcoholism, and provide opportunities for trying out new ways to handle these interactions while the dynamics are still somewhat clear in the minds of those involved.

For example, the ecomap is used to identify and illustrate

whether the client has supportive networks, the kinds of networks available, and how he or she functions in the current life space in social, work, family, and other relationships. The genogram illustrates geneological relationships, instances of alcoholism or alcohol-related problems, significant family events, occupations, losses, cut-offs, role assignments, and communication patterns in the client's life process across generations. Both tools are designed to be developed with the individual client, family, or other system over several interview sessions.[42] They are used with clients whose role dysfunctions, emotional and physical isolation, and stressful transactions with specific organizations or social systems can be revealed graphically during the process of doing the ecomap or genogram.

Both of these tools use small squares to depict males and circles to depict females. The person's age is placed in the center of each circle or square. The quality of relationships between family members and between them and other systems can be expressed by the type of line drawn to connect them; for example, a solid or thick line represents a strong and important relationship. Roles, individual characteristics, and problems such as alcoholism are noted in one or two word descriptions beside the appropriate circle or square. In the ecomap, the nuclear family or members of the household are drawn in a large circle at the center, with other relevant systems depicted in smaller circles surrounding it. The genogram consists of symbols which depict individuals in the current generation (the client system) and the connections between that system and two or more generations of the client's family.[43]

A system's rituals, rules, myths, and secrets can become apparent to the practitioner and client(s) as these tools for illustrating roles and relationships are used. Rituals and rules govern how the interactional patterns, especially those related to alcohol use, are played out daily. Myths are accepted without question usually and stereotypic assumptions about members' attributes dictate their role assignments within the system and outside of it. Included is the typical myth that the alcoholic is weak and needs the protection of other members of a family, work or social system for the system itself to survive.[44] Secrets or open secrets refer to information which various members have about the system's relationships, functioning, or history, but which they all pretend none of them are aware of. All of this hidden and unhidden information underlies the system's dysfunctional patterns of interaction. The discovery and reinterpretation of this information through discussion and the use of visual tools frees the system to adopt new rituals and rules that support abstinence and other improved ways of functioning.

These new ways of functioning are tried out within the system's natural environment in the form of homework assignments. Homework is designed to continue the process of disrupting the system's homeostasis so that the system is more open to the changes indicated and can reorganize around new principles related to these needed changes. These assignments are varied. For example, they can involve having members refrain from acting in the stereotypical roles assigned to them by the system without saying this explicitly to other members. Members who are carrying out this homework assignment can be asked to observe how other members in the system change their behavior in response to the role abdication and to report on the new role they choose for themselves. Other members who are resistive to change may be asked to exacerbate a controlling behavior such as nagging, or even to write down each instance that "requires" nagging. This paradoxical assignment can reduce nagging because the behavior is no longer within the control of the individual involved and other members no longer resist it. If this assignment does not reduce nagging, it may provide important assessment data about the severity of the alcohol-maintaining behaviors within the system.

The elements described such as homework, indicate that systems approaches may be more effective potentially when all members of the alcoholic system involved agree to be included in treatment. These approaches may still benefit clients who are willing to carry out homework assignments that affect family members who do not agree to become involved in treatment. They may be particularly workable in situations in which one or more members of a system are being scapegoated, or assigned stereotyped and dysfunctional roles based on gender or age involving women or elderly clients for example. However, some clients who have been cut off from family members for many years, who are unable to leave environments that involve barriers to networking, such as a skid row type of environment, may be less responsive to these approaches.[45]

Many of these assumptions are supported by research on family systems approaches, primarily involving case studies. In recent years, a small amount of experimental research has been done also to evaluate these approaches. Some of these experimental and nonexperimental studies indicate that alcoholic clients are able to achieve abstinence when families are taught to withdraw role network support that accommodates alcohol-related behaviors, and to alter other reinforcing responses such as conflicting communications about these alcohol-related behaviors.[46]

Other researchers have concluded that it is necessary to extend these efforts to change the alcoholic's environment beyond the family system to social relationships with peers. Clients have been helped to develop appropriate social behaviors and to suppress drinking in alcohol-free social clubs and recreational programs designed for those purposes. Procedures such as verbal and written reminders and the provision of child care services have been used successfully to encourage the attendance and involvement of clients, their families, and their guests.[47]

Some of the existing research on family systems approaches is characterized by small samples and a failure to gather pre-treatment data except very informally. The interventions have sometimes not been clearly described; and various researchers have only labelled them as family therapy, the ecological model, or systems treatment.[48] More follow-up data need to be collected for longer periods than the brief periods that have usually been involved.

On the other hand, the use of case study explorations with these approaches has resulted usually in very clear descriptions of the clients involved, of the other relevant systems involved, and of the outcomes. This research could be improved by the development of more experimental studies, collection of pre treatment and extended follow-up data, and clearer delineations of the interventions involved. Some of the tools for illustrating roles and relationships, such as sculpting and the ecomap, could be developed into more objective measures. They could then be used as pre and post treatment evaluations of changes in the interactional patterns within and between systems and in other alcohol-related behaviors.

The life model has not been researched even to the extent that family systems approaches have been to date. This may be due to its more recent development. However, this deficit needs to be addressed since even some nonexperimental research could help to clarify the interventions being used in this approach and their effects.

This summary about treatment approaches used with alcoholic clients has identified some of the factors that affect explorations and conclusions about practice effectiveness with these clients. Given the present limitations in knowledge about these and other treatment approaches, what guidelines can be developed to help practitioners in the selection of treatment approaches in daily practice?

## DIFFERENTIAL TREATMENT SELECTION

The preceding summary on treatment approaches has indicated that all of them have advantages and disadvantages for particular kinds of alcoholic clients. This conclusion can be extended to other treatment approaches that also have been used with alcoholic clients: transactional analysis, reality therapy, psychoanalytic psychotherapy, gestalt therapy including psychodrama techniques, and the task-centered approach.

Underlying this conclusion is the assumption that the approach selected should therefore be based on the needs involved in each case situation. Some situations may require a specific approach or the use of two or more compatible treatment approaches in combination. In particular, it may be beneficial to supplement other approaches with the AA self-help approach. Similarly, some clients may become more willing to be involved in programs that use these other approaches after an initial positive experience with the AA approach.

A differential selection of treatment should be helpful even though the alcoholism treatment field has not developed a sufficiently sophisticated system of differential diagnosis to date. The field is in transition currently, and careful examination of the effects of differential treatment with clients can improve this diagnostic process. In addition, some authors have noted that treatment programs must incorporate a system of differential treatment in order to serve the full range of problem-drinkers.[49]

A number of factors should be considered as guidelines by social workers and other helping professionals in selecting appropriate treatment approaches for each case situation. These factors include: (1) the kinds of solutions that have worked or have not worked in the past with the particular client and the reasons, (2) the availability of external supports in the client's environment especially if these are essential to the approach, (3) the client's orientation to change or the client's principal mode of learning (visual, auditory, cognitive, emotional, etc.), (4) the nature of other problems in the client's situation that will affect recovery, (5) the client's strengths or areas of adequate functioning, (6) the client's belief system about the nature of his or her alcohol problem(s), (7) whether the client has the skills required to benefit from a particular approach, and (8) the length of time the client has been alcoholic and the severity of the problem.

Any or all of these factors can affect whether a particular approach can be used effectively with a given client. For example, nonverbal clients and older skid row alcoholics may benefit less than others from a psychoanalytic psychotherapy approach. This approach emphasizes the resolution of childhood conflicts through discussions geared toward producing insight as a way of handling current alcohol-related problems and other problems. Also, alcoholic clients whose major problems involve the suppression of feelings may not respond to the task-centered approach unless those feelings themselves are targeted for change as barriers to the completion of tasks. Or this approach may need to be supplemented with an approach such as psychoanalytic psychotherapy which focuses on feelings as part of the process for resolving problems associated with alcoholism.

## SUMMARY

The alcoholism treatment field is in a state of transition in which documentation of treatment effectiveness is a primary concern. This concern not only extends to determining whether specific elements of approaches are beneficial to alcoholic clients, but also to whether they may be harmful by retarding improvement. Methodological problems in existing research and a lack of consensus about outcome criteria are two major barriers to determining practice effectiveness. One way to resolve these problems may be to explore the interactions between clearly described client population groups, treatment approaches, and outcomes in daily practice. This kind of analysis can provide the foundation necessary for developing more rigorous experimental studies on practice effectiveness with alcoholic clients in the future.

## REFERENCES

1. Bakeland, F. and Lundevall, L: Dropping out of treatment: A critical review. *Psychological Bulletin, 82*:738–783, 1975.
2. Armor, D. J., Polich, J. M., and Stambul, H. B.: Alcoholism and treatment. Prepared by the U. S. National Institute on Alcohol Abuse and Alcoholism, Santa Monica, California, Rand Corporation, 1976.
3. Voris, Stephen: Alcohol treatment outcome evaluation: An overview of methodological problems. *American Journal of Drug Alcohol Abuse, 8*:549–558, 1981–82.
4. Wood, Katherine: Case work effectiveness: A new look at the research evidence. *Social Casework, 60*:437–458, 1978.
5. Bennett, Gerald and Woolf, Donna: Current approaches to substance abuse therapy. In Bennett, Gerald, Vourakis, Christine, and Woolf, Donna (Eds.): *Substance Abuse: Pharmacologic, Developmental, and Clinical Perspectives.* New York, John Wiley & Sons, 1983, pp. 341–369.
6. Hill, M. J. and Blane, H. T.: Evaluation of psychotherapy with alcoholics: A critical review. *Quarterly Journal of Studies on Alcohol, 28*:76–104, 1967.
7. Blane, H. T.: Issues in the evaluation of alcoholism treatment. *Professional Psychology, 8*:593–608, 1977.
8. May, S. J. and Kuller, L. H.: Methodological approaches in the evaluation of alcoholism treatment: A critical review. *Preventive Medicine, 4*:464–481, 1975.
9. Voris, op. cit., pp. 551. See also Brandsma, J. M., Maultsby, M. C. and Welsh, R. J.: *Outpatient Treatment of Alcoholism: A Review and Comparative Study,* Baltimore, University Park Press, 1980; Crawford, J. J. and Chalupsky, A. B.: The reported evaluation of alcoholism treatments, 1968–1971: A methodological review. *Addictive Behavior, 2*:63–74, 1977; Caddy, G. R.: Problems in conducting alcohol treatment outcome studies: A review. In Sobell, L. C., Sobell, M. B., and Ward, E. (Eds.): *Evaluating Alcohol and Drug Abuse Treatment Effectiveness: Recent Advances.* New York, Pergamon, 1980.
10. Emrick, Chad D.: A review of psychologically oriented treatment of alcoholism II. The relative effectiveness of different treatment approaches and the

effectiveness of treatment versus no treatment. *Journal of Studies on Alcohol,* *36*:88–101, 1975.

11. Miller, William R.: Controlled drinking: A history and a critical review. *Journal of Studies on Alcohol, 44*:68–83, 1983.

12. Jellinek, E. M.: *The Disease Concept of Alcoholism.* Highland Park, New Jersey, Hillhouse, 1960.

13. Ibid.

14. Miller, op. cit.

15. Alcoholics Anonymous: *Alcoholics Anonymous: The Story of How Many Thousands of Men and Women Have Recovered From Alcoholism,* 2nd edition, New York, 1955. See also Gellman, I. P.: *The Sober Alcoholic: An Organizational Analysis of Alcoholics Anonymous.* New Haven, Connecticut, College and University Press, 1964.

16. See, for example, Cahalan, D.: *Problem Drinkers: A National Survey.* San Francisco, Jossey-Bass, 1970; American Psychiatric Association Task Force on Nomenclature and Statistics: *Diagnostic and Statistical Manual of Mental Disorders (DSM-III).* Washington, D.C., 1980; and World Health Organization, Alcoholism Subcommittee on Mental Health: *Alcoholism Subcommittee Second Report WHO Technical Report Series #48,* Geneva, Switzerland, 1952.

17. Maisto, S. A. and McCollam, J. B.: The use of multiple measures of life health to assess alcohol treatment effectiveness: A review and critique. In Sobell, L. C., Sobell, M. B. and Ward, E. (Eds.): *Evaluating Alcohol and Drug Abuse Treatment Effectiveness: Recent Advances.* New York, Pergamon, 1980.

18. Voris, op. cit.

19. Curlee-Salisbury, Joan: Perspectives on Alcoholics Anonymous. In Estes, Nada and Heinemann, M. Edith, (Eds.): *Alcoholism: Development, Consequences, and Interventions.* St. Louis, C. V. Mosby Company, 1982, pp. 311–318. See also Beckman, Linda J.: An attributional analysis of Alcoholics Anonymous. *Journal of Studies on Alcohol, 4*:714–726, 1980.

20. Ibid.

21. Miller, op. cit.

22. Curlee-Salisbury, op. cit.

23. Grannetti, V. J.: Alcoholics Anonymous and the recovering alcoholic: An exploratory study. *American Journal of Drug Alcohol Abuse, 8*:371–376, 1981.

24. King, B. L., Bissell, L. and O'Brien, P.: Alcoholics Anonymous, alcoholism counseling, and social work treatment. *Health and Social Work, 4*:181–198, 1979.

25. Blake, B. G.: The application of behavior therapy to the treatment of alcoholism. *Behavioral Research and Therapy,* Oxford, *5*:89–94, 1967.

26. Hersen, M., Eisler, R. M., and Miller, P. M.: Development of assertive responses: Clinical, measurement and research considerations. *Behavioral Research and Therapy,* Oxford, *11*:505–512, 1973; and Sobell, L. C. and Sobell, M. B.: A self-feedback technique to monitor drinking behavior in alcoholics. *Behavioral Research and Therapy,* Oxford, *11*:237–238, 1973.

27. Cannon, D. S. and Baker, T. B.: Emetic and electric shock alcohol aversion therapy: Assessment of conditioning. *Journal of Consulting and Clinical Psychology, 49:*20–33, 1981.

28. Criddle, William D.: Rational emotive psychotherapy in the treatment of alcoholism. In Estes, Nada and Heinemann, M. Edith (Eds.): *Alcoholism: Development, Consequence, and Interventions,* St. Louis, C. V. Mosby Company, 1982, pp. 339–348.

29. Blake, op. cit. See also Hunt, G. M. and Azrin, N. H.: A community reinforcement approach to alcoholism. *Behavioral Research and Therapy,* Oxford *11:*91–104, 1973.

30. Hamburg, Sam: Behavior therapy in alcoholism: A critical review of broad spectrum approaches. *Journal of Studies on Alcohol, 36:*69–87, 1975.

31. Bingham, S. L., Rekers, G. A., Rosen, A. C., Sunhart, J. J., Pfimmer, G., and Ferguson, L. N.: Contingency-management in the treatment of adolescent alcohol drinking problems. *Journal of Psychology and Addictions, 109:*73–83, 1981; Miller, W. R., Pechacek, T. F., and Hamburg, S.: Group behavior therapy for problem-drinkers. *International Journal of Addictions, 16:*829–839, 1981; and Olson, R. P., Ganley, R., Devine, V. T., and Dorsey, G. C.: Long term effects of behavioral vs. insight-oriented therapy with inpatient alcoholics. *Journal of Consulting & Clinical Psychology, 49:*866–877, 1981.

32. Ibid; Blake, op. cit.

33. Sobell, M. B. and Sobell, L. C.: Alcoholics treated by individualized behavior therapy: One year treatment outcome. *Behavioral Research and Therapy,* Oxford *11:*599–618, 1973.

34. Voris, op. cit.

35. Hearn, Gordon: General systems theory and social work. In Turner, Francis J. (Ed.): *Social Work Treatment: Interlocking Theoretical Approaches,* 2nd edition. New York, The Free Press, 1979, pp. 333–360.

36. Steinglass, Peter: Life history model of the alcoholic family. *Family Process, 19:*211–226, 1980.

37. Mallams, John H., Godley, Mark D., Hall, George M., and Meyers, Robert J.: A social-system approach to resocializing alcoholics in the community. *Journal of Studies on Alcohol, 43:*1115–1123, 1982. See also Fine, Michelle, Akabas, Sheila, and Bellinger, Susan: Cultures of drinking: A workplace perspective. *Social Work, 27:*436–440, 1982.

38. Steinglass, op. cit.

39. See, for example, Goldenberg, Irene and Goldenberg, Herbert: Theoretical models of family interaction. In *Family Therapy: An Overview.* Monterey, California, Brooks/Cole, 1980, pp. 107–130; Rhodes, Sonya: A developmental approach to the life cycle of the family. *Social Casework, 58:*301–311, 1977; Bowen, Murray: Alcoholism viewed through family systems theory and family psychotherapy. *Annals of the New York Academy of Sciences, 233:*115–122, 1974; Woolen, S. J., Bennett, L. A., Noonan, D. L., and Teitelbaum, M. A.: Disrupted family rituals: A factor in the intergenerational transmission of

alcoholism. *Journal of Studies on Alcoholism, 41:*199–214, 1980; and Germain, Carel and Gitterman, Alex: *The Life Model.* New York, Columbia University Press, 1980.

40. Steinglass, op. cit.
41. Bowen, op. cit.; Papp, Peggy: Family sculpting in preventive work with well families. *Family Process, 12:*197–213, 1973; and Hartman, Ann: Diagrammatic assessment of family relationships. *Social Casework, 59:*465–476, 1978.
42. Freeman, Edith: Multiple losses in the elderly: An ecological perspective. *Social Casework, 65:*287–296, 1984.
43. Ibid.
44. Steinglass, op. cit.
45. Bates, Mildred: Using the environment to help the male skid row alcoholic. *Social Casework, 65:*276–282, 1983.
46. Steinglass, Peter: Experimenting with family treatment approaches to alcoholism, 1950–1975: A review. *Family Process,* 118–123, 1976; Kaufman, Edward (Ed.). *Power to Change: Family Case Studies in the Treatment of Alcoholism,* New York, Gardner Press, 1984.
47. Mallams, op. cit.
48. Janzen, Curtis: Family treatment for alcoholism: A review. *Social Work, 23:*135–141, 1978.
49. Miller, op. cit.

*Chapter Seven*

# FAMILY THERAPY AS A
# TREATMENT MODALITY FOR ALCOHOLISM*

MARION LAZAR USHER, JEFFREY JAY AND DAVID R. GLASS, JR.

Family therapy is emerging as an effective treatment for alcoholism.[1] In the past it was generally not understood or used because clinical models were not available for the clinician; in addition, treatment strategies describing the process of therapy were not available to guide family therapists through the long course of treatment. In this article we describe a clinical model and specific strategies for family therapy as a treatment modality for alcoholism. In the first section, we present theoretical notions that direct our treatment strategy. In the second, we focus on the initial stage of sobriety as a critical component in this treatment. In the last section we present family-therapy techniques and strategies.

## ALCOHOLISM FROM A FAMILY SYSTEMS PERSPECTIVE

How do families and alcoholism interact? The family is an enduring organized system of related individuals; alcoholism is a chronic psychological and physiological condition.[2] The key to the family-therapy model of alcoholism is found in the examination of that relationship: alcoholismic behavior becomes integrated into the family system and becomes part of the family's life

---

*Reprinted by permission from *Journal of Studies on Alcohol,* 43(9), pp. 927–938, 1982. Copyright by Journal of Studies in Alcohol, Inc., Rutgers Center of Alcohol Studies, New Brunswick, NJ 08903.

and stability. The maintenance of one becomes the maintenance of the other.

When viewed as a sociobiological system, the family's viability is seen as a consequence of its own dynamic structures and processes. That is, the family has specific built-in mechanisms for its own functioning and survival. These include roles, organization, boundaries, rules, information exchange and control mechanisms which operate to maintain the family as it satisfies the needs of its members: nurturance, protection and education. These operations, furthermore, tend to be conducted in an orderly fashion and do not deviate far from a prescribed range of tolerated behaviors. When behaviors begin to threaten the family, the system restores the internal order that is necessary to most biological systems. Jackson labeled the relative constancy of the family's internal environment—"maintained by a continuous interplay of dynamic forces"—the "family homeostasis."[3] Since family survival, characterized by "family homeostasis," is paramount to the family, it may enlist even maladaptive behaviors in its idiosyncratic attempt to survive. In families containing an alcoholic the alcoholismic behavior becomes part of the family's homeostatic mechanism.[4]

Although the chaotic and destructive qualities of the alcoholic's behavior are apparent, the tragedy of the family is that it nevertheless relies on that behavior. Researchers have already delineated some of the adaptive consequences for those families.[5] Nowhere is it suggested that such adaptive measures are desirable for meeting the family's needs. Just the opposite: by relying on those rigid and inadequate solutions, the family minimally satisfies the interpersonal needs of its members. The use of alcoholism in family survival may even link alcoholism to those most troublesome areas of family life—those areas where relational skills are the least developed and the subjective threat is the greatest. In the treatment sections of this article we will focus on the clinical implications of this link between the family's incorporation of alcoholism and the relational deficits observed in the families we have treated.

Because of the link between alcohol and specific family functions, the removal of alcohol in the initial phase of family therapy leaves the family vulnerable. They are exposed to their inadequacies and thus experience a threat previously concealed by the alcoholism. At this point the critical family issues move into focus and become visible. Thus, the movement into sobriety has changed the homeostatic balance by changing the part that the alcoholism has played. Consequently, the family's familiar pattern of meeting their needs is also changed. No longer can the family lean on the crutch of the alcoholic stupor to avoid facing intolerable situations. At this time, new affective expressions and interactional skills must be acquired by the family members if they are to constitute a newly functioning family system. The therapeutic task is to facilitate the acquisition of new interpersonal skills and strengths within the family system. Thus, sobriety is a challenge for the family therapist because the family can be expected to restore the status quo. The issue becomes family survival where survival had previously been based on alcoholismic behavior.

## A TREATMENT APPROACH

The initial stages of therapy include engaging the entire family in the treatment process, removing the alcohol from the family system, and then treating the family system as it is without alcohol.

### Engagement in Treatment

Engagement of any family in treatment is often a difficult process, regardless of the presenting problem. We have found this to be no less true for families containing an alcoholic. However, the presence of alcoholism requires specific considerations. The therapist's knowledge of the homeostasis produced by alcoholism directs the interventions from the beginning. The therapist's leverage comes from addressing the relationship of alcoholism to the family homeostasis. Thus, although the therapist joins with the family to facilitate its entrance into treatment, he also confronts the alcoholism directly. The motivation to start treatment comes from the system itself. The therapist capitalizes on this motivation by addressing the family's problems and relating them directly to the alcoholism.

The therapist's role at this point is to (1) make treatment available for the whole family, (2) reframe the problem as a family issue,[6] and (3) help stress the system in ways that increase the family's awareness of the problem, cut through their denial and increase their motivation to change. Specific ways of stressing the system include labeling and eliciting negative feelings, refusing to excuse the alcoholic, and insisting that the family take responsibility for their treatment. In these ways, the therapist takes an effective position which does not connive with the maintenance of drinking. This will contrast with the family's chronic denial of the problem and resistance to altering the alcoholismic homeostasis. The therapist's fear that stressing the system will drive the family away may interfere with his willingness to take a confrontational position, and failure to confront alcoholism directly at the outset of treatment is one way in which therapists unwittingly help to maintain the family's alcoholismic homeostasis and impede change. Addressing the alcoholism is the entry point to altering the family's interactional patterns.

### Removal of Alcohol from the System

Once the family system is engaged in treatment, the first goal is to move the entire family as quickly as possible to a pattern based on abstinence. One must, of course, be aware of the dangers to the alcoholic of a severe withdrawal reaction and take precautions to avoid it. It should be pointed out to the family that medical detoxification and inpatient alcoholism treatment are available if needed but that many alcoholics can successfully achieve abstinence on an outpatient basis. Although families vary greatly, it has been our experience that most families can be helped to confront the alcoholism, and that, with the insistence of family members and the therapist, the alcoholic can be convinced within a few sessions to stop drinking and face the challenge of initial sobriety.

At this point we ask all of the family members to agree to a contract calling for specific behaviors.[7] Such a contract clarifies what has been agreed upon, involves all members in the treatment process, provides structure for the immediate changes, and helps strengthen each individual's resolve. However, without changes in the family system, the alcoholic may find maintaining abstinence extremely difficult. "Slips" in the attempt to stop drinking do occur, and a slip at this point in treatment should not be viewed by family members as a serious setback. However, abstinence remains the goal.

In most of our cases we have found that the family can help the alcoholic to achieve stable abstinence anytime from several weeks to several months into treatment. The leverage provided by the successful involvement of the entire family greatly contributes to the accomplishment of this goal. We have found that in those cases in which abstinence is not achieved, the prognosis for recovery and any major change in the family homeostasis is poor. Even in cases in which there is a reduction in the amount of alcohol consumed, this reduction is usually followed by a gradual increase after termination of treatment, and only modest improvements are made in family relations.

### The Family System Without Alcohol

Alcohol becomes a central organizing principle for the family; it helps members minimally perform certain family tasks and meet affective needs, and it provides an unpleasant stability. Once the alcohol is removed from the family, the system is thrown into flux, into a crisis, and the family in crisis reveals characteristics not readily apparent in the alcoholismic homeostasis, as if alcohol use had disguised the family's more basic problems. During initial sobriety, these problems, though unexpected, are painfully clear to both family and therapist.

The removal of alcohol from the family system reveals an underlying emotional impoverishment, alienation, loneliness, and emptiness in most alcoholic families. The individuals in these families appear emotionally distant from one another, isolated, needing emotional support and closeness, but too empty and fearful to give them or to tolerate them if they are offered. Spouses appear reluctant to approach each other; children, especially older ones, seem hesitant to talk with parents; everyone seems alone and emotionally isolated in the family. Along with this emotional alienation come feelings of depression and hopelessness about their situation since they often feel themselves unable to remedy their isolation.

The family may have used alcohol to explain away their emptiness, and so to maintain it, or heated conflicts around alcohol may have distracted from or covered up their alienation from each other. The conflicts may even have offered some relief from the alienation in that conflict allowed for some interaction and emotional expression. Now, the family in crisis is suddenly aware of the nature of their underlying problem. Their task is to face and deal with the emotional distance between family members and their perceived inability to overcome this distance. While they struggle to do this, they experience the painful emotional emptiness of people needing support and closeness but seemingly unable to offer or tolerate it.

Another major problem area is that of interpersonal skills. Such families tend to be closed and rigid systems. They have not incorporated much from outside their system, nor have they offered an open, flexible environment for the development of ways of relating. They have relied on certain patterns of relating with each other involving alcohol and appear to have very limited relational skills, including skills in affective expression and negotiating. This lack of skills contributes to the family's difficulty in overcoming their emptiness and isolation, and prevents them from more effectively meeting each other's emotional needs.

An additional problem deserving attention involves the unexpected quality of the crisis—unexpected by both family and therapist. When alcohol is removed, several problems become apparent. At this point in treatment everyone will have accepted the goal of abstinence, and an expectation is created that things will improve once it is achieved. The family-systems viewpoint correctly indicates, however, that this cannot be the case. Following a brief "honeymoon" period (characterized by great efforts to please, "walking on eggs," gratitude that the problem is solved, etc.) the family is surprised when their relationships do not suddenly improve and instead are experienced as being emotionally barren.

Giving up alcohol has been stressful for all members of the family. They have accepted the challenge of attempting to relate in new ways. They have faced unfamiliar experiences, such as daily living without alcohol, sex without alcohol, and disagreements without alcohol, with all the fear and uncertainty that these entail. They worked toward abstinence in hope of feeling better and relating better. They find, however, that giving up alcohol did not, by itself, resolve their emotional impoverishment or give them new skills or courage. Old conflicts and anxieties remain, and the family can no longer attribute their lack of success in dealing with these issues to alcohol. The frustration, disappointment, and anger felt by the family and often the therapist as well can be extreme, and are potential barriers to progress or become reasons for returning to the alcoholismic homeostasis.

This crisis in the family is also a crisis in the treatment, and may prove to be a turning point. Four basic types of responses to this crisis have been observed in our clinical work. First, the family can resolve the crisis most easily by reintroducing alcohol into the system, i.e., by returning to their old patterns and reestablishing an alcoholismic homeostasis.

A second type of response to the crisis phase is to maintain sobriety, but split up the family. Families rationalize such an alternative by blaming others for their difficulties and frustrations. Divorce and separation, which are not uncommon following the early phases of treatment, can be seen as instances of families choosing this response. The split is often blamed on some flaw in the alcoholic or on the alcoholic's inability to change his behavior even when sober. Slips following a separation can be interpreted as the family's attempt to return to the familiar alcoholismic homeostasis. Clearly, there are no benefits to the family from either of these responses. In fact, we suggest that it is rare that a split benefits any individual, though it may help some individuals to seek additional treatment or other sources of change.

The third type of response is to begin the difficult process of establishing a new pattern of homeostasis which does not involve drinking. At least two types of such new patterns can be identified. In one case, a new structure or pattern is established in which support from outside the family is relied upon by one or more family members with little change in family interaction patterns. In the extreme, this is a splitting of the family emotionally, although they still live together. In less extreme instances, the family may substitute some other organizing principles from outside the family for drinking and maintain the same basic pattern as before. Excessive involvement in A.A. programs, to the exclusion of family interaction, is one such outcome. Both of these treatment outcomes or developments allow for further changes by motivated families. Genuine changes in family homeostasis remain possible in such cases, although in our view they are not probable.

The fourth, and optimal, solution for the family is a basic change within the family of the family homeostasis, allowing for more effective interaction, closeness, and increased success at meeting each other's affective needs.

### FAMILY THERAPY STRATEGY

From a family-system perspective, alcoholism is neither a symptom to be ameliorated nor simply a cause of other problems. It is an integrated part of family life, and it should be understood as an unfortunate component of survival in families with an alcoholic. The worst mistake that a family therapist can make is to confuse initial sobriety with the completion of therapy. At the time of initial sobriety, the family is facing frightening and destabilizing pressures. Sobriety presents an alteration in the rigid, predictable, and paradoxically stable pattern of alcoholismic family life.[8] It is a time of transition and crisis. Since sobriety is considered healthy, an understanding by the therapist of sobriety in the context of the alcoholismic family is required to realize the challenge of this phase. The therapist's understanding of the relationship between initial sobriety and the family's homeostatic history, as well as the future course of therapy, may be the only gyroscope to steer the family through that transition. If the therapist is unaware of the pressures on the family during initial sobriety, the potential is increased for family resistance to attempts by the alcoholic at sobriety, overt sabotage of treatment by the family, or family dissolution. Furthermore, obtaining sobriety at the cost of family life is not successful treatment. Understanding the challenge of sobriety makes family dissolution less likely.

### Confronting Alcoholism as the First Priority

The initial phase of sobriety is a transition phase. Treatment will contain aspects of crisis therapy. From that perspective, the following family therapy techniques and strategies are offered for working with the alcoholic family in the early and midphase of therapy.

First, in all family therapies an individual's presenting problem is reframed as one component in ongoing family functioning.[9] This transformation of the problem moves the problem from an individual to a family responsibility and often engenders in the family an insistence that the problem really belongs to the labeled individual. Nevertheless, with both firmness and patience, the therapist can reframe the problem in terms of the family. Typically, there is some recognition within the family that each family member has been hurt by and maybe has unwittingly contributed to the problem. At the very least there is acceptance that the family's attempts at solution have been unsuccessful. By speaking with the authority of his experience, and addressing the family's own experience, the therapist can begin to enlist the family system in the therapeutic process.

The approach is the same for the treatment of families containing an alcoholic. The family's insistence on only one person needing treatment is typical. "It's obvious that he is the drinker, not me! What do I have to do with his drinking?" That can be viewed as a question and the therapist can answer it with confidence, "If you want things to be better, which includes not drinking, the only way that can be accomplished is if everyone is involved in the treatment, and there is no drinking." This statement is usually not welcomed by the family. It may take the spouse several months to accept the responsibility of participating in the treatment. But this is a fundamental interpretation and its therapeutic action is that it challenges the family's official presentation of itself. It places the responsibility for change in the shared domain of the family. Finally, this interpretation serves therapy by avoiding a protracted debate over the definition of alcoholism. If the drinking is a problem for the family, then it is a problem to be addressed by the family in family therapy. Denial of "alcoholism" becomes superfluous since treatment requires abstinence regardless of labels. The drinker can be encouraged to achieve the abstinence any way he or she wishes so long as it is understood that not drinking is part of the treatment. If abstinence is not achieved, however, then the therapist takes a more active role in defining treatment toward that end.

Second, the alcoholism can be related to other family problems and placed in a context in which sobriety can be accepted by the family. Often "giving up my drinking for what?" is an important sentiment that the therapist can recognize and elicit in the contract for family change. Whether drinking is seen as a pleasure, defense, or style of problem solving, the family nevertheless has to have a sense of how things might be different once drinking is abandoned. This connection between drinking and other family problems will later become important at several points in the long-term treatment of the family; during the honeymoon phase of initial sobriety it will help the family stay focused on treatment goals. Just the opposite strategy will be available to the therapist when relapses of drinking occur in the face of dealing with the other family problems; the therapist can again interpret the use of alcohol in response to the difficulty of changing family functioning.

### Stabilizing the Family in Therapy

The family can be addressed as individuals who are struggling together to solve a family problem. This addresses the separateness of individual family members while beginning to foster the idea that they are not really alone, that they have allies who not only live together in the same family but who share a common task and purpose, and demonstrates that something is there besides loneliness.

The therapist, in his actions and role, provides a structure for the family while they are in transition from the alcoholismic to a new homeostasis. The therapeutic structure, including the office and the agency of therapy, provides a safe environment. It will help the family trust that they can contain the frustration and anger built up during years of alcoholismic interaction. While the therapist creates those aspects of the therapeutic environment with the family, he can enhance the stabilizing effect by referring the alcoholic to Alcoholics Anonymous, the spouse to Al-Anon and the teen-aged children to Alateen.[10] Just as the therapy provides an "outrigger" to stabilize the changing family system, so, too, can the AA structures provide yet another source of support and stability for the changing family.[11] The family should be encouraged to attend the meetings as part of the treatment contract. As the family becomes engaged in AA, the family therapist can identify for the family those differences in approach that exist between the AA programs and family therapy. In the early parts of treatment, these differences can be understood simply as complementary approaches to obtaining sobriety, one focusing on the family as a unit and the other on family members as individuals. Later, if the family becomes more fully involved in the AA programs, the family therapist will have to gauge the costs and benefits of the two different approaches. An evaluation with the family is necessary to plan how treatment should proceed.

The therapist predicts and interprets the homeostatic pulls back to alcoholismic behavior, thus defusing them. Relapses by the drinker or other family members will occur. These occasions provide a rich opportunity for the family therapist to work with the family toward new understanding and new patterns of relating. A drunken episode with a family can provide the therapist with a different view of the behaviors that become available to the family during intoxication. The family is blind to much of their alcoholic interactions; thus, when a family member comes to the office drunk, the therapist can use the session to examine with the family members what this behavior means to them. Relapses do not constitute failure; inconsistent progress is the rule rather than the exception.

### Addressing the Family's Affective and Interactional Patterns

The therapist addresses the inevitable frustrations of family members. Years of alcoholismic interaction have left everyone disappointed and angry. In addition to this, or perhaps because of it, the initial expectations of the family are unrealistic and, when they are punctured, frustration can become explosive. If the therapist can predict this inevitable frustration, he gains understanding in the eyes of the family, defuses the natural reaction to give up and return to drinking and, most important, begins to address the emotional life of the family. The honest expression and direct acknowledgment of these feelings constitute a new experience for many families. The therapist acts as a guide, teacher, and model in this type of interaction.

The therapist explores the experience and origin of the feelings expressed by individual members, feelings that cannot remain ignored or denied. Loneliness and anger, for instance, are changed through the process of identifying, experiencing, describing and finally sharing feelings. In our experience, the expression of loneliness by one family member leads to identification by other members. It also elicits an examination of how the family members nurture each other. The incapacity to care becomes as frightful as the experience of not being cared for. But the expression of these feelings marks the beginning of change. Attitudes and fears about those expressions need to be addressed as part of trying out new behaviors. Homework assignments extend the work toward connectedness. This is not to say that the family can move easily toward mature caring. Rather, this stage exposes the individual and family difficulties with these behaviors. The continued diagnostic and therapeutic work, however, does lead to change as the family therapist begins to address the traditional areas of family therapy, including appropriate role functions such as parenting, spouse relationships, and child subsystems.

The procedural points described above were not given in a time framework. Each family is different, and any specific timetable will prove to be as much a hindrance as a help. The best guide for the therapist is to monitor the family's response to treatment.

The organizing principle of alcoholism is central to alcoholismic families at the beginning of therapy. If the therapist ignores this he will lose the family or simply never make any progress with them. On the other hand, if he remains tied to a narrow focus on alcoholism he will not help the family to deal with the relationship of alcoholism to other issues of family life. He will thereby fail the family in his overidentification with the problem. The time to make the connection between alcoholism and other family problems, such as its' emotional impoverishment, is in the early phases of sobriety; that is the critical phase when the emotional crisis is most workable. Work on a family level at this time will pay off in the long-term treatment of the entire family.

## REFERENCES

1. Janzen, C.: Families in the treatment of alcoholism. *J. Stud. Alcohol, 38:*114–140, 1977; and Steinglass, P.: Experimenting with family treatment approaches to alcoholism, 1950–1975; a review. *Fam. Process,* Basel *15:*97–123, 1976.
2. Pattison, E. M.: Rehabilitation of the chronic alcoholic. In Kissin, B. and Begletter, H. (Eds.): *The Biology of Alcoholism Vol. 3. Clinical Pathology.* New York, Plenum, 1974, pp. 587–658.
3. Jackson, D. D.: The question of family homeostasis. *Psychiat. Q.* (Suppl. No. 1) *31:*79–90, 1957.
4. Davis, D. I., Berenson, D., Steinglass, P. and Davis, S.: The adaptive consequences of drinking. *Psychiatry, 37:*209–215, 1974.
5. Ibid., and Pattison, op. cit.
6. Minuchin, S.: *Families and Family Therapy.* Cambridge, Harvard University Press, 1974.
7. Berenson, D.: Alcohol and the family system. In Guerin, P. J., Jr., (Ed.): *Family Therapy; Theory and Practice.* New York, Gardner, 1976, pp. 284–297. See also Berenson, D. A.: A family approach to alcoholism. *Psychiat. Opinion, 13:*33–38, 1976.
8. Steinglass, op. cit.
9. Stanton, M. D.: Marital therapy from a structural/strategic viewpoint. In Sholevar, G. P., (Ed.): *The Handbook of Marriage and Marital Therapy.* New York, Spectrum, 1981.
10. Berenson, D.: The therapist's relationship with couples with an alcoholic member. In Kaufman, E. and Kaufmann, P. N., (Eds.): *Family Therapy of Drug and Alcohol Abuse.* New York, Gardner, 1979, pp. 233–242.
11. Davis, D. I.: Alcoholics Anonymous and family therapy. *J. Marital & Fam. Ther., 6:*75–81, 1980. See also Wegscheider, S.: *Another Chance.* Palo Alto, Science and Behavior Books, 1981.

*Chapter Eight*

# MULTIPLE GROUP SERVICES
# FOR ALCOHOLIC CLIENTS*

EDITH M. FREEMAN

The use of many different types of groups for the treatment of alcoholism has become a common practice in most treatment facilities.[1] These groups include Alcoholics Anonymous, treatment groups, and alcohol education groups. Cohen and Spinner noted that "the specific dynamics of alcoholism necessitate a variety of groups corresponding to particular stages in the recovery process, each group possessing its own unique purposes, structure, function, and style of leadership."[2]

This conclusion involves several important underlying assumptions: no particular type of group experience alone is sufficient for effective recovery, a variety of group services in combination can contribute to the overall effectiveness of treatment programs, and the combination of group services recommended and their sequence should depend on the needs of individual clients. Although the literature describes a variety of group services, it contains very little information about the effects of these services in combination or during particular stages of the recovery process.

This chapter includes a brief review of group services that have been provided for alcoholic clients, and the contribution they can make to the overall recovery process of clients either singularly or in combination. Another section is focused on treatment groups in particular, because these groups are designed to achieve two of the

---

*This chapter is a revised version of a paper presented at the 30th International Institute on the Prevention and Treatment of Alcoholism, International Council on Alcohol and Addictions, Athens, Greece, May 27–June 1, 1984.

major goals of treatment: to teach clients generic problem-solving that can be used to resolve a variety of problems and to help them integrate learning from other more specialized groups such as education and relaxation groups. The use of a task centered/ecological approach in one facility will be described to illustrate how group leaders have achieved these goals within their treatment groups.

### REVIEW OF GROUP SERVICES FOR ALCOHOLIC CLIENTS

Before alcohol treatment programs developed, any treatment provided was generally done with clients on an individual basis. There was very little information or experimental data about causes and treatment of alcoholism. The experiences of Alcoholics Anonymous beginning in 1935 established that groups could be useful in the treatment of alcoholics.[3] Alcoholics who were more advanced in the recovery process demonstrated to other alcoholics in these groups that sobriety was possible, and provided mutual support during treatment and throughout the on-going recovery process.

Due to the AA experience, individuals developing treatment programs perceived the usefulness of groups in general, and the need for a variety of groups in the treatment of alcoholics. There was growing recognition that giving up alcohol was only one step in the recovery process, and that these multiple group services were needed to help clients change other alcohol-related behaviors that they had developed. Examples of these behaviors can include: an inability to use leisure time or cope with stress without using alcohol, an inability to identify and use alternatives to drinking, poor social skills and inadequate interpersonal relationships, lack of knowledge and understanding about alcoholism and its effects, poor nutrition habits, low self-esteem, unstable work patterns, impulsive decision-making and minimizing or denying the existence of problems. It was noted that patterns in these behaviors vary from client to client, and that few clients develop all of these behaviors before or during their addiction.[4]

The literature indicates that a number of group services may be useful for addressing some of these problems, including: med-check, Alcoholics Anonymous, relaxation or stress reduction, alcohol education, employment, recreational and treatment groups. These groups will be discussed in terms of the needs which they are designed to meet, and their contributions to the over-all recovery process of clients at particular stages.

## Med-Check Groups

These groups are designed to monitor how well high-risk clients such as the chronically mentally ill, elderly, developmentally delayed, and alcohol dependent use prescribed and nonprescribed medications as instructed. Alcoholic clients who are particularly at-risk for relapse and for mixing contraindicated medications with alcohol benefit even more from these groups. The groups can combine many different types of high-risk clients as well as include alcoholic clients only.

Outpatients are scheduled to attend these groups weekly, biweekly, monthly, or less frequently depending on their individual situations. Inpatients may be monitored daily. Physicians are present to prescribe medications, discuss factual information about medications, observe the effects of medications on clients, and monitor whether clients are using their medications as prescribed.

Family members or others often accompany clients to these groups; this presents an opportunity to increase their understanding of the client's medical regimen and to encourage their support of the client's recovery. Social workers, nurses, alcoholism counselors, and other treatment staff often "sit in" on these groups periodically for this reason and because they can also observe their clients in a different group context.

Although informal data indicate these groups may be particularly helpful to alcoholic clients during the detoxification period and other early stages of recovery, there is little experimental evidence to document this assumption. These groups seem to be linked most closely with the functions of alcohol education groups where clients learn about chemical changes in their bodies related to alcoholism for which medications are prescribed,[5] and Alcoholics Anonymous groups where clients receive support for consistently following their treatment recommendations as a whole.

## Alcoholics Anonymous, Al-Anon, and Alateen Groups

All AA group sessions follow a prescribed pattern related to sharing past experiences involving alcoholism and reviewing how the program's 12 steps toward recovery are being followed. These groups are designed to show alcoholics how to acknowledge their loss of control to alcohol and to eliminate denial of the effects of their drinking on all aspects of their lives. Alcoholics who are more advanced in the recovery process demonstrate how to strive for recovery on a day-by-day basis and provide mutual support as sponsors for new members to prevent relapse. There is a spiritual element to group sessions which seems to work with many clients; they are encouraged to gain control over their lives by acknowledging dependency on a higher power. Abstinence is the goal in all AA groups.

Due to the needs of some special population groups, some specialized AA groups have been developed for racial minorities such as American Indians and for gay clients. Other specialized groups have been developed for family members of alcoholics. Spouses can attend Al-Anon groups that discourage the kind of enabling behavior that impedes the clients' recovery. Spouses or other family members learn to not take responsibility for the alcoholic's drinking or to facilitate drinking, and they learn to not feel guilty about taking care of themselves. They are also taught about the disease process and the systemic effects of alcoholism on all of those involved. These groups are open to spouses even when the alcoholic refuses to attend an AA group. Alateen groups were developed for the children of alcoholics and serve a similar function for them.

Informal estimates about the effectiveness of AA, Al-Anon, and Alateen groups range from 40 to 70 percent.[6] The few systematic studies on these groups indicate that involvement of family members in Al-Anon and Alateen is equally important to involvement of the alcoholic in AA since alcoholism has systemic effects and requires a systemic approach for resolution. In addition, it has been found that combining the client's involvement in AA group with participation in a treatment group increases the likelihood of continued sobriety. AA groups are thought to be helpful during early stages of recovery when abstinence models and mutual supports are needed, and also after the period of active treatment ends when a long-term support group is beneficial.

## Relaxation Groups

These groups were developed to achieve two related goals: to improve mental and physical health by increasing a client's ability to prevent and cope with stress. Alcoholic clients are usually involved in these relaxation groups one or more times weekly, and are taught to use a series of cognitive and behavioral exercises as part of their daily routines. These groups range from the very informal involving some structured and unstructured exercises, to the formal involving a totally structured curriculum of educational content, exercises, practice tapes, and group discussions about nutrition and clients' experiences in using the exercises to reduce stress.[7]

Since poor impulse control, confused thought processes, and low self-esteem are problem areas for some alcoholics that do not get resolved automatically with abstinence, these groups can help clients after the initial period of detoxification and during the on-going phase of active treatment. Clients are expected to continue the exercises after treatment ends. Clients can learn to build a support network since often they are encouraged to pair off outside the sessions to practice exercises with other members. The groups are usually led by alcoholism counselors, physical therapists or recreation specialists. There is no experimental evidence about the effects of these groups on the recovery process, but clients seem to respond more positively to these groups after they have learned about the physical and psychological effects of alcoholism as a disease in alcohol education groups.

## Alcohol Education Groups

These groups are designed for 3 types of individuals: the general public in key settings such as schools, those who are high-risk for alcoholism such as drunk drivers or the children of alcoholics, and those diagnosed as alcohol dependent. Groups are usually closed-ended and meet on a time limited basis ranging from 10 to 20 weeks. Some participants are mandatory referrals due to drunk driving, family violence, or other criminal offenses. Some of the participants may be referred to treatment groups later for follow-up. The combination of the two types of groups is particularly helpful for early stage alcoholics.

The goal of these groups is to change knowledge, attitudes, and behavior related to alcohol use or to encourage abstinence. Educational content on the physical, psychological, and social effects of alcoholism, causes of alcoholism, and alternatives to alcohol use are presented.

Some group leaders have more recently used experimental methods such as control groups and pre and post instruments to measure changes in participants as a result of group sessions. They have found the use of peer co-leaders and provision of alcohol education for collaterals such as parents, spouses, or teachers can be effective.[8] A larger number of these group leaders have used informal observations to evaluate changes without providing experimental documentation to support their claims.

### Employment Groups

These work groups are designed to provide opportunities for clients with unstable work habits and histories to develop work-related skills: regular and prompt attendance, effective follow-through on instructions and assignments, maintenance of cooperative attitudes, and effective management of conflicts at work. An inability to handle stress at work or stress from being unemployed can affect clients' continued sobriety, so these groups can be very beneficial during the recovery process. Additionally, they provide opportunities for clients to collaborate in regular group sessions on major decisions that affect the work and to build self-esteem.

Although these groups sometimes involve maintenance jobs in the treatment facility, they can also involve service contracts with external businesses. Services can include house painting, lawn and garden care, or the development of various marketable products. Clients usually continue in these groups while they are inpatients, until they obtain external employment individually, or are referred for vocational training.

The point in the recovery process when unemployed clients should be involved in work groups depends on the extent of deficits in other areas that can block their use of these groups. Involvement in treatment groups prior to these groups seems to be helpful for such clients, because treatment groups provide a model for problem-solving that can be generalized to the work groups. There is no experimental evidence regarding the effectiveness of these groups; however, they do seem to meet some of the needs discussed in this section when provided along with group services for stress reduction and recreation.

### Recreational Groups

These groups are designed to teach clients how to structure leisure time with abstinent peers and utilize alternatives to drinking. The loss of drinking companions and having long periods of inactivity that were formerly devoted to alcohol consumption make many alcoholic clients vulnerable to loneliness and relapse. Therefore, these groups are most helpful during the early stages of recovery before clients have been able to develop new social networks that encourage sobriety.

Group members enhance their social skills by planning and participating in athletics, movies, plays, parlor games, hobbies, and other activities. They may also spend time in sessions discussing the effects of these activities on their recovery process especially at high-risk times, their experiences in participating with other group members, and ways to involve key individuals in their environments in some of these activities without alcohol being involved. A few investigators have explored experimentally the need to extend counseling beyond traditional services to change clients' social environments. Their results indicate that these groups provide clients with a positive social reference group that reinforces sobriety and can lead to their use of other appropriate social activities.[9]

## Treatment Groups

Treatment groups have been designed for alcoholic clients, family groups and couples. The family and couples groups were developed so that several families or couples can share common experiences and problems related to alcoholism during sessions, and learn how to resolve problems together also. Some family treatment groups do not involve the alcoholic client and are similar to Al-Anon or Alateen in that respect.

In all treatment groups, members are encouraged to identify commonalities and to develop group goals focused on changing aspects of their lives that are problematic. Individual goals are also developed for individual problem areas as a model for future problem-solving after treatment ends. Additionally, these groups are used to provide mutual support, feedback, and reality testing for facilitating problem-solving and an understanding of the recovery process.

These groups are noted in the literature as being important throughout the period of active treatment, but much of the information about what factors make them effective is conflictual. There is some consensus that focusing on environmental supports and barriers to recovery, teaching a clear framework for problem-solving that is useful for all life domains, and providing education about alcoholism can make these groups effective.[10] Most researchers have had difficulties exploring the effectiveness of these groups, however, because the interventions involved are seldom described or implemented in a systematic or measurable manner.[11] Further, many clients for whom these groups are effective seem to benefit also from an ongoing support group such as AA in order to maintain their gains after they are no longer involved in treatment groups.

In summary, all of the groups discussed in this section have the potential for enhancing the recovery of alcoholic clients in various ways. Although experimental evidence about the effectiveness of most of these services is insufficient to date, monitoring how clients utilize these other groups during treatment group sessions can be helpful for recovery. This monitoring process requires that treatment groups themselves be designed to include a productive and therapeutic atmosphere.

## TREATMENT GROUPS IN ONE SETTING

The treatment groups for alcoholic clients described in this section were developed in response to staff complaints in one mental health center about the fragmented and nontherapeutic nature of their groups. Clients also seemed to be frustrated by the slow progress or by what has been characterized as "running in place."[12] Treatment groups have been developed for couples, families (children included), and for individuals. The latter type of treatment group is the focus for this chapter. These integrative groups will be described in terms of goals; staff, clients, and setting; format and structure, and group process.

### Goals

In this setting, over-all service goals have been developed to serve as guidelines for individual client goals. Clients are expected to:

1. Increase their abilities to cope with the internal and external stresses that contribute to their problems with alcoholism and hinder their efforts to achieve sobriety.
2. Identify some of the common problems that group members experience in the recovery process and alternative ways to handle those problems.
3. Learn stages involved in the recovery process and some symptoms of the behaviors of alcoholic clients in each of those stages.
4. Develop a range of alternatives to drinking and a support network that aids in the recovery process.

### The Setting, Staff, and Clients

The setting in which these goals were developed is a substance abuse division of a mental health center in the Midwest. It includes a 23-bed residential treatment program, detoxification services, a reintegration program, outpatient treatment services, and consultation and education services. In addition to treatment groups, the setting provides individual counseling, AA groups, relaxation groups, work groups, and alcohol education groups. Attendance at AA groups, treatment groups, and individual counseling is mandatory. In addition, Antabuse® is prescribed for all clients involved in the program and other medications may be prescribed on an individual basis. The average length of stay in the program is 60 days, but the range is from 30 to 120 days.

The staff consists of six counselors and ten aides. The counselors have BA or master's degrees (MA's and MSW's). Treatment groups are conducted by the counselors, some of whom are recovering persons. All counselors have been trained in alcoholism counseling in addition to their academic training. The six counselors include three males and three females, and their ages range from 25 to 45 years.

Some of the clients who receive services in this setting have been referred by outside agencies: public welfare, mental health centers, industry, probation departments, family service agencies or other types of treatment programs. Some have used other drugs in addition to alcohol, including marijuana, cocaine, or amphetamines. They range in age from 20 to 40 years with the majority being in the 20 to 25 age group. Both males and females are included in all treatment groups, although there is a women's treatment group for clients who want or need this kind of culture-specific group service.

### Format and Structure

In-patient treatment groups are open-ended and meet two times daily. Clients attend these groups for the duration of their residential stay. Out-patient groups are close-ended and meet weekly for a period of 14 to 16 weeks. Group size ranges from 10 to 20 members.

A task-centered/ecological approach has been used by group leaders in their treatment groups. This approach is based on cognitive, problem-solving, and systems theories. It encourages practitioners to help clients change ideas, beliefs, and feelings about problem-solving and other relevant issues that can hinder progress, as well as their actual problem-solving activities.[13] It requires the planning, assignment, and implementation of tasks in a systematic way once problems have been clearly identified and specific goals have been developed.

Goals and tasks cover all life domains based on systems theory: family life, social and recreational, cognitive, spiritual, physical, and work.[14] Task implementation in any of these areas is monitored during each group session by the group member involved, the group leader, and other members who provide feedback and support. This approach uses small incremental task assignments to help clients increase problem-solving skills and self-esteem, and to counter learned helplessness, inappropriate use of support networks, and impulsive decision-making.

### Group Process

A number of strategies are used by group leaders to facilitate clients' integration of learning from other groups and progress in the recovery process. They include: developing specific goals, assigning related tasks to achieve those goals, using paradoxical interventions, and helping members move from superficial to meaningful discussions.

Goals are developed regarding all of the life domains mentioned previously as being consistent with an ecological perspective. This has broadened the range of client interactions which group leaders use for identifying preliminary statements for goal setting. For example, if clients made direct statements about being unhappy with some aspect of their lives, about wanting to see some aspect changed, or about wanting help with solutions to problem areas, group leaders are able to use these obvious opportunities to explore goal-setting.

More frequent, but less obvious opportunities, are also utilized for goal setting: members' complaints about some aspect of another member's behavior (e.g., another member monopolizes the group), members' nonverbal behaviors which indicate strong feelings or the absence of feelings and involvement in the group, members' denial of the existence of problems in general or problems with alcohol, members being inconsistent in what they say compared with what they do, or members' complaints about problems with significant individuals outside the group. In both situations involving direct and indirect expressions of problems, group leaders use exploratory questions to clarify these problems: i.e., who, what, when, where, how, and the effects of these problems. A next step involves exploration by the group leader and other members of what the individual wants to see changed specifically, by whom, and to what extent.

These discussions lead naturally to actual goal setting in the treatment groups. Group leaders have a set of criteria for evaluating goals as they are developed with clients during the group process. They evaluate whether the goals are:

1. Specific (or concrete) and clear.
2. Stated in terms of outcomes rather than methods.
3. Observable and measurable with the method of evaluation implied.
4. Time-limited and future-oriented.
5. Reasonable and achievable within the time-limits involved.
6. Challenging to the client, requiring him or her to "stretch."

An example of this goal setting process involves Wilma, a 37-year-old female inpatient who began crying when other group members were discussing areas of their lives they wanted to change. The group leader acknowledged her tears and explored the underlying feelings with her. Wilma mentioned that her sadness resulted from a growing recognition that she had experienced many losses and did not have the supports she now needed to make progress in recovery. The group leader made normative and supportive comments about her permanent losses (her mother had died in her arms and her husband divorced her due to her alcoholism). When Wilma also mentioned an emotionally-distant relationship with her 19-year-old son, the group leader and other members questioned her about what she wanted changed in the relationship, who would need to change, and to what extent. Wilma stated she wanted to be close to her son after not seeing him for three years.

By using the criteria for evaluating goals, this vague, nonspecific, long-term goal was modified as follows: "By the next group session, Wilma will have reestablished direct or indirect contact with her son as observed by her roommate." Additional time was spent discussing how and when the contact could be accomplished effectively.

This example also helps to illustrate how goal-setting can be used to help clients integrate learning from other groups. As Wilma discussed her losses and her goal, she mentioned that she was going to have a difficult time getting through Mother's Day the following week without drinking. The group leader asked members to think about what they had learned in their alcohol education groups about handling pain. One member noted that some alcoholics use alcohol to hide from pain and losses, and that Wilma might be tempted to drink because of stresses related to the holiday. The group leader asked them to think about alternatives for handling stresses other than drinking, especially at high-risk periods. Some members shared ideas about alternatives that had been discussed in AA sessions, including planning special activities with AA sponsors for high-risk times, developing an absorbing hobby that involves contact with others, or renewing formerly supportive relationships.

Another member shared some of the stress-reduction exercises that she had learned in her relaxation group. On this basis, Wilma developed a second goal related to "Being able to identify and use two or more alternative ways (nonalcoholic) for coping with stressful situations within one week." This short-term goal was helpful because it was related to her first goal, and met the criteria for effective goals.

Goal-setting in this manner facilitates the development of tasks within group sessions and outside of these sessions, a second strategy used by group leaders. The tasks involve specific cognitive, behavioral, or interactive activities. An example of a within session task can be illustrated with Wilma's situation. Group members could have been asked to develop a collective list of alternatives for handling stressful situations. The group leader could have typed the list and distributed it to members for their current and future use.

Another within-session task involves having group members divide into small groups of three to four and discuss different effective responses to situations in which they are being pressured to drink. This task is helpful when members question whether they can resist peer pressures to drink, or will be involved in new social situations where others are unaware of their alcoholism. Other within-session tasks include trust-building exercises, role plays, or gestalt techniques involving the "hot seat" in which the client talks to an absent person about concerns or conflicts. All of these tasks can aid in recovery because they teach or allow clients to practice behaviors in situations in which they are potentially high-risk for relapse.

Tasks assigned to members outside of sessions include a range of activities also (e.g., using communication exercises with a family member or contacting a potential employer). In regard to Wilma's first goal, she agreed to telephone her son before the next group session four days later. The group discussed possible responses by the son, and ways Wilma could respond in turn. Members gave Wilma feedback about positive changes they had observed in her interpersonal skills in other types of groups over the past weeks, which increased her confidence and self-esteem. This allowed Wilma to integrate feedback on her progress in other groups and encouraged her to complete this task.

Tasks are monitored by group leaders and members in subsequent sessions. In Wilma's situation, she was able to complete her task successfully, and the next session was used to focus on why she was successful and development of another task for increasing contacts with her son. Subsequent goals and tasks were developed with Wilma related to obtaining a job and increasing her social skills. In other situations when a task is not accomplished successfully, group leaders encourage members to explore what prevented task accomplishment, what could have been done differently, and how that learning could be generalized to other members' situations as well as to future problem situations of the member involved.

A third strategy, paradoxical interventions, has been used by group leaders at times for moving clients to a point where goals can be developed and tasks planned. Situations in which clients deny the existence or extent of their drinking problems, give excuses about why they cannot change their situations, or otherwise sabotage their own problem-solving efforts are prime opportunities for using these interventions. Paradoxical interventions include utilizing resistance when clients deny problems, reframing, paradoxes, less of the same, advertising, and benevolent sabotage.[15] Initially, group leaders used these interventions without an awareness of when they were using them or why they were effective. They gradually developed skills in predicting when they could be effective and in implementing them appropriately.

All of these interventions involve an assumption that resistance is a precondition rather than a barrier to change, they prescribe the symptom, and help to move group leaders and clients from an impasse in problem-solving. For example, Ed was a nonvoluntary client who had been referred for alcohol education due to a drunk driving offense. He was later referred to a treatment group after staff members diagnosed him as being alcohol dependent. In one session, Ed was trying to convince others that he could drink while driving and that his only problem was to plan how to avoid getting caught. When members' efforts to convince him of the futility of this plan did not work, the group leader noted that he seemed committed to his plan and wondered if he wanted to set a goal around drinking and driving. Ed seemed very surprised and then spent time attempting to set his goal and develop a task related to the goal.

When Ed was unable to develop a goal, the group leader noted that his difficulty might be due to his lack of information about how long he could go without drinking. He was asked to monitor and keep a written record of how long he could refrain from drinking during the following week. This assignment utilized the client's resistance or denial in order to demonstrate to him his lack of control in alcohol consumption, and it eliminated the impasse between Ed and the group. When he reported back during the next group session, he was less confident that he could control his drinking—he was not able to refrain from drinking even for one day.

When Ed wanted to set a long-term goal for abstaining for the rest of his life, other members reminded him about what they had learned in AA group sessions about taking recovery one day at a time, and in the alcohol education group about drinking models. This helped members to integrate learning from other groups. They provided suggestions to Ed about starting with daily goals, how to resist peer pressures to drink, and how to develop a network of abstinent friends. Group leaders also teach clients like Ed to advertise rather than attempt to hide their alcoholism from abstinent friends and others. This reduces the stress from hiding and reframes acknowledging the problem as a positive rather than negative behavior.

A fourth strategy used by group leaders involves helping members move from superficial to meaningful content and interactions. This strategy is very important because staying at a superficial level can delay clients' progress through the recovery process, and encourage the denial of problems noted in the preceding section. Group leaders have gradually developed their skills in this area by identifying their own resistances to meaningful content, such as fears that this content can cause group leaders to lose control of their groups. Group leaders' fears in this area are usually related to their own experiences with alcoholism, as recovering alcoholics or as relatives or friends of alcoholics.

Group leaders have identified some of the factors that indicate whether the content and process in their groups are at a meaningful or superficial level (see Table 8-1). These factors range from how members address other members or share information with each other, to whether the focus in sessions is on the process of interaction as well as on the content, to whether members discuss their learning experiences from other types of groups.

Group leaders have also identified the steps which they must take to move members from a superficial to a meaningful level related to each of these factors. For example, in closed-ended groups, the leaders use get acquainted exercises during the first session to help members learn how to share personal information about themselves. Members might be asked to give their names, marital and family status, employment, etc.; and to provide more personal information about an area which they want to know about the person seated next to them. The person seated next to them has the opportunity to hear this information about another member and then to provide the same information about him or herself. As noted in Table 8-1, this kind of information about other members is helpful in brainstorming problem solutions. Another exercise involves pairing members off and having them interview

## TABLE 8-1.
## SUPERFICIAL AND MEANINGFUL INTERACTION
## IN GROUPS WITH ALCOHOLIC CLIENTS

*When the Content and Process Are Superficial:*

1. Members don't know each other's names.

2. Members refer to each other as "he or she" or talk to other members about issues related to particular members instead of talking to those members directly.

3. Members do not share moderately personal information about their backgrounds or present circumstances. Their lack of information about each other becomes apparent when they discuss problems in the group (they can't help each other anticipate barriers to problem solving or build on strengths.)

4. Members seldom share intimate or confidential information about themselves. They focus on general issues ("the need to stop drinking"), or they focus on intimate information at a superficial level by intellectualizing (e.g., "I need to be more open with people, I know why I drink, If only my spouse understood me better"). Feelings are sometimes expressed indirectly but seldom discussed in the group in terms of the reason for the feelings or how they affect behavior.

5. Members give glowing but general reports on their progress with problems and seldom admit mistakes or relapses. Other members provide them with only positive feedback (automatically) or do not provide feedback at all (e.g., "I think Harry is sincere.").

6. Members give "pat" answers to problem situations being discussed ("you've got to work your program"). They seldom confront each other about inconsistencies or game playing, they are reluctant to disagree with one another or with the leader overtly (they may simply ignore some part of the discussion or show discomfort nonverbally).

*When the Content and Process Are Meaningful:*

1. Members call each other by name.

2. Members generally address each other directly and speak in the first person to each other.

3. Members ask for moderately personal information from other members, share the same about themselves and refer to this information in group discussions on problem-solving (family constellation, marital status, substances used and abused, hobbies and talents, health status, problems and strengths.

4. Members share intimate and confidential information about themselves in the group—their feelings; significant persons and relationships in their lives; significant events; and their *real* concerns. They move toward identifying the significance of these areas when helped to do so (e.g., the effects on their drinking problem and their efforts toward sobriety).

5. Members give specific information about their progress or attempts at work outside the group, or other members and the leader ask exploratory questions to elicit this information (e.g., who, what, when, why, where, how). Members risk admitting to other members when they make mistakes or relapse. Other members provide support and encourage the member to talk about what didn't work and why, and what could be done differently in the future.

6. Members confront and raise challenging questions with each other ("what would happen if . . . , that doesn't fit with what you said before . . . "), they are able to clarify when they disagree with each other and the leader, and the basis for their disagreements. They are able to listen when other members share even when they disagree.

TABLE 8-1 Cont.
## SUPERFICIAL AND MEANINGFUL INTERACTION
## IN GROUPS WITH ALCOHOLIC CLIENTS

*When the Content and Process Are Superficial:*

7. Members make very few references to interactions with other members outside the group sessions, and they label those interactions as positive or negative without exploring them as part of the work of the group. Members seldom discuss experiences in other types of groups that are designed to aid in their recovery.

8. Only a few members become actively involved in group sessions over time; other members seldom get involved except very minimally. Generally, the members' level of involvement is not discussed openly in the group, nor are silent members questioned about their involvement or encouraged to become more involved.

9. Members make very general or out of context comments about what took place in a session, and have difficulty identifying learning unless the session has been focused on them (e.g., "good session," or "Harry's problems are so different from mine—I don't see why he can't stop drinking," or "all of this focus on feelings is a waste of time").

10. Members seldom initiate discussions during the first few minutes of a session; they wait for the leader to start the session, or they open with areas unrelated to the group's purpose and work. They tend to drift from topic to topic so that there is very little focus during sessions.

11. Members seem to be unaware of group goals, norms, and rules, and seldom refer to these aspects during group sessions.

12. Members stay focused on the *content* of sessions only; if the focus is sometimes shifted to group process issues (such as underlying feelings, patterns of interactions among members, or the meaning of messages occurring in the group), members continually distract or divert the discussion.

*When the Content and Process Are Meaningful:*

7. Members make frequent references to ways in which they utilize each other outside the group sessions for support and problem-solving. They use the group to explore how those interactions are helpful or not and what they have learned from them. They also discuss learning from other types of group sessions (AA, relaxation group, education group, etc.).

8. Over time, most of the members become actively involved in sessions, although those actively involved from session to session may vary. Members often comment on or explore the level of involvement for themselves and others, and relate that to the problems members are or should be working on.

9. Members are able to participate in summarizing the content or process of group sessions, or to identify specific things that were useful or that they have learned during a session no matter what the focus has been.

10. Members spontaneously start sessions without prompting by the leader, focused on material from previous sessions or on things related to the group's purpose that have occurred since the last session. Discussions have focus; an effort is made to bring about closure before shifting to other topics.

11. Members discuss group goals, norms, and rules to help orient new members, or during relevant discussions among themselves when specific interactional issues come up in the group.

12. Members can tell each other and the group leader when group process is or is not facilitating the work of the group, and can often identify relevant barriers, explore them, or discuss specific process issues.

and introduce each other to the rest of the group with information beyond the basic name and marital or family status. These kinds of exercises or tasks are used periodically in open-ended groups in which the membership often changes. They are consistent with the task-centered approach used for the treatment groups in this setting.

Group leaders teach members how to focus on group process as another example of steps they must take to keep interaction at a meaningful level (see Table 8-1). They have identified a series of discussion questions to ask clients that help in this area as well as with goal setting and using an ecological focus: what information or messages are being shared during a particular interaction, what does this information mean, what are the unspoken messages involved and how are they affecting the interaction, what are the underlying feelings involved and what are the signs of those feelings, how are those feelings affecting the interaction within and outside sessions in other life domains, how do those feelings and behaviors relate to alcohol dependency and sobriety, how are other members involved or not involved in the interaction, how would members like to see things changed within or outside of the group, and what will have to happen for things to change? These questions not only encourage meaningful interaction, they help members recognize that the same problems they have outside the treatment group can be observed and resolved during those sessions with peers.

## CONCLUSIONS

Group leaders in one facility have developed several strategies for making their treatment groups effective. These strategies seem to be useful because they teach clients a method of problem-solving that can be generalized to other current and future problem areas that affect recovery, and they help clients to integrate learning from other group services. The use of a range of different group services is also assumed to be beneficial in helping clients to maintain sobriety at different stages in their process of recovery. Group leaders in this facility now need to become more systematic in describing and using the strategies that have been discussed. This can make it possible in the future for them to analyze the short and long-term effects of these strategies on clients under experimental conditions.

## REFERENCES

1. Cohen, Mark and Spinner, Allyne: A group curriculum for outpatient alcoholism treatment. *Social Work with Groups, 5:*5–13, 1982.

2. Ibid., p. 5.

3. Curlee-Salisbury, Joan: Perspectives on Alcoholics Anonymous. In Estes, Nada and Heineman, M. Edith (Eds.): *Alcoholism: Development, Consequences, and Interventions.* St. Louis, C. V. Mosby and Company, 1982, pp. 311–318.

4. Shuckit, Marc and Haglund, Robert: Etiological theories on alcoholism. In Estes, Nada and Heineman, M. Edith (Eds.): *Alcoholism: Development, Consequences, and Interventions.* St. Louis, C. V. Mosby and Company, 1982, pp. 16–31.

5. Ibid., p. 22.

6. Curlee-Salisbury, op. cit., p. 315.

7. Brody, Alan: S.O.B.E.R.: A stress management program for recovering alcoholics. *Social Work with Groups, 5:*15–23, 1982.

8. Goodstadt, Michael and Sheppard, Margaret: Three approaches to alcohol education. *Journal of Studies on Alcohol, 44:*362–380, 1983.

9. Mallams, John, Godley, Mark, Hall, George, and Meyers, Robert: A social systems approach to resocializing alcoholics in the community. *Journal of Studies on Alcohol, 43:*1115–1123, 1982. See also Azrin, Nathan: Improvement in the community reinforcement approach to alcoholism. *Behavior Research, Therapy, 14:*339–348, 1976.

10. Bakeman, Frank and Lundwall, Lawrence: Dropping out of treatment: A critical review. *Psychological Bulletin, 82:*738–783, 1975.

11. Ibid., p. 738.

12. Bolen, Jane: Easing the pain of termination for adolescents. *Social Casework, 53:*519–527, 1972.

13. See Reid, William: Task centered treatment, and Hallowitz, David: Problem-solving theory. In Turner, Francis (Ed.): *Social Work Treatment: Interlocking Approaches.* New York, The Free Press, 1979, pp. 479–498 and 93–122. See also Germain, Carel (Ed.): *Social Work Practice: People and Environments.* New York, Columbia University Press, 1979, pp. 7–20.

14. Germain, op. cit.

15. See for example: Shore, Jeffrey: Use of paradox in the treatment of alcoholism. *Health and Social Work,* pp. 11–20, 1981; and also Watzlawick, Paul, Weakland, John, and Fisch, Richard: *Change: Principles of Problem Formation and Problem Resolution.* New York, W. W. Norton Co., 1974.

*Treatment Issues with*
*Special Population Groups*

*Chapter Nine*

# A COMPREHENSIVE TREATMENT PROGRAM FOR CHILDREN OF ALCOHOLICS

JOANNE M. PILAT AND JOHN W. JONES

Drinking and drug use among children and adolescents are of increasing concern for social workers and other helping professionals. Youthful experimentation, peer influence, ineffective role models related to alcohol consumption, and media misrepresentations about substances and the effects are some contributors to the use of chemicals by young people. Increased societal pressures, adolescent unemployment, as well as age and developmental problems add to the difficulties all children and adolescents face in their decisions about whether to use alcohol and other drugs.[1]

The potential for alcohol abuse as well as for emotional and/or physical neglect makes the children of alcoholics a special "at risk" population among the population of children in general. Children of alcoholics include not only infants, latency-age children, and adolescents born to alcoholic parents, but also adults. There are between 27 and 34 million children of alcoholics in the United States alone. Of this total, about 12 to 15 million are schoolage children.[2]

There is a need to identify these children who are more at risk as a preventive measure regarding potential alcoholism. In addition, there is a need to prevent negative reactions to the emotional scarring and inconsistency of growing up with alcoholism in the family system. Social workers in all areas of practice must begin to identify, refer, and treat this special population of children. This chapter will describe a comprehensive treatment program for the children of alcoholics focusing on family dynamics as they pertain to the children in alcoholic families, an assessment instrument and procedures for using it, treatment issues, and the three phase program itself.

### FAMILY SYSTEM DYNAMICS

Alcoholism is often viewed from a family systems' perspective by social workers and other clinicians and researchers. This perspective is appropriate because of the nature of systems' dynamics, the fact that in a system, change in the functioning of one family member is automatically followed by a compensatory change in another family member.[3] The drinking behavior of each alcoholic impacts on the lives of significant others, including members of the family. Many of these significant others are children.

Alcoholic family systems often look fused. The focus of family life is the drinking or on nondrinking. Everyone in the family becomes stuck around the issue of drinking.[4] Alcohol eventually controls the alcoholic's activities, relationships, and thoughts. It is equally true that family members lose their identities to concentrated focus on alcohol.

Roles, rules, and generational boundaries must be clear if a family is to function in a way that allows members to grow. With alcoholism, roles and rules are frequently vague. Generational boundaries are unclear. The nonalcoholic spouse assumes extra roles that have been abandoned by the alcoholic. Older children often adopt a parenting position with their younger siblings and at times with their parents. Older children also cross generational lines at times by functioning as surrogate marital partners. Younger children must often fend for themselves, both emotionally and physically.

All family members' lives become controlled by the alcoholism. For instance, the work and school performances of spouses and children, respectively, are often detrimentally affected by preoccupation with, and emotional worries about, the alcoholic. Some family members seek to escape the alcoholism by becoming overly involved in work, school, community affairs, and/or recreation.

Finally, family members may develop social, emotional, and physical health impairments.

## Dynamics of Children of Alcoholics

Children of alcoholics have a significantly higher rate of alcoholism and problem drinking than the general population. Some researchers note that children of alcoholics tend to have other problems at a higher rate than the general population in addition to alcoholism. Studies have found that marked hostility, fear, depression, impulsive behavior, and sexual confusion are problems experienced by children living in stressful alcoholic family systems. Other problems noted include hyperactivity, antisocial or aggressive behavior, poor social relationships, poor academic achievement,[5] various types of chemical dependency, and other emotional and behavioral problems.[6]

However, the assumption that nearly all children of alcoholics have emotional, behavioral, and academic problems may be stereotypical. There seem to be a number of children who adjust to or cope with the chaotic family system created by parental alcoholism. These children become mediators, junior family therapists, and marriage counselors for their parents and/or typically repress their own feelings.

Evidence shows that children of alcoholics often adopt these seemingly positive roles in their families in order to survive within the system. They are the children who are responsible, who adjust, who placate, who become the family heroes.[7] People marvel at these childrens' adjustment skills. They may excel at athletics and academics and are often school leaders. These children adopt roles that are the most comfortable for them in coping with the fear, anger, loneliness, and unpredictability of the alcoholic family system. They tend to deny feelings, control their environment, protect the alcoholic and other family members in order to save themselves and their family from feelings of fear, embarrassment, and shame. They absorb the pain of the system. For many of these adjusters, a strong facade is the only way to survive.

Often it is these children who adjust well and do not draw

attention to themselves, who will develop greater problems in the future. Usually the children with behavior problems tend to act out their problems, thus coming to the attention of the school social worker, the court social worker, or others. Low self-esteem, lack of confidence, repressed feelings, anxiety, and unresolved anger plague the family heroes in later life.[8] The adjusters may experience difficulties in maintaining intimate relationships and may have problems with trust and control issues in later life. Finally, they often marry alcoholics and are at-risk for becoming alcoholics themselves.

Studies show that children of alcoholics are especially vulnerable because they have difficulty maturing based on a hierarchical scale of needs. Children of alcoholics may get their biological needs met (some do not), but the sense of security, belongingness, confidence, and self-esteem cannot be achieved in a family where inconsistency is the norm. The children are unable to develop a consistent relationship with the alcoholic parent and find that the nonalcoholic parent is also unable to meet their needs.[9]

Finally, children of alcoholics are usually angry with both the alcoholic and nonalcoholic parent. They are resentful about their parents' inabilities to meet both emotional and physical needs, and they are angry about the unpredictability and the demanding nature of the family system. This anger, however, is frequently supressed.

## VIOLENCE IN THE FAMILY

Family violence is not limited to any economic, racial, geographical, or age group. However, alcohol use is consistently associated with violence. Violence in the family, as experienced by the children of alcoholics, is just beginning to be fully understood. Mounting evidence is being accumulated about physical and sexual abuse, emotional violence and their relationship to parental alcoholism and chemical abuse.[10]

Researchers have found a highly significant relationship between alcohol abuse and child abuse. One study conducted at a community alcoholism treatment program found that more than one-half of the alcoholic parents had abused their children.[11]

The violent family or some of its members frequently presents itself to social workers in all areas of practice. The husband who abuses his wife may also abuse the children and/or the abused wife may abuse their children. Sometimes the wife then batters her husband, often supported by the children.

Incest and sexual abuse have been taboo subjects. Social workers need to pay special attention to clues about these aspects in the lives of children of alcoholics. Sexual abuse occurs in closed and secretive family systems where the boundaries are unclear. The alcoholic family system is a closed system and invested in the family secret of alcoholism. The system is out of control around the use of alcohol and may be out of control in other relationships. The drunken behavior of the alcoholic, the emotional deprivation of the alcoholic and the nonalcoholic spouse, and the deterioration of generational boundaries produce a situation where sexual abuse can occur. Even if there is no overt sexual abuse, children of alcoholics frequently assume age-inappropriate emotional relationships with one or both parents. Children can become their parent's best friend. Siblings may sexually act out relationships or the sex abuser may be an extended family member. Children may not be able to receive the familial protection they need in these situations. As an example:

> R. is a 31-year-old recovering alcoholic woman who is also the adult child of an alcoholic. She was raped by a babysitter when she was 7 years old and told by her mother to not dare mention this to her father. Her mother was mad at her for bringing up more trouble when she already had an alcoholic husband to worry about. The mother was afraid that the father would kill the babysitter.

## THE ASSESSMENT PROCESS

The U. S. Department of Health and Human Services notes that only 5 percent of the 12 to 15 million school-age children of alcoholics in the United States are identified and treated.[12] This finding indicates that children of alcoholics are critically in need of services. It has been noted that these children are invisible to professionals.[13] Those who have come to a professional's attention are those who act out their problems, not the many children who adjust. It is urgent that social workers start identifying the many children of alcoholics in their various settings so that these children can receive help.

Screening opportunities are everywhere that social workers practice, in schools, drop-in centers, child guidance clinics, family service agencies, adolescent psychiatric units, youth organizations, community centers, pediatrics departments, and the courts. Screening to obtain data and to identify the children of alcoholics is the first step towards providing help through the available resources.

### A Screening Instrument

The Children of Alcoholics Screening Test (C.A.S.T.) was developed to aid in this identification process.[14] This screening instrument can be used psychometrically to identify children who are living with or have lived with alcoholic parents. The C.A.S.T. is a 30-item inventory that measures childrens' feelings, attitudes, perceptions, and experiences related to their parents' drinking behavior. The instrument items were formulated from real-life experiences that were shared by clinically diagnosed children of alcoholics during group therapy and from published case studies. All items were judged to be face valid by a number of alcoholism counselors and grown-up children of alcoholics.

The C.A.S.T. is presented in Table 9-1. It measures the following related to children: (1) emotional distress associated with a parent's use/misuse of alcohol (item 2), (2) perception of drinking-related marital discord between their parents (item 14), (3) attempts to control a parent's drinking (item 3), (4) efforts to escape from the alcoholism (item 28), (5) exposure to drinking-related family violence (item 7), (6) tendencies to perceive their parents as being alcoholic (item 22), and (7) desire for help (item 26).

The C.A.S.T. can be used to identify latency-age, adolescent, and adult children of alcoholics. Children nine years of age or older can usually complete the C.A.S.T. with little or no assistance. Children eight years of age or younger usually need to have each item read and sometimes explained to them. All "yes" answers are tabulated to yield a total score. The total score can range from zero, indicating no experience with parental alcohol misuse, to 30, indicating multiple experiences with parental alcohol abuse. Even without scoring, talking about the questions with a child can be diagnostic and therapeutic.

## TABLE 9-1.
## CHILDREN OF ALCOHOLICS SCREENING TEST

### C.A.S.T.

Please check (✔) the answer below that best describes your feelings, behavior, and experiences related to a parent's alcohol use. Take your time and be as accurate as possible. Answer all 30 questions by checking either "Yes" or "No."

Sex: Male _____ Female _____ Age: _____

| Yes | No | Questions |
|---|---|---|
| _____ | _____ | 1. Have you ever thought that one of your parents had a drinking problem? |
| _____ | _____ | 2. Have you ever lost sleep because of a parent's drinking? |
| _____ | _____ | 3. Did you ever encourage one of your parents to quit drinking? |
| _____ | _____ | 4. Did you ever feel alone, scared, nervous, angry, or frustrated because a parent was not able to stop drinking? |
| _____ | _____ | 5. Did you ever argue or fight with a parent when he or she was drinking? |
| _____ | _____ | 6. Did you ever threaten to run away from home because of a parent's drinking? |
| _____ | _____ | 7. Has a parent ever yelled at or hit you or other family members when drinking? |
| _____ | _____ | 8. Have you ever heard your parents fight when one of them was drunk? |
| _____ | _____ | 9. Did you ever protect another family member from a parent who was drinking? |
| _____ | _____ | 10. Did you ever feel like hiding or emptying a parent's bottle of liquor? |
| _____ | _____ | 11. Do many of your thoughts revolve around a problem drinking parent or difficulties that arise because of his or her drinking? |
| _____ | _____ | 12. Did you ever wish that a parent would stop drinking? |
| _____ | _____ | 13. Did you ever feel responsible for and guilty about a parent's drinking? |
| _____ | _____ | 14. Did you ever fear that your parents would get divorced due to alcohol misuse? |
| _____ | _____ | 15. Have you ever withdrawn from and avoided outside activities and friends because of embarrassment and shame over a parent's drinking problem? |
| _____ | _____ | 16. Did you ever feel caught in the middle of an argument or fight between a problem drinking parent and your other parent? |
| _____ | _____ | 17. Did you ever feel that you made a parent drink alcohol? |
| _____ | _____ | 18. Have you ever felt that a problem drinking parent did not really love you? |
| _____ | _____ | 19. Did you ever resent a parent's drinking? |
| _____ | _____ | 20. Have you ever worried about a parent's health because of his or her alcohol use? |
| _____ | _____ | 21. Have you ever been blamed for a parent's drinking? |
| _____ | _____ | 22. Did you ever think your father was an alcoholic? |

**TABLE 9-1 Cont.**
## CHILDREN OF ALCOHOLICS SCREENING TEST

| | | |
|---|---|---|
| _____ _____ | 23. | Did you ever wish your home could be more like the homes of your friends who did not have a parent with a drinking problem? |
| _____ _____ | 24. | Did a parent ever make promises to you that he or she did not keep because of drinking? |
| _____ _____ | 25. | Did you ever think your mother was an alcoholic? |
| _____ _____ | 26. | Did you ever wish that you could talk to someone who could understand and help the alcohol-related problems in your family? |
| _____ _____ | 27. | Did you ever fight with your brothers and sisters about a parent's drinking? |
| _____ _____ | 28. | Did you ever stay away from home to avoid the drinking parent or your other parent's reaction to the drinking? |
| _____ _____ | 29. | Have you ever felt sick, cried, or had a "knot" in your stomach after worrying about a parent's drinking? |
| _____ _____ | 30. | Did you ever take over any chores and duties at home that were usually done by a parent before he or she developed a drinking problem? |

TOTAL NUMBER OF "YES" ANSWERS.

### Validity and Reliability of the C.A.S.T.

The test was anonymously administered to 82 clinically-diagnosed children of alcoholics, 15 self-reported children of alcoholics, and 118 randomly-selected control group children. Both latency-age and adolescent children participated in this study. The 82 clinically-diagnosed children of alcoholics lived in a home where at least one parent had been diagnosed alcoholic by a psychiatrist, a psychologist, and a social worker who was a certified alcoholism counselor. The 15 self-reported children of alcoholics stated that at least one of their parents received personal alcoholism counseling, either because of their own or their spouse's alcoholism. Chi-square analyses were computed on this data. It was found that all 30 C.A.S.T. items significantly discriminated children of alcoholics from control group children. In addition, children of alcoholics scored significantly higher on the C.A.S.T. (mean = 17.4 and 19.1) compared to control group children (mean = 3.6).

Since the two children-of-alcoholics groups did not significantly differ in their total C.A.S.T. scores, these two criterion groups were combined thus forming an overall children-of-alcoholics group. The 97 children of alcoholics were scored 2 and the 118 control group children were scored 1. These group scores were correlated with the total C.A.S.T. scores and yielded a validity coefficient of .78 (p < .0001). Finally, it was found that a cutoff score of six or more reliably identified 100 percent of the clinically-diagnosed children of alcoholics and 100 percent of the self-reported children of alcoholics. This cutoff standard also showed that 23 percent of the control group children were "at risk."

Another validation study indicated that the C.A.S.T. appears to be valid with the adult children of alcoholics' population as well.[15]

### An Example of the Screening Process

In order to receive a clearer picture of the numbers of children of alcoholics in ordinary school classrooms, a study was completed in a large metropolitan Chicago-area high school in a predominantly blue-collar, white neighborhood. One hundred seventy-four high school students anonymously answered the C.A.S.T. while attending their gym classes. Twenty-seven percent indicated parental alcoholism and another 17 percent indicated a questionable parental drinking problem. Thus, a full 44 percent of the students were living in a family where parental drinking is an issue. These children need help.

In addition, of the 77 children in this category, 23 percent were in the Honors rank and 58 percent were making passing grades. None of these students had come to the school social worker's attention. These children were doing well in school although they were living with the secret of family alcoholism.[16]

### TREATMENT PLANNING

Social workers and other health professionals have become increasingly willing to see the entire alcoholic family system as the focus of treatment. Professionals once believed that all clinical attention should be focused on the marital dyad and the recovery of the children would automatically follow. It is true that when the parents work on their relationship, pressure is taken from the child. However, since the chronicity of alcoholism indicates that the parental dyad may never reach a functional level, children should not be viewed only as adjuncts to the adults' treatment. Children need specialized help for themselves.

## A Three-Phase Program

A treatment program for children of alcoholics was developed through a large family alcoholism treatment center located near Chicago. The program can be adapted to any setting where children of alcoholics are present, in schools, mental health centers, and community centers. Such settings should have social workers who are both knowledgeable and comfortable in talking to children about alcoholism and its effects on them and their families. In this setting, alcoholics and/or nonalcoholic parents were encouraged to bring their children aged 5 to 19 to the children's groups described below. This was done to discourage any thinking that the sessions were only for children who had problems. It was understood that all family members, including all children, needed to learn about alcoholism, to understand the dynamics that interplay when alcoholism is present in the family system, and to have a safe place to ask questions and to ventilate feelings.

The children attended large 45 minute lecture/discussion sessions with the entire program population two times a week for four weeks. These lectures focused on family issues. These lectures, and one family session, were the only places where the children received treatment/education with their parents. In order to meet the special needs of the children in an alcoholism treatment program, ongoing therapy/education groups were also formed. These groups were for children only. They made up the core of the three-phase treatment program.

### Phase I: Crisis Intervention and Education

The purpose of this phase is to begin to encourage the children to open up and talk about the secret of family alcoholism. Education is a large part of these lecture/discussion sessions because it is less threatening than the experience of talking about personal feelings. Children meet 1½ hours a week for four weeks. They are divided into age appropriate subgroups (e.g., adolescents, latency-age, and prelatency-age children).

There are several clinical issues and themes that emerge during this phase. They include the need for knowledge about alcoholism, the issue of denial, and the expression of feelings. The children learn the basic dynamics of alcoholism; how the illness affects families, how the roles, rules, and boundaries become confused. They learn about relapses, blackouts, and dry drunks. They learn that they did not cause their parent's drinking problem. This educational aspect helps to globalize the childrens' experiences. They see that other children have experienced similar situations. This decreases the sense of isolation and guilt that all children feel. In one case example:

> Two pre-teen girls who were best friends unknowingly met in the children's group. Neither of them knew about the other's parent who had a drinking problem. They and other children described the sense of being the only one in their classroom with a parent with alcoholism. These myths are soon dismissed in the phase I sessions.

Denial as a symptom of alcoholism is present in the children also. In this phase, some children will not admit that a parent is alcoholic, but will be better able to talk about a parental drinking problem. Some children's sense of family loyalty requires them to admit nothing. Even if children are able to talk about family problems associated with drinking, many deny the extent of the effects of parental alcoholism on their own lives. The task of the leaders is to facilitate the children's inclusion into the group and discussion of their experiences at a pace comfortable for each child. In another case example:

> One 12-year-old girl could only talk about the problem. When others would ask her which parent drank, she was unable to talk about any drinking. Her loyalty to the family prevented her from discussing anything but the problem and only in general terms. Even though her parents were in another room discussing a drinking problem, she would not.

Because emotions are often repressed in an alcoholic family system, children are uncomfortable owning and expressing their feelings. Much of the emotional energy in the family goes into managing and controlling the feelings and behavior of others. In Phase I, the aim is to encourage the ventilation of natural feelings such as anger, guilt, love, confusion, and sadness.

Group meetings are centered around different activities that are conducive to allowing expression of feelings, experiences, knowledge about alcoholism, and problem solving. Types of activities include:

1. Artwork-magic markers and chalk are used to produce pictures that depict a particular feeling about the parental drinking, a picture of the family system, or of ways to cope.
2. Clay work involving plasticine and clay, are particularly good for pounding, mashing, manipulation, 3-D sculpting of feelings, and molding scenes that depict family dynamics.
3. Storytelling—"Once upon a time . . . " is not threatening and the children can pretend a story about alcoholism and feelings, especially if they are uncomfortable sharing a personal, family experience.
4. Small Group Exercises and Word Games—geared with a focus on better understanding of themselves and the alcoholism.
5. Therapeutically Focused Discussions—Talk is focused on alcohol-related issues. Members verbally share feelings and experiences related to their own alcoholic family systems. They confront denial in other children and they encourage other group members to better cope with parental alcoholism. This activity is more effective with older children.

### Phase II: Support Group

The aim of Phase II is the continuation of the education and the integration of the clinical issues indicated in Phase I, including breaking through the denial and the expression and owning of feelings. These are vital to the work necessary in Phase II.

The structure is similar to Phase I. The group meets 1½ hours a week, once a week, for 12 weeks. This is considered the support group. It enhances the work already begun in Phase I. Hopefully, all the children will move into Phase II so that the effects of the first phase will enable the group to delve quickly into the tasks of Phase II.

Clinical issues during this phase include coping mechanisms, self-esteem and mastery, generational boundaries, and self-identity. As the children become more open regarding their feelings and the effects of alcoholism on their lives, they are able to begin to share their methods of coping with parental drinking or non-drinking. Both effective and ineffective coping techniques are shared. The children have an opportunity to experiment with the model of a variety of coping skills. Both the development of realistic problem-solving skills and learning how to optimally survive in an alcoholic family system are necessary because of the chronic nature of alcoholism and the length of time which recovery takes.

Self-esteem and mastery relate to problem solving and coping also. An important issue in Phase II is the bolstering of the children's sense of confidence in themselves and in their ability to get help for themselves. Realizing that they can effect some changes in their own lives even though they cannot control parental drinking, leads to an enhanced self-esteem. Alateen, an important community resource helpful in this phase of treatment, is discussed later.

The fact that the children are not in a group with their parents states behaviorally that as children, they are not responsible for their parents' problems, only for their own problems. This helps them to understand generational boundaries in their families. When children are in large groups with their parents, the focus is usually on the parents' problems, especially because of the parents' very real needs and the fact that most treatment programs are more comfortable in dealing with parental issues and spouse issues. In these adult groups children usually are uncomfortable and do not speak or feel very comfortable and then assume an adult role. This adult-like behavior only reinforces the inappropriate responsibility that children in alcoholic families assume. Parenthetically, the group leaders should anticipate that the perfect, adult-like children of Phase I might begin to try out more childlike problem behaviors in Phase II. Boundaries, in general, are a problem for these children. When there are siblings in the same group, they frequently speak for each other. Although in most cases they have not shared their feelings with each other, they still interpret and talk for the other.

Although self-identity is closely related to the above issues, special mention needs to be made about this issue. This second phase is important in its focus on the special opinions, feelings, and attitudes of each child. This focus on some of the differences in the children enables each to become aware of their own separateness. Because of the fusion in most alcoholic family systems, along with the heavy focus on the drinking, it is important that children continue to grow in their own identities. This is difficult to do in an alcoholic family system.

Many of the techniques indicated in Phase I are also used in Phase II. In addition, the following group activities and techniques are used:

1. Role playing and Psychodrama—children play their own roles, their parents', and those of siblings. They act out scenarios designed to aid in understanding the multitude of conflicts that plague alcoholic family systems during the progression and recovery phases of the illness.
2. Collages and montages are made with scissors, paste, pictures, and paper to create themes such as "Who am I?", "What I like to do.", "My different feelings."
3. Films—those geared to children and their feelings, for discussion and problem-solving techniques. Films are starting to be developed that show how children are adversely affected by, and can come to cope with, parental alcoholism. These are especially good for viewing and can be borrowed from alcoholism treatment programs.

In Phase II, children share more personal feelings and family experiences. Their gains are further solidified and expanded by participation in Alateen.

### Phase III: Alateen

Children in the groups were encouraged to attend four beginners Alateen meetings during Phase I of treatment. These Alateen meetings were held once a week at the center. Children younger than 12 had to find a pre-Alateen meeting in the Community. Children are encouraged to find an outside Alateen or pre-Alateen meeting to attend during Phase II. They need to be motivated to attend these meetings at this stage due to their denial that alcoholism is a family problem and that all family members need help. Another difficulty might occur if the children cannot get to the meetings without parental escort. Some children make other arrangements to be taken if their parents are unwilling to see that they get to meetings.

After Phase II, children are encouraged to attend regular outside Alateen meetings. Participation in Alateen meetings allows children of alcoholics to have access to an ongoing peer group that provides a solid program of recovery from family alcoholism.

Alateen is a self-help movement which consists of hundreds of groups of young people who help themselves and each other to learn about alcoholism. Empirical research has shown that children of alcoholics who are members of Alateen are better off emotionally and academically than those who are not.[17] Social workers can work with their clients to help them use the available resources of Alateen.

Any young person between the ages of 12 and 20, whose life is or has been affected by the alcoholism of a parent or someone else is eligible for membership in Alateen. Alateen focuses on ways in which group members can accept the fact that they are powerless over the alcoholic. Members learn to detach themselves emotionally from their parents' difficulties while continuing to love them. They learn to become responsible for their lives and not the lives of their parents. Members of Alateen help each other keep their own lives from being affected too deeply by relationship with an alcoholic parent. Some schools are now allowing Alateen meetings on school premises.

### EVALUATION OF THE PROGRAM

No formal evaluations have been done in terms of this program. These evaluation procedures need to be developed in the future. However, observations of the children who participated in the program, coupled with feedback from both parents and family alcoholism counselors, show that the program is highly effective. Major changes observed in the children include the following:

1. Greater understanding of alcoholism and how it affects family members.
2. Improved communication with other family members including the alcoholic parent and fewer arguments.
3. An increased number of ways to cope within the system. Children were able to problem-solve more effectively.
4. Less intense feelings of anger, fear, and confusion. Increased ability to disclose feelings to others.
5. More assertive and self-confident behaviors.
6. Greater ability to separate one's own behavior and feelings from others, thus, not blaming themselves for the alcoholic's drinking or for other family problems.
7. An unplanned by-product of the program has been the alleviation of guilt on the part of the parents. Parents have felt they are doing something positive for their children that could help them deal with feelings and unpleasant experiences connected to the parent's drinking. Many of the parents were themselves adult children of alcoholics and expressed wishes that a program had been available for them when they were young.

### SPECIAL TREATMENT ISSUES

There are some special issues related to treatment that have become apparent from providing these services to children. Some children have suffered such severe emotional and/or physical abuse that they may need more long-term psychotherapy instead of, or in addition to, this three-phase program. The assessment phase of the program can alert the social worker to the specific needs of individual children and provide the opportunity for further referral if necessary. Some children can make use of the educational aspects of the program while receiving additional help.

Children who themselves are abusing chemicals are a special target treatment group. Because of the high incidence of alcohol abuse among children of alcoholics, it is not uncommon for discussion in some of the group meetings to center on the children's own alcohol and drug use. This is always a lively discussion as all children relate that it won't happen to them. Some refuse at the time to use any chemicals while others experiment. All are concerned about the information regarding generational alcoholism and they wonder about a genetic factor.

Some children who may be identified as alcohol and/or drug abusers by family members or through the group process are referred for a more intensive chemical evaluation. Recommendations are then made and the parents and child are made aware of the various options available to them. The three-phase program can be an important early step in the diagnosis and referral for some child and teenage alcoholics.

This chapter primarily focused on the special needs of children of alcoholics. In addition, it is often helpful for children to be involved in family therapy sessions with the entire family. This is especially important in the renegotiation of the family roles, rules, and generational boundaries. Although children may be relieved that drinking has stopped in the system, this is as difficult an adjustment for them as it is for the parents. Children too, must relinquish some of the roles they assumed during the drinking days, and secondary gains attached to those roles. This is often difficult. In one case example:

> J. is a 16-year-old boy who as the eldest son of an alcoholic father had been the family disciplinarian for his siblings. The father returned from alcoholism treatment and with his new sobriety began to assume an authoritative position with his children. J., who had been on his own for years, had much difficulty with his father's demands that he ask to use the car, check about going out at night, and request permission for things that he had been doing without any questioning.

## IMPLICATIONS FOR SOCIAL WORK PRACTICE

By training, social workers have the skills and the basic orientation to problem solving that can make them especially effective in working with children of alcoholics. Social workers are trained to view the entire system as the client. This means that they must consider the total environment and the relationships in that environment as the treatment focus.

Children are members of family systems. Social workers should be aware of the impact which the family has on all aspects of the child's life. Because social workers know community resources and practice in a wide variety of settings, timely interventions on behalf of children are possible.

## CONCLUSIONS

Children of alcoholics are a vulnerable population. They are at risk for the development of their own alcoholism and chemical problems and/or for establishing other alcoholic family systems in their adult lives by marrying alcoholics. Some children of alcoholics develop severe emotional and behavioral problems in childhood. A greater majority seem to adjust to the inconsistency and pain in the family environment. It is only later in their adult relationships that the scars of survival from their childhood may surface.

Early identification and assessment of the children of alcoholics is imperative. Only then can appropriate resources be made available to them and their families. The three-phase program of education and crisis intervention, support group, and community involvement through Alateen can meet the needs of most children of alcoholics. Empirical research is needed to document the exact effect of this program on the children's feelings, attitudes, and coping skills.

## REFERENCES

1. Stober, B.: Alcohol abuse in children and adolescents. Translated from the German of Alkohol-Missbrach bei Kindern und Jugendlichen, in Gauting, *Fortschritte der Medizin,* 96:1917–22, 1978.
2. Bowen, Murray: A family systems approach to alcoholism. *Addictions, 21:*3–11, 1974.
3. Root, Laura: *Casework with Alcoholics.* Selected papers of the 27th International Congress on Alcoholism, Frankfurt, West Germany, Vol. II, 1964.
4. U. S. Dept. of Health and Human Services. *4th Special Report to the Congress on Alcohol and Health.* Washington, D.C., U. S. Govt. Printing Office, 1981.
5. Pilat, Joanne: Children of alcoholics: Needs and treatment intervention. In

*Proceedings of the International Council on Alcohol and Addictions,* Vienna, Austria, 1981, pp. 486–495.

6. Fox, R.: Children in the alcoholic family. In Bier, D. (Ed.): *Problems in Addiction: Alcohol and Drug Addiction,* New York, Fordham University, 1962, 71–90. See also Chafetz, M. E., and Blane, H.: Children of alcoholics: Observations in a child guidance clinic. *Quarterly J. of Studies on Alcohol, 32:*687–698, 1971; Cork R. M.: *The Forgotten Children: A Study of Children with Alcoholic Parents.* Don Mills Ontario, General Publishing, 1969; Whitfield, C. L.: Children of alcoholics: Treatment issues. *Maryland State Medical Journal,* 86–91, 1980; and Booz, Allen: *An Assessment of the Needs of Children of Alcoholic Parents.* Washington, D.C., National Institute of Alcoholism and Alcohol Abuse, 1975.

7. Black, Claudia: Children of alcoholics. *Alcohol Health and Research World, 4:*23–27, 1979.

8. Wegscheider, Sharon: *The Family Trap.* Crystal, Maine, Nurturing Networks, 1976.

9. Stone, F.: *Alcoholism: The Children's Viewpoint.* Austin, The University of Texas Press, 1979.

10. Hindman, Margaret: Family violence: An overview. *Alcohol Health and Research World, 4:*2–11, 1979.

11. Spieker, Gisela: Family violence and school abuse. *Proceedings of the 24th International Institute of Prevention and Treatment of Alcoholism,* Zurich, Switzerland, 1978.

12. U. S. Department of Health and Human Services, 1981, op. cit.

13. Bosma, W.: Alcoholism and the family: A hidden tragedy. *Maryland State Medical Journal, 21:*34–36, 1972.

14. Jones, John: *The Children of Alcoholics Screening Test (C.A.S.T.),* Chicago, Family Recovery Press, 1981.

15. Jones, John: Psychometrically identifying adult children of alcoholics. Unpublished Manuscript, 1981.

16. Pilat, Joanne: Children of alcoholics: Identification in a classroom setting. *28th International Institute on the Prevention and Treatment of Alcoholism,* Munich, Germany, 1982.

17. Hughes, J.: Adolescent children of alcoholic parents and the relationship of Alateen to these children. *J. of Counseling and Clin. Psychology, 45:*946–947, 1977.

*Chapter Ten*

# ENVIRONMENTAL FACTORS
# IN TEENAGE DRINKING*

ANN WEICK

The subject of drinking among any group in our society is inevitably one which stirs up flurries of misinformation, emotionalism, and concern. When the focus is teenage drinking, the issues become further clouded by the complex behavioral context of adolescence. It is important, then, to sort out the various elements of teenage drinking which can clarify our understanding about this important topic.

In looking at the topic of alcohol and youth, it is immediately apparent that there are distinctive parts of this large subject area. The literature examines why teenagers drink, why some may be problem drinkers, and why some become alcoholics. Although these areas are interconnected, each of them represents different issues for consideration. A helpful way to see their relationship is to establish a common frame of reference. The one to be proposed here uses as its keystone the concept of environment. It is this concept which will help demonstrate some of the subtle linkages among the various aspects of teenage drinking.

All human behavior occurs in and is part of multiple environments. Because of the difficulty we have in conceptually integrating social and physical factors, we tend to view drinking behavior as a social phenomenon, without reference to its physical elements. We can move beyond this narrow dichotomy if we frame behavior within a context which considers environment as com-

*Reprinted by permission from the *Journal of Social and Behavioral Sciences*, 25(2), Spring 1979, pp. 62–68.

posed of both social and physical factors, each of which may be internal or external to ourselves. This simple set of divisions allows us to examine one segment at a time and yet keeps the examination grounded in the common base of environment. It is the complexity of the whole which is the proper perspective for behavioral analysis.

This multiple environment focus is a beneficial one for extending our understanding of teenage drinking. It helps to plot the information already available and also forces us into new areas of investigation.

## THE SOCIAL ENVIRONMENT OF TEENAGE DRINKING

It is not surprising that the definition of teenage drinking as a social behavior has produced a wealth of data about the impact of social environment on drinking habits. The external-social environment, composed of such factors as language, customs, social norms, political and economic arrangements and social control mechanisms, forms the social context within which drinking behavior occurs. It is clear that teenagers drink because they live in a drinking culture. The production, marketing and consumption of alcohol are accepted and supported activities within this society. Society values the presence of alcoholic beverages, as has every other society in recorded history.

There are, however, two provisos which must be added to this acceptance, because our society does not unequivocally support these activities. Lemert suggests that the Protestant middle class value system has had a classical abhorrence of the loss of control over self which is typically associated with heavy drinking.[1] Strains of prohibition still add their flavor to social responses to alcohol. In addition, teenagers, by virtue of their age, at least technically live in an abstaining culture; to drink alcohol as a teenager is illegal, prohibited behavior.

One way of trying to account for the transition of most young people from abstention to drinking can be made in terms of their overall social development. Findings of Maddon and McCall's study of teenage drinking suggests that high school students drink because such an act has the possibility of conferring on them an adult status.[2] Because drinking is an aspect of adult behavior, the act of drinking is seen as a way of moving more closely to the desired goal of being an adult. Jessor and colleagues support this view in their longitudinal study of high-school students. Their evidence indicates that "initiations of drinking (are) ... an integral part of personality, social and behavioral development."[3]

It is important to note that a number of behaviors marking adolescent transitions are age- or status-related. What may be illegal at age 13, for example drinking or driving, will become acceptable at age 18. Therefore, it is anticipated that most young people will begin to adopt behaviors as teenagers which will become legal and acceptable when they become adults.

Jessor's study is particularly interesting because it attempts to identify the pattern of characteristics involved in developmental changes. Their research suggests that initiation of drinking is only one of the behaviors indicating transition to adulthood. They found involvement in political activism, use of marijuana, and experience with sexual intercourse were related measures for determining readiness for adult-oriented change. In support of their thesis, their evidence suggests that "becoming a drinker ... is an integral aspect of the process of adolescent development as a whole."[4] The fact that teenagers drink, therefore, must be understood within this larger social context.

Understanding the external social environment is also important for examining the issue of problem drinking. Although accurate data are scarce, survey data in two studies indicate that the use of alcohol among teenagers is widespread and that it has "increased both in extent and intensity."[5] FBI crime report statistics show that arrests for drunk driving doubled between 1960 and 1970.[6] Among youth there appears to be a general shift toward alcohol as the preferred drug, although a pattern of mixed drug use is also in evidence.[7] Ironically, the return to alcohol is welcomed by many parents who exclaim quietly, "Thank heavens it's not drugs." Because alcohol is legally used by adults, it is not commonly viewed as a drug. It is, however, the most widely used drug.

The picture of problem drinking is blurred by a number of important issues. One is the issue of learning to drink. Unlike some cultures where there are rules and rituals governing the act of drinking, our society presents mixed messages. Alcohol is seen as both a blessing and a curse: an enticing entree to adulthood and as the first step toward alcoholism.

As Maddon and McCall suggest, the complexity involved in learning the social rules leads to a "high probability of discrepancy between statements about what one ought to do about alcohol and what may in fact be permitted."[8] It is worth noting that this failure of training in social roles is not a matter of concern only in the area of drinking; as a society we are similarly remiss in preparing young people for their roles as mates and parents. Education may provide a partial answer, although education itself often gets tangled up in conflicting views and moral rules. Controlling and limiting behavior often takes precedence over providing accurate information and assistance to young people for making their own decisions.

It is important to take into account the influence of the peer culture on teenage drinking. In meeting the challenge of this stage of development, adolescents are faced with the task of establishing their own identity—who they are and what they will become. It is a phase of great self-consciousness and self-awareness. The pain and discomfort during this phase of personal growth is often diminished by strong ties with one's peer group. Group identity is the counterpoint for personal identity. Peer pressure, then, is one popular reason for drinking.[9] This pressure, together with ambiguous social rules about drinking, helps shape the broad social environment in which drinking occurs.

Separating fact from fiction is a major problem in the area of drinking. The field is not clear about why some people have problems with alcohol, particularly those who become alcoholics. A common definition of alcoholism states that: "Alcoholism is intermittent or continual use of alcohol associated with dependency (psychological or physical) or harm in the sphere of mental, physical, or social activity."[10] While there are those who repeatedly drink alcohol in ways that interfere with their health and functioning, there are others whose drinking is only occasionally problematic. We see, then, that there may be various alcoholisms or species of alcohol problems. A teenager whose first experience with alcohol leads to an arrest for drunk driving has problems with alcohol but at a different level than one who keeps a thermos of vodka in a school locker.

Efforts to explain problem drinking have often focused on another part of the social environment, namely, the internal environment. This environment is composed of emotions, attitudes, unconscious beliefs, dreams, and personal histories. Here we see motivational aspects explained at psychological levels. Teenagers are said to drink because of "maladjustive behavior" resulting from pathological relationships between parents and child,[11] because of the need to rebel against parents and society,[12] and because of "dependency conflict and sex-role confusion."[13] The stress and uncertainty which accompany adolescence are also said to contribute to the decreased likelihood that they will "exercise judgment and restraint" in their use of alcohol.[14] These emotional factors play a predominant role in many current theories about alcoholism and account for the predominance of therapy and counseling as a form of treatment. If the problem is thought to reside in the person, then treatment must necessarily attempt to change those personality characteristics that are thought to account for the alcoholic behavior.

## THE PHYSICAL ENVIRONMENT OF TEENAGE DRINKING

This view of the social environment, both external and internal, is the most common framework for viewing and understanding the behavior of drinking and the problems associated with its use. Applied in its broadest sense, the social environment clearly constitutes one of the important environmental contexts for teenage drinking. There is, however, another dimension of equal importance to the social environment—the physical environment. It has not been popular in any behavioral field to study the physical environment, much less to understand its impact on behavior. In the field of alcohol studies, investigation has been relegated to medical and laboratory research. But the physical environment is of crucial importance if we are to begin to understand why it is that some people who drink are not able to control their use of alcohol.

Using again the somewhat arbitrary distinction between internal and external environments, we find that the internal physical environment in each of us is a rich influence on our total state of well-being. Although our culture makes us both self-conscious and neglectful of our bodies, they are of no less importance than our minds.

In fact, the tremendous ability of our bodies to adapt to changes has been largely responsible for our survival as a species. The internal fluid environment, called by Bernard "the internal milieu," replicates the sea water environment which once surrounded our distant ancestors.[15] The fact that the life-giving fluids in our bodies are so similar in composition to the sea environment which gave life to the forms from which we evolved should serve as a reminder to us of our evolutionary history and the wondrous changes which brought us to this level of existence.

Our internal system is a dynamic one, constantly regulating itself in order to maximize well-being and survival. We often think of genetic factors as static elements in this environment, determining our physical and biochemical traits. But even here, it is more accurate to think of genes as establishing, as Dilger said, the "framework of possibilities."[16] Genetic potentials develop in interaction with the environment; some traits may be modified, some may be "lit up" depending upon the factors and circumstances provided by the environment.

In adolescence, the changes in an individual's physical environment are phenomenal. A young person experiences body growth which equals that of early childhood in its speed and complexity.[17] Genital development, with its increase in sex hormones, is a physical change which aptly demonstrates the close relationship between body and mind. Hormonal changes alter the body chemistry in significant ways and, at the same time, reactions to and feelings about this "new self" occur. Once again, we tend to emphasize the psychological and emotional strata of change without always recognizing that the status of the physical environment is also a critical contributor to the individual's behavior.

Perhaps this connection can be made more clear if we recognize an obvious but often neglected fact: our state of physical well-being is totally dependent on outside resources. No matter how well our physical system appears to function, it would not be able to function at all without elements available in the external environment. Oxygen, water, and food, among other elements, are absolutely essential for our continued survival. The fact that many people enjoy a life-span of 60 to 70 years or more, in part demonstrates again the tremendous power of our physical organism to survive, even when the quality of food, water, and air may be less than adequate.

This brings us to a closer examination of the external physical environment—that life space which provides or fails to provide the elements necessary to our well-being. To the extent that our survival depends upon the availability and quality of the physical resources present in our environment, it seems worthwhile to look at how something as specific as food intake may relate to behavior or states of behavior.

If one were to analyze the American diet today, one would see that it is a high fat, high carbohydrate diet. It is commonly estimated that each American consumes the equivalent of over 100 pounds of sugar per year, much of it in candy, soft drinks, cereals, desserts, or hidden in products such as catsup or canned stew.

The diet of many teenagers is an extreme version of this, sometimes called a "junk food" diet. It is composed of such items as cokes, french fries, candy, ice cream, pastries, and salty snacks. As a class, these are foods which have little if any nutritive value. They are not able to deliver to the body the nutritional elements it needs to carry out its complex operations each day. This deprivation is occurring at a time when the body is growing at an exceedingly fast pace and needs the very best materials at its disposal to accomplish its task.

What, one may ask, does this state of affairs have to do with alcoholism? An interesting experiment was performed by a group of researchers to explore the relationship between a "teen-age" diet and voluntary alcohol consumption in animals.[18] Recognizing that all the major alcohol consumption studies had made use of a purified laboratory diet in their tests, these researchers decided to use a human diet known to be marginal in nutrients to test free-choice consumption of alcohol. The diet, pulverized for animal feeding, included an array of glazed doughnuts, hot dogs, soft drinks, pies, spaghetti and meatballs, garlic bread, vegetable salad, cake, cookies, and candy. The control diet was a combination of foods based on the Recommended Dietary Allowances for adults. After testing the individual drinking behavior of the rats, they grouped them on the basis of their alcohol consumption so that each group of eight rats had similar intakes of alcohol. Rats were allowed a choice of water or an alcohol solution which was varied for given time periods by alcohol and sugar content. The groups were fed the teen-age diet for four weeks, the control diet for four weeks and returned to the teen-age diet for six more weeks. Results showed that the highest drinkers consumed large amounts of alcohol on the teen-age diet, but the consumption was significantly reduced when placed on the control diet. A return to the teen-age diet showed them reverting to their previously high drinking pattern. The marginal content of the teen-age diet appeared to produce a progressive preference for drinking the alcohol solution. The investigators suggest the possibility of some metabolic control mechanism which is responsible to dietary factors. They raise the further possibility that the effect of diet during developmental stages may have some yet untested importance for the regulation of alcohol consumption.

Results with laboratory animals are not the same as results with human beings. However, the relationship between diet and alcohol consumption is an intriguing one, particularly when diet is such a pervasive part of each individual's life. The possible connection between diet and excessive alcohol consumption underscores the critical importance of considering human behavior within the broader contexts of the physical environment.

This connection also points up the role of alcohol as a nutritional element. In addition to the well-known drug properties of alcohol which depress the activities of the central nervous system, alcohol is also used by the body as an energy source. The calories of energy produced by the metabolism of alcohol are used as carbohydrates. It is important to note, however, that although it provides usable energy, it does not provide protein, fat, vitamins or minerals—that is, the substances used by the body for growth and maintenance. It is technically a food source but it, like candy and soft drinks, is a junk food. It does not provide real nutrition for the body and ultimately can rob the body of some of the nutrients it needs.

One of the interesting ways that the presence of alcohol affects metabolism is its effect on the level of glucose in the blood. The brain is dependent upon glucose for its functioning and requires a small (less than 2 teaspoonsful) but steady amount in the bloodstream. When alcohol is ingested it receives top priority for metabolism; because it cannot be stored in the body, it continues to be oxidized as long as it is present. Researchers have found that alcohol elevates blood sugar levels,[19] an occurrence often subjectively felt as a heightened sense of well-being or renewed energy. In many people, regardless of nutritional states, they eventually experience a lowering of blood sugar with such symptoms as fuzzy-headedness, weakness, hunger, and jitters. The discomfort associated with this state has been implicated by at least one researcher in the hang-over phenomenon. Forsander[20] has suggested that alcohol in a morning-after drink is often used to cure the very symptoms it causes, namely low blood sugar. Whether or not the impact of alcohol on blood sugar levels is significant for everyone, the relationship does at least suggest a problematic interaction for those individuals who may be more susceptible to slight variations in blood sugar levels.

Within the nutritional realm, one last area seems deserving of mention. It is the area of allergies. The hypothesis that alcoholism was a form of allergy was one of the earliest physical explanations for this puzzling condition. Influenced by Dr. Silkworth's views, Bill Wilson, one of the founders of Alcoholics Anonymous, gave support to this position, even though it was not integrated into the AA approach. For a time, the theory fell into disrepute but has lately been enjoying a renewed interest. Randolph[21] and later Mackarness[22] have both explored the possibility that alcoholic beverages carry the allergenicity of the foods from which they are derived, namely rye, wheat, or corn and that some people's adverse reaction to alcohol is based on a food allergy to a food substance or to congeners in alcohol. Both of these researchers hypothesize a food addiction pattern in which there is continued ingestion of the problem food because it temporarily improves the very symptoms it later causes. While the conception of allergy has been insufficiently supported, it is at least theoretically conceivable that some specific properties of alcohol in its refined form strike peculiar and possibly compelling responses in some drinkers.

The literature which speaks to aspects of the physical environment as ones of possible importance in the development of alcoholic drinking is vast and, when taken together, not easily dismissed. The physical and emotional changes which occur among adolescents mark that group as one especially vulnerable to the impact of alcohol. We know very little about the interaction between the physical and social environments as it affects behavior, but it seems essential that we not continue with our one-eyed view. We must create a place in our thinking and research for physical environmental factors and their impact on behavior.

### ENVIRONMENTAL BALANCE

One way to begin moving toward a synthesis of the physical and social environments is to place a renewed emphasis on health. Rather than continue being seduced by issues of pathology and disease, we might think of health as a goal-point. Understanding behavior in its pathology is only useful if it incorporates a direction away from pathology. Because most theories are not helpful in this task, we must turn out energies toward concepts which suggest new paths.

Alcoholic drinking can be seen as a symptom of disease, whether emotional or physical. But it may also be viewed as a state of ill-health. Given what we know to be the vigorous conditions for maintaining a happy balance between internal and external environments, it is not surprising that the balance may be disrupted. Physical or emotional states, or stresses from the external environment, may tip the balance away from health toward ill-health. When this occurs, whether it is evidenced by excessive eating, drinking, smoking, depression, or skin rash, the goal is to right the balance, that is, to restore health.

Such an approach clearly requires more comprehensive, integrated responses than are usually applied. The point of diagnosis is the individual's total state of health. Because health is seen as a combination of physical and emotional factors, as well as external environmental factors, the plan to restore health must take these into account.

Teenage drinking is not a simple matter, but neither is any other behavior which human beings exhibit. Rather than spurning complexity, we must find ways to formally link the physical and social factors which account for behavior. With such an expanded view of the behavioral environment, it may become possible to discover new approaches to what seems to be a stubbornly recalcitrant problem.

## REFERENCES

1. Lemert, E. M.: Alcohol, values, and social control. In Pittman, D. and Snyder, C. R. (Eds.): *Society, Culture, and Drinking Patterns.* Carbondale, Southern Illinois University Press, 1962.
2. Maddon, G. L., & McCall, B. C.: *Drinking Among Teenagers.* New Brunswick, Publication Division, Rutgers Center of Alcohol Studies, 1964.
3. Jessor, R., and Jessor, S. L.: Adolescent development and the onset of drinking. *Journal of Studies on Alcohol, 36:*27, 1975.
4. Ibid., p. 48.
5. Addeo, E. G., and Addeo, J. R.: *Why Our Children Drink.* New York, Prentice-Hall, Inc., 1975, p. 12.
6. Saltman, J.: *The New Alcoholics: Teenagers.* New York, Public Affairs Committee, Public Affairs Pamphlet No. 499, 1973.
7. Fox, V.: Alcoholism in adolescence. *Journal of School Health, 43:*32, 1973.
8. Maddon & McCall, op. cit., p. 60.
9. Addeo & Addeo, op. cit., p. 73.
10. Davies, D. L.: Definitional issues in alcoholism. In Tarter, R. E. and Sugarman, A. (Eds.): *Alcoholism: Interdisciplinary Approaches to An Enduring Problem.* Reading, Addison-Wesley Publishing Company, 1976, p. 69.
11. Moses, D. A., and Burger, R. E.: *Are You Driving Your Children to Drink?* New York, Van Nostrand Reinhold Company, 1975, p. 13.
12. Saltman, op. cit.
13. Blane, H. T., and Chafetz, M. E.: Dependency conflict and sex role identity in drinking delinquents. *Quarterly Journal of Studies on Alcohol, 22:*1026, 1971.
14. Saltman, op. cit., p. 9.
15. Bernard, C.: *An Introduction to the Study of Experimental Medicine.* New York, Henry Schuman, Inc., 1949.
16. Dilger, W. C.: Behavior and genetics. In Bliss, E. L. (Ed.): *Roots of Behavior.* New York, Harper and Row, 1962.
17. Erikson, E. H.: *Childhood and Society.* New York, W. W. Norton and Company, Inc., 1963.
18. Register, U. D., Marsh, S. R., Thurston, C. P., Hardinge, M. C., and Sanchez,

A.: Influence of nutrients on intake of alcohol. *Journal of American Dietetic Association, 61:*159–165, 1972.

19. Forsander, O. A.: Influences of alcohol on the general metabolism of the body. In Lucia, S. P. (Ed.): *Alcohol and Civilization.* New York, McGraw-Hill Book Company, Inc., 1963. See also Arky, R.: The effect of alcohol on carbohydrate metabolism: Carbohydrate metabolism in alcoholics. In Kissin, B., and Begleiter, H. (Eds.): *The Biology of Alcoholism, Volume I: Biochemistry.* New York, Plenum Press, 1971.

20. Forsander, O. A.: Metabolism of rats as related to voluntary alcohol consumption. *Psychosomatic Medicine, 28:*521–528, 1966.

21. Randolph, T. G.: The descriptive features of food addiction. *Quarterly Journal of Studies on Alcohol, 17:*198–225, 1956.

22. Mackarness, R.: The allergic factor in alcoholism. *The International Journal of Social Psychiatry, 18:*194–200, 1972.

*Chapter Eleven*

# PSYCHODYNAMIC TREATMENT
# OF WOMEN ALCOHOLICS

CHRISTINE HUFF FEWELL

In recent years there has been growing interest in looking at women alcoholics as a separate group and asking such questions as: Does alcoholism have a distinct etiology in women? Does alcoholism manifest itself differently in women and for different reasons? Are there implications for treatment arising from the answers to these questions? For general overviews of the literature on alcoholism and women see Beckman,[1] Schuckit and Duby[2] and Lindbeck.[3]

The actual incidence of alcoholism among women is unknown, but conservative estimates put it at approximately one million in the United States or 20 percent of the total number of alcoholics.[4] In the 1980 Survey of the Membership of Alcoholics Anonymous based on a sample of 24,950 alcoholics, the percentage of women in the U.S. and Canadian sample rose from 22 percent to 31 percent since 1968. Moreover, the percentage of women in the portion of the sample who came to the Fellowship since the last survey is 34 percent indicating that the upward trend continued.[5] This was considered a slight overstatement since women attend meetings slightly more often than men. This figure, however, applied to women in AA, so its exact relationship to women alcoholics is unknown. The purpose of this chapter is to explore this problem of alcoholism in women, including factors that are associated with the problem and treatment implications.

## CHARACTERISTICS OF WOMEN ALCOHOLICS

In her review of the studies in the literature on this topic, Lindbeck[6] says that women who are diagnosed as alcoholic by state hospitals, alcoholism clinics, outpatient clinics or correctional institutions are more likely to have done their drinking in public with others than those who are seen in private practice, private hospitals, or by voluntary community agencies. Thus, it appears that some characteristics of women drinkers are related to socioeconomic status and also to marital status. Additionally, women have been found to be much more likely to misuse multiple substances. Related to this factor, physicians have tended to prescribe drugs to women more readily than they have to men.[7]

Studies indicate that the average woman alcoholic drinks at home alone and tends to hide her drinking.[8] Women tend to telescope their alcoholism into a much shorter period of time.[9] This has been more frequently seen in upper socioeconomic groups of women and may not be true of women alcoholics in general. In a study of alcoholic women in treatment, Corrigan[10] found that of 150 women interviewed in her sample, 28 percent were not daily drinkers or drank less than five drinks daily. She states that, therefore, "the usual definition of heavy drinking is not adequate when applied to women."

Several researchers have compared differences in the patterns of drinking and the amount of consumption between men and women alcoholics. Men and women have been found to respond differently to alcohol as demonstrated by Jones and Jones.[11] Women become more intoxicated than men on the same doses of alcohol, because their body weight is composed of 45 to 55 percent water as opposed to 55 to 65 percent in men. Since alcohol is distributed throughout the body in proportion to the water content of body tissues, alcohol tends to be more diluted in the body of males than females. Additionally, women have more fatty tissue which contains less water than muscle tissue, while men have a greater concentration of the latter tissue.[12] Women's susceptibility to intoxication varies throughout the menstrual cycle. Also, women who are taking oral contraceptives metabolize ethanol more slowly than women who are not.

### EFFECTS OF FAMILY BACKGROUND

It has been frequently said that alcoholism runs in families and apparently this is true for alcoholic women as well, although the rate is not as high as for men.[13] Women alcoholics are much more likely than nonalcoholic women to have parents who were alcoholics, especially their fathers.[14] Losses in early childhood have been found to be an important element in the lives of those who later became alcoholic. In her study, Curlee[15] found that women alcoholics experienced more losses than men of a parent through divorce, desertion, or death and had had more disruption in their early lives. More women than men reported mothers and fathers who were mentally ill.[16]

DeLint,[17] in a study of 451 alcoholic women, found that 166 had lost one or both parents before age sixteen. In a group of 2,005 alcoholic men, only 264 had lost one or both parents before age sixteen. In another study DeLint[18] found that alcoholic women described their mothers as cold and domineering in 78 percent of cases and 51 percent said that their fathers were alcoholic. He found that the loss of one or both parents at an early age was frequently reported by his sample of 276 alcoholic women. Fathers tended to be unavailable due to death, divorce, desertion, psychosis, or alcoholism. When the daughter was raised by both parents, she tended to perceive the mother as the more dominant personality. There was an absence of strong attachment to either parent, so that in crises the girl turned to neither parent but attempted solutions utilizing her own inadequate resources.

Many women who are alcoholics also have husbands who are alcoholic, and it has been noted that it is not uncommon for symptomatic drinking to pass from husband to wife, although it rarely works in the other direction.[19]

### DIFFERENCES AMONG WOMEN ALCOHOLICS

A number of studies have looked at the possibility of different subtypes of alcoholic women. The association between alcoholism and depressive symptoms is well known and depression can be a physiological result from drinking alcohol. However, Schuckit and his colleagues[20] identified a clearly discernable group of alcoholic women who had an affective disorder which either preceded the alcoholism or developed independently. This group was clearly distinguished from the group of "primary" women alcoholics who showed no such characteristics.

Some researchers report that women alcoholics demonstrate a higher degree of serious pathology than male alcoholics. Curlee[21] studied 100 male and female alcoholics. Their treatment histories showed that women alcoholics had been admitted as psychiatric patients more often and for longer periods than men in the sample. Many were complaining primarily of depression. Since women in general are more likely to be treated for psychiatric problems, the relationship of this characteristic to alcoholism is not clear at this point.

Some studies indicate that the pattern of alcoholism as a disease is different in women, and that it is more likely to develop during particular life situations compared to the patterns in men. In Curlee's study, a definite precipitating stressful event could be identified by the women involved which led to alcoholic drinking. Sometimes it was related to a middle-age identity crisis, the death of a husband, divorce, menopause, the marriage of children, or some other disruption in the roles of wife and mother. Another study by Lisansky[22] found that twice as many women as men cited a specific life experience as the point at which they started drinking heavily. However, a study by Morrissy and Schuckit[23] found that this was definitely not so in the sample they studied; Corrigan[24] also did not find this to be true in the alcoholic women she studied.

Black women alcoholics have also been designated as an important subcategory of alcoholic women. It has been found that there is a higher percentage of black women alcoholics than in other racial groups. There is evidence that black women are at higher risk for alcoholism than black men as compared with white women versus white men.[25] Some authors assume there may be more social acceptability for drinking by women within the black culture. However, other authors have noted that this higher rate of drinking may result from stresses related to poverty which often require black women to work while continuing parental and other roles.

## OTHER FACTORS RELATED TO ALCOHOLISM

Sex role conflict has been a major area of investigation in the literature on alcoholism among women. Since women have traditionally been under less social pressure to drink, many speculations have been made about why they drink. Is it because they are assuming the role of drinking like men and thus are acting in more masculine ways?

Several recent studies have had conflicting results. Wilsnack[26] concluded that alcoholic women are consciously feminine but are unconsciously masculine and thus drink heavily to feel more womanly. In another study, Wilsnack[27] found that drinking increased womanliness imagery and decreased scores on power imagery and masculine assertiveness. Parker[28] found that the alcoholics he tested showed unconscious femininity and conscious masculinity.

Scida and Vanicelli[29] found that sex role conflict per se rather than the direction of the stance was related to alcohol misuse. The magnitude of the conflict was the critical factor. They concluded that identity conflict, the discrepancy between how a woman sees herself and how she would like to see herself, may be a general factor in alcoholism in women. They also found that conflict regarding one's sexuality may be of particular importance considering both the centrality of sexuality within the general self-image and the increasing possibilities for sex-role conflict as women take on new roles.[30] Wilsnack,[31] in a recent comprehensive review of the literature on sex role and alcoholism in women, suggests that with the increasing impact of the women's movement, new forms and directions of conflict are more likely to develop.

Low self-esteem also has been suggested as one of the important features of alcoholic women. A study by Beckman compared 120 women alcoholics, 120 men alcoholics, 119 normal controls (women who were not alcoholics and who were not in treatment), and 118 "treatment controls" (women nonalcoholics in treatment for psychiatric and emotional problems). He found that the women alcoholics showed exceptionally low self-esteem, even lower than men alcoholics.[32] This low self-esteem also appeared characteristic of the women in treatment for psychiatric disorders not related to misuse of alcohol and other drugs. While the self-esteem of both women alcoholics and men alcoholics improved during a one-year period, the women showed greater improvement than the men.

## TREATMENT EVALUATION STUDIES

There are no programs for alcoholic women alone which have been evaluated, although some models have been proposed. In her review of alcohol treatment for women, Blume[33] points out that "Outcome studies in general provide a mixed, often conflicting, picture of the results of treatment on male patients and, unfortunately, usually exclude female outcomes altogether." She goes on to point out the conflicting and inconclusive results shown in those few studies that do include women and also asserts that we have little objective data upon which to recommend lengths and types of treatment for men and even less for women.

There is wide divergence of opinion in the field about the treatment of choice for women. Some recommend separate programs for women. Some recommend group therapy and others recommend individual therapy. Some authors recommend all female groups and others mixed male and female groups with supplementary all female groups for exploring issues of concern to women. A few authors have noted that women do better in AA than men and some that they do worse. For reviews of these studies see Braiker,[34] Beckman[35] and Blume.[36] Other authors have advocated having women therapists for female alcoholic patients. One area for investigation is whether the establishment of child care services for women who need to enter treatment would increase the number of women treated as well as improve their prognosis. Blume points out that the highest proportion of female patients in her program is found in the day hospital (43%) as compared to detoxification services (17.5%) and rehabilitation services (23.5%).

## TREATMENT ISSUES IN WORKING WITH WOMEN ALCOHOLICS

What useful principles can be derived from this review of the literature on alcoholism and women? It is clear that the question of whether alcoholism in women is different from alcoholism in men is far from being answered at present. As has been pointed out time and again, the vast majority of researchers have not studied samples of women and theories of etiology have been generalized from men to women without thinking about whether there are differences for women. In addition, there is insufficient direct evidence of how women's traditional devalued status in society has affected the etiology and dynamics of their problems with alcohol.

The greater stigma attached to being a woman alcoholic needs to be dealt with at the outset. In admitting to herself that she has a stigmatized illness, the alcoholic woman will be experiencing this stigma in addition to the low self-esteem that has been found in many studies. She needs the acceptance and nonjudgmental attitude from the therapist which are so important in working with all alcoholics. She should be encouraged to explore her feelings about what it means to be a woman alcoholic. Feelings of shame should be brought out in order to deal with their potential effect in causing a relapse into drinking. Social workers and other practitioners need to be aware of their own values, societal biases, and the biases in some practice approaches which can emphasize an individual deficit perspective toward women alcoholics.

Since the amount consumed by women may be considerably less than men given the different physical reactions to alcohol, looking only at quantity will not be a good diagnostic indicator and may in fact be deceptive. Often the amount of time it takes the woman to develop alcoholic drinking or addiction may be less than for men. Women who tend to drink alone more frequently may have fewer social consequences from their drinking. Blume[37] points out the need for validation of the National Council on Alcoholism's Diagnostic Criteria for women and the need for the identification and subtyping of alcoholism in women.

It is generally agreed that women abuse pills (mainly minor

tranquilizers such as Librium® and Valium®) in combination with alcohol more frequently than men. This has implications for considering physical complications and withdrawal reactions, and for being alert to the woman's involvement with a physician who may be prescribing pills. In taking a history and considering the total involvement of the woman with chemicals, the pattern of mixing pills and alcohol should be asked about. Complaints about not being able to sleep should alert the social worker to ask about what solutions are being used to deal with the difficulty. It seems particularly difficult for women to tolerate insomnia and at times the affect associated with this condition verges on panic. Aside from the physiological effects of alcohol on sleep patterns, it is useful to explore the meaning of the woman's panic and fear when she feels she will not be able to sleep without drinking or taking a pill or marijuana.

Since women alcoholics have been found to seek help more often for marital and family problems while men seek help for job-related problems, social workers, psychologists, and other practitioners in family service agencies, mental health centers, and employee assistance programs need to be aware of these casefinding possibilities. Lawyers have access to women alcoholics when they come seeking divorce. Gynecologists, pediatricians, staff in children's health clinics, family physicians and internists also have opportunities to identify alcoholic women according to Blume.[38] Even practitioners who are aware of the symptoms of alcoholism and chemical abuse may be startled to discover how many single patients, who come for therapy in an urban area ostensibly for difficulty in forming love relationships or for problems related to work, have an abusive involvement with alcohol and/or marijuana and cocaine. In one instance, it took one month of trying to understand the depression of one young professional woman which was making her unable to find another job, before her abuse of alcohol and marijuana came to the surface as a chronic pattern dating back over the last three years.

The finding that alcoholism has often been present in the family of alcoholic women is another important area for exploration during treatment. Feelings about the alcoholic parent as well as the nonalcoholic parent's reactions are of vital importance in recovery. Denial about the parent's alcoholism is frequent and must be worked through in order for the patient to be able to deal with denial about her own present alcoholism. There are often difficulties in accepting the identification with the alcoholic parent depending on the feelings involved. The patient may be angry about having become like a parent who was hated, or feel guilty about having been angry with a parent whose illness is now shared. This may well be one of the mechanisms involved in the transmission of alcoholism from one generation to another.[39] How can the person condemn the alcoholic parent when he or she is no better? It is threatening to alcoholic patients to express the anger, but it is necessary to understand the part that alcoholic behavior played in the parents' attitudes toward them.

As reported previously, losses in early childhood were found in a significant number of women alcoholics. The difficulty in dealing with losses and with the anxiety brought about by unresolved grief is often a major dynamic in the treatment of people recovering from alcoholism as described in a paper by Goldberg.[40] Alcoholics often report drinking more following losses and may have used alcohol to deal with feelings surrounding loss. In addition, alcoholism itself causes many losses to accrue. It is not uncommon to see someone who has stopped drinking suddenly begin to mourn a loss which occurred in the past, perhaps even years before. The person never dealt with the loss at the time it occurred and the alcoholic drinking encapsulated the experience as if in a deep freeze until it emerged when the drinking stopped. Goldberg elucidates a model of treatment for mourning the loss of alcohol and the feelings surrounding its use which then strengthens the ego so that grief surrounding other losses can be resolved. In addition to unresolved grief, losses in the first few years of life can cause separation anxiety and an arrest in the separation-individuation process which results in greater dependency and a need to please authority in order not to feel rejected and depressed. The following case vignette illustrates some of the treatment issues discussed in this section:

> Paula was 65 years old when she came to treatment following her rehabilitation stay. She had been sober for 25 years and then had begun drinking socially which led to uncontrolled bouts resulting in three

detoxification admissions within two years. She had always suffered depressions in the spring and the fall, and any time that she was to go on a trip she would become ill with fever as well as become depressed. In exploring her early experiences, it was learned that her alcoholic mother had very little to do with her care. She was raised in a foreign country by servants who were very loving. When she was five, her father's business required them to come back to the United States. The parents told Paula the nursemaid was coming with them on the boat. It was only when they were out to sea that they revealed the nurse was not there to the great distress of Paula who cried for days. Her fear of being left and her conflicts about it continued throughout her life with her rebellious behavior in high school causing her to be enrolled in eleven different schools. This ambivalence was transferred to her husband whom she found to be critical and demanding but to whom she compliantly submitted without being able to express anger. The anger came out in her drinking bouts when she could contain it no longer.

One very important issue in working with an alcoholic woman such as Paula is to help decipher the dynamics involved in relapses. The dynamics of a drinking episode can usually only be discovered if there was enough sobriety before the episode to set it apart. If the drinking is continuous, it is difficult to identify a dynamic since compulsive repetitious actions are involved.

In the case of Paula who had been sober for 25 years when she began drinking again, it was possible to uncover some underlying dynamics. On one occasion she began drinking when she had to go alone to another city to dispose of the possessions in her dead aunt's apartment and was angry about the responsibility being left to her totally. On a second occasion she began drinking when she was beginning a two-month vacation in the country with her husband with whom she was very angry. On a third occasion she began drinking over a power struggle with her husband about where they should spend their weekends. She said that she felt she had to do something very drastic in order to be heard.

## PSYCHODYNAMIC CONSIDERATIONS
## IN ALCOHOLISM TREATMENT

In the treatment of alcoholism, total abstinence from chemicals is necessary in order to achieve lasting results. However, understanding the role that alcoholism has played in the dynamic conflicts of the person is often of great importance to the therapist in helping the patient to establish a comfortable sobriety and to promote continued growth.

Psychoanalytic theory is one of several theories that provide useful explanations about how people become alcoholics. In terms of this theory, people are assumed to use alcohol because it makes them feel good or produces euphoria. Fenichel says "the specific elation from alcohol is characterized by the fact that inhibitions and limiting considerations of reality are removed from consciousness before the instinctual impulses are, so that a person who does not dare to perform instinctual acts may have both satisfaction and relief with the help of alcohol."[41] Essentially, this means alcohol acts to diminish the demands of the superego. The well-known saying that the superego is "the part of the mind that is soluable in alcohol" refers to this characteristic.

The elation from drinking alcohol also brings about a temporary increase in self-esteem and is in fact one of the predisposing factors in using alcohol. Self-esteem is also the result of a relationship between the ego and the superego. Low self-esteem is a problem in all alcoholics, but particularly so in women.

Alcoholics frequently have a strict, punitive superego. The signs are quite familiar to those working with alcoholic patients: the moralism, the perfectionism, the remorse following drunken actions, and the make-up-for-lost-time attitude the sober alcoholic often shows. Simmel[42] observed that in the group of alcoholics he termed "neurotic alcoholics" there were some serious problems in superego development. He concluded that the parents of most alcoholics he saw were emotionally immature people who permitted themselves enjoyments which they prohibited in their children. This was a way for the parents to deal with their own superegos: to repress in their children what they were unable to repress in themselves. For example, an alcoholic parent or a parent who acts seductively, but represses all evidence of sexuality in the child, a parent who has temper tantrums but allows no expression of feeling in the child, or a parent who is sloppy but very exacting of neatness in the child. This results in the formation of a superego (the internalized demands, prohibitions and permissions) which is both opposed to instinctual demands as well as being in favor of them. The result is great conflict within the superego.

In depression, a greater or lesser loss of self-esteem is present. It is due either to a loss of external resources from a person or situation or it is due to a loss of internal supplies from the superego. If the superego is of a primitive nature, it can be unable to forewarn the ego in a signal way that it should not engage in an activity, but after the impulsive act is carried out it is very punitive in its response to the infraction. The superego of such a person is often unable to forgive and thus causes great suffering to the person.

The case of Sylvia illustrates the need to work with several of these issues which have been commonly observed in alcoholic women:

> Sylvia was depressed, had low self-esteem, had had an alcoholic father and a rejecting mother, had been sexually overstimulated by witnessing violence and had a masochistic manner of relating to people. She was unable to express anger and was sexually inhibited. Her superego was very strict and had conflicting introjects. On the one hand she had to be a good little girl and not express any anger herself, but father and mother and teachers at school all resorted to beatings if she stepped out of line. She was Catholic and was sent to mass seven days a week. She remarked that her family went to mass without fail every Sunday. If she took any initiative to be independent, she was punished.
>
> Sylvia was born in an Irish neighborhood in an urban area, the oldest of three children. Her father was an alcoholic and worked as a laborer. Sylvia's early life was both chaotic and rigid, both full of people and empty. The children were forced by their mother to go to bed at 6:00 o'clock so that when their father returned home at 3:00 A.M. from the bar they would have gotten some sleep. He often woke them up and made the children watch while he beat the mother. If they tried to intervene, the mother told them to stay out of it. Sylvia reacted to these situations with vomiting, headaches, and nose bleeds, all somatic ways of responding to excess stimulation.
>
> Sylvia's father did have several periods of sobriety up to a year in length during which the family life was relatively calm, although the parents did not share joint activities during that time either. During his sober periods, her father was quiet, charming and well-dressed, as opposed to his dirty, slovenly, and violent behavior when drunk.
>
> Soon after graduating from high school, Sylvia met and married a man

two years her junior, a college man whom she thought was the opposite of her immigrant father. In contrast, he was from a well-to-do well-established family, handsome, and not an alcoholic. Soon after their marriage he began to have affairs with other women which he continued throughout their marriage. Finally, her father-in-law convinced her that she should get a divorce, and she tried for three years to care for her three children while her alcoholic drinking continued to progress. She often was unable to remember whether she had fed the children the night before. Her oldest daughter assumed many of the mothering functions which she was unable to perform, and she suffered many falls and blackouts. She gave the children to her ex-husband to care for and three more years passed until she finally achieved a relatively stable sobriety. She was then able through a lengthy legal battle to regain custody of her two youngest children.

When she came to treatment she was engaged to a man she had met two years previously. She had begun drinking again soon after meeting him, and this had resulted in her ending up in a rehabilitation program. When Sylvia began treatment she showed a masochistic character structure with very low self-esteem, great dependency needs, and an inability to express anger with resulting depression. She followed the pattern of her mother with her dependency on men and her inability to express feelings. She thought when she married that she had chosen a man who was better than her father. While he did not beat her physically, he was unresponsive to her needs and beat her emotionally with his affairs and his narcissistic, self-centered need to be admired by her while not responding to her. He needed an attractive wife who would "make beautiful children" for him. He exploited the one area of Sylvia's self-esteem which had received encouragement, her physical attractiveness which her mother enjoyed when it brought compliments from friends and neighbors on Sunday mornings at church.

Her fiance represented a better choice in his abilities to respond to her considerately, but she suffered feelings of shame and disgust which were carried over from her feelings about her father who was dirty and loud-spoken in his alcoholic state. She equated her fiance's interest in hunting and automobiles and his less polished demeanor with her father.

At the same time that her fiance was a better choice than her ex-husband, she had still selected a man who was unavailable to her to a large extent because he had not mourned the loss of his dead wife. In the relationship, the dead wife still presented herself as a powerful force in the fiance's not wanting to change anything about his life.

Treatment had two main focal points: (1) Sylvia's right to have her own opinion and (2) her entitlement to her feelings of anger, of satisfaction, or pleasure. In working on her right to have her own opinion, there was work done on her ego's strength to cope and on assisting her in the separation-individuation process which was arrested, as indicated by her dependence on men and other authority figures and her tendency to merge with the wishes of another.

Early in treatment Sylvia talked about her ex-husband and his opinion that she should send her daughter to live with him since she was not doing well in school. After she related everyone else's opinion, she was asked what she and her daughter wanted to do. She realized with amazement that they both wanted to live together. This was the beginning of a process which resulted a year later in her being able to intervene with her daughter's principal at a point of crisis and initiate meetings which led to testing and uncovered a learning disability. Her daughter was then involved in therapy and this led to Sylvia's being able to intervene in her daughter's sexual acting out by setting guidelines.

This process of individuation was explored in the relationship with her fiance as it was determined which part of the problems were hers and which were his, and which she could express her feelings about without feeling that she would be rejected immediately.

With respect to her sense of entitlement, work was done on making her superego less severe and helping her to introject benign aspects and permissions instead of the many prohibitions which were there. This involved an exploration of feelings about her father's behavior in the past. She had never mourned the death of her father from alcoholism and there were many tears shed as she recalled not only the rage, shame, and humiliation she felt towards him and his violence, but also the tender feelings when he was sober and the loss of the relationship that she could not have with him. Her anger about her mother's beatings and rejection and the related demands on her were also explored. Resolving these familial and individual issues helped to increase Sylvia's self-esteem, eliminated her depression, and helped to maintain her sobriety.

## SUMMARY

Treatment with women alcoholics needs to address issues of femininity and sexuality,[43] grief work relating to various losses, evaluation of the type and dynamics of any depression, and working through feelings related to parental alcoholism or other dysfunctional behavior. While the ego is strengthened through helping it to learn to tolerate delay and frustration with successful ways of coping, the superego's values, prohibitions and judging aspects need to be helped to temper themselves with self-approval, forgiveness and self-love. Abstinence is emphasized as an integral part of this psychodynamic treatment process with alcoholic women. Finally, additional research is needed to clarify other issues related to effective treatment with this population.

## REFERENCES

1. Beckman, Linda J.: Alcoholism problems and women: An overview. In Greenblatt, Milton and Schuckit, Marc A. (Eds.): *Alcoholism Problems in Women and Children.* New York, Grune and Stratton, 1976, pp. 65–96. (a); See also Beckman, Linda J.: Women alcoholics: A review of social and psychological studies. *Journal of Studies on Alcohol, 36*:797–824, 1975. (b)
2. Schuckit, Marc A. and Duby, Jane: Alcoholism in women. In Kissin, Benjamin and Begleiter, H. (Eds.): *The Pathogenesis of Alcoholism: Psychosocial Factors.* New York, Plenum, 1983, pp. 215–241.
3. Lindbeck, Vera L.: The woman alcoholic: A review of the literature. *The International Journal of the Addictions,* 7:567–580, 1972.
4. Beckman (b), op. cit., p. 797.
5. Analysis of the 1980 Survey of the Membership of A.A. Distributed by the General Service Office of Alcoholics Anonymous, New York, 1981.
6. Lindbeck, op. cit., p. 569.
7. Schuckit and Duby, op. cit.
8. Schuckit, Marc A. and Morrissey, Elizabeth R.: Alcoholism in women: Some clinical and social perspectives with an emphasis on possible subtypes. In

Greenblatt, Milton and Schuckit, Marc A. (Eds.): *Alcoholism Problems in Women and Children.* New York, Grune and Stratton, 1976, pp. 5–35.

9. Gomberg, Edith S.: The female alcoholic. In Kissin, Benjamin and Begleiter, H. (Eds.): *The Biology of Alcoholism, Vol. 4, Social Aspects of Alcoholism.* New York, Plenum, 1976, pp. 117–166.

10. Corrigan, Eileen M.: Alcoholic women and treatment: A summary of findings. In Cook, David, Fewell, Christine and Riolo, John (Eds.): *Social Work Treatment of Alcohol Problems.* New Jersey, Publications Division, Rutgers Center of Alcohol Studies, 1983, pp. 109–118.

11. Jones, Ben Morgan and Jones, Marilyn K.: Women and alcohol: Intoxication, metabolism and the menstrual cycle. In Greenblatt, Milton and Schuckit, Marc A. (Eds.): *Alcoholism Problems in Women and Children.* New York, Plenum, 1976, pp. 103–136.

12. Ibid, p. 109.

13. Winokur, G. and Clayton, P. J.: Family history studies. IV. Comparison of male and female alcoholics. *Journal of Studies on Alcohol, 29*:885–891, 1968.

14. Wood, H. P. and Duffy, E. L.: Psychological factors in alcoholic women. *American Journal of Psychiatry, 123*:341–345, 1966.

15. Curlee, Joan: A comparison of male and female patients at an alcoholism treatment center. *Journal of Psychology, 74*:239–247, 1970.

16. Wood and Duffy, op. cit.

17. DeLint, J. E. E.: Alcoholism, birth order and socializing agents. *Journal of Abnormal and Social Psychology, 69*:457–458, 1964.

18. Delint, J. E. E.: Alcoholism, birth rank and parental deprivation. *American Journal of Psychiatry, 120*:1062–1065, 1974.

19. Wanberg, K. W. and Knapp, J.: Differences in drinking symptoms and behavior of men and women alcoholics. *British Journal of Addictions, 64*:347–355, 1970.

20. Schuckit, M. A., Pitts, F. N., Jr., Rich, T., King, L. J., Winokur, G.: Alcoholism. I. Two types of alcoholism in women. *Archives of General Psychiatry, 20*:301–306, 1969.

21. Curlee, op. cit.

22. Lisansky, op. cit.

23. Morrissey, Elizabeth R., Schuckit, Marc A.: Stressful life events and alcoholism in women seen at a detoxification center. *Quarterly Journal of Studies on Alcohol, 39*:1559–1576, 1978.

24. Corrigan, op. cit.

25. See Bailey, M. B., Haberman, P. W. and Alksne, H.: The epidemiology of alcoholism in an urban residential area. *Journal of Studies on Alcohol, 26*:19–40, 1965.; and Roebuck, J. B. and Kessler, R. C.: *The Etiology of Alcoholism: Constitutional, Psychological and Sociological Approaches.* Springfield, Charles C. Thomas, 1972.

26. Wilsnack, Sharon C.: Sex role identity in female alcoholism. *Journal of Abnormal Psychology, 82*:253–261, 1973.

27. Wilsnack, Sharon C.: The effects of social drinking on women's fantasy. *Journal of Personality, 42*:43–61, 1974.
28. Parker, F. B.: Sex-role adjustment in women alcoholics. *Journal of Studies on Alcohol, 33*:647–657, 1972.
29. Scida, Joan and Vannicelli, Marsha: Sex-role conflict and women's drinking. *Journal of Studies on Alcohol, 40*:28–44, 1979.
30. Ibid., p. 42.
31. Wilsnack, Sharon C.: The impact of sex-roles on women's alcohol use and abuse. In Greenblatt, Milton and Schuckit, Marc A. Eds.): *Alcoholism Problems in Women and Children.* New York, Grune and Stratton, 1976, pp. 37–63.
32. Beckman, Linda J.: Self-esteem of women alcoholics. *Journal of Studies on Alcohol, 39*:491–498, 1978.
33. Blume, Sheila B.: Diagnosis, casefinding and treatment of alcohol problems in women. *Alcohol, Health and Research World, 3*:10–22, 1978.
34. Braiker, Harriet B.: The diagnosis and treatment of alcoholism in women. In U. S. National Institute of Alcohol Abuse and Alcoholism. Special Population Issues. (Alcohol and Health, Monograph No. 4). Washington, D.C., U. S. Government Printing Office, 1982, pp. 111–139.
35. Beckman (b), op. cit., p. 812.
36. Blume, op. cit., p. 18.
37. Blume, op. cit., p. 20.
38. Blume, op. cit., p. 15.
39. Smith, Jeffrey: Alcoholism and the forgiving object. Paper presented at a workshop at the New York City Chapter, National Association of Social Worker's Alcoholism Institute, New York City, May, 1982.
40. Goldberg, Marian: Loss and grief: Major dynamics in the treatment of alcoholism. *Alcoholism Treatment Quarterly,* (in press).
41. Fenichel, Otto: *The Psychoanalytic Theory of Neurosis.* New York, Norton, 1945, p. 379.
42. Simmel, Ernst: Alcohol and addiction. *Psychoanalytic Quarterly, 17*:6–31, 1948.
43. Fewell, Christine H.: The integration of sexuality into alcoholism treatment. *Alcoholism Treatment Quarterly,* (in press).

## Chapter Twelve

# NETWORKING COMMUNITY SERVICES FOR ELDERLY CLIENTS WITH ALCOHOL PROBLEMS

BETTY BLACKMON

The elderly in the United States comprise a group that is neglected, maligned and set aside. Increasingly, service providers are confronted with the complex issue of providing services to a growing population of elderly. By the year 2000, persons over the age of 65 years of age will number in the millions. This increased population and diminishing resources will increase the present fragmentation of services into serious gaps in the service delivery system for the elderly.

The aging process can involve continuing loss and change. The loss and changes in the elderly are characterized by physical maladies, loss of meaningful relationships, role and status losses, career changes, diminishing mental faculties, and loss of independence and financial resources. Each change or loss is related to the need to make contact with other systems in their environments. These systems are not always equipped to provide for the needs that occur in the lives of the elderly. Oftentimes one aspect of a need may be recognized while other needs are neglected.[1]

Health care, interpersonal relationships, housing, legal, financial, and transportation issues are but a few of many which are a part of an elderly individual's life. The extent of change often depends on factors such as the socioeconomic background of individuals, but change is a major concern in the later life cycle of most adults.

Change can affect the use of substances in the elderly. For

example, many elderly take prescribed medications due to physical diseases and ailments. Others abuse these medications or nonprescription drugs due to lack of adequate knowledge about the effects or as a way of handling some of the stresses associated with the aging process. With increases in the number of elderly and the inadequate number and quality of resources for meeting their needs, abuse of substances by the elderly and life threatening consequences may also increase.

The purpose of this chapter is to explore problems in drug use by the elderly with particular emphasis on their abuse or addiction to alcohol. Some of the dilemmas in handling these problems within the current service delivery system will also be examined. Finally, a comprehensive plan for networking alcoholism treatment and educational services to this underserved population will be described, along with a specific network program.

## SUMMARY OF DRUG USE IN THE ELDERLY

Presently in this country, persons over 65 years of age number about 23 million, constituting about 10 percent of the total population. As stated earlier, this figure is increasing rapidly due to increased longevity rates in the elderly.[2] Contrary to the myth that the elderly reside in long-term care institutions, only 5 percent of the elderly population are in such institutions, 15 percent live in the community with their children, 25 percent live alone, and 50 percent live with their spouses.[3]

Seventy-five percent of this population utilize some kind of medication, at least one-third of which is obtained over the counter. Twenty-five percent of the medications taken in this country are consumed by persons 65 years and older. In most cases the amount of medication taken by these individuals includes five to six different varieties. For these individuals, the likelihood for abuse of substances increases due to the number of medications being taken. For the purposes of this chapter, substance abuse is being defined as the consumption of one or more psychoactive substances in a pattern that presents hazards to ones health or overall functioning. There are essentially three categories of substance abuse in the elderly. They are abuse of illicit drugs, misuse of prescription drugs in a manner not prescribed, and alcohol abuse.

First, the literature on substance use shows very few documented incidences of illicit drug use among the elderly. However, staff in alcoholism treatment facilites report anecdotally that there are increasing numbers of elderly who are reported to be using drugs such as marijuana. The elderly may be more reluctant than those in other age groups to report using illicit drugs due to societal mores and values about acceptable behavior in the elderly. The extent of any problems in this area and possible solutions clearly need further exploration.

The misuse of prescription drugs is a second area of concern regarding the elderly. The availability of many new drugs means that more people live longer, are healthier, and are far more independent than in past generations. Today's elderly benefit from the availability of drugs, however, there are risks involved that can be life-threatening. These drugs are powerful substances; if they are not used carefully, they may cause serious life-threatening consequences.

The misuse of prescription drugs occurs in a variety of ways, involving underuse, overuse, erratic use, and use in other contra-indicated ways and in lethal combinations. Although a problem of underuse of legal drugs exists, there seems to be a greater risk of overuse, particularly when psychoactive drugs are involved. Acute drug reactions can occur in some circumstances involving the misuse of drugs such as barbituates. An additional 10% of these reactions involves the abuse of Propoxyphene®, a drug given for arthritis-related pain in combination with aspirin, Acetaminophen®, or Darvon Compound®. The latter is a mild narcotic with a molecular structure related to methadone. Snider, Pascarrelli, and Howard, leading authorities on drug dependence, report that almost all acute drug reactions in the elderly are related to the use of prescribed drugs.[4] Many elderly are dependent on depressants, which are usually prescribed by their physicians or purchased by them in the form of alcoholic beverages. The sometimes lethal combination of Librium® or Valium® or alcohol are debilitating to the young and even deadly to the elderly whose bodies react differently to such medicines.

Alcohol use in the elderly is the third and largest area of substance abuse in the elderly. It is further complicated by the aging process. Alcohol has a more pronounced effect behaviorally and physically on older individuals, because it is metabolized at a slower rate. Therefore, smaller amounts may have more debilitating effects. Alcoholism in the elderly is often missed because many signs are attributed to aging rather than to alcohol use. For example, symptoms of confusion, paranoia, disorientation, memory loss, depression, anxiety, aggressive behaviors, and social isolation are often ignored for this reason. This may be a result of practitioners' generalizations about the aging process, and an attitude that a little alcohol doesn't hurt the older individual.

Patterns of alcohol abuse reflect the complex interactional dynamics involved in medical, psychiatric, environmental, and other socioeconomic factors. The stress associated with these factors can increase the likelihood that the elderly will abuse the very substances prescribed or self-administered to cope with these problems. It becomes a vicious cycle that repeats itself if appropriate intervention does not occur.

Drug use patterns in elderly persons are beginning to become clearer; only recently have we come to understand the nature of the more widespread problems of alcohol and other drug abuse. It is important to note that the beneficial use of drugs and their abuse are separated by a fine line in the elderly because of their diminished tolerance for most drugs, the larger quantities they receive, and because of their reasons for taking medications.

Snider, Pascarelli, and Howard state that the medical profession has overprescribed depressants for the elderly.[5] Physicians often tell their elderly patients to take daily doses of alcohol. The reasons for this range from ignorance to wanting to use these substances to pharmacologically subdue persons with difficult medical, psychological, or social problems.[6] Additionally, health and mental health care workers often fail to recognize problems related to the side effects of drugs, drug interactions, and self-medication problems. Some of the reasons for this may be related to attitudes, values, and stereotypes about the elderly and their role in society. For example, elderly persons who sleep during the day and appear to be forgetful are often diagnosed by care givers as being senile.

Persons abusing alcohol are seen as enjoying what few remaining years they have left.[7] Only when the person loses control and becomes dependent on institutions is it seen as a problem to be controlled and not treated.

## THE NEED FOR A NETWORK OF SERVICES

There are a number of problems in the current service delivery system based on the extent of substance abuse problems among the elderly as described in the previous section. The services delivered are not always based on needs of the elderly. For instance, often they are not located within their communities, requiring them to travel long distances if transportation is available. Frequently it isn't available. They are limited in scope usually without consideration of the fact that the elderly may have problems that go beyond the need for food, shelter, and clothing. In addition, the services are not coordinated, thus requiring the individual to interface with a half dozen or more agencies before they have their needs met. Sometimes, as in substance abuse, the needs are not met because they are not identified. The examination of whether elderly individuals are alcohol or drug abusers is a rarity, although like the rest of the population, 10 percent of them are likely to be alcoholic. Further, most of them are taking drugs of some kind. The failure to deliver comprehensive substance abuse services to this population is one of the largest gaps that exist in the delivery of needed services to the elderly.

Recognition of this gap should provide the impetus to develop comprehensive services to the elderly. Programs in existence must recognize the need and indicate a willingness to address the problem through collaborative efforts.[8] Collaboration and interagency coordination will permit services to be offered in a comprehensive systematic manner. Networking of services can prevent agencies from attempting to meet the needs in a fragmented manner. This fragmentation reduces the quality of the services rendered.

The need for a comprehensive collaborative network to enhance the quality of life for the elderly who have substance abuse problems is essential. Efforts should not only be made to provide treatment services for those with existing problems, but should include preventive services for those with potential problems in this area.[9] This increasing population requires that social workers become advocates and assist the elderly in obtaining needed services. Substance abuse among the elderly is out of the closet, along with the need for a comprehensive service network that may save countless lives.

## A COMPREHENSIVE NETWORK OF SERVICES

The comprehensive network necessary to provide substance abuse services will also provide the framework for collaboration between all service providers. The essential components of such a comprehensive network include health care, social services, housing, clergy/church, and family members.

### Health Care

Health care providers such as clinics, private physicians, hospitals, and home health providers are essential members of this service network because of the frequency of their contacts with elderly individuals related to health and physical problems involving drugs. For example, problems of medication misuse/abuse and alcohol use are seen frequently at this level. They may be identified and interventions conducted with the person either through a referral or contact with others who are a part of the abuser's life. Prevention activities can be offered in a systematic and coordinated way if the health care personnel are aware of social services and alcohol and drug programs. In fact, joint programs between health care providers and alcohol treatment staff can be developed and delivered without overwhelming effort on the part of either organization. For example, an alcohol and drug regulating agency in collaboration with a health care association, an alcohol and drug association, and an alcohol and drug treatment program developed a statewide workshop to educate the staffs of all four agencies about alcohol use and misuse among the elderly. Similarly, collaborative activities between health care and other agencies have involved networking for the purposes of direct services to elderly substance abusers.

## Social Services

This group is composed of mental health practitioners such as social workers, psychologists, psychiatrists, and alcoholism counselors. In addition, community centers, nutrition sites, counseling centers and day care service centers for the elderly are included. This group of providers furnish financial assistance, counseling, or supportive services to individuals for maintaining their emotional well being. These providers are contacted by health care providers on occasion, but the issue of alcoholism and drug abuse is rarely addressed during these contacts. This may be due to the ever increasing demands on staffs' time or a lack of knowledge about the issues. Referrals are made to social service agencies primarily at times of crisis. The coordination of services between health care providers and social services staff can occur in two ways. Staff from social service agencies can be utilized to train health care providers about alcoholism in the elderly, or to increase their sensitivity in identifying problem situations or potential problems through informal contacts. A second method is through the development of interagency coordination groups focused on increasing collaborative case finding and follow up.

## Housing

The development of housing complexes for the elderly means that this population is concentrated in some areas, and this is an advantage for outreach activities. Health care can be provided on site, as can mental health services, support groups, and substance abuse services. This requires the development of a collaborative network that also involves staff in the housing site. Substance abuse treatment in the environment can easily involve early intervention, because the services impact on the environment where a person spends a large proportion of time and where others may know about his or her problems with alcohol. Prevention activities can be built in because of the nearness of accessible neighbors for developing alternatives to drinking and other drugs such as recreational activities. Attorneys for housing complexes who resist evicting clients may want to involve another agency to treat the substance abuse problem rather than allow it to continue until eviction cannot be avoided. In one situation, staff from a substance abuse agency, legal aid, a housing development, Alcoholics Anonymous, and a community center worked together to assist an elderly individual to recover from alcoholism. This cooperative effort in one case provided the impetus for an ongoing network of services.

## Clergy/Church

Ministers and clergy are faced with this problem, but often they are not included in the network of helpers who can intervene at all levels. Clergy have frequent contacts with elderly individuals and have the potential for doing preventive activities in churches where elderly persons often congregate. For instance, those seniors who drive may benefit from a refresher course on safe driving skills, and information on drinking and driving laws. Another example could be the inclusion of family members and friends for establishing a support group that encourages independence of the elderly and encourages a positive role for the adult children of these clients. Courses on the side effects of drugs and how to be assertive with your physician are also often needed and could be offered in neighborhood churches. Courses on loss and grief and peer counseling programs are needed. Agencies have staff who can provide basic training and follow-up support to clergy who work with the elderly.

## Family Members

Another part of the network is the family. The family enables the elderly individual to feel loved, and their involvement is essential in the provision of substance abuse services to the elderly. The family may enable the abuser to continue using drugs because of his or her age, frustration about not knowing what to do, or due to denial. Providers who promote a comprehensive network of services will also promote the involvement of family members. The latter can help to plan services as well as monitor the effects of services on their elderly family member.

In summary, comprehensive services to the elderly in the area of abuse of alcohol encompasses every aspect of the individuals' life in a coordinated manner. Social workers should help to develop networks that enhance the provision of services. Collaboration requires talking with other providers, promoting the network, formalizing agreements, and forming on-going interagency groups that are active in the collaborative efforts. These are but a few of the activities that can potentially close the gap in substance abuse services for the elderly.

## THE TENANT ASSISTANCE PROGRAM

The Tenant Assistance Program was developed to provide services to the elderly through trained personnel who were the employees of other community based programs. The housing authority provided full time personnel to coordinate the program. The administration and governing authority of the housing project provided policy and procedural guidelines that supported and enhanced the effectiveness of the program. Providers in health care and social service agencies identified a gap in services to the elderly in the area of substance abuse. Informal case finding sessions between several of these agencies indicated that an increasing number of elderly clients in one housing complex had problems with alcohol and other drugs. A joint meeting was scheduled between those agencies and the housing authority.

One of the elements necessary for the success of any project that coordinates services is a joint meeting. A joint meeting of the key participants provides an opportunity to explore the commitment and degree of participation by each agency involved. The objectives of the project can be developed and key agency or service providers who are responsible for the implementation then can agree on the objectives and procedures of the program. The agreement is formalized by governing bodies or partners through a formalized policy statement that supports staff participation and a signed agreement. These steps occurred as the Tenant Assistance Program was planned. The success of any project is based on the ability of the coordinator to effectively network with a variety of agencies. Substance Abuse personnel can be helpful in coordinating services because of their skills in networking support groups, families, and employers in the care and treatment of alcoholic clients.

As a result of the joint meeting between the housing authority and these other agencies, specific services were developed for this Tenants Assistant Program.

## Preventive Services

Services to new tenants to ease the stress of moving to a new location, recreational activities, transportation, and stress management were among the preventive services that were provided. In addition, a pharmacist was provided during educational sessions to answer questions about the side effects of drugs. A physician came on-site to provide consultation on some of the tenants. Blood pressure screening and nutrition classes were additional services. The above services were provided by persons knowledgeable in these areas. Peer support groups were formed subsequently as resources to elderly who participated in the educational sessions which were held over an eight-week period by the social worker who originally identified the gap in services.

## Treatment Services

Direct services to tenants in crisis were offered during and after the prevention services ended. They were offered on an on-going basis and included resource networking, identifying alternatives to loneliness, and direct counseling activities. The latter involved groups or individual sessions for tenants in crisis. Consultation and education services were provided to staff in the housing complex to enhance their professional development and skills in providing follow-up referral services to tenants whom they might have contact with in the future.

## Family Involvement

If the individual will not get involved, it is permissible to offer services to family members to ease their stress during transition periods. Families may be seen as supports and they can enhance resources, if they are included as part of the elderly persons services. In the Tenant Assistance Program, it was not necessary for significant others to be related to the individual; they only needed to have a strong affiliation with the person. Families received information on intervention strategies they could use with a family member who was using alcohol and drugs in a dysfunctional way. They were invited to attend the educational sessions, and some did attend.

## Peer Support Groups

The Tenant Assistance Program involved peers in a collaborative organized way. They were asked to support the policy and procedures and to assist in the outreach activities before, during, and after the preventive services. In the case of substance abuse, peers may have first-hand knowledge of the problem, and some may be affected by it. This is especially true if the person is disruptive. Support groups are essential for maintaining any gains made with elderly clients by the professional staff. This program provided alternative supports through peers and prevented isolation of some elderly.

## THE ROLE OF SOCIAL WORKERS

Social workers, because of their training and simultaneous focus on the person and their interface with the environment, are the logical leaders to develop networks of services. The various roles which social workers are trained to use include those of broker, enabler, and advocate. All of these are appropriate intervention roles for service delivery with elderly substance abusers.

Brokerage of services is a method that permits social workers in any setting an opportunity to perform an essential function that assists elderly clients to obtain needed services. The linkage between the client and other services often requires an intermediary who is knowledgeable about available community resources and able to make appropriate referrals. Obstacles to the receipt of services are diminished, because the social worker operating as a broker is familiar with other organizations' procedures and operating policies.

When developing a network, the brokerage role facilitates collaboration between agencies. It is often assumed that staff in agencies are familiar with other community resources. This is frequently not true, however. For example, the housing authority did not have knowledge of substance abuse treatment resources, but was willing to collaborate so that their clients could receive a broad range of services.

The enabler role utilized by social workers is a facilitative one that recognizes the need for individual clients to effect changes within themselves and their environments. Social workers may need to support elderly clients as a group in developing programs that meet their needs as defined by them.

Advocacy is often a neglected dimension in social work practice. Social workers should advocate for the elderly in obtaining new and adequate services in the area of substance abuse. They can advocate on the policy level for changes that recognize the elderly as valuable human beings. Advocacy within one's own agency is an essential aspect of the role social workers play in changing institutionalized discrimination against the elderly in policies and practices.

### SUMMARY

Comprehensive service delivery to the elderly involving substance abuse problems is a proactive stance rather than a reactive one. Such a stance requires knowledge of how to network services among staff in health care, social service, legal, religious, and housing agencies. Strategies that are critical for implementing an effective network program include those necessary for consultation, prevention, and treatment services. This kind of comprehensive service delivery has been illustrated by a description of a Tenants' Assistance Program in which services in the substance abuse area were delivered to clients, family members and peers, and staff in an effective manner. The success of this program was enhanced by the advocacy and broker roles utilized by the social worker involved.

## REFERENCES

1. Freeman, Edith M.: Multiple losses in the elderly: An ecological perspective. *Social Casework,* 65:287–296, 1984.
2. Knapp, R. J., and Chapel, W. C.: Drug use among the elderly: Introduction. *Journal of Drug Issues,* 9:1, 1979.
3. Ibid.
4. Snider, D. A., Pascarelli, D., and Howard, M.: Survey of the needs and problems of adult home residents in New York State. Welfare Research, Inc., New York State Department of Social Services, 1979.
5. Ibid.
6. Prentice, Robert: Patterns of psychoactive drug use among the elderly. *The Aging Process and Psychoactive Drug Use,* Department of Health and Human Services Publication No. (ADM) 82-113, 1982.
7. Buys, Donna and Sultman, Jules: *The Unseen Alcoholics: The Elderly,* Public Affairs Committee Publication, 1982.
8. Ibid.
9. Wood, W. Gibson: The elderly alcoholics. In Wood, W. Gibson (Ed.): *Clinical Psychology of Aging,* New York: Plenun Press, 1978.

*Chapter Thirteen*

# ALCOHOL USE AND ABUSE AMONG BLACKS

RUTH G. MCROY AND CLAYTON T. SHORKEY

Alcoholism is the number one health problem today among blacks, the nation's largest ethnic minority population.[1] A brief review of statistics of black drinking patterns reveals the devastating impact that alcoholism and alcohol abuse have had on black individuals and their families. Although the overall drinking rates for black and white males are similar, there is a larger percentage of heavy drinkers among black males than white males.[2] Among black women, we find both more abstainers and more heavy drinkers than among white women.

Cirrhosis of the liver is 44 percent higher among blacks than whites. Similarly, the rate of other alcohol-related illnesses such as heart disease, hypertension, and psychological disorders are higher among blacks than whites.[3] Blacks are more often victims in alcohol-related homicides, have higher arrest rates for drunkenness than whites, and are disproportionately channeled toward prison rather than treatment compared with other ethnic groups.[4]

Despite the serious nature of alcoholism among blacks, there is a paucity of empirical research on alcohol use and abuse in the black community. In his 1976 review of the findings in 40 studies on blacks, Harper reported the following: heavy drinking is increasing among 18 to 25 year olds, and one-third of all black females under 45 as well as one-half of all black youths use or abuse alcohol.[5] Most studies which include data on black drinking patterns use survey research data or correlational designs which report drinking patterns and demographic factors. Although they attribute drinking problems to socioeconomic, cultural, familial or psychological factors, they generally fail to examine complex social and cultural factors related to the development of effective alcohol education prevention and treatment programs.

Just as the problem and consequences of black alcoholism have been largely ignored in the research literature, historically black Americans and the black community have also tended to ignore this issue. This chapter is designed to examine and discuss: (1) the current state of knowledge about black alcoholism; (2) cultural and psychological factors which should be taken into consideration in the development of education and treatment programs for blacks, and (3) some recommendations for social workers involved in education, community outreach and treatment programs designed for black Americans.

## DRINKING PATTERNS

### Black Men

A recent study on racial patterns of alcohol consumption among over 56,000 people who had routine health examinations between 1978 to 1980, found that men of all racial and ethnic groups reported more drinking than women. Daily drinking patterns of black men were found to be similar to those of white and Hispanic men. Black men reported a twofold greater proportion of lifelong abstinence and heavy drinking than whites or Hispanics.[6] However, the consequences of alcohol abuse are especially severe among black men. For example, studies of hospital admissions for medical problems associated with alcoholism reveal that blacks tend to be admitted more often than whites (52% versus 11%), are admitted at a younger age and are more likely to have delirium tremens and alcohol hallucinations.[7]

A number of possible psychological explanations have been given for this pattern of alcohol abuse. For example, Steer et al. studied 103 black men who were being treated for alcoholism and found an overall pattern of depression characterized by dissatisfaction, pessimism, a sense of failure, guilt feelings, and self-dislike.[8] Alcohol has been used by many black men as self-medication for countering the frustration and depression which result from the racial prejudice and self-hatred that many have experienced in this society.[9]

## Black Women

Comparisons of drinking practices of black and white women reveal that black women also have higher proportions of both abstainers and heavier drinkers than whites. Among the factors used to explain the high level of abstainers among black women are: limited resources for the purchase of alcohol, religious beliefs, and differences in life styles. Heavy drinking patterns among black females are generally attributed to the greater alienation or unhappiness found among the economically and culturally deprived. Black female problem drinkers often start drinking regularly and heavily at an earlier age than whites; are more likely to drink with peers, to drink in public, and to drink in the mornings; and are less likely than white female alcoholics to cite male-female difficulties as major causes of drinking problems.[10]

Sterne and Pittman's 1972 study of black female heavy drinkers in a low-income housing project indicated that heavy drinking women were often nonconformists regarding personal achievement, church attendance, and sexual practices. By patronizing taverns and other drinking establishments, these black women used alcohol for meeting both personal and social goals. It is interesting to note that the majority of the heavy drinking females in this study had been reared in large cities outside of the south.[11]

Many black women who are problem drinkers find themselves in a triple bind of oppression by being black, female, and alcoholic. Responsibility for managing a family and possible problems with male/female relationships increase the stress on black women, which may precipitate heavy drinking. Treatment opportunities are less available to black women because of racism, lack of insurance coverage, the scarcity of treatment programs for females (especially black females), and a lack of employment. Also, many may find themselves in situations in which they deny their drinking problem for fear of persecution from family members. Families too often enable the female alcoholic's drinking by protecting her or by refusing to admit the problem exists.[12] As a result, some black women have difficulty maintaining sobriety once the treatment process has begun. Many try to recover alone without the family as a support group and without the benefit of alternative support systems such as self-help groups.

For a variety of reasons, most black women do not have access to employee assistance programs. Many are working in either service occupations, private household jobs, or clerical positions which do not offer special programs for employees. Those who are employed in companies which offer these programs sometimes fail to utilize them due to high costs which often are not included in insurance coverage. Moreover, many industrial social service programs are oriented to the white middle class and have few black service providers or policy makers, thus, many blacks may chose not to participate.[13]

### Black Youth

Although only a few studies exist which compare black and white adolescent drinking behavior, the data that are available indicate that there is little difference between the two groups. In fact, black teenagers tend to be no more likely and often are less likely than whites to be involved in drinking behavior.[14]

A 1978 national survey of drinking practices among senior high school students reported that there were twice as many alcohol abstainers among black students as among white students, and that four times as many white students as blacks drank heavily.[15] Research data on adolescent alcoholism also reveal that blacks are more likely to receive their first drink at home from their parents, whereas, whites often have their first drink with peers outside the home. Black youth also tend to have less knowledge than whites about alcohol and its effects on the body.[16]

A 1980 study of 196 black female high school students from rural backgrounds revealed that slightly over one-third were classified as drinkers. Reasons varied regarding their justification for drinking. Some attributed their drinking to a need to overcome frustrations or to psychological barriers to performance; others indicated alcohol helped them to do things they felt they shouldn't;

some found that alcohol made them more carefree; still others indicated that they drank when they were worried or bothered about a particular incident or to overcome shyness. About one-fourth of the black females surveyed reported that they drank for the sole purpose of getting high.[17]

These findings are significant for the development of effective educational and prevention programs which should be targeted specifically to the needs of black students. Moreover, such programs must demystify the belief that alcohol can lift spirits or that conversely it is a morale bane. Effective programs should educate youth and the community to the realities of alcohol abuse and alcoholism as a disease.

### Black Elderly

The elderly have the lowest proportion of problem drinkers among the black population. Only those elderly without adequate housing, medical care, recreational facilities, activities, or occupations are found to abuse alcohol and experience alcohol related problems.[18] Among many low income black elderly, alcoholism is often a result of ineffective attempts to cope with boredom, loneliness or feelings of low self-esteem.

### FACTORS CONTRIBUTING TO ALCOHOL USE/ABUSE

From the preceding overview of the nature of alcoholism among blacks, it is evident that there is a bimodal tendency among blacks to either be abstainers or to drink heavily. Heavy drinking is a pervasive problem in urban areas especially among low-income blacks who have easy access to taverns and package stores. Although the majority of black women do not drink (51%), those who do are often heavy drinkers.[19]

Several theories have been proposed to explain the etiologies of black drinking behavior. Many of these explanations have focused on psychological causes such as a need to overcome social inadequacies or some other weakness. A means of escape from the frustrations and rejection caused by institutional and individual racism, social stress from living in crowded urban areas, unemployment, and conflicts in male-female relationships are other reasons that have been suggested as affecting black drinking patterns.[20] Frederick Harper has proposed four hypotheses of black drinking behavior which explain drinking patterns from the perspective of both psychological and social factors:

1. Patterns of weekend drinking and heavy drinking as well as abstinence have resulted from the historical ambivalent habits and attitudes thrust upon blacks by white Americans in an attempt to control their behavior. At times during slavery, blacks would be encouraged to drink and at other times discouraged.
2. Accessibility to liquor stores and peer expectations of drinking behavior influence black drinking patterns.
3. Frustrations in being unable to get a job or one that pays enough to fulfill one's financial responsibilities may also cause many blacks to abuse alcohol.
4. Alcohol and drinking are a source of recreation and social activity which satisfy many needs and can allow one to attempt to escape the unpleasant experiences of racial discrimination.[21]

## FACTORS AFFECTING TREATMENT

Bowles has suggested that black clients can develop trust and positive working relationships with white workers if these workers demonstrate the following qualities: openness, an ability to listen and accept differences in values, a capacity to acknowledge their limitations, and a willingness to negate stereotypes and myths about blacks. Having confidence in black clients' capacities for self-understanding is also helpful.[22]

Other factors which are crucial to effective treatment with blacks include an appreciation for strengths in black clients, an understanding of in-group differences, knowledge about defense systems, the need to facilitate the development of a healthy self-concept, and the need to establish positive communication patterns. Further, an understanding of black language is critical for effective cross-cultural communication. In examining the issue of in-group differences, Bell and Evans identified four fluid interpersonal styles within the black culture that can affect treatment: acculturated, bicultural, culturally-immersed, and traditional. Individuals in the acculturated interpersonal style tend to reject black stereotypic behavior and rituals and assimilate into the mainstream white culture. Acculturation is considered a response to the emotional pain of being black in America. Bicultural persons tend to be comfortable functioning in a white world while maintaining pride in black racial identity and culture.

Culturally-immersed individuals may reject white values and assume a pro-black stance. The inner turmoil experienced in this state may make a counseling relationship difficult. Finally, the traditional style includes persons whose survival needs are met in the white world but whose human needs are met in the black world. Often older, these persons generally are accepting of their blackness but dependent on whites for meeting many of their needs. They may be less open and candid in counseling relationships with white counselors.[23]

## TREATMENT APPROACHES

A review of existing counseling approaches reveals that many have elements that can be useful in working with black alcoholic clients. Roderick McDavis has proposed an eclectic approach which draws from behavioral, client-centered, existential, Gestalt, rational-emotive, and reality counseling approaches. The following provides a brief review of the key concepts and techniques useful to alcholism counseling with black clients:

1. *Existentialism*—In keeping with the philosophy that individuals have an inherent right to retain their own identities, make their own choices and provide self-direction, alcoholism counselors should attempt to learn the cultural language, the lifestyle of the culture, and try to understand the experiences of these clients.
2. *Client Centered Approach*—Counselors should be sincere, genuine, open, honest, and communicate acceptance and understanding to black clients. This can help to increase self-esteem

and negate self-criticisms which reinforce alcohol abuse.

3. *Reality Therapy* — By getting involved in the counseling relationship, conveying their own experiences and ideas and avoiding value judgements about clients behavior, counselors can employ the basic concepts of this approach to help clients to objectively identify the consequences of drinking. Counselors should guide clients to evaluate their own behavior rather than evaluate it for clients.

4. *Behavioral Therapy* — The use of goal setting, role playing, modeling, and behavioral contracts for monitoring abstinence rates can help black clients learn to develop new behaviors. In this approach, both counselors and clients are actively involved in the counseling process.

5. *Gestalt Counseling* — Counselors help clients focus on their immediate dysfunctional behaviors by asking "how and what" questions. The sharing allows the client to feel that the counselor is listening, wants to hear more about their concerns, and encourages clients to explore inner feelings that underlie alcohol abuse.

6. *Rational Emotive Therapy* — Counselors help clients to use rational thinking to control their emotions and the stresses which they have routinely hidden by using alcohol in the past. Homework assignments are also used to help clients work on practical solutions.[24]

Selective techniques from each of these approaches rather than one single approach can increase social workers' flexibility and capacity for the development of individualized treatment plans. Social workers should be actively involved in the counseling relationships as well as develop skills in dealing with cultural specific areas of emotional pain in black alcoholic clients.

Social workers and alcoholism counselors must be flexible in their use of these approaches to counsel black clients and be willing to initiate outreach counseling. By leaving the agency and entering the clients world of friends, family, work, and neighbors in the community, social workers may be able to dispel some of the initial mistrust of the alcoholic client. Also, they will be able to better understand the external environmental stresses which may be affecting the black alcoholic's problems and to help the client confront these realities.[25]

## EDUCATION-OUTREACH-REFERRAL

As mentioned earlier in this chapter, blacks utilize traditional alcoholism treatment facilities less often than whites. Of the three major access points (family/friends, job/school, and courts), courts seem to be the major referral source for blacks into the treatment system. Unfortunately, many of these individuals do not receive help until they are in a more advanced stage of their illness.

In 1974 the National Institute on Alcohol Abuse and Alcoholism funded a three-year demonstration traffic safety program, which provided treatment services for persons arrested for driving while under the influence of alcohol. This required a seven-week 14-hour alcohol reeducation program, intensive counseling, referral, and monitoring for those diagnosed as problem drinkers. At the completion of the project, over 60 percent of both blacks and whites had decreased their alcohol intake, and of this total 29 percent of whites and 28 percent of blacks had achieved abstinence at termination and had maintained abstinence for about six months. These positive results indicate that court enforced treatment of problem drinking can be effective.[26] Plans to develop treatment services in the black community should consider the use of such well designed court mandated programs.

Another community outreach program, Alcoholics Anonymous, has been very successful with many white alcoholics but has yet to reach blacks in great numbers. Some believe that the Anglo-Saxon, Protestant, middle-class orientation of most AA groups dissuade most black alcoholics from seeking help. Research is needed to determine how such self-help programs could be redesigned to be more culture specific and address the needs of black alcoholics. Caldwell suggests that effective AA meetings for blacks personalize the traditional abstract issues, emphasize interpersonal relationships, and make greater use of linguistic styles which employ metaphors and analogies.[27]

Another potential area for education and outreach is the church. Traditionally, however, black churches have followed white fundamentalist belief systems and condemned the use of alcohol as sinful. This moralistic orientation has tended to make it difficult to involve ministers in attempts to treat alcoholics; some ministers may also fear that such programs will have an impact on an area where they have had a monopoly. Allaying these fears and re-educating clergy about alcoholism problems and treatment is a necessary step for involving them in outreach efforts.

Employee Assistance Programs (EAP's) which have been very successful in reaching out to problem drinkers in early stages, also potentially offer hope for black alcoholics. However, the number of black clients referred by EAP's is currently under-represented based on the number of black employees in the work setting. Employers need to explore the practices and policies of their EAP's and to redesign them to reflect the needs of all employees.

## CONCLUSIONS

Research on the problems of black alcoholism treatment programs has revealed several major problem areas related to community relations, race relations, and the treatment process. Gaining community acceptance and involving churches in new programs are considered major obstacles which must be overcome. Funding, technical assistance, and staff training also pose problems for the development and continuation of specialized programs in the black community. Racial attitudes among staff, between staff and clients, and between policy makers and administrators pose additional serious problems in the development of programs to reach black alcoholics. Many of these obstacles may be resolved through increased involvement by black citizens in the design of these programs. Joint efforts by citizens and treatment staff are needed to plan and develop effective alcoholism service delivery systems in the black community.

## REFERENCES

1. National Institute on Alcohol Abuse and Alcoholism. *Alcohol Topics In Brief: Alcohol and Blacks.* Rockwell, Maryland, National Clearinghouse for Alcohol Information, 1982; and Bourne, P. G.: Alcoholism in the urban Negro population. In Bourne, P. G. and Fox, R. (Eds.): *Alcoholism Progress in*

*Research and Treatment.* New York, Academic Press, 1973.

2. Harper, Frederick: Alcohol use and abuse. In Watts, Thomas D. and Wright, Roosevelt Jr.: *Black Alcoholism.* Springfield, Ill., Charles C Thomas, 1983.

3. National Institute on Alcohol Abuse and Alcoholism, op. cit.

4. Dawkins, Marvin P.: *Alcohol and the Black Community: Exploratory Studies of Selected Issues.* Saratoga, Ca., Century Twenty One Publishing, 1980.

5. Harper, Frederick D. (Ed.): *Alcohol Abuse and Black America.* Alexandria, Va., Douglass Publishers, 1976; King, Lewis M.: Alcoholism: Studies Regarding Black Americans, 1977–1980. In *Alcohol and Health Monograph No. 4: Special Population Issues.* Rockville, Md., National Institute of Alcohol Abuse and Alcoholism, 1982, pp. 385–407.

6. Klatsky, Arthur L., Seizelaub, Abraham, Landy, Cynthia, and Friedman, Gary: Racial patterns of alcohol beverage use. *Alcoholism: Clinical and Experimental Research,* 7:372–377, 1983.

7. Cahalan, Don and Room, Robin: *Problem Drinking Among Men.* New Brunswick, NJ, Rutgers Center of Alcohol Studies, 1974; and Rimmer, J. F., Pitts, F., and Winokur, G.: Alcoholism, sex, socioeconomic status and race in two hospitalized samples. *Quarterly Journal of Studies on Alcohol,* 32:942–952, 1972.

8. Steer, R. A., Shaw, Brian F., Beck, Aaron T., and Fine, Eric W.: Structure of depression in black alcoholic men. *Psychological Reports, 41:*1235–1241, 1977.

9. Ibid.

10. Dawkins, Marvin P. and Harper, Frederick D.: Alcoholism among women: A comparison of black and white problem drinkers. *The International Journal of the Addictions, 18:*333–349, 1983.

11. Sterne, M. and Pittman, D.: Drinking patterns in the ghetto. Unpublished Research Report. St. Louis, Social Science Institute, Washington University, 1972.

12. Stuart, Lorraine B. and Brisbane, Frances: The black female alcoholic: A perspective from history to 1982. *Bulletin of the New York Chapter of the National Black Alcoholism Council, 1:*5–7, 1982; and Williams, Millre: Blacks and alcoholism: Issues in the 1980's. *Alcohol Health and Research World,* 6:31–40, 1982.

13. Ibid.

14. Lowman, Cherry, Harford, Thomas, and Kaelber, Charles T.: Alcohol use among black senior high school students. *Alcohol Health and Research World,* 7:37–46, 1983.

15. Ibid.

16. Dawkins, Marvin P.: Alcohol use among black and white adolescents. In Harper, Frederick D. (Ed.): *Alcohol Abuse and Black America,* Alexandria, Va., Douglass Publishing Co., 1976.

17. Globetti, Gerald, Alsikafi, Moyeed, and Morse, Richard: Black female high school students and the use of beverage alcohol. *The International Journal of the Addictions, 15:*189–200, 1980.

18. Jarvis, Edna: Alcoholism: A new perspective for black Americans. *The Crisis, 85:*237–239, 1978.

19. Harper, Frederick D.: Etiology: Why do blacks drink? In Harper, Frederick D. (Ed.): *Alcohol Abuse and Black America*, Alexandria, Va., Douglass Publishing Co., 1976, pp. 27–37.
20. Ibid.
21. Ibid.
22. Bowles, Dorcas Davis: Treatment issues in working with black clients. *Smith College Journal*, 4:8–14, 1977.
23. Bell, Peter and Evans, Jimmy: Counseling the black client. *Professional Education*, No. 5, Hazleden Foundation, 1981.
24. McDavis, Roderick J.: Counseling black clients effectively: The eclectic approach. *Journal of Non-White Concerns*, 1:41–47, 1978.
25. Bell and Evans, op. cit.
26. Argeriou, Milton: Reaching problem-drinking blacks: The unheralded potential of the drinking driver program. *The International Journal of the Addictions*, 13:443–459, 1979.
27. Caldwell, Fulton J.: Alcoholics Anonymous as a viable treatment resource for black alcoholics. In Watts, Thomas D. and Wright, Roosevelt Jr. (Eds.): *Black Alcoholism*. Springfield, Il., Charles C Thomas, 1983, pp. 85–99.

*Chapter Fourteen*

# ALCOHOLISM AND THE INDIAN PEOPLE: PROBLEM AND PROMISE

JOHN F. GUNTHER, ERIC J. JOLLY (OOLOOTEEKA)
AND KENNETH R. WEDEL

The problem of alcoholism among Indian people is a tremendously complex issue. Indians who identify a tribal affiliation as well as assimilated urban Indians present very real paradoxes and problems in making any generalized statements about alcoholism and Indian people. Nevertheless, the problem is a staggering one for those who claim the ethnic identity of Indian. It shall be the purpose of this chapter to detail the incidence and prevalence of alcoholism among Indian people,[1] analyze the ensuing sociocultural effects of alcoholism on Indian people, and review current treatment strategies offered to ameliorate the problem. A social work perspective on alcoholism and the Indian people is the guiding theme of the chapter.

## INCIDENCE AND PREVALENCE
## OF ALCOHOLISM AMONG INDIAN PEOPLE

The profession of social work has paid relatively little attention to the problem of alcoholism among Indian people.[2] Yet, this complex issue constitutes the most critical health and social problem confronting the Indian people today. Almost every tribal unit in the U.S. maintains an active alcohol treatment program. Additionally, alcohol-related health, regulatory, and enforcement programs are among the largest financial burdens borne by tribal units across the United States. Alcohol abuse has also been indicated as a primary contributor to violent crime among Indian people, and it is evident in about 90 percent of all Indian homicides and in as many as 80 percent of all Indian suicides. Together with cirrhosis of the liver (including but not limited to Laennec's cirrhosis), homicide, and suicide constitute the three leading causes of death among Indian people.[3]

The U.S. Public Health Service has reported alarming statistics in relation to alcohol abuse among Indian people which indicate that the alcohol-related discharge rate for Indian people treated by Indian Health Services and contract hospitals is higher than that of all other races discharged from U.S. short-stay hospitals. Also, in the 15 to 44 year age bracket (the age group that constitutes high productivity years), the discharge rate of Indian people is four times higher than all other discharges in U.S. short stay hospitals.[4]

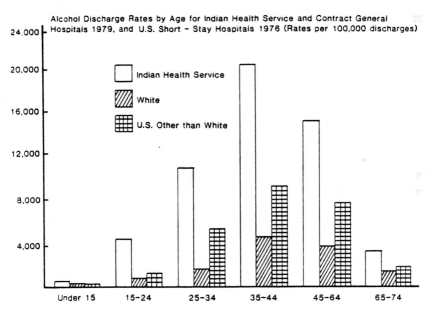

Alcohol Discharge Rates by Age for Indian Health Service and Contract General Hospitals 1979, and U.S. Short - Stay Hospitals 1976 (Rates per 100,000 discharges)

* Chart developed by Indian Health Service, Inpatient Care Branch, Office of Program Statistics, Division of Resource Coordination, 1980.

Figure 14-1

The Public Health Service has also released data profiling the disproportionate amount of alcohol related deaths among American Indians.

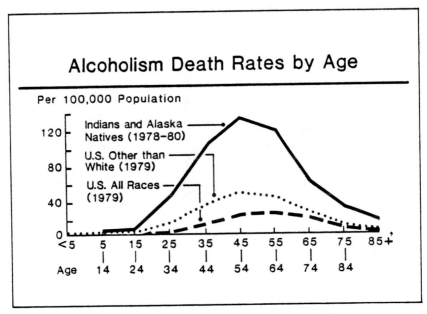

Source: Department of Health and Human Services—
Public Health Service

Figure 14-2

Other researchers commenting on the incidence and prevalence of alcohol abuse have indicated a disproportionate amount of alcohol abuse among Indian people when compared to other groups. Specifically, Oetting, Edwards, and Garcia-Mason found that when compared to a national sample, Indian people in the 7th through 12th grades involved themselves in alcohol experimentation at a significantly greater level (p <.001).[5] May similarly found that when compared to a national U.S. sample, Indian people indicated a somewhat higher incidence of alcohol abuse.[6] However, May does add an important caution to his analysis: "If one were to do surveys on a number of other Indian groups, particularly those with less notorious drinking reputations (i.e., the Pueblo or eastern Oklahoma Tribes) then an incidence similar to or lower than the rest of the nation would probably be established for Indians."[7] Hamer and Steinbring also support May's latter point by noting that "while the volume of alcohol consumed by native people is not disproportionately greater ... the social cost does appear to be disproportionately greater than for other groups."[8] Finally, as May, Hamer, and Steinbring have suggested, alcohol use and abuse statistics on Indian people are not only difficult to find, but once located may have dubious accuracy. Generalizations should therefore be treated with caution.

## SOCIO-CULTURAL EFFECTS OF
## ALCOHOLISM ON THE INDIAN PEOPLE

While most empirical studies in the field describe the severity of the alcoholism problem among Indian people, they do little to explain the factors that contribute to and sustain the problem and the ensuing socio-cultural costs of the problem. However, most studies do indicate that any explanation of alcoholism among Indian people would have to account for the impact of Anglo culture on Indian tribal society and the concommitant effects of role stress, identity confusion and acculturation trauma. The problem of identity trauma from a sociocultural perspective is a particularly acute one for Indian people and has had a direct impact on their social functioning. Kunkel, Dobrec and Wedel emphasize this concern:[9]

> In short when viewed from a minority perspective, the promise of the dominant culture is at least (at best?) a partial lie. The effect on identity for minority persons is to engender ambivalence. Whom to select as a reference group for behavior becomes a critical question of society. Most of the rewards are controlled by the dominant culture. Paradoxically, the dominant culture teaches Indians ... to reject their own cultural origins ... Since American Indians ... recognize that they are unlikely to ever gain unconditional full membership in a dominant culture characterized by institutional racism, they retain an often unfulfilling identification with their own people. Add to this problem the tendency of the dominant culture to produce and perpetuate stereotypes about American Indians ... and the picture of the American Indian identity dilemma begins to come into focus.

Extending the issue of identity trauma into the societal arena Wanberg, Lewis and Foster, in commenting on the social-personal adjustment of Indian people, note that when Indian people are compared to dominant culture groups they indicate a higher degree of disruption in employment, income, and marital status.[10] However, perhaps the most extreme statement concerning the societal context in which alcoholism among the Indian people has grown is offered by French and Hornbuckle. They note that the federal government, through its various legislative enactments, has created both a "physical and cultural genocide" for Indian people. They further elaborate on the social cost of alcoholism for Indian people:[11]

> The Federal Bureau of Investigation's Uniform Crime Reports (1958–77) support these statistics, indicating that Native Americans have the highest conviction rate for crimes of violence. Their conviction rate is twice that of blacks and Hispanics and three times that of whites. Not all Native Americans who drink are involved in violent crime, however. The rate of other alcohol-related offenses such as public drunkenness is eight times that of blacks and Hispanics and over twenty times that of whites.

Other studies have pointed to alcoholism as a contributing factor in suicides of Indian people.[12] Whitaker noted that drinking provided an outlet for aggression and a form of escape from the psychological pressures of low self-esteem and feelings of inadequacy among the Standing Rock Sioux.[13] His study also notes the impact of social influences on the disposition to drink within a tribal society:[14]

> Social norms have a strong influence on the rates of alcohol misuse within a particular society. The overwhelming majority of the respondents said that most of their friends have favorable attitudes towards drinking, ... Another social norm which contributes to drinking is the traditional generosity of the Sioux. In Sioux society, there is considerable mutual support ... Even if a person spends every cent irresponsibly, others comes to his aid. Sharing, in a way, gets the irresponsible drinker "off the hook."

In another study Levy and Kunitz have pointed out that Navaho women are at the greater risk to become alcoholics than Navaho men.[15] While the authors offer no explanation for this phenomenon it does open an area for analysis that has been relatively unexplored in the literature; the differential impact of alcoholism on the Indian woman.

In summary, the inferences that can be made from the current research indicate a sociocultural breakdown of the aboriginal culture of Indian people. From this breakdown an effort has been made within the dominant culture to have Indian people assimilate. The thrust toward cultural assimilation has had devastating social costs and has created a "hostile environment" for Indian people. This "hostile environment" and its parallel cultural stress have significantly contributed to the problem of alcoholism and its ensuing social costs. Such cultural stress and a prevalence of external sources of control have been demonstrated to be correlates to increased alcohol consumption.[16] Essentially what appears to be happening is that the Indian, in looking for a place to integrate within the hostile environment, encounters unresolvable stressors arising from the ensuing weakening of the Indian social structure and his or her aboriginal cultural grouping. One outlet for escaping such stress has become alcohol abuse which may be in part a reaction against the Anglo-culture and self-fulfilling prophecy.[17] For example, in areas with a large population of Indian people it is reported that the police officers "are more prone to look for evidence of drunkenness in cases involving Indians and to see sufficient evidence to warrant arrest . . . "[18] Thus, the alcohol-related arrest incidences of Indians are several times greater than for the United States as a whole,[19] and as much as twenty times greater than those of whites.[20] Reducing the effects of stress by consumption of alcohol is not only a highly effective short-term treatment, but fulfills the expectations of the dominant culture.

## CURRENT TREATMENT STRATEGIES FOR ALCOHOLISM AMONG INDIAN PEOPLE

Most apparent in the problem of alcoholism among Indian people is a paucity of information on treatment approaches. Hall, in an extensive review of the literature emphasizes this noticeable gap[21]: " . . . Indian alcohol literature suffers from a paucity of information on treatment . . . Unitl there is some objective reporting of what was employed and whether or not it worked . . . programs will continue to rely on a seat of the pants approach or whatever-worked-for-me-will-work-for-you-philosophy."

Despite the relatively bleak picture in regards to treatment information some initial attempts have been made. One area that has received attention has been the twelve step program of Alcoholics Anonymous. This program places emphasis on spiritual recovery. Walker has reported on the successful inclusion of A.A. in an Urban Native American alcoholism program.[22] However, Levy and Kunitz note, "the Navaho man does not respond well to group confessionals (characteristic of A.A.) which emphasize the impropriety of behavior."[23] Price, in an extensive anthropological study of Indian drinking patterns notes, "Alcoholics Anonymous works through non-Indian cultural patterns on physiologically addicted individuals, so it is usually effective only with acculturated Indians unless it is radically reworked. . . . "[24] However, Jolly has demonstrated that the spiritual beliefs associated with Indian cultures often manifest themselves in ways which conflict greatly with the type of spiritual approach emphasized within A.A.[25] In addition to the spiritual approach of A.A., Hall notes that a number of other spiritual approaches have been utilized to treat alcoholism among Indian people. These include the Peyote Way, Christianity, and affiliations with nativistic movements.[26]

Another treatment program which reports "substantial success" across several cultural groupings, including Indian people, is the Alcohol Troubled Personality (ATP) model formulated by Willoughby.[27] This model is based on the premise of stress reduction and may therefore be especially appropriate for an ecological treatment perspective. This program identifies the potential ATP client as any person for whom alcohol is "reducing the quality of life in any one (or more) of the following areas: (1) social; (2) financial; (3) physical; (4) emotional and cognitive."[28] The model seeks to enhance the quality of life by reducing stress and eliminating the accompanying consummatory habit patterns.

Comprehensive alcoholic treatment programs for Indian people that have also been organized and conducted by Indian people in urban areas have met with some success. Locklear reports on an early program in Baltimore conducted by the American Indian Study Center which emphasized education, prevention, and treatment through outreach.[29] The Seattle Indian Alcoholism Program, which has also reported successful outcomes, emphasizes a comprehensive program of (1) identification and referral; (2) detoxification; (3) intensive inpatient treatment; (4) intermediate rehabilitation; (5) outpatient follow up; and (7) criminal justice outreach.[30]

Perhaps the most interesting line of research emerging for Indian alcohol treatment concerns locus of control and its impact on alcohol consumption. Locus of control refers to an "individual difference dimension" devised by Rotter. The individual differences dimension indicates the strength of a person's convictions by which he or she can willfully and effectively control his or her life situations.[31] A person who scores high on the locus of control scale is demonstrating a strong belief in individual efficacy. Such persons assume greater responsibility for the positive and negative consequences of their actions. Those who score low on this scale tend to believe that their life consequences are largely under the control of external forces. The locus of control scale has been further subdivided into three subscores which detail specific differences according to belief in control by self, chance, and powerful others.[32] In nonclinical populations, Indian people who score low in locus of control generally exhibit a strong tendency to indicate (perhaps accurately) control by powerful others.[33] The importance of this research to treatment lies in the idea that, if the source of control or its locus is specified and relevant characteristics are understood, treatment intervention at the appropriate psycho/social-cultural level can be implemented. In essence, if the previous notion of "hostile environment" is to hold up under rigors of research, one would expect that Indian people living on reservations who have the support of their cultural group would sense more control of their life situation and thus be less prone to alcoholism. Likewise, those Indian people living off reservations and/or without the support of their cultural group would have a locus of control that is more externally oriented.

While research on this topic is only in its initial stages, a pattern has begun to emerge. Hurlburt, Gade, and Fuqua have noted, "Caucasian alcoholics . . . apparently still perceive themselves as having more potential for self control than Native American subjects."[34] However, it should be noted that the subjects for this study were patients in detoxification programs and, as such, it is understandable that Indians felt less of a potential for self-determination than their Caucasian counterparts. Alternatively, Harris and Phelan have found that, when minority support groups do exist, there is less of a tendency toward externality.[35] Whitley, in studying this phenomenon among Indian people, found some basis for extension of Harris and Phelan's conclusions. Specifically Whitley found that Indian "subjects living on the reservation scored more internally than subjects living outside the reservation."[36] However, American Indians living on the reservation may be more apt to be heavy drinkers than those living outside the reservation. While the two groups have a similar percentage of heavy drinkers, those who live outside the reservation are subject to more stress from other sources than those living on the reservation . . . [37] Although this finding by Whitley may seem contradictory, a plausible explanation can be offered. Even though Indians living on reservations may have higher internality or control scores, they are still likely to drink due to stress from external fragmentation of their aboriginal cultural groups on the reservation as well as stress from sources that exist within the social structure of tribal groups.

## PROPOSED TREATMENT STRATEGIES

Given the current state of research into treatment on Indian alcoholism, a general schema of specific treatment interventions may now be suggested at this point. Essentially, these methods are suggested for immediate implementation into an alcoholic situation, however, the ecological context of each case must be carefully assessed. The first task in any course of treatment should be the development of the relationship. In this regard, client-centered therapy with its emphasis on unconditional positive regard, empathy, and trust is an excellent method to utilize in the early development of a relationship with the Indian alcoholic.[38] Once a relationship is developed, a period of consciousness-raising should ensue. This phase should be engaged in by the Indian alcoholic and facilitated by the social worker to ascertain the level of internal and external control sensed by the alcoholic. Formation of reality as perceived by the Indian alcoholic is a critical consideration during this period, and these perceptions along with their ensuing behavioral manifestations later serve as the base for cognitive/behavioral interventions in the Indian alcoholic's immediate social environment.

Once the perceptual cognitions of the Indian alcoholic are ascertained, both rational-emotive therapy[39] and reality therapy[40] are important methods in helping the Indian alcoholic confront the basic objective reality of his or her situation and begin to move away from the self-defeating ideas that have created an alcoholic "state of mind." Rational emotive therapy is especially effective in counteracting the basic irrational ideas and absolutist thinking that make many Indian alcoholics feel helpless in combatting their own alcoholism. Likewise, reality therapy with its heavy emphasis on responsibility and the need to develop plans in light of present behavior is an important approach in changing the Indian alcoholic from a reactive individual to a proactive individual who has a sense of direction.

Although rational emotive and reality therapies are excellent mechanisms for changing cognitions and perceptions, it is also important to help the Indian alcoholic develop new "non-alcoholic" behaviors. In this case contingency contracting, social skills training, systematic desensitization with progressive relaxation, and covert sensitization are important adjuncts to therapy. Essentially, contingency contracting can extend the plans made through reality therapy by setting up a schedule of reinforcement for movement toward desired changes. Behavioral rehearsal through systematic desensitization can allow the Indian alcoholic to extend and visualize the "rational self-talk" learned through rational emotive therapy in a state of induced relaxation. Covert sensitization through the inducement of noxious states could also be introduced during a period of relaxation. Social skills training could be extended to the Indian alcoholic in relation to his or her most immediate social context including the familial, vocational, educational, and economic. The extension of training into these important contexts involves a wholistic or ecological perspective that is consistent with a social work emphasis on the significance of the client's environment in all problems.

Finally, while there is still a great need for further inquiry into treatment intervention in relation to Indian alcoholism, some important beginnings have been made. Intrinsically, it would seem that programs run by the Indian people themselves can meet with a greater level of success than such programs run by non-Indian counterparts. Also, sociocultural stress seems to be a critical dimension that must be dealt with in any effective treatment regimen. In this regard, the locus of control research is important in assessing the level of internality or externality experienced by the alcoholic. Once stressors are identified, effective treatment can then be implemented on both the individual and ecological level with emphasis directed toward the appropriate level of intervention. However, perhaps the single most important principle in the treatment of individual alcoholism is the necessity to approach the problem from a comprehensive viewpoint that emphasizes multiple treatment regimens rather than reliance on any single method. This principle is suggested because the methods available may not always be the methods of choice. Caution and care must also be given to the ecological concerns of the problem as noted previously.

## TOWARD A SOCIAL WORK PERSPECTIVE
## ON INDIAN ALCOHOLISM

Social work in its finest tradition has always placed an important emphasis on the ecological dynamics that affect individual social functioning. In the case of alcoholism among Indian people, these dynamics seem to be of even greater importance because of the diversity that exists among both acculturated Indians and Indian people who maintain the heritage of their own aboriginal cultural groupings. Thus, in developing a social work perspective for working with alcoholism among Indian people, it is critical to bring forth two dimensions. First, intervention guidelines must be developed so that immediate help can be given to individuals suffering from alcoholism. Secondly, and interwoven with the initial intervention, an ecological perspective must be developed that stresses the sociocultural identity of Indian people and supports Indians in developing their own solutions to Indian alcoholism.

In rendering immediate help to the Indian alcoholic it is critical to establish a working relationship. Undergirding this relationship building phase should be the humanitarian tenents that guide all effective practice: a sense of commitment, concern, warmth, caring sensitivity, and acceptance of differences. Beyond the relationship building stage, it is necessary for social workers to implement comprehensive strategies of change that ultimately impact both the Indian alcoholic and his or her immediate situation. The research on locus of control and sociocultural stress have already been emphasized as a critical knowledge base for these interventions. Additionally, client-centered therapy, rational-emotive therapy, reality therapy, and behavior modification have all been suggested as immediate methods for combatting the problem. However, while all of these approaches can bring some degree of immediate help to the Indian alcoholic, a long-range approach to the problem would emphasize the ownership of the problem by Indian people themselves. To not emphasize Indian control of the problem would simply add to the sociocultural stress that already exists in relation to the problem. In developing this move toward cultural diversity, David and Dobrec[41] have pointed out that there are specific Indian value and belief systems that lead to culturally-related behaviors that are in direct opposition to non-Indian concepts. They note the following differences:

| *Indian* | *Non-Indian* |
|---|---|
| Accumulation of private property is not a cornerstone of Indian social organization. | Material gains and ownership of private property are stressed. |
| Communal sharing of tribal property is emphasized. | Private enterprise is paramount. |
| Silence and generosity are the mark of a highly respected person. | Power, wealth, and status are benchmarks of success. |
| Horizontal power structure in tribal work and community is stressed. | Vertical power structure in corporate structures and community is stressed. |

| | |
|---|---|
| Noncompetitive social structures are emphasized. | Competitive social structures are emphasized. |
| Thoughts and values originate within the framework of tribal consciousness. | Thoughts and values originate within the framework of individualistic society. |
| Community action is based on tribal consciousness. | Community action is based on desires of power blocks. |
| Extended families define the roles and responsibilities of members with child care shared by all. | Nuclear family concept defines roles and responsibilities of parents; child care shared by parents with non-interference of other family members. |
| Work is necessary to make a living; do what is needed, but leave time for life. | Work is performed to make money and gain status. |

In developing practitioners who would facilitate movement toward Indian ownership of the problem, Walker has noted the characteristics that would be intrinsic for a worker in this role. "It is essential that the therapist be sensitive to the different culture-specific, ethical ideologic and semantic systems operant . . . These systems give a different world view and outlook on life from tribe to tribe."[42] While it is most important to recognize the need to move toward Indian control of Indian alcoholism, it must also be noted that the profession still has not fully developed the technology needed to effectively deal with this aspect of the problem. There seems to be a rather large opportunity in this area for the social work education system to fill these most important gaps. Finally, we may conclude by noting that even though the problem of Indian alcoholism is a complex one, it is amenable to social work interventions. Immediate help to Indian alcoholics can be rendered and movement can be made toward Indian control of the problem.

## REFERENCES

1. The phrase "Indian people" is used as the preferred title for Native Americans and American Indians and was selected from the official statement of Indians of all Tribes, Alcatraz Island, December 16, 1969.
2. A review of *Social Work Research and Abstracts* for the period of 1979–84

revealed the following four articles dealing with the subject. Stephens, R. C. and Agar, M. H.: Red-tape-white tape federal Indian funding relations. *Human Organization*, *38*:283–293, 1979; French, L. A. and Hornbuckle, J.: Alcoholism among native Americans: An analysis. *Social Work*, *25*:275–280, 1980; Westermeyer, J., Walker, D. and Benton, E.: A review of some methods for investigating substance abuse epidemiology among American Indians and Alaska natives. *White Cloud Journal*, *2*:13–21, 1981; Burns, T. R.: A survey of attitudes toward alcoholics and alcohol programs among Indian health service personnel. *White Cloud Journal*, *2*:25–30, 1981.

3. French and Hornbuckle, op. cit., p. 275.
4. Indian Health Service, Inpatient Care Branch, Office of Program Statistics. *Alcohol Related Discharges from Indian Health Service and Contract General Hospitals:* Fiscal Year 1979. Rockville, Md.
5. Oetting, E. R., Edwards, Ruth, Goldstein, G. S., and Garcia-Mason, Velma. Drug use among adolescents of five Southwestern native American Tribes. *International Journal of Addictions*, *15*:439–445, 1980.
6. May, Phillip A.: Substance abuse and American Indians: Prevalence and susceptibility. *International Journal of Addictions*, *17*:1185–1209, 1982.
7. Ibid, P. 1189.
8. Hamer, John and Steinbring, Jack: *Alcohol and Native Peoples of the North.* Lanham, Md., University Press, 1980, p. 1.
9. Kunkel, Dale, Dobrec, Antonia, and Wedel, Kenneth: American Indians and mental health. Unpublished paper, University of Oklahoma, School of Social Work, Norman, Ok., 1984, p. 3.
10. Wanberg, Kenneth, Lewis, Ron and Foster, F. Frank: Alcoholism and ethnicity: A comparative study of alcohol use patterns across ethnic group. *International Journal of Addictions*, *13*:1245–1262, 1978.
11. French and Hornbuckle, op. cit., pp. 277–280.
12. Resnick, H. L. and Dismang, L. H.: Observations of suicidal behavior among American Indians. *American Journal of Psychiatry*, *127*:882–887, 1971.
13. Whitaker, James O.: Alcohol and the Standing Rock Sioux Tribe: A twenty year follow-up study. *Journal of Studies on Alcohol*, *43*:191–200, 1982.
14. Ibid., pp. 197–198.
15. Levy, Jerrold E. and Kunitz, Stephen J. Economic and political factors inhibiting the use of basic research findings in Indian alcoholism programs. *Journal of Studies on Alcohol*, Supplement No. 9, pp. 60–72, 1981.
16. Coleman, James C.: *Abnormal Psychology and Modern Life*, 5th Ed. Geneview, Il., Scott, Foresman and Company, pp. 428–429.
17. Merton, Robert K.: *Social Theory and Social Structure*. Glencoe, Il. Free Press, 1957, pp. 421–423.
18. Swigert, V. L. and Farrell, R. A.: *The Substance of Social Deviance*. Sherman Oaks, Ca., Alfred Publishing Co., 1979, pp. 349–350.
19. Stewart, O.: Questions regarding American Indian criminality. *Human Organization*, *1*:61–66, 1964.

20. French and Hornbuckle, op. cit., p. 275.
21. Hall, Patricia D.: American Indian alcoholism: What is not being done? *The IHS Primary Care Provider,* 9:1–5, 1984.
22. Walker, R. Dale: Treatment strategies in an urban Indian alcoholism program. *Journal of Studies on Alcohol,* Supplement No. 9, pp. 171–184, 1981.
23. Levy and Kunitz, op. cit., pp. 66–67.
24. Price, John A.: An applied analysis of North American Indian drinking patterns. *Human Organization,* 34:17–26, 1975.
25. Jolly, Eric, Reardon, R. and McKinney, K. D.: *Cognitive Style and Belief in the Paranormal.* New Orleans, Southeastern Psychological Association, 1982.
26. Hall, op. cit., p. 4.
27. Willoughby, A.: Effectiveness of the ATP Model in Project Good Hope. Personal Communication to Jolly, 1984.
28. Willoughby, A.: *The Alcohol Troubled Person.* Chicago, Il., Nelson-Hall, 1979.
29. Locklear, Herbert H.: American Indian alcoholism: Program for treatment. *Social Work,* pp. 202–207, May, 1977.
30. Walker, op. cit., pp. 171–184.
31. Rotter, J. B.: Generalized expectancies for internal versus external control of reinforcement. *Psychological Monographs, 80,* 1966.
32. Lefcourt, H. M.: *Locus of Control: Current Trends in Theory and Research.* Glencoe, Il., Free Press, 1980.
33. Jolly, Eric and Reardon, R.: *Correlates of Locus of Control,* Unpublished paper, 1984.
34. Hurlburt, Graham, Gade, Eldon, and Fuqua, Dale: Sex and race as factors on locus of control scores with an alcoholic population. *Psychological Reports,* 52:517–518, 1983.
35. Harris, H. F. and Phelan, J. G.: Beliefs in internal-external control of reinforcement among Blacks in integrated and segregated high schools. *Psychological Reports, 32:*40–42, 1973.
36. Whitley, Gary P.: Reservation versus non-reservation American Indians' loci of control and consumption of alcohol. *Psychological Reports,* 46:431–434, 1980.
37. Ibid., p. 443.
38. Rogers, Carl: *Client Centered Therapy.* Boston, Ma., Houghton-Mifflin, 1951.
39. Ellis, Albert: *Reason and Emotion in Psychotherapy.* New York, Lyle Stuart, 1962.
40. Glasser, William: *Reality Therapy.* New York, Harper and Row, 1965.
41. David, Jay: *The American Indian: The First Victim.* New York, William Morrow and Company, 1972; and Dobrec, Antonia: *Indian Child Welfare.* Norman, Ok., The University of Oklahoma, School of Social Work, p. IV-1 to IV-13, 1983.
42. Walker, op. cit., pp. 183–184.

*Chapter Fifteen*

# ALCOHOL USE AND ABUSE
# AMONG MEXICAN AMERICANS

RUTH G. MCROY, CLAYTON T. SHORKEY AND EUNICE GARCIA

Mexican Americans constitute the largest percentage of Hispanics in the United States. The Hispanic population also includes the following: Puerto Rican islanders, mainland Puerto Ricans, Cubans, and the more recent immigrant groups from Cuba, Venezuela, Argentina, El Salvador, Nicaragua, Guatemala, Honduras, and other countries in Central and South America. By early 1983, the Bureau of the Census reported an estimated 15.9 million Hispanics in the country including 9 million of Mexican origin and 6.9 million of "other Spanish origin."[1]

The 1979 National Survey of Alcohol Use and Alcohol Problems among adults in the U.S. revealed that Hispanics, when compared with blacks and Anglos, have the highest proportion of heavy drinkers and alcohol-related problems. For Hispanic males the incidence of drinking with loss of control or dependence was over twice as high as that for blacks and whites.[2] Although incidence data related to specific Hispanic groups is very limited, an examination of the prevalence of alcohol related problems among Hispanics revealed that the Mexican American population has higher death rates from cirrhosis of the liver and are arrested for alcohol-related offenses at a higher rate than other groups in the general population.[3]

Alcohol problems are significantly impacting on many Mexican-American families in destructive ways. Not only do Mexican-American men continue to drink at higher rates than other population groups, but drinking problems are increasing among

Mexican-American women who are becoming more acculturated. Moreover, alcohol is now disrupting the adaptive developmental process for many Mexican-American youths.

The purpose of this chapter is to examine the factors contributing to the higher overall rate of alcohol use and abuse in the Mexican-American community and to explore cultural factors which are of significance in developing culturally relevant prevention, outreach and treatment programs in the Mexican-American community. Practice issues related to the role of social workers who help Mexican-American clients resolve alcohol problems will also be discussed.

### FACTORS ASSOCIATED WITH ALCOHOL USE AND ABUSE

Research on the etiology of the high rate of alcoholism among Mexican Americans reveals a number of interrelated possible causes. Minority group status, physiological tolerance, cultural factors, and acculturation stress are among the variables which have been identified as being important in alcoholism and alcohol abuse among Mexican Americans.

Several authors have speculated that the Mexican-American population may have a greater physiological tolerance for alcohol than other groups, but no definitive studies have been conducted. However, research on alcohol metabolism, anatomical makeup, acetaldehyde accumulation, and enzyme systems is needed to ascertain if differences in alcohol response do exist among different populations.[4]

Belonging to a minority group which has experienced varying degrees of discrimination, prejudice, and low social status can create emotional stress and anxiety. This may lead to higher incidences of alcohol use among a large percent of Mexican Americans. Stress associated with acculturation is the most frequently cited factor in the literature as contributing to high rates of alcoholism.

Based on the "acculturation stress theory" of alcoholism, Madsen noted that the highest rate of alcoholism was found among Mexican Americans who had abandoned their native culture but had not yet found acceptance by the dominant culture. Similarly, Graves found that Mexican Americans who had the highest rates of problem drinking had adopted the Anglo culture but had not yet attained assimilation and economic success.[5] Even those who were assimilated into the Anglo culture experienced higher rates of alcohol abuse and associated problems if they were also having economic problems.

Alcohol problems are most severe among children of Mexican-American immigrants who lack the Mexican cultural identity. First generation children of immigrants have to cope with the lack of sensitivity of enculturating institutions and often develop a resentment towards these institutions. They may find themselves trapped in an inescapable cycle of poverty without hope for change in the future.

Alcohol problems also exist among more recent illegal aliens who have migrated from rural areas of Mexico, and/or to Mexican border towns, prior to entering the United States.[6] Some are men who may use alcohol to mitigate the stress associated with the acculturation process and the separation from their families. Once in the United States, the illegal alien is further subjected to a restricted life-style and is often in the company of others in social groups that encourage the use of alcohol. Furthermore, the marginal legal status of these people also affects their access to the community resources designed to address problems of alcohol abuse and other needs.

## MEXICAN-AMERICAN DRINKING PATTERNS

One necessary condition for an individual to become a problem drinker is the existence of cultural norms that permit heavy drinking in social situations at least occasionally.[7] There are often positive sanctions for the use of alcohol in Mexican-American rituals and special events such as weddings, baptisms, patriotic and religious holidays. Also, Mexican-American literature and music often depict alcohol as a mitigating agent which is used by individuals to cope with the harshness of life and its vicissitudes.

The male in the Mexican-American traditional culture is considered the head of the household and the ultimate authority figure. Machismo, the ideal of manliness, is often associated with the ability to drink and to hold one's liquor frequently and in quantity. However, negative sanctions exist for losing control when drinking. While it is considered macho to drink, dignity, honor, and responsibility are expected to be maintained. Due to these high and often conflictual expectations placed on Mexican-American men, men who show "weakness" in drinking feel humiliated and experience heightened anxiety and stress which often leads to more drinking.[8]

Studies of Mexican-American drinking patterns have found that Mexican-American men are more likely to drink frequently and heavily than are Mexican-American women. According to Paine, the differential drinking patterns of Mexican-American men and women can be explained in terms of values that exist in the Mexican-American community related to drinking. For example, in a study of 138 families in Mexican-American neighborhoods in Houston, Texas, 72 percent of men drank, compared to 16 percent of women. Seventy-one percent of drinkers drank with friends, 27 percent in the family, and 4 percent alone.[9] Men's drinking has been traditionally sanctioned positively by both men and women, and drinking by women has been viewed negatively. Mexican-American women who drink find rejection and stigmatization and are often victims of physical and/or verbal abuse.

Although the percentage of female Mexican Americans who use/abuse alcohol is low compared to the general population, recent research evidence has also revealed that alcohol use and abuse is increasing among Mexican-American women who are young, heads of households, and who are having to cope with less lucrative vocational options, cultural conflicts, and problems associated with single parenthood. The incidence of drinking and alcohol problems is also higher among more acculturated Mexican-American women who have completed high school or have finished some college, especially among women in professional fields.[10]

Although there is a greater percentage of alcohol problems among Mexican-American men compared with whites and blacks, recent statistics reveal that the percentage of Mexican-American youth who drink or are classified as problem drinkers is about the same as the national average for other groups. The research data available on drinking patterns of Mexican-American youth indicate the following: (1) Mexican-American youth begin using alcohol at an earlier age than their white counterparts, but by the age of eighteen are generally surpassed by Anglo youth; (2) Frequent users are generally males from all socioeconomic backgrounds who seem to mistrust family, school, and religious institutions; (3) Higher alcohol use by Mexican-American youth is associated with lower grades and higher rates of dropping out of school; (4) Higher incidences of alcohol use by Mexican-American youth are associated with use of alcohol or a positive view of alcohol by the father; (5) Mexican-American youths often use alcohol as a means of becoming an adult, whereas Anglo youths generally use alcohol for celebrating or as a means of having fun; and (6) Male Mexican-American youths, as well as adults, are more likely to drink in the presence of male peers, whereas Anglos are more likely to drink with male and female peers; and (7) Recent studies indicate that the use of alcohol by Mexican-American youth is increasing while the use of soft drugs is decreasing.[11]

## CULTURAL FACTORS

Attention has been given, if only briefly, to the historical and socioeconomic context of Mexican Americans as it impacts on rates and identified patterns of alcohol abuse. However, consideration of in-group cultural variants is also essential for understanding individual differences in beliefs, attitudes, values, and customs related to the use and abuse of alcohol.

As a whole, Mexican Americans range from the more traditional Mexican culture-oriented to the more acculturated dominant culture-oriented individuals and families. Thus, by placing these variations within a continuum, it is possible to identify traditional Mexican Americans, bicultural Mexican Americans, and the more acculturated Americans of Mexican origin.

Traditional Mexican Americans are more oriented to the culture of Mexico. They are included in the group of 11 million Hispanics who speak Spanish in the home. Gomez and Becker stress the significance of the bilingual characteristic among Mexican Americans which helps to maintain ethnic authenticity and ensures survival in the dominant society.[12]

Another salient characteristic of the traditional Mexican American family is that the value placed on the family supersedes the importance of its individual members. Thus, contrary to individualism, this value serves to direct the individual's development toward the protection and survival of the family. The compadrazgo system serves principally to extend family ties to nonrelated members of the community who are selected as co-parents (compadres) upon the christening of children. Therefore, the traditional value which makes a family responsible for taking care of its own serves to extend an interdependent network of families throughout the Mexican-American community.

The family is the single most important support network in the Mexican-American culture. Traditional Mexican Americans tend to solve emotional problems within the family and barrio context rather than to expose themselves to Anglo institutional services. Moreover, the Mexican American, feeling a strong sense of identification with the family, often believes that his or her problems are a reflection on the family.[13]

Mexican Catholic tradition is another characteristic linking the majority of Mexican Americans. Among traditional families, this involves a form of Catholicism which developed in the 16th century as a consolidation of the Roman Catholic Church and the native religious belief systems of the conquered Mexicans. It characteristically includes folk culture, as well as church doctrine, and is abundant in rituals for every aspect of life.

Traditional Mexican-American culture may also be considered in terms of its humanitarian philosophy. "Respecto" is valued; it is the requirement that one person respect others and expect the same in return. A related concept, "personalismo," requires a person to shed his or her social and professional status in order to interact with the other party on a person-to-person level. This type of people-oriented world view permeates all interactions, regardless of economic resources or the lack of them.

There are conflicting opinions regarding the role of folk medicine and healing within various Mexican-American subcultures. Researchers have found that in some Mexican American communities in the southwest, the healer occupies a very esteemed position, while others have minimized the role of the curandero.[14] The

1979 President's Commission on Mental Health, Special Populations Subpanel on the Mental Health of Hispanic Americans
reported that up to 75 percent of the Mexican-American clients
have consulted folk healers.[15] While the curandero (healer) may
not exist in every community, the traditional family continues to
have access to hierberos (healers who use herbs), the sobadores
and hueseros (healers who massage sprained muscles and set bones
respectively), parteras (midwives), and the healers who use botanic,
religious, spiritualist and magical tools related to the physical,
social and emotional complaints of their patients. Cuaranderismo
may then be considered as an alternative health system which
offers family and cultural reinforcement in an accessible fashion.

Traditional culture holds to the increasingly controversial value
of "Machismo." Above all, the Mexican-American male is held
responsible for protecting the family against all real and alleged
dangers. As an attitudinal and behavioral pattern expressing an
individual as well as a social value, machismo is characterized by
aggressive and dominant behavior. It requires strength of character, leadership, and a commitment to one's word. While it may
encompass all the other less positive aspects of male domination
and sex discrimination now commonly identified as male chau-
vinism, machismo is meant to provide protection and support of
the family in a hostile environment and to reinforce personal and
gender identity.

Bicultural Mexican Americans hold to many of these traditional value systems. They speak Spanish and simultaneously
embrace the use of English and selected aspects of the dominant
culture in American society. They are, in fact, bilingual and
bicultural in terms of world view and value systems. They vary
greatly, however, within the continuum of acculturation and cultural identity.[16]

In turn, the acculturated families of Mexican origin are farthest
from the traditional Mexican culture but may hold some of the
traditional values and customs while they direct most of their
world view toward the dominant culture. While many more acculturated families of Mexican origin may be strong family units,
family members exist as more of a support system for individual
development rather than for the survival and development of the

family. As with the bicultural individuals and families, many variations occur within acculturated families.

## PREVENTION, TREATMENT, AND OUTREACH PROGRAMS

Studies have shown that the most effective alcohol treatment programs for Mexican Americans are implemented by staff who are bilingual and are trained to resolve problems within the family context, including cultural assessments and culturally individualized treatment plans. More specifically, such programs should involve the family, reinforce the Mexican American cultural value system, and use the machismo ideal in a way that is non-threatening to the client's self-image.

Cuellar, Harris and Jasso have developed an acculturation scale for Mexican Americans which can be particularly useful in the assessment process in alcohol treatment centers. The 20-item scale can be administered in English, Spanish, or both languages, and it differentiates five distinct types of Mexican Americans ranging from very Mexican to very Anglicized. Derived from a 126-item questionnaire developed at Casa Del Sol, a culturally-relevant alcoholism treatment program for Mexican Americans in San Antonio, Texas, this scale includes such questions as: "What language do you speak? What language do you prefer? How do you identify yourself? Which ethnic identification does your mother use? (your father?). What contact have you had with Mexico? Can you write in English? (in Spanish?) Which do you do better? How would you rate yourself (from very Mexican to very Anglicized?)" These questions, scored on a five-point Likert scale, have been found to be very reliable indicators of the degree of acculturation.[17]

Using this type of assessment of the individual client in the context of the family, it is possible for workers to design interventive strategies which are culture-specific. For example, Sanchez and Atkinson found that Mexican-American college students who expressed a strong commitment to the Mexican-American culture expressed the strongest preference for an ethnically-similar counselor and were the least open to self disclosure.[18] The desire for personalismo may explain this preference for an ethnically-similar counselor. Personalismo refers to relationships of a close nature which are characterized by trust, confidence, and a blending of similar personalities.

Similarly, "carnal" is used to describe a brother, sister, or close friend whom one can trust and respect. Carnalismo or personalismo is a high priority among many Mexican Americans and sometimes is rated higher than demonstrated competency in the alcoholism counseling field. Bilingual and bicultural Mexican-American counselors, trainers, paraprofessionals, and support givers are essential in an effective alcoholism treatment program designed for Mexican-American clients.

Successful alcohol treatment programs should be designed to include a strong community outreach component and close community involvement. On a national level, organizations such as the National Spanish Speaking Commission on Alcoholism (NSSCA) and the Mexican American Commission on Alcohol and Drug Abuse (MCADA) were organized to develop outreach guidelines and criteria for cultural-specific treatment programs.[19] "La Comunidad," the desire for a strong sense of a community, is a highly valued concept within the Mexican-American culture. Through outreach efforts the negative stigma attached to alcoholism may be overcome. Community picnics and parties to help educate youth about the problems of alcohol abuse along with the development of referral services in the community have been found to be effective means to reach the community and to make treatment and prevention of alcoholism more effective. Attempts to involve the community should also include the church and other religious groups. Many clergy are willing to help individuals with alcohol problems. As members of the clergy are often viewed with respect and trust by the community, they can help educate the community about the nature of problems associated with alcohol abuse and support the use of the services available in the community by clients in earlier stages of alcoholism.[20]

A cultural strategy that has been used successfully in treating alcoholic clients that allows them to maintain respect and status in the community is the making of a manda. By telling others they have a manda (a promise to a saint or God), alcohol abusers can justify their decision to refrain from drinking and thus resist pressure from social circles to continue drinking. In such a context, services can be provided to assist the individuals in keeping their promise.

Alcohol treatment and prevention programs in the occupational context must not be overlooked. Since the critical period in the development of alcoholism often is early in life, detection and treatment at this stage are essential. Occupational alcoholism programs can be effective in identifying and providing opportunities for treatment before the individual loses his job due to continued alcohol abuse. At this time specialized employee programs for Mexican Americans are very rare.[21]

## IMPLICATIONS FOR SOCIAL WORK PRACTICE

The preceding discussion of cultural issues in development of alcohol treatment and prevention programs for Mexican Americans has identified several principles which social workers, alcoholism counselors, and other professionals who are working with alcoholics and their families should incorporate in their treatment strategies. Among these are:

1. Consider carefully demographic characteristics such as age, marital status, religion, educational level, life-style strivings, medical sophistication, etc., in any assessment of a Mexican-American client.
2. Be aware of the client's cultural traditions and language preference. It is important to assess the level of acculturation.
3. Assess the role folk medicine plays in the lives of the clients and their families and consider the integration of folk practices and conventional treatment procedures.
4. Gain an understanding of the concept of "machismo" and utilize it in a way that does not threaten the individual's self-image and self-esteem.
5. Cultural sensitivity and flexibility are essential in working with Mexican-American clients and their families with alcohol problems. Operationalize the values of personalismo, carnalismo, and respeto in practice.
6. Encourage the expression of feelings in individual interviews and use group techniques such as art and drama in

assessment of problems that may exist in the home.

7. Assess the role of the compadrazgo system in the family and when necessary engage key members in the treatment plan.
8. Increase awareness of the institutional barriers and familial factors which have resulted in underutilization of services by Mexican Americans. Design programs which are responsive to these issues.
9. Develop community outreach efforts which serve to establish credibility and relevance of alcoholism treatment programs to Mexican-American communities.
10. Finally, social work practitioners must be aware that many persons with alcohol problems experience feelings of depression, hopelessness, personal deficiency, and a sense of meaninglessness in life. Alcohol often is used as an escape. Interventive programs must address this basic existential need for security, belongingness and enthusiasm for life.

### CONCLUSIONS

Although Mexican Americans today have the highest rates of alcoholism of any population group, alcoholism services have not been sufficiently targeted to address the problem. Further, only limited evaluative research is available on the components of effective culture-specific programs. The moral weakness model of alcoholism attributes drinking to sin. The disease or medical model of alcoholism assigns responsibility totally to problems within the individual and fails to consider the contextual factors which may influence drinking patterns.

Use of alcohol is a part of the social role of Mexican Americans. Therefore, programs committed to treatment and prevention of alcohol abuse must acknowledge the role that the community and broader society play in their drinking patterns. Recently, Mansell Pattison developed a public health model of alcoholism which identifies a broader range of behavioral factors and reformulates alcoholism and alcohol abuse as a general population problem and emphasizes situational and cultural variables as well as problems within the individual.[22] This model provides a broader framework for developing programs targeted at different cultural groups.

More research is needed to develop this and other models for application to Mexican-American treatment programs.

## REFERENCES

1. Bureau of the Census, Condition of Hispanics in America today. Washington, D.C., September 13, 1983, 1–13.
2. Caste, Carlos A.: Alcoholism among Hispanics. In *Proceedings of the National Hispanic Conference on Alcoholism*, September 7–10, San Antonio, Texas, Department of Health and Human Services Publication No. (ADM) 81-1130, 1981.
3. Garcia, Louis S.: Alcohol related problems and the Hispanic. *Agenda*, 7:21–23, 1977.
4. Alcocer, Anthony M.: Alcohol use and abuse among the Hispanic American population. In *Alcohol and Health Monograph 4: Special Population Issues*. Rockville, Md., National Institute on Alcohol Abuse and Alcoholism, 1982, pp. 361–382.
5. Madsen, William: The alcoholic agringado. *American Anthropologist*, 66:355–361, 1964; and Graves, Theodore, D.: Acculturation, access and alcohol in a tri-ethnic community. *American Anthropology*, 69:306–321, 1967.
6. Chavez, Leo R.: Mexican immigration and health care utilization: The case of San Diego. A lecture presented at the University of Texas at Austin, Texas, May 1, 1984.
7. Paine, Herbert: Attitudes and patterns of alcohol use among Mexican Americans. *Journal of Studies on Alcohol*, 38:544–553, 1977.
8. Johnson, L. and Matre, M.: Anomie and alcohol use: Drinking patterns in Mexican American and anglo neighborhoods. *Journal of Studies on Alcohol*, 39:894–902, 1978.
9. Paine, op. cit.
10. Zavaleta, Anthony: Drinking patterns of low-income Mexican American women. *Journal of Studies on Alcohol*, 40:480–484, 1979; and Reyes, Martha: Consulta familiar: Alcoholism treatment for women with dependent children. In Andrew, Sylvia Rodriquez and Hall, Phillip A. (Eds.): *Alcoholism: Culture and Family*. San Antonio, Worden School of Social Service, Our Lady of the Lake University, 1980, pp. 18–24.
11. Bruno, J. and Doscher, L.: Patterns of drug use among Mexican-American potential school dropouts. *Journal of Drug Education*, 9:1–10, 1979; Dominquez, Eleanor: Alcohol and youth. *La Luz*, 4:34, 1975; and Estrada, Antonio, Rabov, Jerome, and Watts, Ronald K.: Alcohol use among Hispanic adolescents: A preliminary report. *Hispanic Journal of Behavioral Sciences*, 4:339–351, 1982.
12. Gomez, Ernesto and Becker, Roy: *Mexican American Language and Culture: Implications for Helping Professionals: Part I*. San Antonio, Worden School of Social Service, Our Lady of the Lake University, 1979.
13. Ibid.

14. Kiev, Ari: *Curanderismo: Mexican-American Folk Psychiatry.* New York, The Free Press, 1968; and Wecleu, Robert V.: The nature, prevalence, and level of awareness of "curanderismo" and some of its implications for community mental health. *Community Mental Health Journal, 11*:145–154, 1975.

15. Caste, op. cit.

16. Garcia, Eunice: La familia, cultural diversity and its implications for social work practice. Austin, Texas, Audio Visual Resource Center School of Social Work, The University of Texas at Austin, 1978, Color Videotape, 60 minutes.

17. Jasso, Ricardo: An acculturation scale for Mexican American normal and clinical populations. *Hispanic Journal of Behavioral Sciences, 2*:199–217, 1980.

18. Sanchez, Arthur and Atkinson, Donald: Mexican American cultural commitment, preference after counselor ethnicity, and willingness to use counseling. *Journal on Counseling Psychology, 30*:215–220, 1983.

19. Alcocer, op. cit.

20. Harrison, John: The church and alcoholism: A growing involvement. *Alcohol Health and Research World, 1*:2–10, 1977.

21. Fidelia, Masi: Occupational alcoholism: An area of action for Hispanics. In Szapacnik, Jose (Ed.): *Mental Health, Drug and Alcohol Abuse: An Hispanic Assessment of Present and Future Challenges.* Washington, D.C., National Coalition of Hispanic Mental Health and Human Service Organizations, 1979, pp. 71–82.

22. Pattison, E. Mansell: Cultural level interventions in the arena of alcoholism. *Alcoholism: Clinical and Experimental Research, 8*:160–164, 1984.

## Chapter Sixteen

# THE PROBABILITY OF RELAPSE
# AMONG POOR ALCOHOLICS

E. Thomas Copeland, Jr.

Relapse among poor alcoholics is a complex issue due to the lack of valid and reliable research data and clinical findings from primary care providers for these clients. Associated with this phenomenon is the prominent belief that low socioeconomic status in clients results in poorer treatment effects and higher relapse rates than are found in the general population. The purpose of this chapter is to explore issues related to relapse in poor alcoholics and variables which coalesce and complicate the recovery process in these individuals.

## CHARACTERISTICS OF THE POOR

Poor or low socioeconomic status clients include largely minorities—blacks, Hispanics, native Americans, Asian Americans, poor whites, and others. The number of poor Americans encompasses roughly 14 percent of the total population. Figures available from the 1979 Census indicate that 30 percent of black Americans, 24% of Hispanics, 14% of Asian Americans and 9% of white Americans reported incomes below the poverty level for that year.[1]

The poor are typically different in their life-styles, have diverse cultural backgrounds, have few or virtually no economic resources, and usually have little hope for long-term employment as compared to white middle-class clients. They are usually limited in formal education and may have different or unclear family relationship patterns.

242

It has been noted that amount of education and size of income are directly related. Some four million poor families are headed by individuals who have eight or less years of education. Sixty-one percent of breadwinners in poor families did not go beyond the eighth grade. Poverty is also common to the aged. One-third of all poor families are headed by a person 65 years old or older. Poverty also is very common in agricultural areas; about one-fourth of all farmers are poor. Poverty can be found in families headed by women. As a result of divorce or death of the husband, these families are apt to be very poor. About one-half of all families headed by women are poor.[2]

## PREVELANCE OF ALCOHOLISM

Alcoholism is a major health problem that affects an estimated 9 to 13 million Americans.[3] This fact is compounded by a number of indirect manifestations in terms of the impact alcoholism has on other individuals who may come into contact with the alcoholic. An additional 45 million persons may be included in this group. Despite the vastness of the problem, the percent of those receiving treatment for alcohol dependence is relatively low. Brandsma, Maultsby, and Welsh estimate that less than 10 percent of those who are dependent on alcohol receive any formal treatment.[4]

Many studies find that majority of problem drinkers are poor, but the proportion of those who drink is greater within higher socioeconomic status groups.[5] Alcohol, however, is more likely to constitute a threat to the poor because they are more easily affected in a negative way by external stresses.

## STEREOTYPES AND DEFINITIONS RELATED TO ALCOHOLISM

When a person is labeled an alcoholic, a host of stereotypic images and/or value assumptions are engendered. Some people have the stereotyped image of an alcoholic as a skid-row derelict or "bowery bum" sleeping on the sidewalk with a bottle of wine in his hand. Although this person is probably alcoholic, skid-row alcoholics constitute only about 3 to 5 percent of alcoholics in the

United States.[6] Overall, most alcoholics are undistinguishable from other persons with problems in that they are likely to be encountered when their drinking is not apparent to others or when they are in a sober state.[7]

Alcohol addiction, alcohol habituation, alcohol dependence, alcohol misuse, or problematic alcohol usage are all terms that have been used at one point in time to describe alcoholics. The use, misuse, abuse, and dependence on alcohol represent an accepted continuum from responsible use to problem drinking to addiction. This consensus has not led to the construction of an adequate definition of the disease or diagnostic procedures. The conflicts about the definition and the diagnosis of alcoholism have resulted from the impact of various social, political, legal, and medical goals. Each of these goals involve a different definition of alcoholism.

For the poor, a definition which is more comprehensive and addresses the physiological, emotional, behavioral, and cultural interactional factors seems more appropriate. For example, Bell and Evans defined alcoholism as: "A primary, progressive, pathological love/trust relationship with a mood-changing chemical, alcohol. The chemical is used at the repeated expense of a person's values and goals. It can be diagnosed, treated and prevented most successfully when taking into account the cultural context in which the alcohol abuse developed."[8]

Regardless of how alcoholism is defined, it is encountered at every socioeconomic level in every type of person.

## EFFECTS OF SOCIAL CLASS ON TREATMENT

There are some issues related to treatment effectiveness that are associated with being poor. For example, there are stereotypes about clients related to their socioeconomic status that can put poor clients at a disadvantage. Alcohol treatment programs are most often geared to the upper and middle-class clients.[9] These clients usually present with resource-positive environments. It is usually easy for treatment providers to relate to them, understand their presenting problems, and develop traditional plans utilizing client resources such as money, employment, or marketable skills. They are also likely to have the support of family members. For these clients, successful treatment and lower relapse rates are usually assumed, despite the complexities involved in the recovery process for all alcoholic clients.

Compared to upper and middle-class clients, poor clients differ in life orientation, which is assumed to interfere with effective alcohol treatment. On the whole, they tend to be less preoccupied with how they relate to life on an abstract level. They live on such limited economic resources that stresses are likely to produce major crises. They tend to be unskilled, have irregular employment patterns, have less formal education, and some show more family instability. For these clients, unsuccessful treatment and higher relapse rates are usually assumed.

The same biases which negatively affect the availability of general health care to the poor affect their access to alcoholism treatment. When social class, area of residence, and ethnic differences co-exist as they do with poverty, the overall picture for recovery looks bleak.[10] The number of poor alcoholics admitted to treatment-based on epidemiological data is extremely low. Once the poor are engaged in treatment, the effects for some of them are similar to those of higher socioeconomic groups, but the consequences of limited access are severe. Poor alcoholics are more likely to go to jail, prison, or remain actively drinking in their communities than to be engaged in and remain in treatment successfully.

However, according to much of the research data, no significant differences seem to exist between middle and upper-class alcoholics and poor alcoholics in terms of their relapse rates.[11] Nevertheless, the factors that affect those relapse rates may be different for poor clients compared to others. Thus, social class variants are at least as important as physiological and psychological variants when one tries to understand relapse in poor alcoholics. What seems to be a clinical consensus is that unstable clients have lower remission rates and higher relapse rates, regardless of their social class.[12]

Based on this concensus, there are concerns about treatment effectiveness with alcoholics in general that are also relevant to treatment with poor alcoholics. For example, the rate of improvement for treatment of alcoholism in formal programs has been estimated as high as 70 percent for the general population.[13] This rate indicates a relapse rate of about 30 percent and up. Most outcome data are collected during single observations at 6 and 18-month intervals. Since alcoholism tends to follow a cyclical pattern between stages of drinking, abstinence, and normal drinking these data are viewed with skepticism.

The results of the Rand Report contrast with many of the claims related to effective alcohol treatment.[14] Their findings indicate about 7 percent of alcohol-dependent clients in their sample were abstinent throughout a four-and-one-half-year post-treatment evaluation. Similar results were obtained by Miller and Hester in that 26 percent of the clients in their sample remained abstinent or showed improved drinking behavior one year after treatment.[15] Therefore, valid and reliable remission, recovery, and relapse rates are unavailable at the present time.

Successful treatment rates are based on criteria ranging from completing treatment as required as judged by the primary giver to extensive follow up over several years. It is not surprising that published remission rates range from 90 percent to 7 percent.[16] The latter results are probably closer to actual success rates. An analysis of various evaluation outcomes could support the contention that the problem of relapse is related to factors outside of the direct effects of treatment.[17]

## THE ISSUE OF RELAPSE FOR POOR ALCOHOLICS

### Definition

Relapse is one of the most critical issues encountered in the field of alcoholism. The results and overall course of alcohol treatment parallel those encountered in the treatment of any chronic illness or disorder. A relapse essentially involves a slip-back into a former state, especially after an apparent recovery from an illness. Clinical experience indicates that relapse in alcoholism is analogous to the acute-chronic illness differential. An acute disorder suggests a rapid onset and progression of symptoms. The time between physical deterioration and debilitative symptoms is extremely short. The person does not have time to adapt to the symptoms but is acutely aware of his or her loss of functioning.

On the other hand, a chronic disorder such as alcoholism suggests a gradual onset of progressively more severe symptomatology. The time between physical deterioration and debilitating symptoms is long and drawn out. The person has the time to adapt to the symptoms because they unfold in a step-by-step progression. Thus, the person has the opportunity to compensate in an attempt to retain functional ability. Since adaptation and compensation occur over a long period of time, permanent personality, life-style, and social changes are also likely to occur. This process seems quite clear in the remission-recovery process of alcoholism. Some dysfunctional symptoms of alcoholism are elicited or triggered by drinking and others are triggered by abstinence. These permanent dysfunctional symptoms developed over time continue or are initiated during abstinence. Their presence influences whether abstinence can be maintained or whether relapse occurs.

## Drinking Patterns Related to Relapse

There are many variations in drinking patterns exhibited by poor alcoholics as there are by middle and upper-class alcoholics. A number of patterns, however, are somewhat common among those alcoholics who are poor. These patterns can increase the probability of relapse during and after treatment.

The following case vignettes illustrate some of the social influences and patterns which commonly compound relapse in poor alcoholics.

### Case 1

Mr. B. J. was a 39-year-old black male from a large urban city in the Midwest. He lived with his wife and two children in a rented tenement apartment. He was employed and worked in a low-skilled, heavy-labor position which he held for about eight years. He had a regular pattern of excessive drinking on weekends. He was paid on Friday and continued to drink on and off, from that point, until Sunday. On Sunday, he started his sobering process in order to start work on Monday. For B. J., alcohol was a reward for hard work during the week. He did not drink during the week because he usually did not have the money. Although this pattern produced serious stress on his family, it was tolerated. B. J.'s friends exhibited a similar pattern and that was the way most men in his immediate community conducted themselves.

## Case 2

Mr. J. G. was a 35-year-old white male who lived in a small town in the Midwest. He was single but had lived with several women for short periods of time over the years. He worked for 6 years in a fiberglass plant on a swing shift which changed every two weeks. This schedule continued throughout his work at the plant. His pattern consisted of drinking small quantities of alcohol throughout his shift each day. J. G. indicated most of the men in the plant engaged in the same type of drinking behavior. This pattern occurred for several years and did not significantly interfer with his work or alcohol intake. Drinking was considered as the way to cope with the stagnation and harshness of the job. If one did not engage in similar drinking behavior, he was ostracised or scapegoated by the rest of the workers.

## Case 3

Mr. R. S. was a 38-year-old Hispanic male who was married, had five children, and resided in an urban area in the southern part of the Midwest. His employment was irregular, but when he worked, he was engaged in manual labor positions. His pattern consisted of drinking cases of beer with friends, all day long everyday. His friends were in similar circumstances in terms of their employment and family situations. Drinking with his friends was an important part of his socialization and ethnic identity. If he did not drink with his friends, he believed he would be socially isolated in his community.

## Case 4

Mr. G. W. was a 54-year-old white male who was seen for an evaluation subsequent to incarceration for felony criminal damage to property and misdemeanor theft. He returned from California to a midwestern town to visit his ailing father whom he had not seen in several years. He was drinking heavily at the time. Upon entering the town, he went to what he believed was his parent's home. When he did not find anyone at home, he broke the lock and proceeded to take a bath and prepare a meal. To his surprise, he was later arrested because he was in the home of someone else.

Mr. G. W. lived a somewhat nomadic existance for the past three or four years. He took odd jobs and associated with people in similar social situations. He started drinking heavily when he entered the military in 1947. Since his honorable discharge in 1954, he had married four times, had been hospitalized twenty times in alcohol treatment units, and had experienced auditory hallucinations for the past four years. He had periods of abstinence which lasted from four months to two years over the past thirty years. An emotional crisis usually precipitated his relapses.

These four case vignettes describe some of the drinking patterns and other factors that can contribute to relapse in poor alcoholics. Weekend binges, continuous sipping, cultural norms that support heavy drinking in a group, can counteract treatment and compound relapse in poor alcoholics. Although these vignettes represent some typical drinking patterns and implications for treatment with poor alcoholics, they should not be generalized to all clients in this population.

## Other Environmental Factors Affecting Relapse

Certain environmental conditions create a greater than usual risk to some poor clients should they relapse and resume drinking. For some, the resumption of drinking may result in the termination of marginal employment or the breakup of the family. For others, the resumption of drinking may result in incarceration. Relapse may be part of the conflicting philosophical argument surrounding the definition of alcoholism and criteria for treatment success for some. If clients adopt the position that "once an alcoholic, always an alcoholic," one drink or moderate drinking after treatment is considered a failure by these clients.

The goal of total abstinence from drinking may be unrealistic for all alcoholics in general and for some poor alcoholics in particular. Relapse is a common phenomenon in alcoholism treatment, and seems to occur especially during the early weeks or months of sobriety and again about a year after direct treatment.[18] Resumption of drinking does not always necessarily proceed immediately to addiction and dependence, although it does for some clients even in a gradual manner. For other clients, there are periods of weeks, months, or even years of controlled drinking without the onset of the signs and symptoms of alcoholism.

A life crisis, disappointment in sobriety, emotional conflicts, excessive mood swings, pressures to drink socially by persons significant to the alcoholic are all events which may precipitate the onset of drinking. Poor clients have qualitatively different problems in that giving up alcohol and its related activities may involve social and human loss with few accompanying gains. For example, for many poor alcoholics their worlds consist only of friends who drink, and they may maneuver within a larger system that includes hospitals, jails, flophouses, and the like. In this system, the client feels secure, receives warmth, food, personal recognition, and attention to his or her basic needs at critical periods. Life without alcohol may seem no better or even worse for these clients than life with alcohol. Therefore helping professionals should be acutely aware of the disadvantages to abstinence and the losses that can be incurred when helping poor alcoholics to change their life-styles as alcoholics. Ignoring these consequences or failing to help the poor alcoholic to anticipate and deal with them can increase the probability of relapse.

The extent to which a poor person's values and cultural perspectives coincide or conflict with those of staff in alcohol treatment programs is crucial to effective treatment outcomes and recovery. For example, a poor alcoholic from a rural community may experience cultural shock if he or she is referred to an inner city alcoholism treatment program. This client may feel continuously uncomfortable and out of place and may not be able to identify with other clients there. A person from an Hispanic background may experience communication problems if he or she speaks very little English. In addition, if he or she is referred to a treatment center where there are no Spanish-speaking treatment staff, relapse or premature termination may occur.

An assessment of the content and procedures included in some culture-specific programs for minority clients or poor alcoholics has indicated that their efforts may only represent "window dressing." That is, staff members of a program may have similar backgrounds to those of the clients involved but the structure, content, and values manifested in these programs are usually traditional. Program content, counseling styles, and suggestions about coping strategies for clients in a treatment program should reflect the perceptions and values of program participants. Staff members should have some input into the design and content of the program, but some effort should be made to consider the environmental context that the clients involved come from and usually return to. Typically, coping strategies that are alien to a client's culture or that are not reinforced by his or her community can mean that treatment gains are lost once the client leaves the program and returns to that community. Therefore, a focus on building skills and competencies necessary for poor clients to negotiate their environments more successfully are more appropriate. In this manner, the life stress issues that can precipitate relapse may be more effectively addressed during treatment.

## CONCLUSIONS

Poor alcoholics are reported to come to treatment at a disadvantage and present with behaviors which are characteristically against optimal outcomes. Although expectations of failure may influence both diagnosis and the willingness to provide treatment, it seems clear that little has been done to develop approaches to treatment which are appropriate to the needs of poor alcoholics. A less conventional approach based on a system's view appears more appropriate.

There are several reasons why psychologists, social workers, doctors, and alcoholism counselors should view alcoholism from a system's perspective when dealing with the poor. First, it is less productive, or perhaps even harmful, to rehabilitate an alcoholic in isolation and return him or her to the same destructive environment that created or maintained the problem. Second, many components of the poor alcoholic's family or community may be under as much stress and may be in need of as much help or attention as the poor alcoholic.

Alcohol dependence and related dysfunctional behaviors should not be thought of as the fault of the client, but as a reaction or mode of behavior in response to forces encountered as the client moves in space and time. Cause, therefore, is to be sought in the dynamic interaction between the nature of the individual and the nature of his or her environment at a particular point in time. For example, if a rock hits a piece of glass and the glass breaks, one may wonder if the rock caused the window to break, or whether it was the brittleness of the glass, the nature of the surrounding medium, or the velocity with which the rock was traveling. It seems clear the breaking was caused by an interaction of all of these factors and many more. According to Thomas and Chess, problems stem from an interaction between three factors; the host, the agent, and the environment.[19] The host, within this framework, is the individual. It includes his or her knowledge about alcohol, the attitudes that influence drinking patterns, and drinking behavior itself. The agent is alcohol. This includes the content, distribution, and availability of alcohol which is influenced by the cultural and group norms. The environment consists of the setting in which drinking occurs and the environmental or community mores which influence the alcoholic. Intervention at all of these points appears essential for effective treatment and for the prevention of relapse in poor clients. An awareness of the pluralistic, multifactorial origins of any dysfunction broadens the helping professional's understanding and increases the therapeutic potential.

## REFERENCES

1. U.S. Bureau of the Census, Supplementary Report. Provisional estimates of social, economic, and housing characteristics. Washington, D.C., U.S. Government Printing Office, 1982.
2. Sowell, Thomas: *Ethnic America.* New York, Basic Books, 1981; and U.S. Bureau of the Census, op. cit.
3. Cohen, Sidney: *The Substance Abuse Problems.* New York, The Haworth Press, 1981; and Brandsma, J. M., Maultsby, M. C., Jr., and Welsh, R. J.: *Outpatient Treatment of Alcoholism: A Review and Comparative Study.* Baltimore, University Park Press, 1980.
4. Brandsma, Maultsby, Welsh, *op. cit.*
5. Cahalan, Don and Cisin, Ira H.: Drinking behavior and drinking problems in the United States. In Kissin, Benjamin and Begleiter, Henri (Eds.): *Social Aspects of Alcoholism.* New York, Plenum Press, 1976, pp. 77–115.
6. Blumberg, Leonard, Shysler, Thomas E., and Shandler, Irvin W.: *Skid Row and It's Alternatives: Research and Recommendations from Philadelphia.* Philadelphia, Temple University Press, 1973; and Wiseman, Jacqueline P.: Skid row alcoholics: Treatment, survival, and escape. In Pattison, Mansell and Kaufman,

Edward: *Encyclopedic Handbook of Alcoholism.* New York, Gardner Press, 1982, pp. 946–953.

7. Polich, Jim, Armor, O. J., and Braiker, H. B.: *The Course of Alcoholism: Four Years After Treatment.* Santa Monica, The Rand Corporation, (NIAAA), 1980.
8. Bell, Peter and Evans, Jimmy: *Counseling the Black Client: Alcohol Use and Abuse in Black America.* Center City, Hazelden, 1981.
9. Westermeyer, J. and Lang, G.: Ethnic differences in use of alcoholism facilities. *International Journal of Addictions, 10:*513–520, 1974.
10. Coleman, R. P. and Rainwater, L.: *Social Standing in America.* New York, Basic Books, 1978.
11. Polich, Jim, Armor, D. J., and Braiker, H. B.: Patterns of alcoholism over four years. *Journal of Studies on Alcoholism, 41:*397–416, 1980; and Hunt, A., Barnett, L. W., and Branch, L. G.: Relapse rates in addiction programs. *Journal of Clinical Psychology, 27:*455–456, 1971.
12. *Ibid.*
13. Polich, Armor, and Braiker, *op. cit.*
14. Polich, Armor, and Braiker, *op. cit.*
15. Miller, W. R., and Hester, R. K.: Treating the problem drinker: Moderate approaches. In Miller, W. R. (Ed.): *The Addictive Behaviors: Treatment of Alcoholism. Drug Abuse, Smoking, and Obesity.* New York, Pergamon Press, 1982.
16. Hunter, C., Jr.: Freestanding alcohol treatment centers: A new approach to an old problem. *Psychiatric Annals, 12:*346–408, 1982.
17. Argeriou, M.: Reaching problem-drinking Blacks: The unheralded potential of the drinking drivers programs. *International Journal of Addiction, 13:*443–459, 1978; and Shore, J. H., and Non Fumetti, B.: Three alcohol programs for American Indians. *American Journal of Psychiatry, 128:*1450–1454, 1972.
18. Pattison, E. M., Sobell, Mark B., and Sobell, Linda C.: *Emerging Concepts of Alcohol Dependence.* New York, Springer Publishing Company, 1977.
19. Thomas, A. and Chess, S.: *The Dynamics of Psychological Development.* New York, Brunner/Mazel, 1980.

# PART THREE: RESEARCH

# OVERVIEW

## Edith M. Freeman

The chapters in this section involve research on alcohol problems. The chapters by Harford and by Moos et al. examine the effects of environmental factors on alcohol use in adolescents, and on coping patterns within families in which one member of the marital dyad is an alcoholic. Because of their ecological foci on clients in their environments, their research is particularly relevant to practice in general and to other sections of this book. In addition, each of these authors effectively dispells several myths about specific clients and alcohol problems: black adolescents and the spouses of alcoholics.

The chapter by Mandell on evaluation helps to identify barriers to good research, and thus to evaluation of practice. He proposes a set of evaluation criteria that can not only be used for program evaluations by alcohol treatment facilities, but that can be used to evaluate the work of state alcohol problem control agencies.

Wechsler and Rohman's chapter focuses on one other aspect of the client's environment that is frequently ignored in evaluating the effects of treatment on clients with alcohol problems. They speculate on the effects of practitioners' knowledge levels and attitudes on practice outcomes by comparing doctors, nurses, counseling and social work students in these areas. They make a compelling case for the legitimacy of growing concerns about practitioner bias on treatment outcomes.

*Chapter Seventeen*

# A CRITICAL OVERVIEW OF EVALUATIONS
# OF ALCOHOLISM TREATMENT*

WALLACE MANDELL

Alcoholism treatment evaluations have made an important
historical contribution to the advancement of the service field
by providing evidence that alcoholics can abstain from alcohol
and return to social productivity at rates that destroy recent stereotypes. Having served that function, it is time for evaluation studies to move forward to new tasks. The methodologies that have
sufficed to demonstrate the possibility of recovery are not adequate to these new tasks. These tasks can be conceptually organized in terms of three questions: (1) Which treatments are most
effective? (2) For whom are particular treatments most effective?
(3) How can treatment programs be better managed?

## METHODOLOGICAL ISSUES IN
## DETERMINING TREATMENT EFFECTIVENESS

The reliability and validity of the data reported on treatment
outcome have not been established, and the data are not properly
analyzed to establish the durability of treatment effects.

In order to evaluate treatment outcomes, it is necessary to
define in measurable terms the goals and objectives of treatment.
The immediate goal of alcoholism treatment programs is to provide service to alcoholics and people with alcohol-related prob-

*Reproduced by permission from *Alcoholism: Clinical and Experimental Research*, *3*:4, October 1979, pp. 315–323.

lems. Many evaluation studies do not measure the long-term goals of treatment established by service providers and the public. These goals must be defined operationally in terms of reliably recognizable and measurable outcomes. These outcomes must be translated into measures that unambiguously describe the status of the patient before and after treatment. Many of the evaluation studies currently available in the literature do not measure the patient's status before treatment along the same dimensions that will be used to describe patients after treatment. In addition, status before treatment is described for a short, inappropriate period of 30 days prior to treatment, usually a crisis period that is not representative of the patient's status either for the year prior to treatment or for the period prior to the onset of illness. As a result, such evaluations can only report that the patient has improved compared to his status during crisis.

Alcohol treatment evaluations do not use an adequate array of measures. In 265 studies of alcoholism treatment, 80 percent had used alcohol consumption as the principle outcome measure. This does not appear to be an adequate criterion. Alcohol consumption has the advantages of being specifiable in quantitative terms and of being related to a measuring system that can be generally understood, however, the use of this outcome measure places "alcohol consumption" at the center of the illness model of alcoholism. Indeed many alcoholics believe that the act of drinking alcohol is the illness. This concept of illness is not appropriate in either medical or psychologic science. Neither a single behavior nor a chemical substance can be an illness, though they may be part of the definition. An illness is defined in terms of a pattern of signs and symptoms with a known course, etiology, and mechanisms of action.

If "alcohol addiction" is the central mechanism in the illness condition, then change in addiction must be the goal of treatment. Similarly, if other psychologic or physiologic mechanisms are part of the alcoholic illness, then an adequate measure of the effect of treatment must involve evidence of change of these functions.

Emrick and Pattison find in their literature reviews that alcoholics who stop or moderate their drinking do not necessarily improve in other areas of function, especially not in their vocational and marital adjustment.[1] Gerard and Saenger found that abstinence was not related to improvement in related psychologic problems, indeed, many of his subjects were overtly more disturbed in psychologic functioning after abstinence.[2]

In the evaluations by Armor et al. of the federally funded alcohol treatment centers' data, the correlations between alcohol consumption and behavioral impairment at 6 and 18 months was less than .70.[3] This indicates that less than half of the reported behavioral impairment observed in these patients after treatment could be predicted by the level of alcohol consumption. Similarly, treatment could be associated with improvement in social functioning without producing reduction in alcohol consumption.

This author in his 1970 review, found that between treated and untreated patients, the major difference supported by research was mortality.[4] Alcoholic patients have been reported to have two to four times the annual risk of death compared to peers (2% to 4% per year).

Goals set by patients should also be used as a basis for evaluating treatment outcomes. What many alcoholics want from treatment may be quite different from the external criteria applied by evaluators. The outcomes they seek are a sense of self-acceptance (based on feeling worthwhile), a decrease in experienced inner psychologic conflict (related to feelings of being a "whole person"), and freedom from "subjugation" to a chemical that continually produces experiences of mortification and demoralization (feeling powerless and ineffective).

This brief review suggests that to be defined as effective, treatment must change the projected natural course of the illness. The variables that are critical to the medical, psychologic, and social definitions of alcoholism must be included in evaluation, i.e., physical and/or psychologic dependence, health status, vocational adjustment, marital adjustment, legal comportment, and mental functions. When the illness is in remission, there should be an arrest of both physical and mental deterioration, illustrated by increased longevity and decreased memory loss and irritability, respectively. A recovery of related social functions should also occur.

The basic reason that the alcoholism treatment evaluation field does not use the above described variables as outcome measures is because of the lack of standardized measuring instruments that can be applied systematically before and after treatment.

Evaluations in the alcoholism treatment field have also been characterized by an inattention to basic research methodological assumptions that weakens most of the conclusions currently reported in the literature. Little attention has been given to the validity of the data used in evaluation studies. In only a few studies have the self-reported data on alcohol consumption been examined for validity. Simple measures, such as corroboration of reports by significant others, have not been undertaken. Particularly problematical in outcome studies are the self-reports of individuals claiming to drink at moderate levels. Methodological studies have shown in several samples that blood alcohol levels and self-reports of moderate drinking do not agree by as much as 10 to 50 percent of drinkers. Simple lying is not an explanation for this variation. Sobell and Sobell have found that heavy social drinkers are not able to accurately estimate their blood alcohol levels after administration of varying quantities of alcohol.[5] Nor are experienced alcohol treatment staff able to make such estimates based on observations of patient behavior.[6]

Alcohol interferes with memory functions, including the inability to remember the amount consumed. It seems likely that researchers are asking patients for information they cannot accurately provide. This suggests that breath samples and other physiologic measures may be required to establish the validity of consumption data reported as outcome measures.

The system currently used for classifying types of drinkers along a quantity-frequency dimension of consumption has confused the interpretation of some evaluation study findings. Drinkers are often classified as abstaining, moderate, or heavy drinkers. Little et al. have demonstrated that considerable information is lost by the use of this type of classification.[7] Additionally, there is considerable variation among studies in the definitions of these terms. The most common definitions derive from the study by Cahalan, Cisin, and Crossley of American drinking patterns.[8] "Heavy drinkers drink nearly every day with 5 oz or more per occasion at least once in awhile or about once weekly with usually five or more" (p. 19). "The reasoning behind this assumption is that only very few of those who never drink as many as five drinks on any occasion would be likely to become intoxicated or to have serious present problems related to drinking" (p. 15). However, recent NAPIS data indicate that on the average, patients entering alcoholism treatment programs consume the equivalent of 16 oz of whiskey per day, while the driving-while-intoxicated (DWI) population entering treatment consumes, on the average, the equivalent of about 4 oz of whiskey per day.[9] Both groups would be classified as heavy drinkers by general population norms. I would argue that these groups should reasonably be considered distinct alcoholic and alcohol-problem populations. The non-DWI treatment population could cut their drinking in half to 8 oz of whiskey and still be classified as heavy drinkers, perhaps still alcoholic. They would be consuming twice as much absolute alcohol as the DWI population. Certainly most clinicians would agree that patients consuming 8 oz of whiskey daily are in great danger. Several authors have concluded that evaluations will provide more useful information by using measures of daily absolute alcohol consumption, such as those proposed by Little, Schultz, and Mandell.[10]

Whatever the measure of outcome may be, the durability of effect must be considered in evaluating a chronic illness. The reports by Armor et al. and Paredes et al. bring into focus the issue of measuring the durability of treatment outcome.[11] Ten percent of those who abstained during the first six months had gone back to problem drinking. Similarly, 21 percent of those who had abstained for 1 month by the 6 month follow-up had gone back to drinking at 18 months, and 32 percent of those who were "normal" drinkers at 6 months had returned to drinking at 18 months. Thus, with an increased period of observation, the proportion of patients still in remission decreases. The present procedure of reporting proportions of patients who are in a specific category or remission at 6 months or 1 year follow-up is insensitive to variation in short-and long-term treatment effects. I have proposed using a measure of effectiveness, i.e., the number of months in which the patient has met the criteria for remission after treatment. Thus, a treatment can be described as producing on-the-average months of remission during the study period, which is a measure sensitive to the duration of effect.

Most currently available evaluations tend to attribute patient outcome status to treatment without an adequate research design that would take into account "natural remission." Unless a randomly assigned control group or adequately matched alternate treatment group is available for comparison, the outcome should not be attributed to treatment. When alcoholism is not treated by a formal agency, Emrick reports abstinence rates ranging up to 30 percent and improvement rates up to 54 percent at 6–8 months after initiation of treatment.[12] Armor found that 50 percent of the clients with minimal treatment contact in the alcohol treatment centers report remission compared with 70 percent who received five or more treatment contacts.[13] Edwards found that individuals assigned to a single encounter in which advice was offered had outcomes similar to a group receiving extensive counseling.[14] On reviewing the data reported on untreated control groups in 12 studies, this author found that the abstinence rate at 1 year ranged from 20 percent to 49 percent.[15]

These studies suggest that as many as 40 to 50 percent of the population seeking alcoholism treatment will, if left untreated, discontinue drinking or reduce alcohol consumption. This being the case, studies attempting to attribute improvement to treatment must have comparison or control groups that provide information about the normal rates of discontinuing alcohol abuse in the relevant population, so that the treatment's additional contribution can be evaluated. Caution in interpretation is advisable, since not participating in the treatment program under study does not mean that the potential patients remain untreated. Studies of treatment dropouts find that alcoholics try many different treatments, for example, A.A., religion, or even other treatment programs.[16] Such alternate treatment must be taken into account in evaluating recovery rates in nontreated groups.

There are several other problems that must be overcome when differences between treated and untreated groups are examined. One major source of error results from not taking into account missing cases who are not located at the follow-up period. The rates of nonresponse are quite large in many alcohol treatment studies, ranging from 20 to 40 percent of the sample. Some of the major reasons for nonresponse are mortality, morbidity, criminality, and leaving the geographic area. Several studies have indicated that the nonrespondents are not similar to those individuals who do respond, in these above-listed characteristics. The non-response rates are large enough so that findings of improvement would be significantly changed if the non-located individuals were taken into account.

Barr et al. were able to locate follow-up data on 81 percent of a study sample; they then contacted an additional 10 percent of the original group.[17] Almost all of the latter group were doing poorly. Bowen and Androes found similar results.[18] Sobell and Sobell found that of the five very difficult-to-locate subjects in their study, four functioned much more poorly than their appropriate comparison group and the fifth was also slightly below average.[19]

Evaluations of alcoholism programs must also take into account the effect produced by exclusion of patients who do not fit treatment program criteria. Excluded patients may be "more-difficult-to-treat" individuals.

Another problem related to interpretation of findings is the tendency to attribute to the treatment program patient successes or failures that are more properly related to the social and economic environment in which the patients live. Environmental opportunity and support systems may have significant impact on the measures of patient status. In communities with high unemployment rates, alcoholics may remain unemployed after treatment or may only find employment in jobs below their skill and experience levels. In communities where only limited health care is available, alcoholics treated by alcoholism treatment programs may have high mortality rates.

There is substantial evidence available that the rate of consumption of alcohol and alcohol-associated problems vary systematically through time and geography.[20] These variations are known to be associated with economic factors, as well as cultural factors. Thus, during a period of increasing alcohol use and abuse, it might be anticipated that individuals would be more resistant to improvement, and during a period of decreasing abuse, more of the alcohol abusers might spontaneously remit. Similarly, in communities experiencing high rates of unemployment or marital instability, fewer remissions will be associated with increased employment or marital stabilization. This can be overcome by random assignment of subjects to a control group that allows appropriate testing of the difference produced by the treatment procedure. None of the studies reported thus far evaluate the contribution of historical changes in society to outcome or community-environment conditions that may influence the rate of alcohol problems. In order to estimate these influences and discount their effects, time-series data are urgently needed to estimate the expected remission rates as a baseline against which to compare the contribution of the treatment.

### WHICH TREATMENTS ARE MOST EFFECTIVE?

A major problem in evaluating treatment program comparisons is the composite nature of the treatments being studied. What is often provided as treatment includes a main treatment, such as counseling or group therapy, and other services, such as education and follow-up. Even these components are not described with enough detail to be reproducible in other settings. Interpretation of results is further confounded by the fact that the therapist may be a major unstudied factor influencing the outcome. Certainly the intensity and duration of treatment must also be considered in estimating treatment effects.

Only three studies report random assignment of subjects to comparable treatments. Bruun[21] found that multidisciplinary treatment is more effective than psychiatric treatment alone, and Corder et al.[22] found that couples' therapy added to an inhospital program produced significant improvement in abstinence and employment. Edwards and Gutherie compared patients who had been randomly assigned two months of inpatient or outpatient treatment and, in both cases, group therapy and A.A., found no difference in outcome.[23] At this time there is no evidence from either inhospital studies or outpatient studies that a specific type of treatment makes a difference in outcome.

## FOR WHOM ARE PARTICULAR TREATMENTS MOST EFFECTIVE?

There is general agreement that there is no single alcoholic personality. This makes the hypothesis that specific treatments will be more effective with specific patient types very attractive. However, there has been no experimental demonstration of this phenomenon.

Some of the effects attributed to treatment may be more properly attributed to the type of patients in the treatment program. Patients who have families, employers, and those who are skilled workers return to their previous roles after treatment. Pattison has documented how programs may selectively serve populations with different resources and competencies.[24] Individuals with high levels of competency may do well without treatment and those with poor competencies do poorly despite substantial sophisticated treatment.

Very few evaluation studies have examined patient characteristics as these may interact with the type of treatment. It must be of considerable concern that of the alcoholics who voluntarily come to treatment, 50 percent leave after the first few contacts. The common explanation of this phenomenon is that the alcoholic is either ambivalent or not motivated for treatment. It could well be that many of these potential patients do not find the treatment offered to be acceptable.

Evaluators in the alcoholism field confront a social-class bifurcation among the patient populations of treatment agencies that is related to differences in mission, constituencies, and technologies. Middle- and upper-class individuals receive treatment that is either covered by their medical insurance or paid for by their employers. The lower socioeconomic groups do not purchase their treatment, as do the middle and upper groups, by fee-for-service or increased productivity. State and local governments pay for alcoholism treatment for the lower groups as a response to public concern for greater behavioral conformity to community approved norms, thus reducing the welfare burden and preventing public disorder. This variation in patient population and treatment goals is reflected in location, style of operation, and staff values. This in turn produces mutual selection or matching between patients and treatment programs.

Kissin's group has pointed out that acceptability of treatment is an important factor in its outcome.[25] Acceptors of particular types of treatment did better when a wide array of treatments was available, than did those who rejected a treatment.

Clinicians and evaluators have tended to consider the differences they observe among patients as personality differences. There has been an unfruitful debate as to whether there is an alcoholic personality. The term "personality," as currently used in the alcohol literature compared to the way it is used in the psychologic literature, is ambiguous and refers to such things as drinking patterns and skid-row winos. The personality-differences issue has diverted attention from the life experience or life-style variables that seem to account for most of the differences in outcomes among programs.

In relation to matching patients to treatment the variables that are studied are social class, cultural-ethnic background, scores on symptom checklists (like the MMPI), and life-style variables including marital status, social marginality, vocational adaptation, and criminality. Each of these characteristics has been shown to predict successful outcomes after treatment. Social and economic competence measures stand out as predictors of treatment outcome.[26]

The hypothesis that certain treatments will be more effective for some patients than others has not been adequately described so that they are reproducible or comparable. Patient characteristics have not been adequately described to allow comparison of treated populations. Comparison studies of treatment procedures have not randomly assigned subjects or provided statistical controls to allow analysis of the independent contributions of various types of treatment.

## HOW CAN TREATMENT PROGRAMS BE BETTER MANAGED?

At the present time there are three evaluation strategies used to improve the management of treatment programs. The first evaluation technique used to manage programs is the systematic application of a set of standards put forth by an accrediting body. The best known standards in the alcohol field are those of the Joint Commission on the Accreditation of Hospitals (JCAH). These standards are created by panels of experts who may or may not reflect the current level of practice by treatment agencies in the field. The standards describe the nature of the physical facilities, the availability of appropriate staff, and the adequacy of the record-keeping system of a treatment program.

Standards such as those of the JCAH are beyond the resources available to many public programs. Since health insurers use these standards as the basis for reimbursement, public programs are often excluded. This is now operating to create a two-tier system of treatment in which private sector facilities are accredited and receive insurance reimbursement while public sector facilities are not. Since public agencies are not accredited, they treat few middle-class individuals, but these few are required to pay for their treatment and do so through insurance programs. This situation has resulted in pressure to lower JCAH standards, but it is argued that these standards should be maintained, so that public programs can be stimulated to meet them. Based on the experience of state mental hospitals, only a small proportion of state-funded facilities will reach JCAH standards. A number of state governments have moved to create their own alternative licensing standards to be used as a basis for insurance reimbursement. There are no empirical studies available that have examined whether different sets of standards make any difference in treatment outcomes. Such studies require comparison of outcomes in accredited and nonaccredited facilities with all the previously discussed methodological issues taken into account. The lack of data reduces present discussions about standards to a political process related to the desire to capture funds for treatment. Evaluation research is not playing any part in this important decision process.

The second strategy used in evaluation of treatment programs is generally known as management by exception. In this approach, each treatment program or program component is required to produce statistical data about key indicators of the care provided to patients. The data collected usually include information about the volume of patients treated and the size and cost of operating the program. These data are accumulated on a statewide or national basis and reduced to ratios indexing the productivity of the program per unit of cost and the volume and duration of services received by the average client. Treatment programs that report productivity, staff turnover, or cost data below the average are identified for intensive management scrutiny and administrative intervention. The central assumption of management by exception is that productivity, more units of treatment, more patients treated, and lower cost are the desired outcomes of the programs. Programs are encouraged to bring their indices of performance to the average level. The effectiveness of this method of management evaluation is dependent on the items of information that are selected as indicators of the quality of program performance. An illustration of a data system that can be used for management by exception purposes is the National Alcohol Program Information System.[27]

As Hagedorn has pointed out, intake and discharge procedures in treatment programs use expensive staff time.[28] These workload factors can be taken into account in assessing program productivity by weighting measures of staff effort by type of activity, producing a measure of workload.

The amount of workload units produced by a program can be examined in relation to the size of the staff and reported in terms of full-time equivalents (FTE). (Full-time equivalents are defined as the total number of treatment hours available per week divided by the standard number of hours in the work week, usually 40.) The ratio of workload units to FTE yields a ratio describing the productivity of the average program staff member.

Another representative measure that can be derived from this system is the number of patients-to-FTE ratio, indicating the intensity of care the average patient is likely to receive. Intensity of care is also reflected in number of hours of treatment per month. Such ratios may also be examined in relation to cost, yielding familiar indices such as cost per unit of treatment or cost per patient treated.

When such ratios are accumulated for a group of programs, average and modal tendencies can be calculated. This allows administrators to set standards of performance based on the current or usual practice in the field. Unfortunately, productivity indicators have not been studied in relation to outcomes of treatment. As a result, management by exception has the unintended consequences of providing incentives to program directors to produce good productivity statistics rather than good outcomes. This is sometimes done by selecting as patients individuals who will keep appointments, thus decreasing the unused hours in the program and thereby increasing the productivity ratios. This effect can also be achieved by retaining in treatment patients who miss few appointments.

A third type of program evaluation just beginning to be used in the alcohol program evaluation field has been called cost-benefit analysis, and this attempts to overcome reliance on productivity measures. Cost-benefit analysis rests on the proposition that the benefits from services provided should outweigh their costs.[29] A prerequisite assumption that must be met is that it is possible to estimate the outcomes of a service and to place a monetary value on these outcomes as well as on the costs of providing the service.[30] A second assumption that must be met in order to use this approach is that future costs and benefits can be estimated and discounted to present value.[31]

Very few such evaluations have been carried out because of the lack of investment in gathering outcome data that meet the methodological requirements for such studies. As discussed in the preceding section, alcoholism programs often do not identify present and future benefits that can actually be linked to the program. An overriding difficulty in evaluating human service programs is that it is often impossible to place a value on principal benefits, such as an increased lifespan or sense of self-worth. Administrators committed to a cost-benefit approach tend to finesse this problem by selecting particular benefits that they believe to be important to funding agencies and limiting their analyses to these outcomes. In most evaluations of alcoholism programs, the principal benefit examined is economic productivity of patients. An analysis of published evaluation studies suggest that for many alcoholics, changes in economic productivity are either not possible or irrelevant to the treatment goals of the patients and their families. None of the evaluation studies in the alcohol services field has adequately accumulated costs of treatment or applied appropriate discount methods to the present costs and future benefits of treatment programs.

One subcategory of cost-benefit study that has been proposed for the alcoholism field should more properly be called cost-effectiveness analysis. In these studies, only the dollar costs of the treatment program are considered in relation to specified program outcomes. These outcomes are not valued in dollar terms, but are described in terms of units of the desirable, e.g., months of abstinence. This approach is useful in allowing comparisons between programs in the same state in effectiveness units per dollar of cost. There is as yet no method for determining the economic value or even utility of effectiveness units. The method cannot be considered a true cost-benefit study, since some programs may produce more abstinent months per dollar while others produce more months of life per dollar.

Studies using effectiveness units produced per dollar of investment have, as yet, not taken into account the relative difficulty of particular populations being treated, e.g., young uneducated alcoholics, and the support systems in the communities in which the program operates, e.g., high employment rates. The methodology for producing this kind of sophisticated evaluation is available in linear regression prediction equations and if it is applied to this problem, it will make this technique more useful in program evaluation by state agencies.

One area in which empirical evaluation studies have not yet been applied is in state government agencies for alcoholism. Discussions with governors and their advisors have suggested that indices are desired to afford them evidence that state programs are being well managed. The question is being raised by state legislatures as to whether their state programs are cost-effective. At this time, many state governments do not have management information systems that allow intra- or interstate comparisons of how adequately citizens are served. In this sense, the evaluation effort is at a primitive level. The state alcohol problem control agencies have not generated data that will allow the basic comparisons needed for effective leadership. In part, this has been the result of a lack of articulation of key indicators for such evaluation. It seems reasonable to propose that indices used to evaluate treatment programs be applied to state agencies.

The following six indices are suggested as providing a minimal set with which to measure the effectiveness of state agency programs.

1. Measure of effectiveness in resource mobilization

   Ratio: Total of funds from all sources spent in state on alcoholism control/Dollars spent on operating state alcoholism agency

2. Treatment capacity of the state

   Ratio: Units of capacity for treatment/Adult population of the state

3. Cost per unit of treatment capacity

   Ratio: Units of capacity for treatment in state/Dollars allocated to treatment

4. Cost of a unit of treatment provided

   Ratio: Units of treatment actually provided in state/Dollars allocated to treatment

5. Cost of a unit of treatment effectiveness

   Ratio: Treatment effectiveness units/Dollars allocated to treatment

   Treatment effectiveness units are defined as: months of life for treated population, months of alcohol consumption, months of employment, months not incarcerated.

6. Cost of alcohol problems prevalence reduction

   Ratio: Prevalence of alcohol problems effectiveness units/ Dollars allocated to alcohol programs

   Prevalence of alcohol problems effectiveness units are defined as: rate of medical facility admissions due to alcohol problems, rate of arrests related to alcohol problems, rate of highway accidents related to alcohol problems.

The evaluation technology for empirically evaluating treatment and state programs for the control of alcohol-produced problems is now available. As a result of the work of many pioneers, there is now available excellent careful specification of the assumptions and methodological requirements for good evaluations. Evaluation efforts are now able to move forward to more significant contributions to improving the care of alcoholic individuals. The leaders of the alcoholism treatment field must make a commitment to investing the resources necessary for effective evaluations on which to base new advances in technology.

## REFERENCES

1. Emrick, C. D.: A review of psychologically oriented treatment of alcoholism: I. The use and interrelationships of outcome criteria and drinking behavior following treatment. *Q J Stud Alcohol,* 35:523–549, 1974. See also Pattison, E. M.: A critique of alcoholism treatment concepts with special reference to abstinence. In Pattison, E. M., Sobell, M. B., and Sobell, L. C. (Eds.): *Emerging Concepts of Alcohol Dependence.* New York, Springer, 1977, p. 260.
2. Gerard, D. L., and Saenger, G.: *Outpatient Treatment of Alcoholism.* Toronto, University of Toronto Press, 1966.
3. Armor, E. J., Polich, J. M., and Stambul, H. B.: *Alcoholism and Treatment.* Santa Monica, The Rand Corp., June 1976.
4. Mandell, W.: Does the type of treatment make a difference? *Md State Med J.,* pp. 80–83, March 1975.
5. Sobell, L. C., and Sobell, M. B.: Self-feedback technique to monitor drinking behavior in alcoholics. *Behav Res Ther,* 11:237–238, 1973. (a)
6. Midanik, L.: Early dropout in two sites of a comprehensive alcoholism treatment program. Doctoral dissertation, Johns Hopkins School of Hygiene and Public Health, Baltimore, 1979.
7. Little, R. E., Schultz, F. A., and Mandell, W.: Describing alcohol consumption: A comparison of three methods and a new approach. *J Stud Alcohol,* 38:554–562, 1977.
8. Cahalan, D., Cisin, I., and Crossley, H.: *American Drinking Practices: A National Study of Drinking Behavior and Attitudes.* New Haven, College and University Press, 1969.
9. NIAAA National Alcoholism Program Information System, data for 1978. Rockville, NIAAA, 1978.
10. Little, Schultz, & Mandell, op. cit.
11. Armor, Polich, & Stambul, op. cit. See also Paredes, A., Gregory, D., Rundell, O. H., and Williams, H.: Drinking behavior, remission and relapse: The Rand Report revisited. *Alcoholism,* 3:3–10, 1979.
12. Emrick, op. cit.
13. Armor, op. cit.
14. Edwards, G., Oxford, J., Egert, S., Gutherie, S., Hawker, A., Hensman, C., Mitcheson, M., Oppenheimer, E., and Taylor, C.: Alcoholism — A control trial of "treatment" and "advice." *J Stud Alcohol,* 38:1003–1030, 1977.
15. Mandell, op. cit.
16. Sobell, L. C., and Sobell, M. B.: Second-year treatment outcome of alcoholics treated by individualized behavior therapy: Results. In Pattison,

E. M., Sobell, L. C., and Sobell, M. B. (Eds.): *Emerging Concepts of Alcohol Dependence.* New York, Springer, 1977, p. 300. (b)

17. Barr, H. L., Cohen, A., Hannigan, P., and Steinberger, H.: Problem drinking by drug addicts and its implications. In Seixas, F. A. (Ed.): *Currents in Alcoholism, Vol. 2.* New York, Grune & Stratton, 1977, p. 269.

18. Bowen, W. T., and Androes, L.: A follow-up study of 79 alcoholic patients: 1963–1965. *Bull Menninger Clin, 32:*26–34, 1968.

19. Sobell and Sobell (b), op. cit.

20. Brenner, H.: Trends in alcohol consumption and associated illness. *Am J Pub Health, 65:*1279–1292, 1975.

21. Bruun, K.: Outcome of different types of treatment of alcoholics. *Q J Stud Alcohol, 24:*280–288, 1963.

22. Corder, B. F., Corder, R. F., and Laidlaw, N. D.: An intensive treatment program for alcoholics and their wives. *Q J Stud Alcohol, 24:*432–442, 1963.

23. Edwards G., and Gutherie, S.: A comparison of inpatient and outpatient treatment of alcohol dependence. *Lance, 1:*467–468, 1966.

24. Pattison, op. cit.

25. Kissin, B., and Begleiter, H.: (Eds.). *The Biology of Alcoholism: Treatment and Rehabilitation of the Chronic Alcoholic, Vol. 5.* New York, Plenum, 1977.

26. Rudie, R. R., and McGaughran, L. S.: Difference in developmental experience, defensiveness, and personality organization between two classes of problem drinkers. *J Abnorm Soc Psychol, 62:*659–665, 1961. See also Singer, E., Blane, H. T., & Kasschau, R.: Alcoholism and social isolation. *J Abnorm Soc Psychol, 69:*681–685, 1964; and Sugerman, A., Reilly, D., and Albahary, R. S.: Social competence and the essential-reactive distinction in alcoholism. *Arch Gen Psychiatry, 12:*552–556, 1965; and Goldfried, M. R.: Prediction of improvement in an alcoholism outpatient clinic. *Q J Stud Alcohol, 30:*129–139, 1969.

27. NIAAA National Alcoholism Program Information System, op. cit.

28. Hagedorn, H., Beck, K., Neubert, S., Werlin, S.: *A Working Manual of Simple Program Evaluation Techniques for Community Mental Health Centers.* Cambridge, Arthur D. Little, 1976.

29. Williams, A.: The cost-benefit approach. *Br Med Bull, 30:*252–256, 1974.

30. Klarman, H. E.: Present status of cost-benefit analysis in the health field. *Am J Pub Health, 57:*1948–1953, 1967.

31. Conley, R.: Issues in benefit-cost analyses of the vocational rehabilitation program. *Am Rehabil, 1:*19–23, 1975.

## Chapter Eighteen

# DRINKING PATTERNS AMONG BLACK AND NON-BLACK ADOLESCENTS: RESULTS OF A NATIONAL SURVEY*

### Thomas C. Harford

Alcohol abuse is regarded as one of the greater health problems of the black community in the United States.[1] Cirrhosis mortality rates are disproportionately high among black Americans. Rates among black men and women, aged 25 to 34, are several times higher than for white men and women of the same age. For all age groups up to 65 years of age, the cirrhosis mortality rate for black Americans is nearly twice that for white Americans. When examining racial differences in cirrhosis mortality rates, it is important to acknowledge the potential contributions made by such factors as nutritional differences, genetic differences, bias in recording information on death certificates and psychosocial differences. While alcohol is not the exclusive cause of cirrhosis of the liver, prolonged heavy drinking is recognized as a major contributor.

High cirrhosis rates in the black population are a historically new phenomenon. They did not begin to exceed rates in the general population until the late 1950's. Herd has shown that the abrupt rise in cirrhosis mortality among blacks in the late 1950's and 1960's was in part a reflection of a transformation in black drinking patterns initiated at the turn of the century and the massive population shifts which began at that time.[2] The increase in cirrhosis mortality among black cohorts born in the early

*This chapter is a revised version of a paper presented at the 29th International Institute on Prevention and Treatment of Alcoholism, International Council on Alcohol and Addictions, Zagreb, Yugoslavia, June 27–July 1, 1983.

decades of this century are strongest in the high urban areas which were the major centers of black migration over the past century.

## ALCOHOL USE AMONG BLACK ADOLESCENTS

Although cirrhosis mortality rates are disproportionately high among black Americans, yet, in one important segment of the black population, high school students, alcohol abuse and even use are at relatively low levels.

In a review of the 1960–75 literature, Blane and Hewitt noted that the majority of studies of alcohol use among black adolescents were derived from surveys of high school students.[3] These surveys indicated lower rates of lifetime as well as current alcohol use among black high school students compared to non-black students. While many of these surveys are limited by small subgroup sizes and nonrandom samples of students, several national surveys support these findings. The 1974 national survey of junior and senior high school students indicated that black students had the smallest proportion of current drinkers when compared to white and other ethnic/racial groups of students.[4] Blacks also had the lowest proportions of moderate and heavy drinkers. These findings were also replicated in the 1978 national survey of senior high school students.[5] In a national household survey on drug abuse, Fishburne, Abelson, and Cisin reported that approximately 38 percent of white respondents, age 12 to 17 years, were current drinkers compared to 20 percent among black and other races.[6] Similar findings were reported for the years 1972, 1974, 1976 and 1977.

Several explanations may be offered to account for the lower prevalence of alcohol use among black high school students. Surveys of adolescent alcohol use, while indicating that older students drink more than younger students and that boys drink more than girls, also have shown that other demographic variables relate to alcohol use in this population.[7] Lower levels of alcohol consumption have been reported for teenagers living in southern geographic regions, those affiliated with Protestant religious denominations, and those that attain higher academic status in school work.[8] The conservative or fundamentalist Protestant upbringing of many blacks, for example, may be an important factor in accounting for the differences in drinking levels among black and non-black youth. These and other demographic variations in the samples of black and non-black students may account for the differences in alcohol use reported by these students in surveys. A few studies, however, indicate that differences between black and non-black youth in drinking prevalence persist when demographic factors are controlled.[9]

A second explanation for differences in drinking prevalence between these two groups of students relates to differences in underreporting of alcohol consumption. Blacks, as members of a minority group, may withhold or underreport their use of alcohol in national surveys. This is a reasonable point, especially for black students in predominantly white schools or white neighborhoods. The national surveys on drug abuse, however, revealed little variation in the use of illicit drugs among white and black respondents aged 12 to 17 years. It seems unlikely that blacks would conceal the use of alcohol but not other illicit drugs. Moreover, Harford, Lowman and Kaelber examined the drinking patterns of black students in predominantly white schools and black students in predominantly black schools.[10] It was hypothesized that black students in predominantly black schools would be less likely to withhold information on drinking practices than would black students in predominantly white schools. Statistical analyses of beverage specific consumption were not significant. There was no evidence of selective underreporting of alcohol consumption. Nor was there evidence of variations in the self-reports on the frequency of the use of marijuana between black and white students.

A third explanation relates to the fact that surveys of school populations exclude the school dropouts, and these dropouts have been shown to have higher levels of problems associated with alcohol.[11] Studies of institutionalized, delinquent, and school dropout populations, however, are inconsistent with respect to patterns of alcohol use among white and black teenagers—some reported lower rates of problem drinking among blacks, others reported higher rates, and others reported no differences.[12] In addition, the U.S. Bureau of the Census figures indicate that white dropout rates are similar to or slightly higher than black rates up to 18 years of age.[13] At 18, school dropout rates for black males and females begin to increase steeply and to exceed rates for white students.

A fourth explanation may be found in variables which differentiate exposure to and involvement with alcohol among black and non-black students. Harford, Lowman, and Kaelber noted that the onset of drinking was grade-related among black students but was characterized by a later onset relative to non-black students.[14] A delay in the exposure to alcohol may underlie the reported differences in drinking prevalence. Other studies, however, suggest a commonality of drinking correlates among both black and non-black students. Jessor and his colleagues have developed a comprehensive network of variables encompassing personality, the perceived environment, and behavior patterns that account for over 50 percent of the variance in adolescent involvement in problem drinking and marijuana use.[15] Their system of variables has been shown to constitute psychosocial risk for problem behavior in subsamples of adolescents differing in gender and ethnic background. Despite the fact that similar predictors of drinking may apply to both racial/ethnic groups, little is known about the processes underlying the differences in drinking prevalence for these two groups.

The overall objective of the present study was to identify factors which relate to the use of alcohol within each of these racial/ethnic student groups. The 1978 national survey was limited to senior high school students and the overall sample of black students was 496.[16] The present study draws upon the earlier 1974 national survey which encompassed a wider age spectrum and a larger sample of black students.[17]

## MATERIALS AND METHODS

Data for the present study were obtained from a 1974 cross-sectional survey of a nationwide probability sample of all junior and senior high school students in grades 7–12 in the contiguous 48 States and in the District of Columbia.[18] A stratified two-stage sample was used. The primary sampling frame was stratified by census regions, by community size, and by ethnic characteristics.

A sample of 50 primary sampling units (PSU's) consisting of counties or groups of counties was chosen within each selected PSU, the number of homerooms and the number of students enrolled were determined for each of the six grades, either for all schools (rural areas) or for a sample of schools (metropolitan area). The homerooms were stratified into three grade strata: grade 7–8, 9–10, 11–12. A sample of approximately five homerooms per grade stratum was selected within each of the 50 PSU's. A self-administered, 35-page questionnaire was completed by students in the cooperating classes in the sample during the regular school hours at the school facilities. Useable questionnaires were completed by 13,122 students from 643 classrooms. Of the original 717 classes in the sample, 223 (31.1%) were lost because cooperation could not be obtained from State or local school officials. The overall response rate was 72.7 percent including replacement classrooms which were selected by the same sampling procedures described above.

The present analysis compared students who indicated in the questionnaire that they were "Black", not of Hispanic origin (N = 930) and all other non-black students (N = 12,192).

Measures of alcohol consumption were obtained from beverage specific estimates of the typical frequency of alcohol use (every day, 3–4 days a week, 1–2 days a week, 3–4 days a month, once a month, less than once a month but at least once a year, less than once a year, never), and from beverage specific estimates of the number of drinks consumed per typical occasion (12 or more, about 9, 6, 5, 4, 3, 2, 1, less than 1, do not drink).

The beverage specific quantity-frequency information was used to estimate overall frequency (most frequently used beverage) and overall quantity (highest beverage amount).

In addition to alcohol information, the questionnaire contained several items of relevance to alcohol use. The items are organized into the following sets of variables: demography, drinking models, attitudes, and behaviors. Item descriptions and mean scores for the samples of non-black and black students are presented in Table 18-1.

Demographic factors included gender, grade in school, an index of socioeconomic status using a combination of parents' occupa-

TABLE 18-1.
## VARIABLE DESCRIPTION AND MEAN SCORES
## FOR SAMPLES OF BLACK AND NON-BLACK STUDENTS

| *Demographic* | *Item Description* | Non-Blacks (N = 12,192) | Blacks (N = 930) | t-test |
|---|---|---|---|---|
| Gender | boys = 1; girls = 2 | 1.52 (0)+ | 1.52 (0) | 0.49 |
| Grade in school | 7th through 12th | 9.35 (0) | 9.28 (0) | 0.95 |
| Socioeconomic index | Low = 0; high = 9 | 6.23 (0) | 5.44 (0) | 10.40** |
| Region | non-South = 1; South = 2 | 1.27 (0) | 1.35 (0) | 5.48** |
| Religious affiliation | Baptist/Methodist = 1; other = 2 | 1.74 (916) | 1.33 (123) | 25.56** |
| Family intactness | both parents = 1; other = 2 | 1.21 (312) | 1.41 (65) | 14.26** |
| Number of older siblings | none = 2; twelve = 14 | 3.97 (1150) | 4.89 (99) | 12.04** |
| Number of younger siblings | none = 2; twelve = 14 | 3.66 (1755) | 4.34 (153) | 10.18** |
| Number of peers | none = 1; nine or more = 10 | 5.99 (98) | 5.95 (5) | 0.50 |
| Number of older peers | None = 1; older = 2 | 1.14 (197) | 1.19 (22) | 4.05** |
| *Drinking Models* | | | | |
| Parental drinking | both = 1; one = 2; none = 3 | 1.83 (416) | 1.95 (79) | 5.07** |
| School peers drinking | none = 1; all = 5 | 3.24 (268) | 2.77 (76) | 12.71** |
| Friends drinking | none = 1; all = 5 | 3.05 (263) | 2.54 (77) | 10.57** |
| *Attitudes* | | | | |
| Social effects | not important = 1; important = 4 | 2.71 (449) | 2.37 (96) | 9.54** |
| Status reasons | not important = 1; important = 4 | 1.87 (494) | 1.96 (108) | 2.84* |
| Personal effects | not important = 1; important = 4 | 1.88 (501) | 1.99 (107) | 3.86** |
| Conforming reasons | not important = 1; important = 4 | 1.94 (559) | 1.85 (113) | 2.51* |
| *Behaviors* | | | | |
| Academic grades | A's = 1; D's and F's = 7 | 3.32 (0) | 3.79 (0) | 9.45** |
| Religiosity | low = 5; high = 20 | 13.54 (670) | 14.70 (182) | 8.00** |
| Access to alcohol | no = 1; always = 4 | 2.34 (1242) | 1.77 (151) | 14.14** |
| Amount of spending money | none = 1; more than $11 = 5 | 2.99 (85) | 3.09 (4) | 2.28* |
| Extent of deviant behavior | low = 12; high = 48 | 17.61 (705) | 16.80 (139) | 3.94** |
| Marijuana frequency | none = 1; eleven or more = 12 | 2.97 (718) | 2.82 (116) | 1.13 |

+ Figures within parenthesis indicate number of missing cases.
*p < .01
**p < .001

tion and education, geographic region, religious affiliation, family intactness (both parents in household), number of older siblings, number of younger siblings, size of peer network (How many kids do you hang around with?"), and number of older peers.

The influence of drinking models was assessed by three items which included parental drinking (1 = one or both drink regularly, 2 = one or both drink sometimes, 3 = parents do not drink), number of kids in school who drink (1 = none to 5 = all of them), and number of kids you hang around with who drink (1 = none to 5 = all of them).

Attitudes related to drinking assessed the overall importance of drinking in each of the following areas: (1) social effects ("to have a good time"; "it's a good way to celebrate"); (2) status functions ("people think you've been around if you drink"; "it's part of becoming an adult"); (3) personal effects ("when there are too many pressures on me"; "makes things like doing well in school seem less important"; "keeps my mind off problems"); (4) conforming functions ("not to be different from the rest of the kids"; "to be a part of the group").

Behavioral factors include academic grades, religiosity (a five-item scale of the importance placed upon religious teachings, practice and counsel for the direction of daily life developed by Rohrbaugh & Jessor),[19] ease of access to alcohol, amount of spending money, extent of deviant behavior (based on twelve-item scale developed by Jessor & Jessor),[20] assessing involvement in stealing, fighting, property destruction, truancy and other transgressions, and number of times the student reported using marijuana in the past 6 months.

## RESULTS

Among the sample of black students, 33.3 percent of the boys and 43.2 percent of the girls reported that they either abstained from the use of alcohol or drank less than once a year. Abstinence and infrequent drinking were lower for non-black students. About 23 percent of the boys and 30.8 percent of the girls abstained or drank less than once a year. Overall, 38 percent of black students and 27 percent of non-black students abstained or drank less than once a year.

While the proportion of abstainers is high among black students, Harford et al. have indicated that alcohol use is grade-related among both black and non-black students.[21] The results of the 1974 survey on students who reported drinking once a month or more supports that conclusion. Sixty-five percent of non-black students in the 7th grade drink to that extent compared with 85 percent of 12th graders. Forty-eight percent of black students drink to that extent in the 7th grade compared to 75 percent in the 12th grade. This means that the onset of drinking among black students is grade related, as it is among non-black students, but the onset of drinking is delayed among blacks in grades seven through nine. It is important, then, to examine the nature of the differences both within and between each of the two ethnic/racial groups.

Statistical analyses of the variables under study in Table 18-1 indicated that the sample of black students differed significantly from the non-black sample on most of the variables.

Comparisons between the two groups revealed that blacks did not differ from non-blacks with regard to gender or grade in school. Blacks were of lower socioeconomic status, of Baptist/Methodist affiliations, from less intact families, from families with greater numbers of both older and younger siblings (larger families), and older peer networks.

In addition to differences in demographic characteristics associated with socioeconomic status, there were significant differences with respect to the alcohol-related variables. Blacks, when compared to non-blacks, reported less parental drinking and less drinking among both school peers and friends.

With regard to the importance of attitudes related to drinking, blacks rated social and conforming factors as less important reasons for drinking and status and personal effects as slightly more important than did non-blacks.

Blacks did less well academically and were higher on religiosity scores. They had less access to alcohol, slightly more spending money, and less deviant behavior patterns. The overall direction of these differences are such as to expect a lower drinking prevalence among black students. Blacks, for example, reported fewer drinking models, placed less importance on reasons for drinking, and had less access to alcohol than did non-blacks. Black students, while indicating poorer academic performance than non-black students, had higher religiosity scores and less involvement in deviant behavior patterns. Consistent with other studies, however, black students did not differ from non-black students with regard to the use of marijuana.

### Differences Between Drinkers and Abstainers

Table 18-2 presents the mean scores by drinker status (abstainer versus drinker) within each of the two samples for each of the variables under investigation. One-way analyses of variance for the four groups (drinker status by racial/ethnic group) were significant (p < .01) on every variable. Table 18-2 also indicates significant differences associated with planned comparisons within the four groups. Of initial concern are the differences within each of the two ethnic/racial groups.

Among the non-black sample, the majority of variables were significantly related to drinker status. Drinkers, compared to abstainers, were more likely to be boys, older, of higher socioeconomic status, from non-southern regions and of non-Baptist/ Methodist religious affiliation. Drinkers tended to be from less intact families (one or both parents absent), had fewer younger siblings, a greater number of peer networks, and more older peers.

Drinkers, compared to abstainers, reported greater numbers of models for drinking, placed greater access to alcohol, greater involvement in general deviant behavior and marijuana use, and less involvement in religion and school performance. These findings are consistent with the results obtained by Jessor and his colleagues in studies of adolescent problem drinking.

Within the sample of black students, black drinkers tended to be boys and older in age. Unlike non-black drinkers, however, there were few other demographic differences between black abstainers and drinkers. There was a tendency for black drinkers to have fewer older siblings and to have a greater number of older companions in their peer group.

A pattern similar to that of non-blacks emerged with respect to

TABLE 18-2.

## MEAN SCORES ON DEMOGRAPHIC AND ALCOHOL-RELATED VARIABLES FOR SAMPLES OF BLACK AND NON-BLACK STUDENTS

| | Non-Black Students | | Black Students | | Comparisons | | |
| | *Abstainers* | *Drinkers* | *Abstainers* | *Drinkers* | | | |
| *Demographic* | *(1)* | *(2)* | *(3)* | *(4)* | *(1)(2)* | *(3)(4)* | *(1)(3)* | *(2)(4)* |
|---|---|---|---|---|---|---|---|---|
| Gender | 1.59 | 1.49** | 1.59 | 1.48 | ** | ** | NS | NS |
| Grade in school | 8.81 | 9.55** | 8.88 | 9.55 | ** | ** | NS | NS |
| Socioeconomic index | 5.94 | 6.34** | 5.31 | 5.51 | ** | NS | ** | ** |
| Region | 1.35 | 1.24** | 1.38 | 1.34 | ** | NS | NS | ** |
| Religious affiliation | 1.64 | 1.78** | 1.31 | 1.35 | ** | NS | ** | ** |
| Family intactness | 1.19 | 1.21* | 1.39 | 1.42 | * | NS | ** | ** |
| Number of older siblings | 4.02 | 3.95 | 5.18 | 4.71 | NS | * | ** | ** |
| Number of younger siblings | 3.75 | 3.62** | 4.49 | 4.24 | ** | NS | ** | ** |
| Number of peers | 5.53 | 6.17** | 5.84 | 6.03 | ** | NS | NS | NS |
| Number of older peers | 1.09 | 1.16** | 1.16 | 1.22 | ** | * | ** | ** |
| *Drinking Models* | | | | | | | | |
| Parental drinking | 2.17 | 1.70** | 2.13 | 1.84 | ** | ** | NS | ** |
| School peers drinking | 2.69 | 3.44** | 2.36 | 3.04 | ** | ** | ** | ** |
| Friends drinking | 1.96 | 3.46** | 1.88 | 2.96 | ** | ** | NS | ** |
| *Attitudes* | | | | | | | | |
| Social effects | 2.09 | 2.93** | 2.01 | 2.59 | ** | ** | NS | ** |
| Status reasons | 1.85 | 1.88 | 1.91 | 2.00 | NS | NS | NS | ** |
| Personal effects | 1.85 | 1.89* | 2.01 | 1.98 | NS | NS | * | NS |
| Conforming reasons | 1.83 | 1.98** | 1.83 | 1.86 | ** | NS | NS | NS |
| *Behaviors* | | | | | | | | |
| Academic grades | 3.11 | 3.40** | 3.63 | 3.89 | ** | * | ** | ** |
| Religiosity | 15.21 | 12.93** | 15.47 | 14.20 | ** | ** | NS | ** |
| Access to alcohol | 1.53 | 2.66** | 1.47 | 2.19 | ** | ** | NS | ** |
| Amount of spending money | 2.61 | 3.14** | 2.85 | 3.24 | ** | ** | ** | NS |
| Extent of deviant behavior | 14.50 | 18.70** | 14.90 | 18.09 | ** | ** | NS | * |
| Marijuana frequency | 1.20 | 3.60** | 1.32 | 3.79 | ** | ** | NS | NS |

*$p < .001$
**$p < .01$

drinking models, attitudes and behaviors. Black drinkers, compared to black abstainers, reported greater models for drinking, placed more importance on the social effects of drinking, greater access to alcohol, greater involvement in general deviant behavior and marijuana use, and less involvement in religion and school performance.

These results indicate a similar pattern of the correlates of drinker status among both black and non-black students with respect to the alcohol-related variables.

In order to assess the relative contributions of these variables with respect to drinker status, particularly those associated with demographic factors related to socioeconomic class, a discriminant function analysis was conducted separately for each student group. Because of the larger number of missing cases associated with some of the variables, their inclusion would drastically reduce the sample size for multivariate analysis. This is especially critical in view of the number of black students in the sample. For this reason, several of the variables were omitted from the analysis. The majority of these variables related to demographic factors, factors shown to be nonsignificant in the univariate tests with black students. The one exception to the demographic factors was access to alcohol. Because of its theoretical content, the discriminant analyses were conducted with this variable included. Its inclusion reduced the sample size of black students available for analysis from 594 to 530. Comparable results were obtained with the "access to alcohol" variable. The standardized discriminant function coefficients for black and non-black students reflect the relative contributions of each variable controlling for the effects of all other variables. The cannonical correlations in both analyses were highly significant ($p < .001$) both for blacks (.569) and non-blacks (.540). The results from the two analyses yield very similar findings. Among both black and non-black samples, the major variables distinguishing abstainers and drinkers were parents' drinking, friends' drinking, importance of social effects of drinking, extent of deviant behavior, and amount of spending money. Grade in school, conforming reasons for drinking, and amount of spending money made relatively high contributions in the black student sample. Access to alcohol made a substantial contribution in the non-black sample.

## Black and Non-Black Drinking Patterns

In order to assess the relative contributions of these factors with regard to the frequency of drinking and the number of drinks per typical occasion, the same set of variables used in the discriminant analysis was used in multiple regression.

Measures of the typical frequency of alcohol use and of the number of drinks consumed per typical occasion were regressed in a step-wise fashion on the set of predictor variables. The regressions were done separately for non-black and black students. Each coefficient reflects the effects of a particular variable after the effects of the others are controlled. Among black students, the following variables were related to the frequency of drinking: gender, friends' drinking, social effects, access to alcohol, amount of spending money, extent of deviant behavior, and marijuana frequency. More frequent drinking occurred among boys and among students with drinking friends, access to alcohol, greater involvement in deviant behavior and use of marijuana, more spending money, and attitudes viewing the social effects of alcohol as important. These same variables were significant among non-black students. In addition, the following variables were also significant for non-black students: grade in school, number of peers, parental drinking, conforming reasons for drinking, academic grades, and religiosity.

Among both samples of non-black and black students, the following variables were significantly related to the amount of consumption: gender, grade in school, friends' drinking, social effects, access to alcohol, extent of deviant behavior, and marijuana frequency. Heavier consumption occurred among boys and older students and students with drinking friends, attitudes viewing social effects of alcohol as important, access to alcohol, greater involvement in deviant behavior, and more frequent use of marijuana. In addition, the following variables were significantly related to the amount of consumption among non-black students: social class, number of peers, status reasons, academic grades, religiosity, and amount of spending money.

An examination of the beta coefficients for alcohol quantity reveals a pattern similar to that of drinking frequency. Among black students, however, grade in school (age) predicts amount of consumption but not the frequency of consumption.

With regard to both samples of students, the regression analyses would suggest that the factors associated with the use of alcohol are similar for both black and non-black students alike.

### Black and Non-Black Abstainers

In light of the similarity of predictor variables within both samples of students, comparisons between both black and non-black abstainers may reveal factors associated with the later onset of drinking among black students. Table 18-1 summarizes the results of statistical comparisons between the two ethnic/racial groups within each drinker status group. For both abstainers and drinkers, there were significant differences with respect to demographic factors associated with socioeconomic status. It was noted earlier, however, that these variables did not significantly differentiate black abstainers from black drinkers. The results may be interpreted as reflecting more persuasive social class differences between blacks and non-blacks in general. Aside from socioeconomic status, one would expect that black and non-black abstainers would not differ with regard to the alcohol-related variables. This is true for the most part but some exceptions can be noted. Among abstainers, non-black students reported higher proportions of school peers to be drinkers.

A second factor significantly differentiating these two groups relates to the importance of the personal effects of alcohol. Black abstainers, compared to non-black abstainers, viewed the personal effects of drinking as more important reasons for drinking. Since both groups are nondrinkers, this variable may reflect basic differences in the perception of alcohol between these two groups of students.

In order to assess the overall contributions of these variables while controlling for the effects of demographic differences, a discriminant function analysis was conducted with the two groups of abstinent students. The cannonical correlation was .19 ($p <$ .001) and the highest standardized coefficients were school peer drinking ($-.61$) and personal effects ($.58$). Next in magnitude of contribution were grade in school (.31), socioeconomic status (−.31), and academic grades (.36). These findings indicate that both environmental exposure to drinking models and attitudes regarding the use of alcohol distinguish non-black and black abstinent students.

## SUMMARY AND CONCLUSIONS

The overall objective of this study was to identify factors which relate to the use of alcohol among black and non-black students and which might serve to explain the lower prevalence of drinking among black students.

Black students were shown to differ from non-black students with respect to both demographic variables associated with social class and variables associated with exposure to and involvement with alcohol. Multivariate analyses, controlling for the effects of demographic status, yielded several predictors of the frequency and quantity of alcohol consumption. Among the major predictors of alcohol use were exposure to friends as drinking models, attitudes emphasizing the importance of social effects of alcohol, ease of access to alcohol, and behavior patterns of social transgressions and illicit drug use. While degree of religiosity and attainment of good school grades were inversely related to frequent and heavier use of alcohol among non-black students, they were not related to patterns of alcohol use by black students. For the most part, however, there were more similarities than differences in the predictors of alcohol use among black and non-black students. These findings suggest that environmental factors associated with the use of alcohol are similar for black and non-black students.

While the overall use of alcohol is lower among black students, the onset of drinking is grade-related but later in onset relative to non-black drinkers. Despite the fact that the same predictors of drinking are common to both black and non-black students, there is need to identify environmental factors which delay exposure to a more extensive network of peer drinking models and access to alcohol.

Comparisons between black and non-black abstainers revealed that black abstainers reported lower proportions of school peers to be drinkers. This differential exposure to drinking models between black and non-black abstainers may be implicated in the delay of onset of drinking among black students.

A second factor which may be implicated in the delay of onset of drinking among black students related to differences in the perception of alcohol between blacks and non-blacks. Black abstainers, compared to non-blacks, viewed the personal effects of drinking as more important reasons for drinking. These reasons stress the use of alcohol as a coping mechanism to deal with personal stress and problems.

Future studies need to address the status of these variables with regard to their implications in delaying the onset of drinking among black students, and their implications for effective prevention and treatment of alcohol-related problems with adolescents.

## REFERENCES

1. Bourne, P., and Light, E.: Alcohol problems in blacks and women. In Mendelson, J. H. and Mello, N. K. (Eds.), *The Diagnosis and Treatment of Alcoholism.* New York, McGraw-Hill, pp. 83–124, 1979; See also Harper, F: *Alcohol Abuse and Black America.* Alexandria, Va., Douglas Publishers, 1976.

2. Herd, D.: Migration, cultural transformation and the rise of black cirrhosis. Paper presented at the Alcohol Epidemiology Section, International Council on Alcohol and Addictions, Padova, Italy, June, 1983.

3. Blane, H. T., and Hewitt, L. E.: *Alcohol and youth: An analysis of the literature 1960–75.* Report No. PB-268-698. Springfield, Va., U.S. National Technical Information Service, 1977.

4. Rachal, J. V., Williams, J. R., Brehm, M. L., Cavanaugh, B., Moore, R. P., and Eckerman, W. C.: *A national study of adolescent drinking behavior, attitudes and correlates.* Report No. PB-246-002; NIAAA/NCALI-75/27. Springfield, Va., U. S. National Technical Information Service, 1975. (a)

5. Rachal, J. V., Guess, L. L., Hubbard, R. L., Maisto, S. A., Cavanaugh, E. R., Waddell, R., and Benrud, C. D.: *Adolescent Drinking Behavior Volume 1: The Extent and Nature of Adolescent Alcohol and Drug Use: The 1974 and 1978 National Sample Studies.* Research Triangle Park, N.C., Research Triangle Institute, 1980.

6. Fishburne, P. M., Abelson, H. I., and Cisin, I.: *National survey on drug abuse: Main findings: 1979* (Contract No. 271-78-3508). Rockville, Md., National Institute of Drug Abuse, 1979.

7. Rachal (a), op. cit.

8. Ibid; and Blane & Hewitt, op. cit.

9. Bachman, J. G., Johnston, L. D., and O'Malley, P. M.: Smoking, drinking,

and drug use among American high school students: Correlates and trends, 1975–1979. *American Journal of Public Health,* 71:59–69, 1981; and Harford, T. C., Lowman, C., and Kaelber, C. T.: Current prevalence of alcohol use among white and black adolescents. Paper presented at the National Council on Alcoholism Conference, Washington, D.C., April, 1982.

10. Ibid.
11. Cockerham, W. C.: Drinking patterns of institutionalized and noninstitutionalized Wyoming youth. *Journal of Studies on Alcohol,* 36:993–995, 1975. See also MacKay, J. R., Phillips, D. L., and Bryce, F. O.: Drinking behavior among teenagers: A comparison of institutionalized and noninstitutionalized youth. *Journal of Health and Social Behavior,* 8:46–54, 1967.
12. Blane & Hewitt, op. cit.
13. U. S. Bureau of the Census. School enrollment—Social and economic characteristics of students: October 1980 (Advance Report). Current Population Reports Series P-20, No. 362. Washington, D.C., U. S. Department of Commerce, May, 1981.
14. Harford, Lowman, & Kaelber, op. cit.
15. Donovan, J., and Jessor, R.: Adolescent problem drinking: Psychosocial correlates in a national sample study. *Journal of Studies on Alcohol,* 39:1506–1524, 1978, Jessor, R., and Jessor, S. L.: *Problem Behavior and Psychosocial Development: A Longitudinal Study of Youth.* New York, Academic Press, 1977. (a); and Jessor, R., Chase, J. A., and Donovan, J. E.: Psychosocial correlates of marijuana use and problem drinking in a national sample of adolescents. *American Journal of Public Health,* 70:604–613, 1980. (b)
16. Rachal (b), op. cit.
17. Rachal (a), op. cit.
18. Ibid.
19. Rohrbaugh, J., and Jessor, R.: Religiosity in youth: A personal control against deviant behavior. *Journal of Personality,* 43:136–155, 1975.
20. Jessor & Jessor (a), op. cit.
21. Harford, Lowman, Kaelber, op. cit.

## Chapter Nineteen

# THE PROCESS OF RECOVERY FROM ALCOHOLISM II. COMPARING SPOUSES OF ALCOHOLIC PATIENTS AND MATCHED COMMUNITY CONTROLS*

RUDOLF H. MOOS, JOHN W. FINNEY AND WENDY GAMBLE

Three contrasting perspectives have dominated an extensive search for unique characteristics of the spouses of alcoholic patients. One set of studies has tried to identify personality traits which increase the probability that individuals will select alcoholic or prealcoholic mates and then nurture their partner's tendency toward alcohol misuse. A second set of studies has focused on the stress created by being married to an alcoholic partner and has suggested that such spouse characteristics as depression, anxiety, complaints of physical symptoms and poor health are a direct result of this stress. A third set of studies has described alternative ways in which spouses cope with their alcoholic partners and establish satisfactory life-styles even though they are enmeshed in disturbed marriages. The first perspective assumes that alcoholics' spouses suffer from long-standing personality deficits, while the second contends that they are essentially normal people who show the effects of being under intermittent stress. The third perspective argues that many spouses can cope adequately with the stress they experience and lead essentially normal lives.[1]

*Reprinted by permission from *Journal of Studies on Alcohol*, 43(9), pp. 888–909, 1982. Copyright by Journal of Studies on Alcohol, Inc., Rutgers Center for Alcohol Studies, New Brunswick, NJ 08903.

## THE PERSONALITY PERSPECTIVE

Research on the spouses of alcoholics began with a series of clinical descriptions of the wives of heavily-drinking men. These women, the majority of whom had sought help for themselves, were described as demanding, dependent, aggressive, sadistic, psychopathic, and frigid.[2] Although less is known about the husbands of women alcoholics, they have been characterized in generally negative terms as introverted, unsociable, feminine, passive, emotionally distant, self-righteous, sadistic, and defensive.[3]

In a related group of studies some investigators noted instances of depression, psychological or psychosomatic illness, and the development of problem drinking among the wives of alcoholics who became abstinent.[4] These results were interpreted as favoring a "decompensation" hypothesis, which asserted that the spouse's personality characteristics created a "need" for an alcoholic partner. The spouse's functioning was thought to deteriorate because this "need" was no longer met when the partner stopped drinking. However, the failure of several investigators to find that spouses of current or recovered alcoholics were characterized by neurotic or disturbed personality traits[5] raises questions about the disturbed personality and decompensation hypotheses, and bolsters an alternative view — the stress perspective.

## THE STRESS PERSPECTIVE

The stress hypothesis has been tested by comparing spouses whose mates were abstinent (but who had been heavy drinkers) with spouses of currently heavily drinking alcoholics. For example, Kogan and Jackson contrasted the MMPI (Minnesota Multiphasic Personality Inventory) responses of 26 wives of recovered or inactive alcoholics with those of 50 wives of active alcoholics and 50 wives of nonalcoholics.[6] Wives of nonalcoholics had the lowest rate of personality disturbance, wives of actively drinking alcoholics had the highest rate, and wives of recovered or inactive alcoholics were in-between. Bailey[7] and Haberman[8] found that women whose husbands were abstinent (although problem drinking had occurred earlier in the marriage) reported fewer psychophysiological symptoms than women whose husbands were currently drinking, and Paolino et al.[9] noted that spouses of alcoholics in treatment showed significant decreases in anxiety and depression as their partner's drinking problems improved. These results support the stress hypothesis, since wives of abstinent alcoholics (who should be under less stress) were less "impaired" than wives of active alcoholics.

The return to sobriety of an alcoholic, however, does not necessarily alleviate stress-related disturbances in other family members.[10] Characteristics of the alcoholic partner (such as anxiety, depression, and poor occupational functioning), which may remain after the cessation of alcohol misuse, can create continuing stress for the spouse. Some wives perceive their husbands as emotionally distant, suspicious, angry, and depressed regardless of whether they are drinking heavily,[11] indicating that alcohol misuse may not be the primary marital problem.[12] The finding that spouses of recovered alcoholics are not functioning quite as well as spouses of nonalcoholics, therefore, is not inconsistent with the stress perspective and does not necessarily imply that spouses of alcoholics are disturbed individuals or that they have an emotional investment in their partner's continued dysfunction.

## THE COPING PERSPECTIVE

Whereas the personality and stress perspectives have focused primarily on the deficits of spouses of alcoholics, the coping perspective emphasizes the personal resources that spouses bring to bear in adapting to the alcoholism of their mates. For example, James and Goldman found that wives of alcoholics frequently used such active behavioral coping responses as protection (pouring out or hiding the husband's liquor, asking his employer to intervene) and safeguarding family interests (hiding money from the husband, keeping the children out of his way), and such avoidance responses as withdrawal within marriage (wife's avoidance of husband coincident with her feelings of anger and helplessness) and acting out (trying to make husband jealous, getting drunk, and threatening suicide).[13]

In conceptually similar work, Orford et al. identified ten styles of wives' coping behavior and noted that some of these styles were more likely than others to be linked with a good prognosis for the alcoholic partner.[14] Active behavioral coping responses, such as the wife's pleading or arguing with her husband, which imply a degree of engagement or involvement between the partners, were related to improvement in the husband's drinking behavior. Wiseman has described an alternative type of coping pattern by which some wives of alcoholics manage to create independent existences for themselves while remaining married.[15] These women increase their work and hobby skills, gain job promotions, schedule their time to avoid contact with their husbands, and make their own friends and social plans. The coping patterns adopted by spouses may affect their level of functioning as well as the course of their partner's recovery.[16]

## LIMITATIONS OF PREVIOUS RESEARCH

This body of research raises provocative questions about the characteristics of spouses of alcoholics and the effects of a partner's alcoholism. Very few definite conclusions can be drawn from these studies, however, due to four fundamental limitations.[17]

1. Samples of spouses have been small, self-selected, and unrepresentative. Most studies have focused on spouses who are in acute alcoholism-initiated crisis situations or who have sought help for themselves. Spouses who seek help tend to be more dependent, lower in self-esteem, and function less well than spouses who do not.[18]

2. Spouses have not been compared with adequately matched control groups. For example, Kogan and Jackson asked women participating in Al-Anon to recommend friends who were wives of nonalcoholic husbands.[19] This referral process could have created a biased control group, since wives of alcoholics may have friends who are more disturbed or symptomatic than randomly chosen community controls. In addition, since spouses of abstinent alcoholics have not been matched with spouses of drinking alcoholics, the differences between these two groups may be due to factors other than the severity of their partner's alcohol misuse (e.g., socioeconomic status).

3. Spouses have generally been classified into groups on the basis of their reports of their partners' drinking habits rather than on independent information obtained from the partner (but see Orford[20]) and Paolino et al.[21] Spouses who feel anxious or depressed may overestimate the severity of their partners' drinking problems in an attempt to justify their own negative mood. Furthermore, few studies have obtained information on aspects of the current functioning of the alcoholic partner other than drinking behavior, even though such aspects (such as depression or occupational functioning) may substantially affect the spouse.

4. Research on spouses of alcoholics has progressed independently of work on spouses of other "dysfunctional" or normal marital partners. Since the stress of being married to an alcoholic individual may be similar to that of being married to a depressed, physically ill, or unemployed person, spouses of alcoholics need to be studied using a general framework that is applicable to other groups of spouses as well.[22]

## COMPARING MATCHED GROUPS OF SPOUSES

This paper, the second in a series probing posttreatment factors and the process of recovery from alcoholism, tries to avoid these limitations by comparing spouses of recovered and relapsed alcoholic patients with sociodemographically matched spouses of community controls. Patients and their spouses were studied two years after treatment and the patients independently provided information about their drinking patterns and levels of functioning. We address three issues here:

1. Do spouses of recovered alcoholic patients (that is, patients who are able to abstain or control their drinking) function as well as spouses of matched community controls? If so, doubt would be cast on the personality hypothesis, since predisposing personal "deficits" should be relatively enduring and produce current deficits in functioning.

2. How do spouses of relapsed alcoholics compare in social, occupational and health-related areas with matched spouses of controls and recovered alcoholics? Evidence that spouses of relapsed

patients function more poorly (for example, complain of more depression and physical symptoms) than spouses of recovered patients would be consistent with the hypothesis that the stress of being married to a heavily drinking partner detrimentally influences an individual's current functioning. Since such stress should be most evident when the partner is drinking heavily, we also distinguish between spouses of current heavily drinking relapsed patients and those of relapsed patients who are making another effort to control their alcohol misuse.

3. In an attempt to develop a more comprehensive framework to explain spouse functioning, we explore the "effects" of five sets of variables on alcoholic and control spouses. The five sets measure sociodemographic factors, the functioning of the alcoholic or matched control partner, life-changing events, coping responses, and socio-environmental resources. Since characteristics of the partner in addition to alcohol consumption may induce stress for the spouse, we conceptualize indices of the partner's mood, health, and employment as "predictors" of spouse functioning. The inclusion of life-change events explicitly acknowledges that stressful factors other than the partner's current level of functioning may affect the spouse. On the other hand, personal coping skills and social resources available to the spouse should help to mitigate the effects of stress and enhance the spouse's functioning.

## METHOD

### Spouses of Alcoholic Patients

The patients were drawn from a larger sample of 429 persons who were treated for alcoholism at one of five residential facilities.[23] On completing a follow-up questionnaire six to eight months after release from treatment, the 157 patients who had returned to family settings were asked if they and their families would participate in an additional study. In all, 124 patients and their families, or 79 percent of those eligible, participated in the first wave of data collection. One hundred thirteen of these 124 patients (96% of the 118 persons who were still living) were followed up 18 months later, as were seven additional patients whose spouses had not participated previously. Seven of the total group of 120 patients were dropped from this study because they were either not married or not living with their spouses at the six-month follow-up. We obtained data from 105 spouses (84 wives and 21 husbands) of the remaining 113 patients who participated in the two-year follow-up; these spouses constitute the sample for the analyses presented here.

The severity of alcohol misuse at the time of intake to treatment among the patients can be conveyed by their mean alcohol consumption from all beverages on a typical drinking day having been 13.8 oz, that 93 percent had been on "binges" and 72 percent had experienced delirium tremens (DTs) during the past month, and that 90 percent had had physical symptoms, 85 percent had missed meals, and 80 percent had memory problems due to drinking. Sixty percent of the patients had been treated for alcoholism previously during the past three years.

Two groups of patients were identified on the basis of their drinking histories during the two years after treatment. Patients in the recovered group (N = 55) met the following five criteria at both six-month and two-year follow-ups; (1) no rehospitalization for alcoholism during the follow-up interval; (2) alcoholism not a problem which prevented the individual from working during the follow-up period; (3) no problems from drinking (with the exception of "family arguments");[24] (4) abstaining or drinking less than 5 oz of 100 percent ethanol on a typical drinking day in the month prior to follow-up; and (5) quantity-frequency (QF) index (average consumption of 100% ethanol per day) of less than 3 oz. The relapsed group was composed of 58 individuals who either were rehospitalized for treatment of alcoholism or whose drinking was so severe that they could not be classified as recovered moderate drinkers. Data were obtained from 54 spouses of recovered alcoholics and 51 spouses of relapsed alcoholics.

### Spouses of Matched Community Controls

In general, we tried to identify a sociodemographically-matched control family from the same census tract as each treated family.[25]

We obtained a representative community sample of 267 families which were tested twice, 12 to 15 months apart (members of 249 or 93% of the families were successfully followed). The subsample of 105 spouses used here was selected to match the spouses of the alcoholic patients as closely as possible on six sociodemographic factors: sex, age, ethnicity, religion, education, and family size. Families in which drinking problems were reported or which included a family member who had been treated for alcoholism or who was a heavy drinker (more than 3 oz of ethanol per drinking day) were eliminated from the control group.

We were able to select 81 of the 105 controls from the same census tract as the treated families. In the other 24 cases we selected a match from either an adjacent census tract or from a nearby area composed of residents who were sociodemographically comparable to those in the census tract in which the treated family resided. The results shown in Table 19-1 indicate that the spouses of the patients and the community controls were closely comparable. It should be noted that these were groups of stably married people, as indicated by the average length of marriage being 22 years for the control spouses and 21 and 17 years for the spouses of the recovered and relapsed patients, respectively.

## Measures

In addition to sociodemographic characteristics, six sets of variables were measured using three structured, self-administered questionnaires that were completed individually by each respondent: (1) The Health and Daily Living Form (HDL) is a questionnaire containing items adapted from several sources[26] which cover a broad array of personal, social, and health-related information.[27] (2) The Family Environment Scale (FES) measures ten dimensions of a respondent's perceptions of his or her family setting.[28] (3) The Work Environment Scale (WES), which is composed of ten subscales that measure an individual's perception of his or her work setting, was completed by respondents who were currently working in nonsolitary occupational situations.[29] Sociodemographic characteristics, as well as the following set of indices, were used in the present analyses. More detailed

TABLE 19-1.

## COMPARISONS BETWEEN RECOVERED AND RELAPSED
## ALCOHOLIC SPOUSES AND THEIR CONTROLS
## ON MATCHING VARIABLES

| Matching Variables | Spouses of Community Controls (N = 105) | Spouses of Recovered Alcoholics (54) | Spouses of Relapsed Alcoholics (51) | F - Value |
|---|---|---|---|---|
| Sex | 84 women 21 men | 43 women 11 men | 41 women 10 men | < 1.00 |
| Mean age (yrs) | 45.5 ± 11.3 | 49.8 ± 9.5 | 47.9 ± 12.9 | 2.72 |
| Ethnicity (% White) | 80.8 | 83.3 | 82.4 | < 1.00 |
| Education (% beyond high school) | 61.5 | 63.0 | 47.1 | 1.80 |
| Religion (% Protestant) | 44.1 | 55.6 | 47.1 | < 1.00 |
| Percentage of families with children | 53.3 | 50.0 | 41.2 | 1.01 |
| Avg. no. of children in families with children | 1.98 ± 1.00 | 2.04 ± 0.90 | 2.05 ± 1.20 | < 1.00 |
| Occupational status (1–7 rating on Hollingshead scale) | 3.85 ± 1.31 | 3.53 ± 1.50 | 3.66 ± 1.35 | < 1.00 |

descriptions of these indices are provided in the first paper in this series.[30]

### Alcohol Consumption (3 indices)

(1) Do you drink alcoholic beverages (yes/no)? The (2) number of ounces of ethanol drunk in a typical drinking day was calculated for wine, beer and distilled spirits together, as was (3) an overall quantity-frequency (QF) index.

### Mood and Health-Related Functioning (6 indices)

Four indices are related to current mood and health status: (1) depression ($a = .71$)—the number of "yes-no" responses to seven phrases, such as "felt that your memory wasn't all right," and "felt sad or blue"; (2) anxiety ($a = .64$)—the number of "yes" responses to five phrases, such as "felt weak all over" and "restlessness, couldn't sit still"; (3) physical symptoms ($a = .66$)—the number of "yes" responses to 12 symptoms, such as poor appetite, insomnia and headaches experienced fairly often in the past 12 months; and (4) medical conditions—whether the respondent had one or more of 14 more serious medical conditions, such as cancer or diabetes.

The other two indices focus on the use of health services: (5) medication use—the number of "yes" responses to using each of a set of ten medications, such as amphetamines and sleeping pills, frequently during the last 12 months; and (6) doctor visits—the number of times the respondent saw a doctor during the last year (1–5 scale).

### *Personal Resources* (4 indices)

(1) Social competence—an overall index derived from the respondent's age, education, and marital and occupational history. Respondents were also asked about how they had coped with a recent personal crisis or stressful life event. (2) Active behavioral coping was measured by the number of "yes" responses to six action-oriented alternatives, such as "tried to find out more about the situation." (3) Active cognitive coping was assessed by the number of "yes" responses to six cognitively oriented alternatives, such as "tried to step back from the situation and be more objective." (4) Avoidance coping was measured by the number of "yes" responses to five alternatives indicative of avoidance or tension reduction, such as "sometimes took it out on other people when I felt angry or depressed." These measures have adequate psychometric properties and are related to the type of event and outcome experienced by individuals.[31]

### *Social Functioning* (3 indices)

(1) Social contacts—the number of times during the past month the respondent visited with friends or relatives; (2) social activities— the number of social, cultural and recreational activities in which the respondent participated with family members during the past month; (3) religious participation—"How often did you attend religious services?" (answered on a six-point scale ranging from never to once a week).

### Occupational Functioning (3 indices)

(1) Respondents were asked whether they were currently working either part-time or full-time and (2) whether they had changed jobs during the past year. (3) They were also asked to estimate their total annual income.

### Life-Change Events (3 indices)

Events occuring during the past year were checked from a list of 23.[32] Seven were considered positive events (e.g., marital reconciliation and job promotion), ten were judged to be negative (e.g., death of a close friend and trouble at work), and six were judged to be ambiguous (e.g., child left home and began new job). The number of positive, negative, and total life-change events were used to compare the three groups.

### Social-Environmental Resources (13 indices)

The social network of the respondent was measured by the number of confidants with whom the respondent could discuss personal problems. The family environment was assessed by the respondent's perceptions of six of the ten dimensions of the FES: cohesion, expressiveness, conflict, active-recreational orientation, moral-religious emphasis and organization. The work environment was assessed by the respondent's perceptions on six of the ten dimensions of the WES: involvement, peer cohesion, task orientation, work pressure, clarity and physical comfort.

### RESULTS

Two preliminary analyses were conducted. To explore gender differences, we compared the husbands of women patients with a matched (age, ethnicity, education, religion, occupational status, number of children) group of wives of men patients on the seven sets of variables just described. Since essentially no differences were found (t-tests), the husbands and wives of patients were combined in subsequent analyses. Additional analyses (t-tests) indicated that there were no differences between those control spouses who were matched to the spouses of recovered patients and those matched to the spouses of relapsed patients. Therefore, spouses of both recovered and relapsed patients were contrasted with the total control group.

The three groups were compared using one-way analyses of variance (ANOVA) and the Student-Newman-Keuls Multiple Range Test to identify significant differences among the groups. Analyses of covariance (ANCOVA) controlling for sex, age, education, ethnicity, and number of children currently living at home were conducted to determine the extent to which group differences were still significant after these sociodemographic characteristics were taken into account. The adjusted means and the statistical significance levels of the Fs obtained using ANCOVA were virtually identical to those obtained using ANOVA. Thus, the unadjusted means and standard deviations and the ANOVA F-values are presented here.

### Alcohol Consumption and Mood and Health-Related Functioning

The proportion of spouses who were current drinkers was about the same among the community controls and the relapsed alcoholics, but was somewhat lower among the recovered patients (Table 19-2). Although the spouses of the relapsed patients consumed more alcohol than the other two groups of spouses, their average daily ethanol intake (quantity-frequency index) was still within normal limits. The only significant difference in mood and health-related functioning was that the spouses of the recovered alcoholics were less depressed than either of the other two groups.

### Personal Resources and Social and Occupational Functioning

There were no differences among the spouses in their social competence or in their use of different types of coping responses. Spouses of both groups of alcoholics reported fewer informal social contacts than did spouses of community controls, but there were no differences among the groups in social activities or religious participation, or in the proportion of people who were

TABLE 19-2.

COMPARISONS BETWEEN RECOVERED AND RELAPSED
ALCOHOLIC SPOUSES AND CONTROLS
ON ALCOHOL CONSUMPTION AND MOOD
AND HEALTH-RELATED FUNCTIONING

| Variable | Spouses of Community Controls (N = 105) | Spouses of Recovered Alcoholics (54) | Spouses of Relapsed Alcoholics (51) | F–Value |
|---|---|---|---|---|
| Drank alcohol during past month (% yes) | 90.4[a] | 63.0 | 78.4[c] | 9.19‡ |
| Total quantity ethanol drunk (oz of ethanol) | 2.05[b] ± 1.23 | 1.93[c] ± 2.16 | 3.39[b,c] ± 4.65 | 4.18* |
| Mean daily ethanol consumption (oz of ethanol) | 0.49[b] ± 0.59 | 0.73 ± 1.30 | 1.53[b] ± 3.67 | 4.11* |
| Depression (No.yes of 7) | 2.52 ± 2.13 | 1.81[c] ± 1.73 | 2.76[c] ± 2.17 | 3.21* |
| Anxiety (No.yes of 5) | 1.05 ± 1.43 | 1.06 ± 1.14 | 1.20 ± 1.36 | < 1.00 |
| Physical Symptoms (No.yes of 12) | 3.11 ± 2.52 | 2.46 ± 2.19 | 2.92 ± 2.29 | 1.30 |
| Medical conditions (% 1 or more) | 34.6 | 35.2 | 43.1 | < 1.00 |
| Medications (No.yes of 10) | 1.87 ± 1.46 | 2.02 ± 1.41 | 1.86 ± 1.89 | < 1.00 |
| Doctor visits (1–5 scale) | 2.17 ± 1.02 | 2.24 ± 1.08 | 2.27 ± 1.10 | < 1.00 |

[a,b,c]Means that share a similar superscript differ significantly (p < .05) by the Student-Newman-Keuls Test
*P < .05
‡P < .001

currently employed or who had changed jobs during the past year. As expected, and in agreement with their partners' reports,[33] the spouses of relapsed alcoholics stated that they had lower family incomes than did the spouses in the other two groups.

### Life-Change Events and Social-Environmental Resources

The spouses of relapsed patients reported more negative events than did the other two groups of spouses. With respect to the family setting, the spouses of the relapsed alcoholics perceived less cohesion than those in the other two groups, and the spouses of both recovered and relapsed patients perceived less active-recreational orientation than did the spouses of the community controls. However, there were no differences in social networks or perceived work environments among the three groups.

*Spouses of Heavily Drinking Relapsed Patients*

All of the patients in the relapsed group had either been rehospitalized for treatment of alcoholism or had been drinking excessively sometime during the two-year posttreatment interval. However, some relapsed patients were making an attempt to reduce or control their alcohol consumption, whereas others were drinking as heavily as when they initially entered residential treatment for alcohol misuse. To test the hypothesis that the spouse is under greater stress when the alcoholic partner is drinking excessively, we compared the spouses (N = 14) of relapsed patients whose partners were drinking more than 12 oz of ethanol per day with the spouses of controls.

The differences between the groups were similar to those just reported, although the results for the spouses of heavier drinking relapsed patients were more extreme. For example, these spouses were more depressed (mean, 3.57) and anxious (mean, 2.00), engaged in fewer informal social activities (mean, 7.93), and reported more negative life-change events (mean, 1.57). In addition, they complained of more physical symptoms (mean, 4.36) and medical conditions (64.3% reported one or more), and were more likely to have visited doctors (mean, 2.86) and to have changed jobs during the past year (57.1%). They also reported using more avoidance coping methods (mean 1.93) and saw their families as characterized by more conflict (mean, 4.50) and less cohesion (mean, 5.21), organization (mean, 4.43), and recreational orientation (mean 3.14).

*Predicting Spouse Functioning*

In order to develop a clearer understanding of the "determinants" of the functioning of spouses of alcoholics and matched controls, we conducted regression analyses using five sets of variables (background characteristics, the level of functioning of the alcoholic or matched-control partner,[34] life-change events, coping responses, and family environment) to predict six indices of spouse functioning.[35] Partial and multiple correlations between these five sets of variables and the spouse's level of functioning were then analyzed.[36]

The spouses of alcoholics are affected by the current functioning of their partners. Specifically, spouses whose partners were drinking more alcohol and reporting more drinking problems complained of more anxiety, depression, and physical symptoms, and visited doctors more frequently. The extent to which the partner reported anxiety, depression and physical symptoms was related to the spouse's mood, physical symptoms, and use of medications. The set of six partner characteristics accounted for significant increments in predicting four of the criteria of spouse functioning.

With some exceptions, the current functioning of the partner was not related to the six criteria for the spouses of the controls. Spouses with partners who showed poor occupational functioning reported more anxiety and more frequent doctor visits. Spouses with more anxious and physically distressed partners reported taking more medications. In addition, the partner's level of alcohol consumption was positively related to the spouse's level of consumption. However, partner characteristics as a set did not add a significant increment to the predicted variance for any of the criteria among the control spouses.

The life-event indices added incremental variance to the prediction of three criteria for spouses of alcoholics but to only one for spouses of controls. Negative life events were related to depression in both groups; they were also related to alcohol consumption among spouses of alcoholics. Positive events were related to the use of medications, but only among spouses of the alcoholics. Although the use of avoidance coping was related only to depression among spouses of controls, it was strongly related to five of the six criterion indices among spouses of alcoholics.

The partial correlations between the FES subscales and the criteria were similar in the two groups, but family conflict was more highly related to anxiety, depression, and physical symptoms among spouses of alcoholics. Spouses in both groups who were in family environments that lacked cohesion tended to experience more mood and health-related dysfunction. Also, as might be expected, there was less emphasis on expressiveness in families in which spouses were more depressed. The finding that moral-religious emphasis was related to physical symptoms and use of medication in both groups may be due to health problems often eliciting a search for a deeper pattern of meaning to explain life events.[37]

## DISCUSSION

We have used samples of spouses of alcoholic patients and spouses of matched community controls to focus on three questions: (1) Do the spouses of recovered alcoholic patients function as well as the spouses of their nonalcoholic community neighbors? (2) Do the spouses of relapsed patients function more poorly than those of recovered patients and of community controls, and, if so, in what areas? (3) Can a general framework that incorporates such factors as partner characteristics, life-change events, and coping responses contribute to a better understanding of functioning among spouses of alcoholics and normal controls?

### Spouses of Recovered and Relapsed Alcoholics

There were only three differences between the spouses of recovered alcoholic patients and those of community controls. The spouses of the recovered alcoholics were less likely to have drunk alcohol during the past month, and they reported fewer social contacts and less emphasis on an active-recreational orientation in their families. In conjunction with the recovered patients functioning about as well as their nonalcoholic community counterparts,[38] these findings show that some recovered alcoholics and their spouses can attain essentially normal functioning.

In comparison with the controls, the spouses of relapsed alcoholics drank more alcohol, experienced more negative life events, participated in fewer social activities, and enjoyed less cohesion and active recreation in their family environments. Furthermore, the spouses of currently heavy drinking alcoholics also experienced more drinking problems, depression and medical conditions, and tended to change jobs and visit doctors more frequently.

In corroboration of previous research,[39] the overall results indicate that individuals suffer some stress effects from living with an alcoholic partner but that these effects diminish when the partner makes an effort to control his or her excessive drinking. The magnitude of the stress effects that we identified may have been relatively small because most of the spouses of the relapsed alcoholics had been married to their partners for some time and were used to variations in the severity of their alcohol misuse. Furthermore, the spouses were generally not in serious crisis situations at the two-year follow-up, since most of their partners were currently maintaining themselves in the community.

### Predictors of Spouse Functioning

Spouses of alcoholic partners who were functioning more poorly complained of more anxiety, depression, and physical symptoms and reported visiting doctors more frequently. However, the amount of alcohol drunk by the alcoholic partner was only one among several of the partner's characteristics that were related to the spouse's mood and health. In contrast, there was little relationship between the level of functioning of the spouses of the controls and the characteristics of their partners. This is probably because almost all of these nonalcoholic partners were functioning relatively well.[40]

Life events and aspects of the family environment were related to functioning in the two groups of spouses. That spouses in both groups who experienced more negative events reported more depressed effect is consistent with research indicating that life stress can precipitate depression.[41] The influence of negative events on alcohol consumption among spouses of alcoholics extends our earlier results showing that some of these spouses were quite labile in their drinking habits.[42] The findings on the family milieu are consistent with earlier work which showed that family cohesion and conflict are related to physical symptoms and depression (as well as to alcohol consumption) among the alcoholics.[43]

Avoidance-coping responses were more closely related to functioning among spouses of alcoholics, even though, on the average, they were no more likely to use such responses than were the controls. Previous studies have shown that the spouse's avoidance and tension-reduction coping is related to poorer treatment outcome for the partner;[44] the present results indicate that it is also related to poorer "outcome" for the spouse. Avoidance coping may be more predictive of functioning among the alcoholics' spouses because their partners are more prone to engage in such coping than are the partners of the controls.[45] Marriages in which both the husband and wife tend to avoid dealing with stress and to engage in impulsive acting-out are more likely to create problems for both partners.[46]

### Implications for Personality, Stress, and Coping Perspectives

The results provide no support for the hypothesis that, relative to spouses of controls, spouses of alcoholics are more likely to suffer from disturbed personalities. Nor is there support for the idea that their functioning is detrimentally affected by their partner's successful control of alcohol misuse. Although spouses of recovered alcoholics complained of some depression, anxiety, and physical symptoms, their complaints were no more serious than those of spouses of community controls. The most parsimonious conclusion is that spouses of alcoholics are basically normal people who are trying to cope with disturbed marriages and behaviorally dysfunctional partners. Previous findings supporting the personality and decompensation hypotheses may be due to many of the spouses having been in crisis situations, having sought help for themselves, and not having been compared with adequately matched controls.

Our findings are consistent with the stress and coping perspectives. Spouses who are under more stress because their alcoholic partners are drinking heavily experience more mood and health-related dysfunction than spouses of controls or of recovered alcoholics. Furthermore, spouses are affected by their partners' other characteristics (such as mood and physical symptoms) as well as by stressful life-change events (such as loss of income and legal problems) that may be related to the partners' drinking problem. These results indicate that complaints of depression and health-related problems among spouses of abstinent alcoholics do not necessarily provide support for the disturbed personality hypothesis since such spouses may experience high levels of stress due to their partners' continuing dysfunction in other areas. Future studies of spouses of alcoholics need to consider more than just their partners' level of alcohol consumption to accurately portray the amount of stress they experience.

With respect to the coping perspective, the manner in which the spouses of alcoholics respond to stress is predictive of their level of functioning. Spouses who use avoidance-coping responses that are oriented toward handling the emotions aroused by a stressful situation rather than toward actively handling the situation itself complain of poorer mood and health and report using more alcohol and medications than do spouses who do not use such responses.[47] Additional regression analyses showed that variations in the spouses' tendency to use avoidance-coping responses significantly predicted their mood and health-related functioning even after the partners level of alcohol consumption was taken into account. Spouses who had partners who were currently drinking heavily but who did not use avoidance-coping resources were doing as well as those who had used such responses even though their partners were either abstaining or drinking moderately.[48]

Our findings underscore the need to study spouses of alcoholics using a general conceptual framework that can be applied to other groups of spouses as well. Such a framework should be broad enough to include the five sets of "predictors" of spouse functioning used here and to incorporate potentially relevant personality factors. The framework should recognize that the characteristics of the dysfunctional partner can affect spouse functioning directly (the partner's drinking "elicits" drinking in the spouse) as well as indirectly by, for example, increasing life stressors and decreasing coping and social resources. Furthermore, such a framework should enable one to probe the direct effects of life-stress events and coping responses on the spouse's functioning, as well as the extent to which their effects are mediated by the kind of family environment they help to create. The procedures we have used to formulate and estimate models to "explain" the posttreatment functioning of alcoholic patients[49] may be applicable to focusing on their spouses as well.

This type of perspective can serve to reorient research on the spouses of alcoholics in at least three important ways. First, it explicitly recognizes that the effects of any one characteristic of a partner (such as his or her high level of alcohol consumption) on a spouse must be evaluated in light of the partner's adequacy of functioning in other areas. Second, it is flexible enough to include personality, stress, coping factors, and their mutual inter-relationships as potential "determinants" of spouse functioning. It enables an investigator to study the influence of personality factors on functioning without the need to assume that spouses of alcoholics are disturbed or abnormal. Third, by considering an array of factors impinging on spouse functioning, it may orient clinicians toward focusing on specific needs (training in coping skills) and capitalizing on existing resources (family cohesion) in their treatment of spouses.

## REFERENCES

1. Cloptin, J.: Alcoholism and the MMPI: A review. *J. Stud. Alcohol, 39*:1540-1558, 1978; Edwards, P., Harvey, C., and Whitehead, P.: Wives of alcoholics: A critical review and analysis. *Q. J. Stud. Alcohol, 34*:112-132, 1973; Jacob, T., Favorini, A., Meisel, S. and Anderson, C.: The alcoholic's spouse, children and family interactions: Substantive findings and methodological issues. *J. Stud. Alcohol, 39*:1231-1251; and Paolino, T. J., Jr. and McCrady, B. S.: *The Alcoholic Marriage: Alternative Perspectives.* New York, Grune & Stratton, 1977.

2. Price, G. M.: A study of the wives of twenty alcoholics. *Q. J. Stud. Alcohol, 5*:620-627, 1945. See also Rae, J. B. and Forbes, A.: Clinical and psychometric characteristics of the wives of alcoholics. *Br. J. Psychiat., 112*:197-200, 1966; and Whalen, T.: Wives of alcoholics: Four types observed in a family service agency. *Q. J. Stud. Alcohol., 14*:632-641, 1953.

3. Busch, H., Kormendy, E. and Feuerlein, W.: Partners of female alcoholics. *Br. J. Addict., 68*:179-184, 1973; Fox, R.: The alcoholic spouse. In Einstein, V. W. (Ed.), *Neurotic Interaction in Marriage.* New York, Basic Books, 1956, pp. 148-168; Rimmer, J.: Psychiatric illness in husbands of alcoholics. *Q. J. Stud. Alcohol, 35*:281-283, 1974.

4. Kalashian, M. M.: Working with the wives of alcoholics in an outpatient clinic setting. *Marriage & Fam., 21*:130-133, 1959. See also MacDonald, D. E.: Mental disorders in wives of alcoholics. *Q. J. Stud. Alcohol, 17*:282-287, 1956; Mitchell, H. E. and Mudd, E. H.: The development of a research methodology for achieving the cooperation of alcoholics and their nonalcoholic wives. *Q. J. Stud. Alcohol, 18*:649-657, 1957; and Rae, J. B.: The influence of the wives on the treatment outcome of alcoholics: A follow-up study at two years. *Br. J. Psychiat., 120*:601-613, 1972.

5. Ballard, R. G.: The interrelatedness of alcoholism and marital conflict: Symposium, 1958 III. The interaction between marital conflict and alcoholism as seen through MMPIs of Marriage partners. *Am. J. Orthopsychiat.,*

29:528–546, 1959. See also Corder, B., Hendricks, A. and Corder, R.: An MMPI study of a group of wives of alcoholics. *Q. J. Stud. Alcohol*, 25:551–554, 1964; and Paolino, T., McCrady, B., Diamond, S. and Longabaugh, R. Psychological disturbances in spouses of alcoholics: An empirical assessment. *J. Stud. Alcohol*, 37:1600–1608, 1976.

6. Kogan, K. L. and Jackson, J. K.: Stress, personality and emotional disturbance in the wives of alcoholics. *Q. J. Stud. Alcohol*, 26:486–495, 1965.

7. Bailey, M. B.: Psychophysiological impairment in wives of alcoholics as related to their husband's drinking and sobriety. In Fox, R. (Ed.) *Alcoholism: Behavioral Research, Therapeutic Approaches.* New York, Springer, 1967 pp. 134–144.

8. Haberman, P. W.: Psychological test score changes for wives of alcoholics during periods of drinking and sobriety. *J. Clin. Psychol.*, 20:230–232, 1964.

9. Paolino, T., McCrady, B. and Kogan, K.: Alcoholic marriages: A longitudinal empirical assessment of alternative theories. *Br. J. Addict.*, 73:129–138, 1978.

10. Jackson, J. K.: Alcoholism and the family. In Pittman, D. J. and Snyder, C. R., (Eds.), *Society, Culture, and Drinking Patterns.* New York, Wiley, 1962.

11. Kogan, K. L. and Jackson, J. K.: Role perceptions in wives of alcoholics and nonalcoholics. *Q. J. Stud. Alcohol*, 24:627–639, 1963 (a); and Kogan, K. J. and Jackson, J. K.: Patterns of atypical perceptions of self and spouse in wives of alcoholics. *Q. J. Stud. Alcohol*, 25:555–557, 1964 (b)

12. Paolino & McCrady, op. cit.; and Orford, J.: Alcoholism and marriage: The argument against specialism. *J. Stud. Alcohol*, 36:1537–1563, 1975 (a)

13. James, J. E. and Goldman, M.: Behavior trends of wives of alcoholics. *Q. J. Stud. Alcohol*, 32:373–381, 1971.

14. Orford, J., Gutherie, S., Nicholls, P., Oppenheimer, E., Egert, S. and Hensman, C.: Self-reported coping behavior of wives of alcoholics and its association with drinking outcome. *J. Stud. Alcohol*, 36:1254–1267, 1975.

15. Wiseman, J. P.: An alternative role for the wife of an alcoholic in Finland. *J. Marriage & Fam.*, 37:172–179, 1975 (a)

16. Ibid; and Wiseman, J. P.: The "home treatment": The first steps in trying to cope with an alcoholic husband. *Fam. Relat.*, 29:541–549, 1980 (b)

17. Edwards, Harvey, & Whitehead, op. cit.; Jacob, Favorini, Meisel, & Anderson, op. cit.; and Paolino & McCrady, op. cit.

18. Hurwitz, J. I. and Daya, D. K.: Non-help-seeking wives of employed alcoholics: A multilevel, interpersonal profile. *J. Stud. Alcohol*, 38:1730–1739, 1977; Jackson, J. K. and Kogan, K. L.: The search for solutions: Help-seeking patterns of families of active and inactive alcoholics. *Q. J. Stud. Alcohol*, 24:449–472, 1963. See also Gorman, J. and Rooney, J.: The influence of Al-Anon on the coping behavior of wives of alcoholics. *J. Stud. Alcohol*, 40:1030–1038, 1979.

19. Kogan & Jackson, op. cit.

20. Orford, J.: A study of the personalities of excessive drinkers and their wives, using the approaches of Leary and Eysenck. *J. Consult. Clin. Psychol.*, 44:534–545, 1976 (b)

21. Paolino & McCrady, op. cit.
22. Orford (a), op. cit.
23. Bromet, E., Moos, R. H., Bliss, F. and Wuthmann, C.: The posttreatment functioning of alcoholic patients: Its relation to program participation. *J. Consult. Clin. Psychol.*, 45:829–842, 1977.
24. Given the belief in the ineffectiveness of any course other than total abstinence, we felt that some patients might experience family arguments due to drinking, even if they were confining their alcohol consumption to moderate levels.
25. Moos, R. H., Finney, J. W. and Chan, D. A.: The process of recovery from alcoholism. I. Comparing alcoholic patients and matched community controls. *J. Stud. Alcohol,* 42:383–402, 1981.
26. Langer, T. S.: A twenty-two item screening scale of psychiatric symptoms indicating impairment. *J. Health & Hum. Behau,* 3:269–276, 1962; Bradburn, N. M. and Caplovitz, D.: *Reports on Happiness.* Chicago, Aldine, 1965; Gough, H. G. and Heilbrun, A. B., Jr.: *Manual for the Adjective Check List.* Palo Alto, Calif., Consulting Psychologists Press, 1965; and Holmes, T. H. and Rahe, R. H.: The Social Readjustment Rating Scale. *J. Psychosom. Res.,* 11:213–218, 1967.
27. The HDL is available from the Ralph G. Comer Alcohol Research Reference Files (CARRF), Center of Alcohol Studies, Rutgers University, New Brunswick, N.J. 08903.
28. Moos, R. H. and Moos, B. S.: *Manual for the Family Environment* Scale. Palo Alto, Calif., Consulting Psychologists Press, 1981. See also Moos, R. H.: Evaluating family and work settings. In Ahmed, P. and Coelho, G., (Eds.), *New Directions in Health.* New York; Plenum, 1971, pp. 337–360. (a)
29. Moos, R. H.: *Manual for the Work Environment Scale.* Palo Alto, Calif., Consulting Psychologist Press, 1981. (b)
30. Moos, Finney, & Chan, op. cit.
31. Billings, A. G. and Moos, R. H.: The role of coping responses and social resources in attenuating the stress of life events. *J. Behau Med,* 4:139–157, 1981.
32. Holmes & Rahe, op. cit.
33. Moos, Finney & Chan, op. cit.
34. The index of the partner's drinking problems, which was used as a predictor of functioning for spouses of alcoholics, was not appropriate for the spouses of controls because of the exclusions of individuals with drinking problems. The control partner's self-confidence (the accuracy, as rated on five-point scales, of six items as self-descriptors: aggressive, ambitious, confident, dominant, energetic and outgoing) was thus substituted as an alternative predictor.
35. Similar analyses were conducted for social and occupational functioning, but the results are not shown since only a chance number of significant relationships was found between predictor variables and these criteria.

36. Preliminary regressions indicated that the other background variables were not significantly related to the criteria.

37. Moos, R. H.: *Coping with Physical Illness.* New York, Plenum, 1977. (c)

38. Moos, Finney, & Chan, op. cit.

39. Edwards, Harvey & Whitehead, op. cit.; Jacob, Favorini, Meisel, & Anderson, op. cit.; and Paolino & McCrady, op. cit.

40. Moos, Finney & Chan, op. cit.

41. Brown, G. and Harris, T.: *Social Origins of Depression.* New York, Free Press, 1978.

42. Finney, J., Moos, R. H. and Mewborn, C. Posttreatment experiences and treatment outcome of alcoholic patients six months and two years after hospitalization. *J. Consult. Clin. Psychol.,* 48:17–29, 1980.

43. Ibid.; See also Rae, J. B. and Drewery, J.: Interpersonal patterns in alcoholic marriages. *Br. J. Psychiat., 120:*615–621, 1972; and Bromet, E. and Moos, R. H.: Environmental resources and the posttreatment functioning of alcoholic patients. *J. Health Soc. Behav, 18:*326–338, 1977.

44. James & Goldman, op. cit.; and Orford, Gutherie, Nicholls, Oppenheimer, Egert, & Hensman, op. cit.

45. Moos, Finney & Chan, op. cit.

46. Moos, R. H., Bromet, E., Tsu, V. and Moos, B.: Family characteristics and the outcome treatment for alcoholism. *J. Stud. Alcohol, 40:*78–88, 1979.

47. Pearlin, L. and Schooler, C. The structure of coping. *J. Health Soc. Behav, 19:*2–21, 1978.

48. Jackson & Kogan, op. cit.

49. Cronkite, R. C. and Moos, R. H.: Evaluating alcoholism treatment programs; an integrated approach. *J. Consult. Clin. Psychol., 46:*1105–1119, 1978. (a); Cronkite, R. C. and Moos, R. H.: The determinants of posttreatment functioning of alcoholic patients: A conceptual framework. *J. Consult. Clin. Psychol., 48:*305–316, 1980. (b)

## Chapter Twenty

# FUTURE CAREGIVERS' VIEWS
# ON ALCOHOLISM TREATMENT*
# A POOR PROGNOSIS

HENRY WECHSLER AND MARY ROHMAN

Public concern over the incidence and costs of alcohol-related problems has led to the development of many initiatives directed toward the prevention, identification, and treatment of drinking problems. Although many of these initiatives involve the creation of specialized treatment programs, it is clear from the small proportion of problem drinkers who actually seek or obtain help from any source that much could be done to facilitate the seeking of help and to improve the professional response to problem drinking.

As the size and scope of alcohol-related problems increase, the responsibility for identifying or treating these problems has fallen, and will continue to fall, on professionals in many different sectors of the human-service system. Shaw et al. found a disproportionate number of problem drinkers among those seeking help at many types of generic agencies.[1] This pattern of seeking help occurs not only because problem drinkers tend to experience medical, psychosocial, and family problems more frequently than non-drinkers or "normal" drinkers, but also because they seek to avoid the stigma of the label of alcoholic associated with receiving treatment from alcoholism agencies.

It is important, therefore, that professionals in such fields as

*Reprinted by permission from *Journal of Studies on Alcohol*, Vol. 43, pp. 939–955, 1982. Copyright by Journal of Studies on Alcohol, Inc., Rutgers Center of Alcohol Studies, New Brunswick, NJ 08903

nursing, medicine, social work, and counseling be prepared to identify and deal with actual or potential drinking problems among their patients. Unfortunately, previous research has presented a discouraging view of the manner in which professional education and training programs have prepared students to respond to problem drinkers. Both professionals (such as physicians, nurses, and social workers) and students preparing for careers in these fields have been found to have unfavorable attitudes toward alcoholics. Mackey[2] found that professionals in various caregiving and mental health roles—i.e., welfare workers, guidance counselors, police officers, social workers, psychiatrists, and psychologists—attributed negative traits to alcoholics, as did the nurses, chaplains, clerks and health professionals studied by Sowa and Cutter.[3]

One reason for these negative perceptions is that, despite educational efforts to the contrary, attitudes of professionals reflect the dominant views of the society around them, which tend to characterize alcoholism as a moral or character defect. The alcoholic is often seen as a morally weak person who lacks the willpower and motivation necessary for his recovery. In a study of 35 family-practice residents, Fisher et al. found that physicians rated alcoholics as sicker, weaker, and more aimless and hopeless than average people.[4] Wolf et al. reported that emergency-ward physicians perceived alcoholism as a disorder occurring primarily among derelicts.[5] Similarly, Knox[6] found that psychiatrists, psychologists, and social workers at Veterans Administration hospitals believed that alcoholism was caused by such character defects as low tension tolerance, excessive dependency, and poorly restrained impulses.

The attribution of negative traits to alcoholics and the association of alcoholism with moral or character defects generate a self-fulfilling prophecy regarding poor treatment outcome for people with drinking problems. Chafetz has shown that professionals who responded negatively to patients who were alcoholics considered them poorly motivated and, consequently, difficult to treat.[7] In a study of the members of the American Psychiatric Association and the National Association for Mental Health, 90 percent of the psychiatrists interviewed considered alcoholics "more difficult" or "much more difficult" to treat than other patients.[8] In fact, 27 percent felt that the task was impossible. Fewer than 30 percent of the social workers studied by Bailey and Fuchs had a favorable prognosis for alcoholics in treatment under any method.[9] Although 58 percent of those social workers who had worked with alcoholics felt "partly effective," only 16 percent felt "moderately effective" or better. The frustration and discouragement caused by this prognostic pessimism result in low motivation to treat alcoholics and a reluctance to diagnose alcoholism except in the most extreme cases. Thus, a barrier to treatment is created for patients who are in the early stages of alcoholism when they might benefit most from professional intervention.

Other factors have also been associated with the disinclination of professionals to diagnose or treat problem drinking. Shaw et al., in a study of the helping community's response to problem drinkers, found that many professionals in health, mental health, and social service agencies were reluctant to deal with the issue of alcohol misuse.[10] These professionals tended to feel insecure about treating a patient's drinking problem; they felt that they lacked the knowledge and skill to deal effectively with alcohol-related problems. Furthermore, they did not know where to go for additional information and support. They tended to doubt the legitimacy of their role; that is, they were uncertain as to whether drinking problems fell within the sphere of their professional responsibility, and they questioned their right to ask patients about their drinking. Finally, many of these professionals avoided problem drinkers out of a sense of hopelessness, feeling that these patients would never be able to change their behavior.

Professionals' awareness of and sensitivity to issues related to alcohol misuse have a marked effect on their ability and willingness to respond to alcohol-related problems. Reluctance to question or respond to a patient's drinking presents a serious barrier to the recognition and treatment of problem drinkers. To the extent that professionals doubt the adequacy or legitimacy of their professional role, are pessimistic in their prognosis, or feel uncertain about their own drinking, they are unlikely to respond positively or effectively to problem drinkers.

The aim of this study was to investigate future caregivers' expectations and attitudes regarding the treatment of people with alcohol-related problems. We surveyed a random sample of graduate students preparing for careers in medicine, nursing, social work, and counseling—fields in which they might be called upon to treat patients with alcohol-related problems. The survey was designed to elicit information regarding students' awareness of and sensitivity to issues of alcohol use and misuse, focusing on those attitudes which might influence their response to problem drinkers. We wanted to know the extent to which students were prepared to deal with drinking problems, the extent of their interest in and willingness to treat problem drinkers, and their feelings about the diagnosis, treatment, and prognosis of patients with alcohol-related problems.

## METHOD

The findings presented here are based on data collected in a mail questionnaire survey conducted in 1979. A random sample of approximately 2000 students, stratified by college class, was drawn from four schools of nursing, four medical schools, four schools of social work and three counseling programs affiliated with seven major universities in or near the Greater Boston area. The sample size at each school ranged from 90 to 160 students, depending on the total enrollment. The medical, social work, and counseling student samples were composed of students enrolled in graduate degree programs. Since there were comparatively few graduate nursing students, we included some third-and fourth-year undergraduates in the sample of nurses.

Questionnaires were mailed in spring 1979 with a cover letter describing the nature and purpose of the survey, the sample selection procedures, and the methods by which respondents' anonymity would be protected. Two weeks after the initial mailing, a second questionnaire and follow-up letter were sent to nonresponders. The 15-page questionnaire contained items covering a wide range of topics, including demographic characteristics, exposure to alcohol education, knowledge of facts about alcohol, perceptions of the cause of alcoholism, willingness to treat people with alcohol-related problems, preferred treatment modalities, prognosis for alcoholics, and attitudes toward problem drinkers as patients.

A total of 1106 students responded to the initial mailing and one follow-up, for an overall response rate of 52 percent. The response rate was partially influenced by the timing of the survey, which limited opportunities for follow-up mailings. Given differences in the calendars of some sample schools, follow-up mailings would have coincided with final examination periods or changes in residence associated with residencies, practicums, or other required off-campus work experiences.

The comparatively low response rate might have serious implications for the generalizability of the data. Sampling bias may have been introduced, particularly if our respondents had been somewhat more interested in or sensitive to alcohol-related issues and problems than nonrespondents. The students who did respond to the survey, however, appeared to be representative of the students at their schools with respect to race and sex composition. In addition, a comparison of early and late respondents revealed no significant differences. Respondents to the first and second mailings did not differ on such variables as exposure to alcohol education, interest in treating people with alcohol-related problems, personal drinking practices, experience with alcohol-related problems, or sex. Nevertheless, bias related to other variables which we have not identified may be present. Therefore the data presented here should be interpreted with care.

## RESULTS

### Characteristics of Respondents

Of the 1106 students who responded to our questionnaire, 364 were enrolled in nursing programs, 370 in medical schools, 236 in social work programs, and 133 in counseling programs. Slightly less than one-third of the students (32%) were pursuing an M.A., M.S., or M.Ed. degree, and about two-fifths (42%) were in Ph.D. or M.D. programs. The remainder of the sample (26%) were third- and fourth-year nursing students.

Although the average student had been enrolled in his current program for 2.5 years, a large number (82%) had some prior professional experience in their major field.

The majority of the students surveyed were white (92%) and a substantial proportion were women (66%). The highest proportions of women were found in nursing (96%), social work (79%), and counseling programs (60%). Less than one-third (31%) of the medical students were women. The average age of the respondents was 27 years, students in nursing and medical schools tending to be somewhat younger than those in counseling and social work programs.

The sample was fairly evenly divided according to religious affiliation. Although the largest single proportion of the students was Catholic (36%), there were also sizable proportions of Jewish (23%) and Protestant (21%) students. The majority of these students reported that they never attended religious services (45%) or attended only on major holidays (26%).

The majority of the students (64%) were single, particularly those in nursing (73%) and medical (65%) schools. Slightly more than one-quarter of the students were married (27%), and approximately 9% were unmarried but living with a partner.

## Drinking Practices

Since personal drinking practices might be related to beliefs and attitudes toward the use and misuse of alcohol, a number of items in the questionnaire dealt with the students' own drinking practices. Nearly all of the students in this sample (95%) had used alcohol in the past year. However, most of them drank infrequently, a few times a month or less often (46%), or not more than once or twice a week (34%). Very few drank every day or nearly every day.

Wine appeared to be the most popular beverage among respondents (33%), which may be related to the large proportion of women in this sample. Few of the students preferred beer or distilled spirits.

Students' drinking practices were classified according to the quantity and frequency of their usual alcohol use. The majority of both men (66%) and women (64%) surveyed were classified as frequent-light drinkers; that is, they drank at least weekly but not more than 4 cans of beer, 3 glasses of wine, or 3 drinks containing distilled spirits at one sitting. In contrast to the findings of Wechsler and McFadden among undergraduate students,[11] there were no significant differences between the drinking patterns of men and women. Significant differences were observed, however, in the drinking practices of women in different fields of study. Nursing students, for example, who tended to be somewhat younger than social work or counseling students, were more likely than other students to be classified as intermediate and frequent-heavy drinkers.[12]

Although students generally did not drink large amounts of alcohol on any one occasion, some did report experiencing negative consequences in relation to their drinking, such as saying or doing something they would not ordinarily say or do (67%) or forgetting what had happened while they were drinking (25%). Fewer than 5 percent reported more serious consequences, such as getting into trouble with authorities, causing an automobile accident or other type of accident, getting into fights, or losing a friend.

Twenty-nine percent of the students reported that they worried, at least a little about their drinking. About 10 percent of the entire sample (and 18% of the counseling students) said that they had tried to stop drinking at least once, and a few (3%) reported seeking help for a drinking problem.

Among the reasons most often given by the students for not drinking, or not drinking more than they did, were: concern about health (74%), not wanting to get drunk (62%), interference with school work (56%), not liking the effect (55%), and not wanting to become dependent on alcohol (53%).

### Career Expectations

In order to examine the receptivity of these future caregivers to treating patients with alcohol-related problems, a series of questions concerning career expectations was included in the questionnaire. Although the majority (88%) expected that they would treat patients with drinking problems during the course of their careers, many felt unprepared for or uninterested in dealing with problem drinkers. For example, nearly one-fourth of the students (23%)

reported that they were not interested in treating patients with alcohol-related problems, and a similar proportion (24%) agreed that they were "not the type of person who could deal effectively with a problem drinker" in a therapeutic situation.

Students in different fields of study did vary significantly on other measures of willingness to treat and interest in treating alcohol problems. Medical students expressed the greatest willingness to treat people with alcohol-related problems. Social workers and counseling students were the least likely to be interested in taking on a person with a drinking problem, and most likely to indicate that they would spend little or none of their professional time on the care of people with drinking problems.

## Knowledge and Interest

As a measure of their interest in and attitudes toward alcohol-related issues, students were asked their views on several alcohol control issues, their beliefs about the prevalence of drinking problems, and their interest in alcohol education.

Exposure to some kind of alcohol education was fairly common among the students in our sample. Fully 79 percent had taken a course which at least touched on issues of alcohol use and misuse. Such exposure was particularly prevalent among students in nursing (87%) and medical programs (81%), and somewhat less common among social work (73%) and counseling students (65%). An even larger proportion of students (86%) felt that they needed to know more about alcohol and alcoholism, particularly social work (92%) and counseling (90%) students.

Respondents were also asked a series of questions about the prevalence, etiology, and consequences of alcohol misuse. We found that students were well-informed about some basic facts, such as diminishing sex differences in drinking behavior, the maximum legal blood alcohol level for operating a motor vehicle in Massachusetts, and the number of drinks it might take to reach that level. On the other hand, we found that students tended to underestimate some of the economic and social costs of problem drinking (.e.g, alcohol-related suicides, homicides or automobile accidents).

Regarding their views on alcohol control policies, we found that, although many students (69%) agreed that warning labels should be required on alcoholic beverages and that alcoholics should be held responsible for their behavior while drinking (86%), there was less consensus on other policy issues. For example, less than half (44%) supported the new 20-year minimum-age law for the purchase of alcoholic beverages in Massachusetts, or agreed that people arrested for drunken driving should have their licenses immediately suspended (43%).

Interest in issues and problems related to alcohol misuse, as measured by prior or intended exposure to alcohol education courses, was found to be closely associated with a student's willingness to treat people with alcohol-related problems. Students who were most willing to take on alcoholic patients were also far more likely to have been exposed to some kind of alcohol education. Interest was not, however, associated with other attitudes toward alcoholics or alcoholism treatment.

Awareness or knowledge of facts about alcohol misuse was not significantly related to interest in or willingness to deal with alcohol-related problems. To summarize, neither students' awareness of the problems and consequences of alcohol misuse nor their interest in alcohol education was related to attitudes toward alcoholics as patients, prognosis, or drinking practices.

### Causes of Alcoholism

The disease concept of alcoholism presents the alcoholic as a victim of a physical illness which renders him unable to control his drinking. Although it appears that the majority of the students surveyed agree with this concept, the data reveal some ambiguity in students' perceptions of the etiology of alcoholism.

Nearly every student (91%) agreed that alcoholism is a disease. However, a smaller proportion agreed with other statements associated with the disease concept. Overall, 56 percent of the respondents felt that general hospitals should offer alcoholism treatment, and 51 percent agreed that some people are genetically predisposed to alcoholism. On the other hand, nearly half (48%) felt that an alcoholic is seldom helped by medical treatment. This pessimism regarding the efficacy of medical treatment was more prevalent among medical (56%) and counseling (51%) students than among students in nursing (42%) or social work programs (41%).

Students' possible ambivalence regarding the etiology of alcoholism was also reflected in their responses to several items dealing with other possible causes of alcoholism. Apparently, agreement with the disease concept did not preclude agreement with other perspectives, as a number of students seemed to feel that alcoholism was primarily the result of underlying emotional problems or a sign of character weakness.

There were interesting differences between students in different fields of study on these items. Counseling students were far less likely than any other group to agree that alcoholism was a disease, and medical students were less likely than any other group to believe that alcoholism was the result of emotional problems. There were no significant differences between the proportion of students in each group who agreed that alcoholism was a sign of character weakness.

Taking this analysis one step further, we examined the proportion of students who agreed or disagreed with various combinations of these perspectives on the etiology of alcoholism. The largest single proportion of students (42%) agreed that alcoholism was both a disease and the result of underlying emotional problems. Twenty-three percent agreed only with the disease perspective; 6 percent agreed only with the emotional problem perspective; and less than 1 percent agreed only with the character weakness perspective. Nearly one-fifth of the students (19%) agreed to some extent with all three perspectives.

## Attitudes Toward Problem Drinkers

Professionals' attitudes toward patients with drinking problems play a major role in shaping the nature of their therapeutic interaction and affect their willingness to respond to drinking problems. In an attempt to uncover some of their attitudes toward patients with drinking problems, students in this sample of future professionals were asked if they agreed or disagreed with statements reflecting a range of attitudes toward problem drinkers. Responses to these statements indicated that, although a number of students agreed with many negative stereotypes, they were more apt to agree with statements concerning the negative characteristics of alcoholics as patients than those reflecting moralistic or negative attitudes towards alcoholics in general.

Sixty-one percent of the future caregivers agreed that alcoholics were "very demanding" or "difficult and uncooperative" patients. Nearly half felt that alcoholics were "harder to relate to than people whose problems were not self-inflicted." This latter attitude was particularly prevalent among nursing and medical students.

In comparison, there appeared to be somewhat less consensus among students that alcoholics could not be honest about their drinking, that alcoholics had no one to blame but themselves for their problems, or that alcoholics felt little of no remorse about their drinking until they got into serious trouble.

## Impaired Professionals

Control over professionals who have a drinking problem is a controversial but important issue. To approach this topic, students were asked to respond to a series of questions dealing with the locus of responsibility for problem drinking among professionals.

Students generally favored strict public control of professionals with drinking problems. Approximately three-fourths of the students felt that professionals engaged in direct service (i.e., doctors, nurses, therapists) should not be allowed to practice if they are active alcoholics, and that professional organizations should take an active role in restricting the practice of members with drinking problems. Very few felt that professionals should be able to decide for themselves if their drinking interfered with their work. In spite of this attitude in support of professional control, two-fifths of the students said that they would be reluctant to report a colleague who had a drinking problem.

## Prognosis

Students were asked to indicate the proportion of their alcoholic patients that they would expect to achieve total abstinence, resume family and social responsibilities, or show no improvement at all after a year of treatment. Although proportionately few students were totally negative in their prognosis, there was more optimism regarding improvement in social and personal functioning than in the alcoholic's ability to achieve total abstinence. Most of these future caregivers felt that at least half of their patients would show some improvement after a year of treatment, but very few believed that the majority of their alcoholic patients would be able to achieve abstinence, even at the end of a year of treatment.

When questions concerning an alcoholic's prognosis were phrased in more general terms—that is, when they did not apply to the professionals' personal expectations of success with their own patient—their responses were even more pessimistic. More than one-third of the students agreed that "few people are able to overcome their drinking problems, even with treatment." About two-thirds agreed that "even if the alcoholic could stop drinking, chances are that he or she would take it up again," and about half agreed that "alcoholics are seldom able to follow through with treatment plans."

Comparing the responses of students in different fields of study on these items, we found that medical students were most pessimistic, particularly with regard to an alcoholic's ability to achieve and maintain abstinence. Medical students were more likely than other students to feel that alcoholics are unlikely to maintain abstinence, follow through with treatment plans, or overcome their drinking problems.

In the caregiver sample as a whole, we found significant ($p <$ .001) intercorrelations between summary attitudes toward alcoholic patients, and their willingness to treat alcohol-related problems. Prognostic pessimism was closely associated ($r = .329$) with negative attitudes toward alcoholic patients and an unwillingness to become involved in the treatment of problem drinkers ($r = .219$).

## Treatment Modalities

Many types of therapeutic resources are available for the treatment of people who misuse alcohol. To learn which modalities were preferred by this sample of professionals, students were asked to rate ten types of treatments as very good, good, fair, or poor. These resources included Alcoholics Anonymous, social casework, medical treatment, individual psychotherapy, alcohol education, family therapy, group therapy, drug therapy, halfway houses, and behavior modification.

A certain amount of pessimism regarding the treatment and prognosis for alcoholics was reflected in responses to these items. Nearly one-fifth of the students (18%) did not consider any of these treatments to be a "very good" therapeutic resource for alcoholism. This pessimism was particularly prevalent among medical students. Thirty percent of the medical students, compared with 16 percent of the counseling students, 12 percent of the nursing students, and 10 percent of the social work students did not rank any of these modalities as very good resources.

Among the more optimistic students there was widespread agreement on the value of Alcoholics Anonymous. Fewer than a third of the students agreed, however, on the value of other kinds of therapy. After A.A., the treatment modalities, in descending rank were group therapy, family therapy, and halfway houses.

All other types of treatment on our list were more often considered poor than very good treatment resources. Approximately one-fifth of the students felt that drug therapy was a poor resource, and the same proportion (20%) felt negative about alcohol education. Medical treatment was ranked as a poor resource by 18 percent, individual therapy by 17 percent, behavior modification by 13 percent, and social casework by 7 percent.

There were significant differences in the treatment preferences of students by field of study. Medical students were less likely than other students to rank drug therapy or medical treatment as a very good resource. Relative to other groups, social work students were most likely to rank group therapy, halfway houses, social casework and drug therapy as good resources, and nursing students were most likely to favor family therapy, alcohol education, individual therapy and behavior modification. It is interesting to note that about one-third of the counseling students felt that group and family therapy were very good resources, while only 9 percent ranked individual therapy as a very good resource for the treatment of alcoholism.

## DISCUSSION

Successful identification and treatment of alcohol-related problems are contingent on the caregiver's willingness and ability to recognize and respond to problem drinkers. This response, however, can be encumbered by a lack of appropriate knowledge and skills, moralistic attitudes and prognostic pessimism. In order to heighten students' awareness and sensitivity to alcohol problems and mitigate the effects of negative attitudes, many professional schools have promoted alcohol education programs.

In this survey of future caregivers, we found a high rate of exposure to some type of alcohol education and a great deal of interest in learning more about problem drinking. A majority of the students also agreed, to a greater or lesser extent, with the disease concept of alcoholism. It would appear then that the schools have been successful in promoting an awareness of alcohol-related problems, particularly in nursing and medical programs. However, we also found that exposure to alcohol education or acceptance of the disease concept of alcoholism was not necessarily associated with positive or accepting attitudes toward problem drinkers. A substantial number of students, social work and counseling students in particular, expressed a reluctance to become involved in the treatment of people with alcohol-related problems.

Perhaps part of this reluctance can be traced to students' attitudes about the prognosis for alcoholic patients. Their pessimism is reflected in the large proportion of students who felt that there was little hope that an alcoholic would be able to achieve and maintain abstinence. Even within their own professions, there was a general feeling among the students that there were few really good therapeutic resources for alcoholism treatment. Furthermore, regardless of their agreement with the disease concept, many students felt that medical treatment was not an effective therapeutic resource. Similarly, few students felt that therapy — either group, individual, or family — was effective for the treatment of alcoholism.

Prognostic pessimism can be a serious barrier to treatment. Professionals are understandably reluctant to treat patients whose chances for recovery are poor, especially if they feel that their professional skills will not be effective. Prognostic pessimism can also lead to a self-fulfilling prophecy of treatment failure. In short, if a professional does not believe that a problem can be solved or that a patient can be helped, chances are slim that he will respond effectively if at all, to that patient.

Generalizing about future behavior on the basis of attitudinal data such as ours is hazardous. The relationship between knowledge, attitudes, and behavior in this case is not at all clear. However, the data raise some serious questions about the way in which professional programs prepare students to deal with the problems of alcohol misuse. Alcohol education in this context has traditionally focused on the disease concept of alcoholism in an effort to increase knowledge and awareness as well as to reduce moralistic attitudes and ensure humane treatment. Our findings, however, suggest that belief in the disease concept by itself is not sufficient to attenuate negative attitudes. There remains a close relationship between prognostic pessimism, negative attitudes, reluctance to respond to problem drinkers, and the lack of faith in available therapeutic resources.

Many resources exist for the treatment of alcohol-related problems, but few of these have been rigorously evaluated. Questions of special population needs and program effectiveness must be addressed in professional education programs so that our future caregivers develop confidence in their professional skills as well as concern for and willingness to treat drinking problems.

## REFERENCES

1. Shaw, S., Cartwright, A., Spratley, T., & Harwin, J.: *Responding to Drinking Problems.* Baltimore, University Park Press, 1978.
2. Mackey, R. A.: Views of caregiving and mental health groups about alcohol-

ics and drug addicts. *Q. J. Stud. Alcohol, 71*:225–234, 1969.

3. Sowa, P., & Cutter, H.: Attitudes of hospital staff toward alcoholics and drug addicts. *Q. J. Stud. Alcohol, 35*:210–214, 1974.

4. Fisher, J. C., Mason, R. L., Keepley, K. A., & Fisher, J. F.: Physicians and the alcoholic: The effect of medical training on attitudes toward alcoholics. *J. Stud. Alcohol, 36*:949–955, 1975.

5. Wolf, I., Chafetz, M. E., Blane, H. T., and Hill, M. J.: Social factors in the diagnosis of alcoholism: Attitudes of physicians. *Q. J. Stud. Alcohol, 26*:72–79, 1965.

6. Knox, W. J.: Attitudes of psychiatrists and psychologists toward alcoholism. *Am. J. Psychiat., 127*:1675–1679, 1971. See also Knox, W. J.: Attitudes of psychologists toward alcoholism. *J. Clin. Psych., 25*:446–450, 1969; and Knox, W. J.: Attitudes of social workers and other professional groups toward alcoholism. *Q. J. Stud. Alcohol, 34*:1270–1278, 1973.

7. Chafetz, M. E.: Research in the alcohol clinic and around-the-clock psychiatric service of the Massachusetts General Hospital. *Am. J. Psychiat., 124*:1674–1679, 1968.

8. Curlee, J.: Attitudes that facilitate or hinder the treatment of alcoholism. *Psychotherapy, 8*:68–70, 1971.

9. Bailey, M. B., and Fuchs, E.: Alcoholism and the social worker. *Social Work, 5*(no. 4):14–19, 1960.

10. Shaw, Cartwright, Spratley, & Harwin, op. cit.

11. Wechsler, H., and McFadden, M.: Drinking among college students in New England: Extent, social correlates and consequences of alcohol use. *J. Stud. Alcohol., 40*:969–996, 1979.

12. For the purposes of this study, intermediate drinkers were those who usually drank 5 to 6 cans of beer, 4 glasses of wine or 4 drinks with distilled spirits 1 to 3 times a month, or 4 cans of beer, up to 3 glasses of wine or 3 drinks with distilled spirits once or twice a week. Frequent-heavy drinkers usually drank 5 to 6 cans of beer, 4 glasses of wine or 4 drinks with distilled spirits more than twice a week, or 7 or more cans of beer, 5 or more glasses of wine or 5 or more drinks with distilled spirits 1 to 2 times a week.

# PART FOUR: TRAINING FOR THE PRACTICE AREA

# OVERVIEW

## Edith M. Freeman

The two chapters in this section describe training programs for practitioners in the alcohol treatment field. They address some of the needs noted in Wechsler and Rohman's chapter in the previous section on "Future Caregivers . . . " They noted that knowledge and skills are important, but that their use may be mitigated by the attitudes of practitioners toward clients with alcohol problems.

In their chapter, Corrigan and Anderson propose a training program for graduate social work students which addresses all three areas, and which links the course work with other relevant aspects of the curriculum such as research, human behavior classes, and the practicum. It is in the latter that practitioners' attitudes and values about alcoholic clients are operationalized and become apparent. Therefore, the practicum would seem to be an especially critical area of training in terms of their proposed program.

Similarly, Freeman's chapter proposes guidelines for designing inservice training programs for practitioners who are already in this field. An important aspect of those guidelines is the focus on knowledge, attitudes, and skills and suggestions for evaluating learning and the application of learning with clients. Since a future direction for this practice area is increased emphasis on evaluation, effective evaluation of training programs may demonstrate to staff in the best way the importance of evaluation in their work with clients.

*Chapter Twenty-One*

# GRADUATE SOCIAL WORK EDUCATION IN ALCOHOLISM

EILEEN M. CORRIGAN AND SANDRA C. ANDERSON

There are more than 10 million alcoholics in this country, and most social service agencies have a significant number of problem drinkers among their clientele. While social workers are in unique positions for prevention and early intervention, they frequently lack the requisite attitudes, knowledge, and technical skills to be of maximum effectiveness. Many social workers continue to associate alcoholism with moral or character defects and perceive themselves as inadequate to deal with alcohol-related problems. It is clear that, in general, graduate programs in social work have failed to prepare students to address this major public health problem.

This chapter will address the current status of social work training in alcoholism, the basic components of training, specific course content, and various training models in social work. One specific training program will be discussed in depth and, finally, guidelines will be presented for designing a social work training program in the field of alcoholism.

## CURRENT TRAINING PROGRAMS

It has been noted that directors of training programs in alcoholism treatment rarely publish program descriptions or evaluations, resulting in a lack of information and communication in this area.[1] Descriptions of successful curricula in graduate social work programs are particularly sparse. Data compiled in 1981 by the

335

National Clearinghouse for Alcohol Information shows that only 12 U.S. universities or colleges offered an M.S.W. degree with a concentration or specialty in alcohol studies. While many additional schools offer some content on alcoholism, the extent and nature of this content is unknown at present.

## COMPONENTS OF TRAINING

There appears to be agreement that the major goals of social work training in alcoholism are attitude change, knowledge acquisition, and technical skill development.[2] In discussing each of these components, attention will be given to relevant empirical data and to specific substantive content.

### Attitude Change

It is generally accepted that negative attitudes toward the alcoholic are detrimental to the processes of diagnosis, relationship building, and ongoing treatment.[3] Professionals who respond negatively to alcoholics consider them poorly motivated and, consequently, difficult to treat.[4] Conversely, when professionals expect improvement, clients often show such progress.[5]

It has been well-documented that social workers have negative attitudes toward alcoholics. Fewer than 30 percent of the social workers studied by Bailey and Fuchs[6] considered prognosis to be favorable for alcoholics receiving any type of treatment. Of those who had worked with alcoholics, only 16 percent felt that their intervention had been at least moderately effective. Knox[7] found that social workers were pessimistic about the prognosis for long-term abstinence but were more willing to treat alcoholics than were psychologists and psychiatrists. More recently, a study of graduate social work students by Peyton et al.[8] found a strong bias against selecting alcoholics as clients. Contrary to expectations, students with previous work experience with alcoholics were no more willing to treat them than those without prior experience. A replication of this study in 1981[9] corroborated the earlier findings. Of the 15 categories of clients, alcoholics were selected least often; 42 percent of the students expressed ambivalence or a negative bias toward alcoholics. Consistent with Peyton's findings, 69 percent of those expressing a negative bias had worked previously with alcoholics. Finally, Wechsler and Rohman[10] surveyed 1106 graduate students in four fields (medicine, nursing, social work, and counseling) and found that social work and counseling students were the least interested in treating clients with drinking problems. According to the authors, "Prognostic pessimism was closely associated with negative attitudes toward alcoholic patients and an unwillingness to become involved in the treatment of problem drinkers."[11]

In view of these consistently negative findings on the attitudes of social work students and practitioners, it is not surprising that social work training programs have attempted to produce attitude change in participants. The effectiveness of this pursuit is variable. For example, the first effort to evaluate the impact of training on the attitudes of social work practitioners was conducted by Bailey.[12] She found that a 30-hour training program was not effective in changing attitudes and, in fact, there was a slight change toward increased moralism. Waring[13] found that an eight-week training program did not produce significant change in the custodial (authoritarian) attitudes of management-level social workers. Manohar, et al.[14] report more positive results. They found that a 12-hour program for social work practitioners resulted in positive attitude change, but note that the most consistent participants had the most positive attitudes at baseline.

Effectiveness studies of graduate school programs also show contradictory results. Corrigan and Anderson[15] report quite positive outcomes, while Kilty and Feld[16] report that students participating in a demonstration project learned little about alcoholism, evidenced no change in attitudes toward alcoholics, and became less interested in working with alcoholics.

While there is some anecdotal evidence that acceptance of the disease model of alcoholism is resulting in more accepting attitudes, many students still view alcoholics as morally weak and difficult to treat. Thus, training programs need to continue to support the disease concept of alcoholism and stress empirical data supporting the fact that alcoholism is a treatable illness. Connor[17] believes that information dissemination through lectures and reading is ineffective in changing attitudes; to effect real change, feelings and old ideas must be critically examined and a relearning process must occur. She accomplishes this by simulating "town meetings" in which students alternately assume roles of program advocates or adversaries. It has been noted[18] that successful efforts in changing medical students' attitudes have involved the use of intensive small-group discussions focusing on personal attitudes and affective states. There is a clear need for more experimentation and evaluation of innovative methods of changing attitudes in the classroom setting.

### Knowledge Acquisition

Given some movement toward the goal of attitude change, the next objective is the acquisition of information on alcoholism and related problems. Many social workers report that they feel inadequate when faced with an alcoholic client, and are unwilling to handle problems associated with the disease.[19] In spite of experience in treating alcoholics, social work students believe that they lack the knowledge and skills for effective diagnosis and treatment of these clients.[20] Shaw, et al.[21] found that, in addition to recognizing a lack of knowledge and skills, many professionals do not know where to seek additional information or support. They question their right to ask patients about their drinking, and avoid problem drinkers out of a sense of prognostic pessimism. As stated by Wechsler and Rohman:

> Reluctance to question or respond to a patient's drinking presents a serious barrier to the recognition and treatment of problem drinkers. To the extent that professionals doubt the adequacy or legitimacy of their professional role, are pessimistic in their prognosis, or feel uncertain about their own drinking, they are unlikely to respond positively or effectively to problem drinkers.[22]

Shaw, et al.[23] found a disproportionate number of problem drinkers among clients at several types of generic agencies; many clients attempt to avoid the stigma associated with treatment at an alcoholism agency. One study[24] found that only 9 percent of clients with a drinking problem acknowledged this as a presenting problem; 44 percent instead cited marital problems and 28 percent cited interpersonal difficulties or problems with their children. Social workers often fail to identify clients at risk for alcoholism or those in early stage problem drinking who are seeking help for other problems. Their ability to do so is seriously hampered by their lack of training. Diagnostic skills involve knowledge about the disease, familiarity with the principles of taking an adequate history, and the ability to effectively use the skill of questioning.

It appears that significant gains in knowledge are easier to achieve in training programs than are attitude changes. Several studies report substantial gains in cognitive learning in programs for alcoholism counselors[25] and professional social workers.[26] As Blacker[27] points out, most training programs cover the same basic content but vary somewhat in emphasis and method of instruction. Examples of course content from two schools of social work will be presented later in this chapter. In terms of instructional method, some programs utilize predominantly lecture and discussion, while others also use seminars, film, role play, actual and simulated case presentations, student presentations, site visits, and various types of exercises. The relative efficacy of these methods is unknown at present.

### Technical Skill Development

The final component of training is the teaching of technical skills. In teaching graduate social work students, this component includes the techniques associated with the roles of counselor, educator, social broker, and mediator. In work with alcoholics, the techniques of attentive listening, warmth, empathy, genuineness, questioning, confrontation and supporting and redirecting defenses are of particular importance. In addition, students should be familiar with the various treatment modalities (individual, family, and group) utilized in intervening with alcoholics and their families. Skill development can be addressed in both the field and classroom settings through the use of process recordings, direct observation of interviews, and audio and video-taping. The use of video-taped role-play and playback analysis is also helpful in developing assessment and intervention skills with alcoholic clients.

## COURSE CONTENT

Graduate schools of social work vary greatly in the availability of alcohol-specific courses and field placements. The courses discussed below are reflective of alcohol content taught by core sequence.

### Direct Human Services

A direct service practice course entitled "Social Work with Alcoholics and Their Families" is taught by one of the authors at the Portland State University School of Social Work. Teaching methodology includes lectures, discussion, film, case studies, and role plays.[28] Course content is as follows:

*Definition of the Problem*
    A. Epidemiology of Alcoholism
    B. Physical and Psychosocial Consequences of Alcoholism
    C. Attitudes Toward Alcoholism
  II. *The Fetal Alcohol Syndrome and Fetal Alcohol Effects*
    A. Description of FAS and FAE
    B. Dose-Related Risk Factors
    C. Implications for Prevention and Intervention
  III. *The Development of Alcoholism*
    A. Stages in Development
    B. Screening Instruments for Alcoholism
    C. Diagnostic Criteria
    D. Types of Alcoholism
       1. Primary
       2. Secondary
          a. affective disorders (unipolar and bipolar)
          b. antisocial personality
          c. schizophrenia and borderline personality disorders
       3. Reactive
       4. The Early Problem Drinker
    E. Overview of Physiological, Psychological, and Sociological Theories of Alcoholism

IV. *Early Treatment Issues*
  A. Initial Interviews with Client and Significant Others
  B. Principles of History-Taking
  C. Engaging in Treatment; Dealing with Resistance
  D. Developing the Therapeutic Contract
V. *Individual Therapy*
  A. Stages and Techniques of Treatment
  B. Relationship Issues; Transference and Countertransference
  C. Defense Structure of the Alcoholic
  D. Working with Resistance
VI. *Group Therapy*
  A. Indications and Contraindications
  B. Phases in Group Development
  C. Problems Specific to Alcohol Groups
  D. Evaluation
VII. *Family Therapy*
  A. Characteristics of Alcoholic Families
  B. Treatment Models and Techniques
  C. Evaluation
VIII. *Drug Treatment of Alcoholism*
  A. Disulfiram®
  B. Minor Tranquilizers
  C. Major Tranquilizers
  D. Antidepressants
IX. *Alcoholics Anonymous Model*
X. *Behavior Modification Model*
  A. Aversive Techniques
  B. Operant Techniques
  C. Relaxation Techniques
  D. Cognitive Treatment
XI. *Special Populations: Skid Row, Adolescents, Elderly, Women, Lesbians and Gays*
XII. *Controlled Drinking*
  A. Review of Research
  B. Implications for Treatment Planning
XIII. *Evaluation of Treatment Methods*

    A. Methodological Issues
    B. Findings of Outcome Studies

### HUMAN BEHAVIOR IN THE SOCIAL ENVIRONMENT

A human behavior and social environment course entitled "Alcohol and other drugs" is taught by one of the authors at Rutgers University School of Social Work. Teaching methodology includes lectures, discussion, AA visits and invited speakers.[29] Course content is as follows:

    I. *Overview of Drug Use*
        A. Values, Attitudes and Behavior
        B. Social Work and Self-Help
        C. Classifying Drugs
    II. *Epidemiology*
        A. Male—Female
        B. Social Class
        C. Racial—Ethnic
    III. *Action of Drugs*
        A. Specific and Non-specific Effects
        B. Tolerance, Loss of Tolerance and Cross Tolerance
    IV. *Metabolism and Intoxication*
        A. Alcohol Beverage Equivalents
        B. Blood Alcohol Level and Metabolism
        C. Intoxication and Degree of Impairment
    V. *Multiple Drug Use and Drug Interactions*
        A. Polydrug Use and Abuse
        B. Drug Interactions
    VI. *Theories of Alcohol and Other Drug Abuse*
        A. Psychodynamic—personality
        B. Biological (genetic)
        C. Sociological (sociocultural)
    VII. *The Disease Concept of Alcoholism*
        A. History of a Movement
        B. Jellinek's Contribution
    VIII. *Stages of Alcoholism and the Diagnosis of Alcoholism*
        A. Progression
        B. Criteria for diagnosis

IX. *Physiological and Social Consequences of Alcoholism*
   A. Physiological
   B. Social
X. *Other Cultures and Special Population Groups*
   A. Minorities
   B. Youth
   C. Elderly
   D. Gays and lesbians
XI. *Treatment; Goals and Evaluation*
   A. Abstinence and controlled drinking
   B. Criteria for evaluation
XII. *Prevention*
   A. Models of prevention
   B. State of the art

## SOCIAL WELFARE RESEARCH

A research course in alcoholism could address the methodological issues specific to alcohol research, critical analysis of outcome studies in the literature, and the current state of empirically-based knowledge in the field. Content might include conceptual frameworks for alcohol treatment evaluation, problems of definition and description, issues in selection and assignment to control or comparison groups, research designs, measurement, and data analysis. Methodological issues specific to alcoholism research could be highlighted. These might include, for example, the use of abstinence as the sole criterion for success, reliability and validity of self report by alcoholics, differential criteria for men and women alcoholics, and problems locating alcoholic clients for follow-up.

Critical analysis of the outcome effectiveness literature could include examination by program type (residential, outpatient, emergency room), modality (individual, family, group), and treatment method (drug, cognitive-behavioral, psychodynamic, task-centered). At the completion of the course, students should be familiar with research methodology in this field and capable of being critical consumers of the alcoholism literature.

## ADDITIONAL COURSES

In addition to courses in direct human services, human behavior and the social environment, and social welfare research, courses in social policy and planning, and management can be focused upon alcohol content. A social policy course could address the determinants of social policy in the area of alcoholism, differences between formal and informal policy, and the effects of social policy on alcohol use and abuse. In addition, specific existing or proposed policies could be critically examined. These could include, for example, warning labels on alcoholic beverages, warning signs in bars and liquor stores, and minimum age laws for driving and purchasing alcohol. There is relatively little in the literature on program and clinical management of alcohol programs, and curricula development in this area is sorely needed.

## TRAINING MODELS IN SOCIAL WORK

There are several different models of training which can be utilized by graduate schools of social work. Some programs offer specialized training in alcohol studies to select students from the graduate student body. These students take core curriculum courses in addition to specialized courses and practicum training in alcoholism. Other programs attempt to integrate material on alcoholism into the existing core curriculum as opposed to offering training to a select few. Finally, some programs combine specialized training of a selected group with some general training on alcoholism for all graduate students.

### Rutgers School of Social Work

The curriculum in schools of social work allows for electives which can be used to form a number of sub-specialties. Such an approach allows students to gain depth in substantive areas such as alcohol studies. Usually such subspecialties are developed by students according to their interest or they can be formalized by the faculty when they designate a number of subspecialties. It is this latter approach that was followed at Rutgers School of Social Work.

The faculty agreed that six classroom and six field credits would constitute a subspecialty. Three courses already in the curriculum were available for a subspecialty in alcohol studies; Alcohol and Other Drugs; Direct Intervention with Alcoholics and Their Families; Social Policy and Planning in Alcoholism and Alcohol Abuse.

These courses were initially stimulated by a training grant from the National Institute on Alcohol Abuse and Alcoholism (NIAAA) which offered support for students and faculty. The grant was pivotal in attracting faculty who had knowledge and experience in the area. The domain of alcoholic minority women had been the focus of the training grant, and 20 minority women students were recruited to study in this area; a total of 31 students received training in alcohol studies through the mid to late 1970's. At the last followup of these students more than half were practicing in settings which allowed them to use their alcohol expertise.[30]

Each course is lodged in an administrative unit of the school's curriculum. The introductory course, Alcohol and Other Drugs, was part of the Human Behavior and Social Environment Sequence and was considered the foundation course for the subspecialty. The course concerned with Direct Intervention was an elective in the Casework Sequence while the Policy course could be used in lieu of a required Policy course. It was expected that the Direct Practice students would opt for the Direct Practice course while Policy and Planning students would choose the Policy course. All were required to take the introductory course unless they could demonstrate having had the content in prior formal courses.

Students could decide to take the three courses and also register for more than the minimum of six credits in the field practicum. Since all the courses and the practicum have been recognized by the state's certification board it is to the student's advantage to take these credits while in the school of social work if they later wish to become certified as counselors. Many decide to do so since it gives them an advantage in securing certification. The students are informed clearly that the certification process is completely separate from their social work degree; the Direct Practice students, however, are quick to see the advantage of adding to their competencies in a specialized area which enhances their attractiveness to prospective employers.

Clearly formalizing a subspecialty has a number of advantages for both the school and the students. Recruitment of students is decidedly improved, especially for those potential students who are already interested in pursuing a course of study in the alcohol area. Since relatively few schools have such a specialty this has been an attractive feature of the curriculum. The students obviously are pleased to find faculty who share their interest and enthusiasm for this important new area of social work practice. Course availability is a traditional mechanism to sensitize students to a social and public health problem which affects the majority of the clientele of social workers.

The courses over the years have always had sufficient enrollment. It was not until NIAAA support ceased however that the long-term results of the faculty efforts could be evaluated. The faculty's approval of a structure for subspecialties was no doubt immensely useful in providing the continuity beyond a funded training effort.

Since 1981 when the training grant ceased, there has been a steady increase in enrollment in the courses which are offered once yearly. The introductory course now has enrollment of between 50 to 60 students; the Direct Intervention course which has a cap of 30 students is always over-subscribed; the Policy course has more recently edged up to being completely subscribed.

Students who complete the requirements for the subspecialty are given a certificate at the time of their graduation and this is highly prized. The school is now seen as a source of prospective employees by community agencies and inquiries increasingly are coming to the attention of the faculty about job openings. A designated section of the school's student bulletin board now is available for a variety of announcements such as conferences and job availability.

## GUIDELINES FOR DESIGNING A TRAINING PROGRAM

The basic ingredient for developing and designing a training program is the presence on the faculty of a committed and knowledgeable faculty member. The faculty member must be knowledgeable not only about the content needing to be incorporated in the curriculum but also in relation to the school's structure and curriculum organization. The power relations in committee structure must be analyzed and a plan developed based on such an analysis.

Only one faculty member is needed to make a difference in the content. Interest in the alcohol area cannot be expected to be an interest or priority of other faculty. If any allies are found among the faculty that is an asset but it cannot be expected. The support may come in time, possibly from others who have an interest in another specialty area and are sympathetic to an effort which seems similar to their own. If the primary curriculum need is in the area of intervention then a course in this area needs to be designed first. If the faculty member does not have the necessary knowledge to design such a course the assistance of Direct Practice faculty and agency clinical staff can be sought to assist in this first effort. It is clearly important to formalize the structure for the new content. Student interest in the area can be used to support a faculty effort and certainly should be included as appropriate to the school's organization.

As stated early in the paper there is mixed evidence to support the expectation of a change of attitude following training. The emphasis in this chapter has been on offering a cluster of courses while students are in the process of becoming social workers. This is based on an educational philosophy that the exposure of social work students to instructors with a positive and optimistic attitude towards alcoholics and concomitant knowledge will begin to help students to examine the basis for negative attitudes. Interest in acquiring skills to treat would then follow. Students report a shift in their use of self following even an introductory course on alcohol and drugs, and this course does not provide skill training.

There is no question that there are specific techniques to be learned about treating the alcoholic and others affected by the alcoholic. Yet the basic skills of the social worker can be brought to bear for alcoholics, the same as they are for every social and public health problem. As students are given the opportunity to examine their fears and concerns while learning they are then able to deal effectively with the barriers formerly placed between themselves and a particular category of client, the alcoholic.

The learning environment of the student often provides relatively little support. They may also be receiving invalid explanations about alcoholics and alcoholism in many of their other courses. Some practice instructors may be tied to formulations that are presented as knowledge for the profession when they are assumptions which have no empirical base.

An area that has not previously been noted to any extent in this paper concerns the field practicum. This is one of the most influential learning environments for students and is where their professional self emerges. The student is frequently influenced to seek out knowledge in the area of alcohol studies because the agency setting exposes them to alcoholic clients or families of alcoholics. If students have the opportunity then to enroll in courses in this area there is a good fit between practice needs and a school's curriculum. Such students who receive support in their agency setting for their new learning are likely to synthesize the classroom teaching and experiential learning more quickly and more meaningfully. Students who have only the classroom teaching are somewhat disadvantaged as are those students who only have the agency experience without any formal knowledge base. Many agencies, of course, have extensive in-service training to conpensate for the professional school's lack of preparation.

## CONCLUSIONS

This is an area of practice that schools can ill afford to ignore. Recently there has been attention nationally to concerns around the drinking age since youth under 21 tend to drive and become involved in accidents at a higher rate than the general population. Knowledge about the newly identified fetal alcohol syndrome has also caused ripples of concern and has been given wide attention in the media. Both issues are of high interest to students personally and professionally. It may well be that many schools have not formalized a concentration or subspecialty in alcohol studies, but there is a good likelihood that courses in this area are finding their way into the curriculum. A survey is in progress which should provide detailed information on the status of alcohol education in schools of social work.[31] No longer is this a practice area for specialized agencies only. Many community agencies now have a wider range of programs to treat alcoholics and their families. The schools of social work are expected to meet the practice needs of communities by developing and expanding their curriculum in response to what is now recognized as an immense social and health problem: alcoholism.

## REFERENCES

1. Blacker, Edward: Training for professionals and nonprofessionals in alcoholism. In Kissin, Benjamin and Begleiter, Henri (Eds.): *Treatment and Rehabilitation of the Chronic Alcoholic.* New York, Plenum Press, 1977, pp. 567–592.
2. Ibid.; Manohar, Velandy, Des Roches, Joyce, and Ferneau, Ernest W.: An education program in alcoholism for social workers: Its impact on attitudes and treatment-oriented behavior. *British Journal of Addictions, 71:*225–234, 1976.
3. Hanna, Eleanor: Attitudes toward problem drinkers: A critical factor in treatment recommendations. *Journal of Studies on Alcohol, 39:*98–109, 1978; Leake, George J. and King, Albert S.: Effect of counselor expectations on alcoholic recovery. *Alcohol Health and Research World, 1:*16–22, 1977; Sterne, Muriel W., and Pittman, David J.: The concept of motivation: A source of institutional and professional blockage in the treatment of alcoholics. *Quarterly Journal of Studies on Alcohol, 26:*41–57, 1965.
4. Chafetz, Morris E.: Research in the alcohol clinic and around-the-clock psychiatric service of the Massachusetts General Hospital. *American Journal of Psychiatry, 124:*1674–1679, 1968.
5. Leake and King, op. cit.
6. Bailey, Margaret B., and Fuchs, Estelle: Alcoholism and the social worker. *Social Work, 5:*14–19, 1980.
7. Knox, Wilma J.: Attitudes of social workers and other professional groups toward alcoholism. *Quarterly Journal of Studies on Alcohol, 34:*1270–1278, 1973.
8. Peyton, Sarah, Chaddick, James, and Gorsuch, Richard: Willingness to treat alcoholics: A study of graduate social work students. *Journal of Studies on Alcohol, 41:*935–940, 1980.
9. Duxbury, Ruth A.: Willingness of graduate students to treat alcoholics: A replication study. *Journal of Studies on Alcohol, 44:*748–753, 1983.
10. Wechsler, Henry and Rohman, Mary: Future caregivers' views on alcoholism treatment: A poor prognosis. *Journal of Studies on Alcohol, 43:*939–955, 1982.
11. Ibid., p. 952.
12. Bailey, Margaret B.: Attitudes toward alcoholism before and after a training

program for social caseworkers. *Quarterly Journal of Studies on Alcohol, 31:*669–683, 1970.

13. Waring, Mary L.: The impact of specialized training in alcoholism on management-level professionals. *Journal of Studies on Alcohol, 36:*406–415, 1975.

14. Manohar, Des Roches, and Ferneau, op. cit.

15. Corrigan, Eileen M., and Anderson, Sandra C.: Training for treatment of alcoholism in women. *Social Casework, 59:*42–50, 1978.

16. Kilty, Keith M., and Feld, Allen: Professional education in understanding and treating alcoholism. *Journal of Studies on Alcohol, 40:*929–942, 1979.

17. Connor, Bernadette: A course in humanistic education for alcohol specialists. *Journal of Alcohol and Drug Education, 26:*76–79, 1980.

18. Kinney, Jean, Bergen, Bernard J., and Price, Trevor R. P.: A perspective on medical students' perceptions of alcoholics and alcoholism. *Journal of Studies on Alcohol, 43:*488–496, 1982.

19. Dorsch, Graydon and Talley, Ruth: Responses to alcoholics by the helping professions in Denver: A three-year follow-up. *Quarterly Journal of Studies on Alcohol, 34:*165–172, 1973.

20. Duxbury, op. cit.; Wechsler and Rohman, op. cit.

21. Shaw, S., Cartwright, A., Spratley, T., and Harwin, J.: *Responding to Drinking Problems.* Baltimore, MD, University Park Press, 1978.

22. Wechsler and Rohman, op. cit., p. 941.

23. Shaw, Cartwright, Spratley, and Harwin, op. cit.

24. Demone, Harold W., Hoffman, Herbert J., and Hoffman, Ludmulk W.: *Alcoholism: An Evaluation of Intervention Strategies in Family Agencies.* Boston, United Community Planning Corporation, 1974.

25. Gideon, William L., Littell, Arthur S., and Martin, David W.: Evaluation of a training program for certified alcoholism counselors. *Journal of Studies on Alcohol, 41:*8–20, 1980.

26. Manohar, Des Roches, and Ferneau, op. cit.; Waring, op. cit.

27. Blacker, op. cit.

28. The text utilized in this course is Sheldon Zinberg, *The Clinical Management of Alcoholism.* New York, Bruner/Mazel, 1982.

29. The text utilized in this course is Oakley, Ray, *Drugs, Society and Human Behavior,* St. Louis, C. V. Mosby, 1983. Extensive supplementary reading in the alcohol literature.

30. Corrigan, Eileen M., and Anderson, Sandra C.: Training for treatment of alcoholism in women. Research report, 1981.

31. Corrigan, Eileen M., and Humphreys, Nancy A.: Survey of Alcohol Content in Schools of Social Work, (in progress).

## Chapter Twenty-Two

# INSERVICE TRAINING PROGRAMS FOR STAFF IN ALCOHOLISM TREATMENT CENTERS

EDITH M. FREEMAN

M any authors have become increasingly concerned about the quality of inservice programs for alcoholism treatment staff. These concerns can be summarized by the following questions: (1) to what extent do these programs achieve the specific objectives developed for them, (2) what are the specific effects of these programs on the participants' job performance and job satisfaction; (3) do changes in the participants' knowledge, attitudes, and behaviors lead to improved treatment outcomes with clients including improved abstinence rates, and (4) what is the cost/benefit balance of these training programs for the treatment facilities involved?[1]

These questions about quality become even more complex when the range of different mental health practitioners involved in these treatment facilities is considered. For example, these practitioners include social workers, psychologists, doctors, nurses, alcoholism counselors, and paraprofessional aides. Despite some commonalities, these practitioners have different educational backgrounds, job requirements, and training needs that must be considered when interdisciplinary training programs are developed.

The quality of programs for this broad range of personnel has been of concern for additional reasons. Often, these programs have focused only on short-term effects without also focusing on long-term effects, or without providing experimental data to support conclusions about the effects noted. Many others have monitored changes in the participants in only one or two of three important areas: knowledge, attitudes, and skills. Further, when some programs have been found to be effective in these areas, the program components that contributed to that effectiveness often have not been isolated and clarified.[2]

This chapter will summarize some of the components that have been noted as being effective with a variety of treatment personnel, and will relate those components to the four questions about program quality. A final section involves discussion on some of the implications for roles related to these training programs. Social workers and other mental health practitioners are challenged to assume these roles in order to enhance the quality of training programs.

### SUMMARY OF PROGRAM QUALITY ISSUES

Questions about the quality of inservice programs automatically encourage a focus on components that can potentially improve those programs. They also make it possible to generalize some conclusions about these components across settings and training programs, despite many situational differences. Therefore, each of the four questions about quality identified in the introduction will be discussed in general, along with related program components that address those questions. At a base level, one of the simplest ways to evaluate a program is to determine the extent to which its' objectives have been achieved. Other increasingly complex ways to evaluate program quality can be developed by focusing on each of the succeeding three questions addressed in this section.

### To What Extent Are Program Objectives Achieved?

This first question related to quality focuses on whether inservice programs for alcoholism treatment staff fulfill the purposes for which they are developed. Several components must be included in programs to address this question: a comprehensive needs assessment, behavioral objectives, related content areas, evaluation of changes in participants related to the objectives, and the use of expert trainers.

A comprehensive needs assessment is the first critical component to be considered. The results of recent program evaluations are often helpful in identifying staff training needs. Administrative staff also can often provide preliminary information about training needs, but that information should only be a beginning effort toward obtaining the staff's view of their needs. Staff members may have specific concerns that administrative staff are unaware of.[3] In one facility, administrators requested training for staff in the use of behavioral approaches. Direct contact with the staff revealed their growing concerns about handling clients with seizure disorders and other emergency or crisis situations appropriately, areas which administrators had not identified as a training need. The number of emergency situations in the setting had gradually increased over the previous months. This area became the focus for training later, along with other related topic areas.

Methods for doing the assessment can include the use of written questionnaires with staff (open-ended, structured, or a combination of both), interviews with all staff or a random sample of staff, and an analysis of actual staff performance in specific areas compared with job requirements to identify deficits and training needs. All of these methods have advantages and disadvantages. For example, the latter method is advantageous because it can be done by administrative staff, the consultant-trainer, and/or the treatment staff themselves.

When treatment staff complete their own analyses, while also receiving feedback from another objective source, the process of discovery can increase their motivation and involvement in their own learning. This factor may be a particular advantage for nonvoluntary participants or for staff who are burned-out from work with alcoholic clients. The analyses can be accomplished from tapes, written records, or from direct observation of staff performance with clients. This method also has disadvantages. It requires more time and effort than the other two methods. Additionally, it can discourage some staff who may ignore the strengths identified and become overwhelmed by their deficits. However, these situations can be used to help staff recognize how alcoholic clients sometimes feel during initial social assessments, and effective ways to respond.

Some needs assessments produce conflicting information about training needs. These results may be due to interdisciplinary differences or to individual staff differences. They may require separate but related training for staff from different disciplines and educational backgrounds, or a consideration of those differences within the same sessions by providing separate small group discussions, exercises, and learning assignments for different disciplines. Special needs of some staff that are due to differences in skill levels can also be taken into consideration in the design of the training. However, some individual staff differences may need to be addressed through assigned readings or through supervision provided administratively.

A comprehensive needs assessment helps in developing the second component of training: behavioral objectives that address the needs and priorities that have been identified. The objectives should also focus on knowledge, attitude, and behavioral areas.[4] For example, objectives for staff who wanted to learn more about teenage alcoholic clients indicated they should be able to:

1. List important developmental issues and problems that affect how teenagers function generally between the ages of 13 to 19 years. (Knowledge)
2. Discuss common motivations for drinking and the dynamics and consequences involved in alcohol misuse by teenagers. (Knowledge)
3. Discuss values, beliefs, and attitudes that influence the effectiveness of their work with teenage alcoholic clients. (Attitudes)
4. Identify specific practice strategies (including environmental interventions) that can be used to diagnose and resolve alcohol misuse by teenage alcoholics, and situations in which these strategies can be used effectively. (Skills)

Behavioral objectives such as those listed above make it possible to develop content that is consistent with each objective, the third program component. This consistency insures that content will be relevant to the participants' training needs. Content areas consistent with the set of objectives identified in the previous example about training staff to work with teenage alcoholics include: (1) specific developmental issues and problems experienced by teenagers from 13 to 19 years of age and typical responses to these issues and problems including the use of alcohol; (2) familial, peer, and individual factors that influence alcohol misuse in teenagers and the consequences of that misuse; (3) attitudes, beliefs, and values (including those of practitioners) about teenage drinking and related areas, the effects on practice with this age group, and ways to prevent or handle those effects; and (4) alternative strategies for diagnosing and treating teenage drinking problems and related environmental influences, and typical situations in which those strategies can be used effectively.

Content areas can be used to aid in evaluating whether program objectives are achieved, the fourth component.

Achievement of objectives can be evaluated through the use of written pre and posttraining questionnaires focused on the content areas, responses to structured exercises and practice simulations during sessions, and informal observations of changes in staff participation during sessions related to the content and objectives.[5] The effects of training versus no training conditions can be compared by using these measures with staff in another setting who have not received the training. Pre and post data from the second setting can be used as a control for the setting in which the training occurs in order to evaluate achievement of objectives at the point when the training ends. An effort should be made also to identify other sources of learning outside training sessions that might contribute to achievement of objectives. Independent reading, other workshops, supervision sessions focused on a particular practice area, or other intervening variables may influence changes that might be assumed erroneously to result from the training itself.

The final component related to whether objectives are achieved is the use of expert trainers who can teach the content that has been specified and evaluate its effects on participants. Trainers should be knowledgeable and skilled in general adult education and in the specific area of focus for the inservice. In the previous example, the trainer selected had extensive experience as an effective consultant-trainer, and was an expert in the area of alcohol treatment with adolescents and general adolescent development. He was able to clarify and discuss critical practice dilemmas of concern to the participants during sessions, as well as share his own successful and unsuccessful experiences in the practice areas involved.[6]

The five components discussed in this section have focused on short-term changes within the duration and context of the inservice program involved. Even more important to the issue of program quality is whether those changes are generalized beyond the duration of the program to another context: to actual practice situations. This issue is also important for insuring continuity with future training programs.

## How Do Changes in Participants Affect Job Performance and Job Satisfaction?

This second question about quality focuses on the generalization of training effects to actual practice situations over time, and on whether participants are satisfied with these changes in job performance. The components relevant to this question are: the monitoring of short-term changes in job performance, monitoring long-term changes in job performance, and providing incentives to participants for the application of learning.

Monitoring short-term changes in job performance, the first component, can be accomplished by providing participants with opportunities to practice what they are learning within sessions and outside of sessions to actual practice situations. Allowing them opportunities to first try out new skills under simulated conditions in sessions can help them to then apply the skills in a more informed way in actual practice. Further, this process enhances program quality by encouraging participants to integrate knowledge and skill areas as they apply what they have learned.

Simulated conditions that can be provided within sessions include: the use of actual clinical cases of alcoholic clients for discussing and role playing problem-resolution, structured small group discussions, review sessions, site visits that illustrate practice dilemmas and their resolution, and the use of speakers who pose or answer questions related to practice issues and reinforce the content areas being taught.[7] In the training example discussed previously about practice with teenage alcoholics, a speaker from another treatment facility who had extensive experience with teenage female alcoholics discussed some examples of cases from her setting. She used the examples to stimulate discussion about how the participants might have handled those cases and the potential consequences, in addition to discussing how the cases were actually handled in her setting.

Applying new learning under simulated conditions is really a means to an end and should be followed by assignments for participants to try out new skills in actual practice. Only then can short-term changes in job performance be monitored and documented systematically. Examples of assignments outside of sessions that can be used to monitor changes in actual job performance include having participants: write up a social assessment from one of their client interviews based on criteria taught during training, try out a practice strategy taught during training with a real case situation in which they are at an impasse, or analyze to what extent an intervention was or was not effective based on a method of analysis taught during training. This monitoring process can be accomplished through the review of tapes or written records and by direct observation of participants' interviews with clients by the trainer or other evaluators.[8]

Monitoring long-term changes in job performance is the second component, and it can be accomplished by using these same methods. Monitoring should be done at specific and consistent time intervals after training ends, e.g., three months, six months, nine months, and one year. The goal is to determine to what extent participants are continuing to use specific knowledge areas and skills they have learned as they perform daily job requirements. The feedback can be shared with staff to improve job performance, to evaluate the training program involved, and to improve the quality of future programs.[9]

A third component, providing incentives for the application of new learning, can improve the quality of job performance and increase job satisfaction. Alcoholism treatment staff may be particularly resistive to changes due to the demanding nature of their practice and high relapse rates for alcoholic clients. They may lack confidence about their abilities to change clients, and yet resist giving up related practice behaviors they are comfortable with for new behaviors with which they are unfamiliar.

Linking the application of training to particular incentives can reduce this resistance and influence job satisfaction and attitudes in a positive direction beyond the effects of training itself. In one facility, staff who demonstrate their application of learning and improved job performance during the follow-up monitoring process can select other workshops to attend or have access to limited consultation services.

Another kind of incentive involves including administrative staff in training sessions. Administrators can remind staff about other incentives that are available for applying learning when they do not respond positively to assignments to try out skills in actual practice. More importantly, they can help to anticipate and resolve organizational and individual barriers to the application of learning. This kind of administrative support and approval can be an incentive in itself, and should not be overlooked when ways to increase job satisfaction are considered.[10]

Job satisfaction can be evaluated before training, on a short-term basis immediately after training ends, and on a long-term basis at periods when performance is also being monitored. Several authors have developed scales and questionnaires that measure job satisfaction and attitudes related to specific aspects of performance and to practice in general with alcoholic clients.[11]

The components discussed in this section are important for assessing the quality of training programs, but they should not be viewed in isolation. Changes in job performance and satisfaction must be analyzed in terms of another quality issue: the effects of these changes on treatment outcomes with clients.

### How Do Changes in Participants' Knowledge, Attitudes, And Behaviors Affect Treatment Outcomes With Clients?

This question emphasizes one of the most important issues related to quality, whether changes in participants' knowledge, attitudes, and behaviors benefit clients and in what specific ways? Additionally, it directs attention to the specific changes in job performance that achieve the desired outcomes with clients. This question related to quality can be addressed through the following components: administrative review of treatment outcomes, peer review of treatment outcomes, and feedback from clients about treatment outcomes.

Administrative review involves the collection of data on the quantity and quality of changes. Relevant statistical data should be collected on global client outcomes: relapse rates, the number of AA meetings attended, the number of individual and group counseling sessions attended, compliance rates for taking prescribed medications appropriately, the number of legal offences, and work stability. These data are usually collected routinely on a monthly basis, so they can easily be reviewed and analyzed at the same time intervals that changes in job performance are monitored.

Qualitative treatment outcomes can also be evaluated through administrative review. The outcomes to be evaluated depend on the specific focus of the training involved. For example, a training program in one facility was focused on helping staff to improve initial social assessments and the monitoring process for ongoing treatment. In terms of ongoing treatment, the administrative review evaluated changes in clients' abilities to: identify concerns or sources of stress that influence drinking, set goals that enhance sobriety, complete steps to achieve those goals, identify and use alternatives to drinking, identify and use support networks to refrain from drinking, discuss and resolve conflicts with significant others in the environment that affect sobriety, and identify individual and environmental strengths that can be used to maintain sobriety.[12]

Administrative review can be accomplished by reading records, direct observation, and listening to taped client interviews on a random basis before training and during the extended follow-up period after training ends. In the previous example, staff members tended to record only a few general statements about clients' problems and seldom recorded anything about their strengths prior to training. The training program included social workers and alcoholism counselors, with separate but related sessions for paraprofessional aides. Training for the former emphasized the importance of identifying with clients their specific problems or concerns as a lead-in to effective goal-setting, exploring strengths to assess the likelihood of recovery, and the process for accomplishing both steps.

Administrative review of tapes and written records of client interviews was completed in this setting prior to training, immediately after training, and at intervals of six months and one year. These reviews of treatment outcomes showed that after the training ended, more clients were able to identify specific concerns and to identify at least one strength. Additionally, the tapes revealed some of the changes in job performance that facilitated these positive outcomes with clients: Staff members asked for examples of areas clients wanted to see changed in their lives, asked how these areas would have to change for clients to be satisfied, stated that everyone had strengths that they needed to be aware of for aiding the recovery process, and asked what clients liked about themselves or felt they could do well.

Parallel reviews of daily progress notes recorded by aides indicated that they had begun to record more specific behavioral data about clients after their training ended, rather than judgmental and general statements about progress. This information helped social workers and alcoholism counselors to more accurately assess client's strengths and problems during on-going treatment and to achieve related positive treatment outcomes with clients.

A second component, peer reviews, can be used to address this quality issue of treatment outcomes in a similar fashion. Peer reviews are important because they involve the staff themselves in monitoring changes in treatment outcomes. Two methods can be used, case consultation and review of written records. The focus of case consultation should be on those treatment outcomes that relate to the training involved. Staff should rotate in presenting active cases, at designated points in treatment that are consistent with the focus of training. This reduces the likelihood of selection bias. Cases in which clients' progress does not meet expectations should be discussed and staff performance should be compared with what has been taught during training.

In the previous training example, case consultation indicated that a large number of clients were still not achieving goals after training ended. The staff's performance in developing goals was discussed. These discussions revealed that they were failing to encourage clients to set smaller numbers of goals or to set achievable goals, as they had been trained to do. This process tended to reinforce the self-defeating behavior of many alcoholic clients. The discussion included a review of a handout from the training on how to set reasonable achievable goals. Subsequent case consultations showed improvements in staff's goal setting skills and in actual goal achievement rates by clients.

Peer reviews of written records involve assigning each staff member a designated time period in which to review case summaries that are selected on a random basis from all open cases after training ends. Specific treatment outcomes in case situations that are related to training are rated in a structured written format by reviewers. Ratings for one staff member over time or ratings across staff members can be summarized to identify patterns in treatment outcomes prior to and after training. Information about these patterns can be shared with staff to enhance the quality of the training program involved.

The third component related to treatment outcomes involves obtaining feedback from clients. Specific information on their perceptions about outcomes, the effective interventions that were used, and their level of satisfaction about the process can be obtained through exit interviews or written questionnaires at the point of termination. If this kind of feedback is obtained from clients routinely, whether or not any training is occurring, it's less likely that the process will become an intervening variable for outcomes when training is occurring. Feedback on treatment outcomes for the specific periods prior to and after training can then be reviewed and the changes analyzed.

Selection of clients for obtaining feedback can be done on a random basis or all clients can be included, depending on the number of clients involved and the method chosen to obtain the data. Either method of client feedback has advantages and disadvantages. Exit interviews require more time, and some clients may be less candid face to face, even though someone other than the practitioner involved conducts the interview. However, interviews can be used to encourage clients to elaborate on or clarify any unclear feedback. In terms of questionnaires, unclear feedback usually cannot be used since it canot be clarified. Some clients may be more resistive to writing feedback than to sharing it verbally, although questionnaires make it easier to keep clients' responses anonymous.

The three program components discussed here can help to clarify whether changes in performance affect treatment outcomes and how that occurs. It is often also helpful to examine how efficiently these outcomes are achieved as another important issue related to the quality of training programs.

### What Is The Cost/Benefit Balance of Training Programs for the Facilities Involved?

This fourth question related to program quality focuses on whether the desired effects from training have been accomplished with minimal costs to the treatment setting when the benefits are considered.[13] If the other three questions related to quality issues have been addressed adequately by a particular training program, those same procedures need only be extended to analyze the cost/benefit issue. Additionally, two other program components help to address this latter issue: comparison of training outcomes with the costs involved and comparison of initial costs/benefits with subsequent costs/benefits.

The first component involves a comparison between the costs of training versus training outcomes. The costs of training include financial as well as other types of costs: the costs for hiring the trainer, for training materials, for the amount of time and number of staff involved in the training, for monitoring the effects of training over time, and for changing policies and operational procedures related to training within the facility.

Benefits for staff and clients should include quantitative and qualitative treatment outcomes. This means that the cost/benefit balance will not be totally quantifiable. Changes in staffs' knowledge, in attitudes that affect performance such as burn-out and dissatisfaction, and in performance areas are as important as the amount of time and number of clients seen in direct service contacts. Equally important for this analysis are changes in the drinking behavior of clients, rates for continuance in treatment, and social functioning levels such as coping adequately with stress. As in all of the analyses discussed in this chapter, intangibles must be translated into tangible observable behaviors, e.g., coping with stress can mean completing life tasks such as regular attendance at work while under stress.

Although collection of such data can involve an objective process, conclusions drawn about what constitutes an acceptable cost/benefit balance are subjective. Thus conclusions about program quality related to this component can vary from situation to situation even when the data are similar. The use of external evaluators can often provide a more objective process and set of conclusions.

The second component, analysis of initial versus subsequent costs/benefits, focuses on both short- and long-term effects of training programs. The cost/benefit balance can change during follow-up periods after training ends, since the long-term effects of changes may not be apparent until then. Often, unanticipated benefits become apparent also during the follow-up period. In the previous example about training staff to improve their social assessments, informal observation indicated that some of them increased their skills in setting and evaluating their annual job targets as they increased their skills in setting goals with clients. Extending existing procedures for monitoring changes in staff performance levels and treatment outcomes to a *formal* cost/benefit analysis can be beneficial to the setting in general, as well as in evaluating the quality of training programs.

In summary, some important questions related to the quality of inservice programs for alcoholism treatment staff have been identified. In addition, thirteen program components that address these questions have been summarized. In order for the potentially positive effects of these components on training outcomes to be realized, a number of related roles must be assumed by mental health professionals within treatment facilities.

## IMPLICATIONS FOR ROLES RELATED TO TRAINING

Social workers and the broad range of other mental health personnel involved in treatment settings can enhance the quality of inservice programs by assuming certain roles based on their designated functions. The functions of consultant-trainers, administrators, and line staff will be discussed in relation to these roles.

## Consultant-Trainers

It should be clear that not all inservice training programs are designed to address each of the four quality issues. Ideally, every program should do so; whether this is possible depends on the realities involved in each situation. The role of trainers is to clarify with administrators and themselves which of these questions will be addressed within the training program, and the manner in which these questions are interrelated. Minimally, every training program should address the issue of whether the training objectives have been achieved and include a needs assessment, objectives, and other related components. Clarifying the quality issues to be addressed helps trainers and administrators to identify the program components that should be included, and then to identify the kinds of outcomes that should be expected and analyzed given the design of the program. The trainer's role is not only to complete the training in an effective manner, but to be active in planning what a particular program can be reasonably expected to accomplish as outcomes. This role should also involve providing training and follow-up consultation to supervisors and administrators focused on helping them to understand and reinforce the application of training by staff.

## Administrators

Social workers and other mental health personnel who are also administrators have an equally important role in training programs. This role requires active involvement including sitting in on training sessions for staff, providing incentives for the application of training, and resolving organizational barriers that block this process. Ideally, many of the components that enhance the quality of inservice training programs should already be a part of agency operational procedures. When they are not, however, this requires changes in organizational procedures that are most effectively initiated at administrative levels.[14]

For example, determining program quality based on treatment outcomes can be addressed in part by the collection and appropriate use of client feedback. This requires the development of a supportive philosophy and set of data collection procedures by administrators that extend beyond the value of client feedback to the training program.

Additionally, administrators should utilize conclusions about training outcomes to improve the quality of future programs and to insure that training occurs in a systematic organized manner. This may often involve effectively interpreting training needs and outcomes to board members and other key individuals who influence how decisions about training are made.

## Line Staff

The role of line staff is a crucial one since only they can directly apply what they have learned in training to the benefit of clients. They should have an active role in assessing their training needs. If this input is omitted, they should request the opportunity from administrators before training begins or from trainers when assessment conclusions and training objectives are being discussed during initial training sessions.

This opportunity for input can be used more effectively if line staff are familiar with some of the literature on alcoholism treatment. This can often help them to articulate nonspecific concerns into common practice dilemmas that are being explored in the literature. It can also help them to look at their training needs in a more systematic manner in order to enhance related areas of professional development. Training is then more likely to be relevant to their daily practice and to be applied by them appropriately.

Familiarity with the quality issues discussed in this chapter is also an important aspect of the role of line staff. The development of new treatment programs (such as those for women and elderly alcoholic clients) are often dependent on existing practice skills of staff, so some opportunities for training may be missed. When line staff understand quality issues related to training, they can become more assertive about the training necessary to practice effectively in these new programs and in general with alcoholic clients.

## CONCLUSIONS

Questions about the quality of inservice training programs for alcoholism treatment staff must be clarified in the process of designing these programs. Often, these quality issues are not fully understood by trainers and agency administrators alike, so some of their conclusions about the effectiveness or ineffectiveness of particular programs may be inaccurate. Further, these conclusions may be based on unreasonable expectations because program components most likely to achieve a given outcome may not have been included. Trainers, administrators, and line staff have related roles in planning effective programs and in insuring that the learning is generalized to direct service contacts with alcoholic clients.

## REFERENCES

1. See for example, Cartwright, A. K. J.: The attitudes of helping agents towards the alcoholic client: The influence of experience, support, training, and self-esteem. *British Journal of Addictions, 75*:413–431, 1980. Also Gideon, W. L., Lettell, A. S., and Martin, D. W.: Evaluation of a training program for certified alcoholism counselors. *Journal of Studies on Alcohol, 41*:8–20, 1980. Manohar, V., Des-Roches, J. and Ferneau, E. W., Jr.: An education program in alcoholism for social workers: Its impact on attitudes and treatment-oriented behavior. *British Journal of Addictions, 71*:225–234, 1976.
2. Ewan, Christine and Whaite, Ann: Evaluation of training programs for health professionals in substance abuse. *Journal of Studies on Alcohol, 44*:885–898, 1983. (a)
3. Buttram, J.: Assessment of training needs. *Journal of Drug Education, 7*:347–351, 1977.
4. Ewan and Whaite, (a), op. cit., pp. 887–895.
5. Ibid.
6. Ewan, Christine and Whaite, Ann: Training health professionals in substance abuse: A review. *The International Journal of the Addictions, 17*:1211–1229, 1982. (b)
7. Ibid, pp. 1218–1221.
8. Ewan and Whaite (a), op. cit., pp. 892–895.
9. Waring, Mary L.: The impact of specialized training in alcoholism management-level professionals. *Journal of Studies on Alcohol, 36*:406–414, 1975.
10. Doelker, Richard E. and Lynett, Patricia: Strategies in staff development: An ecological approach. *Social Work*, 380–384, 1983.

11. Ewan and Whaite (a), op. cit., pp. 889–892.
12. Freeman, Edith and Blackmon, Betty: *Improving Clinical Effectiveness with Substance Abuse Clients: A Training Manual.* Kansas City, University of Kansas, 1983.
13. Schinke, Steven Paul: Measuring the impact of continuing education. *Journal of Education for Social Work, 17:*59–64, 1981.
14. Doelker and Lynett, op. cit.

# Author Index

Steinglass, Peter, 95, 96, 97, 99, 106, 107, 113
Stewart, O., 219
Stober, B., 141
Stone, F., 144
Strauss, Murray, 26
Stuart, Lorraine B., 205
Sugarman, A., 163, 268
Sultman, Jules, 193
Sunhart, J. J., 93
Swartz, Mark, 57
Swigert, V. L., 219

**T**

Talley, Ruth, 338
Tarter, R. E., 163
Taylor, C., 264
Teitelbaum, M. A., 95
Thomas, A., 252
Thum, D., 9, 11
Thurston, C. P., 166
Trice, H. M., 43, 45
Tsu, V., 309
Turner, Francis J., 95, 129

**V**

Vannicelli, Marsha, 176
Vogel, Susan R., 30
Voris, Stephen, 83, 85, 87, 94
Vourakis, Christine, 83

**W**

Waddell, R., 277
Walker, D., 214
Walker, R. Dale, 220, 221, 226
Wanberg, Kenneth W., 174, 218
Ward, E., 85
Waring, Mary, 337, 357
Watts, Ronald, 233

Watts, Thomas D., 202
Watzlawick, Paul, 133
Weakland, John, 133
Wechsler, Henry, 9, 11, 321, 337, 338
Wecleu, Robert V., 234
Wedel, Kenneth, 217
Wegscheider, S., 116, 144
Welsh, R. J., 85, 243
Werlin, S., 270
Westermeyer, J., 214, 244
Whaite, Ann, 352, 354, 355, 356, 357, 358
Whalen, T., 293
Whitehead, P., 292, 295, 307
Whitfield, C. L., 143
Whitley, Gary P., 222
Whitaker, James O., 218
Williams, A., 271
Williams, H., 263
Williams, J. R., 10, 11, 12, 277
Williams, Millre, 205
Willoughby, A., 220
Wilsnack, Sharon C., 176
Winokur, G., 174, 175, 203
Wiseman, Jacqueline P., 244, 295
Wodarski, J. S., 20
Wolf, I., 316
Wood, H. P., 174
Wood, Katherine, 83
Wood, W. Gibson, 194
Woolen, S. J., 95
Woolf, Donna, 83
Wrich, J., 41, 46, 49
Wright, Janet, 38
Wright, Roosevelt, Jr., 202
Wuthman, C., 297

**Z**

Zavaleta, Anthony, 232
Zinberg, Sheldon, 340

# Subject Index